FISHERMEN'S DIGEST

8th Anniversary
De Luxe Edition

Edited by Erwin A. Bauer

Assistant Editor — Parker Bauer

FOLLETT PUBLISHING CO.
CHICAGO

T-0217

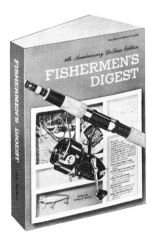

OUR COVERS

Two outfits by Garcia decorate the covers of the 8th edition of FISHERMEN'S DIGEST. Our front cover pictures a spinning combination of the Mitchell 300 reel and a Garcia 2508 light action spinning rod, while an Ambassadeur 5000C baitcasting reel mounted on a Garcia 2521 medium action rod grace our back cover.

FISHERMEN'S DIGEST is published by Digest Books, Inc., Milton Klein, President, 540 Frontage Rd., Northfield, Ill. 60093. Copyright © MCMLXXI by Digest Books, Inc. All rights reserved. Reproductions or use of editorial or pictorial content without express permission is prohibited.

ISBN 0-695-80217-8   Library of Congress Catalog Card Number 75-148727

CONTENTS
FISHERMEN'S DIGEST

This 26-pound coho held the state record for just two months.

Great Lakes Salmon Today

by Tom Opre

A fisherman who's a glutton for sport—or perhaps for punishment—can catch Great Lakes salmon as early as April this year and not stop until November. That's two-thirds of 1971, quite a change from four short years ago when the angling lasted only two months.

"We've been aiming toward as big a sport fishery as possible," Dr. Wayne Tody, chief of the Michigan fish division, said, "and 1970 marked the first year for what might be called 'all-season' fishing."

The changes for 1971 should include even more areas to search for salmon, better facilities for visiting fishermen and improved methods of taking both coho and chinook. From April on, the season gets nothing but better. Fish are plentiful and not too finicky, although the size of fish you want and the way you want to fish dictates when and where you go. Tourist accommodations aren't much of a problem (with isolated exceptions), reliable charterboats are in fairly good supply, boat rentals are available in some spots and campground space is dotted from one end of the lakes to the other.

The only real disappointment to Dr. Tody and his biologists has been the dismal salmon return on Lake Huron. Lakes Erie and Ontario haven't produced any salmon boom either, so that leaves the two upper lakes—Michigan and Superior—the spots anglers should head for.

On these two, the parasitic lampreys which attack salmon and other game fish have been partially controlled, and a new "zone management" approach for commercial fishermen helps keep gill nets out of fish populations meant for sportsmen. Michigan biologists blame the problems in Huron not only on a delayed lamprey control program (due to inconsistent and unsure federal funding) but also on Canadian commercial fishermen who reputedly take big hauls of cohos along their shoreline each spring.

A good idea of what's awaiting anglers on Lakes Michigan and Superior is provided by state planting records for the past few years. Cohos, or silver salmon, mature after 1½ years in the big lakes. Lake Michigan's 1970 coho plant alone totaled 3,484,000, and these will run spawning streams this fall, providing most of the summer open-water fishery.

Wading produces salmon at the mouth of Thompson Creek, near Manistique in Michigan's Upper Peninsula.

Mature coho comes to net for Capt. Ralph Fairbanks.

Chinook, or king salmon, mature at varying rates, so many of the 2¾ million stocked since 1967 will still be in the lakes this year.

Sizes? The top hook-and-line coho so far weighed slightly more than 27 pounds. A 33-pound coho was taken from a state harvest weir on the little Manistee River last fall, and it was a new world size record. But the biggest ever taken by angling was a 30-pounder from the Pacific Coast.

Michigan chinook averaged about 25 pounds last year, with many topping 35 pounds and the biggest just over 42. Averages this season should be more than 30 pounds. The 50-pound barrier may be broken this season too, and some biologists look for a 60-pounder. Most of these big fish will be caught later in the season, just before or during spawning runs, when they've fully matured.

When the action begins, in April and May, salmon run much smaller. Most of the cohos range between 1½ and 3 pounds when they move into the shallow southern reaches of Lake Michigan, jamming up onto the offshore areas from Milwaukee around to Holland, Michigan. This is where winter's ice first disappears and the water begins warming to the 50 to 55°F. range cohos prefer.

Light tackle is the rule for this sporty fishing. Conventional freshwater gear of any type—casting, spinning or fly —can be used. Remember that young cohos tend to fight more like young rainbows—leaping, twisting and ripping off unbelievable runs on light gear. Your fishing rod should have some backbone for this and 6- to 12-pound test line is the norm.

The most conventional method of fishing is trolling, from all manner and size of boats. Popular lures are usually the minnow immitators, such as Tadpollies, Flatfish and Rapalas in smaller sizes, along with small to medium spoons and spinners. Silver, blue, gold, white, fluorescent orange— all these colors (singly or in combination) seem to work well. Streamer flies trolled separately or in combination with chrome dodgers or flashers (to attract attention) can be used on fly rods, especially if your boat has some type of outrigger setup, conventional or home-made.

Evidence seems to indicate, too, that these lures and the trolling method work best once the water has warmed near 50°. In colder water a simple worm fished on the bottom off piers, breakwaters and boats seems to work well with the sluggish early-season fish. Pier fishing also pays off later, when live bait and lures are cast in the shallows. The thousands of warm water factory discharges and river or drainage channel outlets (cohos seem impervious to pollution for a short while) attract the salmon even closer to shore. Chicagoans take home salmon from the waterfront before or after their work shifts.

Trollers will find they don't need much in the way of sinkers, either. Spring salmon stay pretty close to the surface and have no trouble coming after what they want. Four ounces of lead can destroy much of the fun on light tackle, for instance, and it only gets the lure down about ten feet under the surface.

Of course, springtime accommodations along the southern Lake Michigan shoreline are probably more plentiful than anywhere else where Great Lakes salmon fishing is found. Many Hoosiers head for the Michigan City area to do their fishing, a spot where tackle shops, marinas and the city administration promotes the heck out of it. Up into Michigan, the New Buffalo, Benton Harbor, St. Joseph, South Haven and Holland areas have everything the visiting angler needs.

But if southern Lake Michigan's compacted population isn't your cup of tea, the next best spring salmon fishing can be found along the spectacular Lake Superior shoreline of Michigan's Upper Peninsula and Wisconsin's Apostle Islands.

Coho jumps behind stern of Capt. Ralph Fairbanks' boat "The Hunter."

You'll have to wait until late May when weather and water temperatures improve a bit. But if past years are any indication, you'll have the fishing pretty much to yourself. The entire Superior shoreline is relatively wild and uncluttered. Spectacular scenery provides the background, and the pristine crystal waters in most areas of the lake are a delight.

May and early June—in fact, the period through August —finds cohos hanging up on the inshore shallows or in the top 40 feet of water with a great many lake trout and steelhead (lake-run rainbow trout). Frankly, the lake trout is the leading sport species, but few days pass without hitting schools of salmon. Again, it's light tackle fishing with the trolling methods mentioned earlier working for all three species of fish, and trolling with little or no sinkers will tend to produce more salmon and steelhead than lakers.

Cohos will be small, perhaps between one and three pounds all summer. Cold water conditions and no alewife population account for smaller fish in Lake Superior. Water temperatures seldom exceed 48° even in early September, and fish grow at much slower rates. Since there have been few chinook planted in the lake, you needn't worry too much about larger salmon tearing up your light tackle.

But, if you decide to add some weight to your lines, beware of the lakers. Four to eight pounds is a common range for lake trout here, with plenty of 12- and 15-pounders caught each season. I once witnessed a spring salmon fisherman land an unexpected 25-pound laker with very skillful manipulations of his tackle.

Considering the remoteness of this beautiful area, accommodations are surprisingly plentiful, probably because of the long standing popularity with summer tourists. Federal and state campgrounds are unbeatable (and usually uncrowded) in both parks and forests. Major ports for boat launching include (from east to west): Grand Marais, Munising, Marquette, L'Anse, Ontonogan and Black River Harbor, all the Upper Peninsula, and Ashland and Bayfield in Wisconsin. There are a few marinas on the Apostle Islands, too, reached by auto ferry from Bayfield.

If you'd prefer the expertise of a professional skipper, charterboats can be found in nearly all the towns mentioned, with the largest single fleet berthed at Black River Harbor, about 12 miles from Bessemer, Michigan. Rates are usually a bit cheaper than downstate Michigan, too.

Throughout Lake Michigan, June and early July find most fishermen concentrating on lake trout, a species that has recovered remarkably since the lamprey era, thanks to a federal stocking program. In fact, you're liable to find an occasional laker in your salmon catch all season long, especially if the salmon are deep and you fish near bottom.

In past years, there's always been a slump in salmon fishing from mid-June to mid-July. Fish are still caught, of course, but they move further offshore, and only the larger boats usually run the 8, 10 or even 20 miles to the big schools of fish. Most of this action comes between Benton Harbor and Muskegon on the Michigan side, progressing slowly northward with the passage of summer.

Frankly, no one theory has fully explained this phenomenon. The salmon certainly are there. And some biologists think that a great many salmon actually don't migrate to the southern end of the lake in spring, but stay offshore in northern waters. If so, few fishermen are catching them and many are trying for lake trout. Nobody can say for sure why the fish seem to move out in the lake, either. The occasional salmon is caught inshore, even from breakwaters by perch fishermen. But there's no denying that major schools of cohos are somewhat scarce in early summer.

Pier fishermen along the Great Lakes take their share of salmon during early spring or spawning runs in the fall.

Popular holes along spawning streams are usually crowded with bait fishermen.

Throughout the midsummer period, salmon gain weight rapidly (two-thirds of their total weight at spawning is put on in wild feeding frenzies the last four months of their lives). They gradually become more available, too, showing up inshore along Lake Michigan from Muskegon up past Ludington, Manistee, Frankfort, Platte Bay, around into Grand Traverse Bay, Little Traverse Bay and off Charlevoix. Prime salmon fishing begins to peak by early August, if weather conditions are stable, improving weekly in a northward pattern. Arrival of the first big schools does vary from year to year, however, and until late August a telephone call could eliminate a useless auto trip.

The fishing from this time until October, when most of the spawning runs begin, can be nothing short of fabulous. Two days last August proved that to me.

I'd traveled to Ludington at the invitation of Skipper Marv DeWitt who heads the West Michigan Charter Service there. "You can't believe how the fish are coming in," he'd said on the telephone the night before. "I'm filling limits for two parties a day—and I could catch more!"

Not being hard to convince, I was aboard Marv's boat by dawn as we headed out a full ten miles offshore. Marv uses a specialized device called a "downrigger" that enables him to keep several trolled lures at exact depths practically under the boat's stern. Tests with a thermometer showed the preferred water temperature to be at 40 to 70 feet, and blips on the boat's recording fathometer indicated that it was the best depth for fish.

Setting seven lines takes a few minutes. But Marv hadn't put the fourth one down when the first broke loose from its downrigger, a coho swirling wildly behind the boat as it rose to the surface. Fifteen minutes later we lost two more and then boated a second one, then tallied three more quickly. All around us boats were netting fish, filling coolers with cohos weighing between 8 and 18 pounds.

A full hour's lull allowed us to stow gear and settle down, but then we hit another school of fish—or found the first school again—and bouncing rods and aching wrists were the order of the morning. The limit for three of us was 15 fish, and we lost quite a few that struck and were gone. But we still managed to lay 14 fish on the cleaning dock by noon, and it was then I discovered that one of our catch was a fat 12-pound steelhead no one had noticed in the flurry of activity, since cohos and steelhead look much alike.

Boats at least 16 feet long—and preferably even larger—are required for trolling offshore lake waters.

An armada of chinook salmon anglers gathers at the south end of Manistee Lake.

infisherman takes heavy salmon below Croton Dam on the Muskegon River.

Capt. Fairbanks slips the net under a coho.

After a short drive up the shoreline, I spent the next morning fishing with Capt. Ralph Fairbanks whose 30-footer, The Hunter, is berthed in Manistee. Ralph's an old friend and one of the finest skippers on the coast, and we'd spent many a day the past few years researching the habits of salmon and lake trout. In a repeat of the previous day, we were back at noon to lay 14 cohos on the dock all caught in a wild melee of whirring freespool reels, barked knuckles, tangled leaders and straightened hooks.

Emil Dean's "Mary E", berthed alongside, had done even better with an hour's more time, tallying 22 cohos.

Of course these tales whet a fisherman's appetite to a keen edge, but don't let the travel posters or promotional agencies make you think it happens all the time. It doesn't.

But from mid-August to spawning time, there's plenty of action, sometimes for days on end if a furious storm—something Lake Michigan is famous for—doesn't push the fish around and the fishermen off the lake. I've sat in port three days or more many times, waiting for the wind to die.

Which brings up an all-important point. Weather is the Great Lakes fisherman's biggest and most dangerous bugaboo. Don't challenge the lakes recklessly, because they'll win.

Many incoming tourist fishermen are inclined to bring their usual backyard craft—the popular cartop boat. These

12- to 16-foot aluminum boats, powered by 5- to 18-horsepower outboards, are suitable in some areas, but very risky in others. The Great Lakes spawn savage storms, ones that can pop up with but few minutes warning. The entire nation heard of the blow in 1967 when seven fishermen drowned in a few hours. And each season since, the lakes have claimed their victims.

We'll go into the safer spots for smaller boats a bit later, but for now, if you want to fish more open areas or go further offshore in exposed areas such as the Lake Michigan shoreline from Muskegon to Frankfort, you need at least a 16- to 18-foot boat, the bigger the better.

The size of salmon available in late summer—and the good chance of snagging onto a really large chinook—dictate the use of fairly stout rods, the so-called light salt-water variety. You'll find a medium or fast-action tip helpful, though, in providing enough leverage to sink hooks in cohos' touchy mouths without ripping the lure loose again. Trolling or spinning reels with tough, smooth drags are a must, equipped with at least 300 feet of 12- to 15-pound test line, more if possible.

Light tackle enthusiasts who can handle their gear well often catch these big salmon but should be prepared to spend lots of time landing each fish.

Another reason for heavier tackle—if you can't use downriggers—is the amount of lead needed to put lures where the salmon are. No one can say for sure how deep salmon will be at any one time. Fifty- to 55-degree water can be anywhere from the surface to 150 feet. Both a thermometer and a fathometer will help you pinpoint this level and the fish.

But if you have none of that fancy stuff, remember these figures: four ounces of lead takes a lure down about 10 feet, eight ounces to 20 feet, 12 to 40 feet, 16 to 60 feet and 20 ounces to 80 feet. They're based on letting out 150 feet of 15-pound-test monofilament from your boat.

Such a load of lead takes some of the zip out of a salmon fight, though, so many anglers opt for the "slip-sinker" devices sold in most local tackle stores. These release the lead when salmon hit, leaving an unweighted line between fisherman and fish. On days like the two previously mentioned, you'd need a good supply of sinkers, obviously.

Other anglers favor the planing devices that work something like airplane wings when pulled through the water. They're angled to drag trailing lures downward in the water when trolled. These, too, are available in local tackle shops, complete with full directions for their use.

I have seen late-summer salmon take lures right on the surface and I've also seen them hang 150 feet down, if lack of wind has allowed the big lakes to stratify—cooler temperatures sinking deeper down. If indications are that fish are

It takes stout tackle to keep wild salmon out of the brush in Michigan's snag-choked rivers.

Bill Gardiner of Lansing checks average-sized midsummer coho.

much below 80 feet, you'd be better off with the traditional wireline outfits used to take lake trout from deep bottom shoals. Fortunately the fish are seldom that far down.

There are perhaps as many lures purported to catch salmon as there are salmon. Surprisingly enough, when the fish are really hitting, most of these lures will work. But the favorite baits of charterboatmen are Tadpollies, Flatfish, Rapalas, Dardevles, Bayou Specials, Manistee Wobblers, Burke Tail-Spins, Canadian Wonder Spoons, Williams Wablers and Bolo, Mepps and Hep Spinners.

Silver and silver-blue color combinations probably take the most salmon. But fluorescent orange, yellow, white, red-and-white, fluorescent lime-green, gold and combinations of these often work, too.

Generally speaking, as spawning time approaches the salmon schools move even closer to parent streams, becoming more accessible inshore. It's then that such hotspots as Platte Bay, north of Frankfort around Pointe Betsie, begin to produce large catches and give smaller boats a better chance.

Grand Traverse Bay, particularly along the west arm from Traverse City up to Northport, picks up steadily as fall approaches, and Little Traverse Bay off Petoskey switches from a lake trout to a salmon society.

Several relatively uncrowded—and as yet unproven—spots exist in fairly protected waters along Lake Michigan's Upper Peninsula shoreline. Little Bay de Noc (the nearest large town is Escanaba) hosts returning salmon by September, headed for the Whitefish River. Salmon have been planted in the Big Cedar River, too, which reaches Lake Michigan at the town of Big Cedar northeast of Menominee on the Wisconsin line. The Menominee River has salmon, too.

September usually marks the start of spawning runs at Thompson Creek, near Manistique in the Upper Peninsula. A mixture of early-spawning Alaska strain cohos and regular west coast U.S. fish have been stocked here. Fishing from small boats or while wading off the river mouth is often excellent. St. Martins Bay north of St. Ignace in the Straits of Mackinac is another good bet. The Carp River there hosts one bunch of returning salmon, a new access road has been built, and fishermen have been ignoring it. In prevailing winds, St. Martins offers good protection inshore for smaller boats.

Inland lakes through which salmon must pass to reach spawning streams shouldn't be overlooked, either. Both coho and chinook will enter these in many cases by late September and passage of fish continues through October. Better bets include Muskegon Lake at Muskegon, Manistee Lake at Manistee, Loon and Platte Lakes on the Platte River (the river itself is usually closed to fishing until late fall since egg-taking operations are underway at the upstream hatchery), and Lake Charlevoix at Charlevoix and Boyne City.

We should say a word about pesticide levels, too, since DDT use by agricultural interests has found its way into fish here as well as elsewhere around the country.

The number of salmon usually eaten by most individual fishermen and their families each year isn't enough to cause any worry over pesticides—although levels in fresh fish of the mature size make them unmarketable according to the U.S. Food and Drug Administration. Most of this pesticide residue concentrates in the fat of the fish, and by cutting away the belly flanks, skin and meat along the backbone you can eliminate most of it. Practically all the remainder is gone after the fat drips away from a broiling fillet.

So there's no need to avoid eating your catch, at least according to the best studies to date. Of course the salmon are delicious.

By October, much of the fishing action has switched to the spawning rivers themselves, most of which are open to sport fishermen under very liberal regulations. In certain sections of streams, a somewhat restricted form of snagging is permitted, although the law calls it "accidental foul-hooking." Officials figure it's better for sport fishermen to utilize the salmon than have them spawn, die and go wasted. Michigan's fishery program depends mostly on hatchery-raised fish stocked each spring, and though natural spawning adds to the production, it isn't absolutely necessary for good salmon fishing.

The regulations governing this brand of snagging, along with the streams open to it, are spelled out in the annual fishing digest provided with the fishing license.

From south to north in the Lower Peninsula, these are the streams which host spawning runs and are generally open to fishing: St. Joseph, Kalamazoo, Grand, Muskegon, Pere Marquette, Big Manistee, Little Manistee (open for steelhead fishing only above the state harvest weir) and Platt (closed until late fall). Other stocked streams are too small to be open to general fishing pressure, although the river mouth areas are usually open. The Menominee, Whitefish, Carp, Big Cedar and Manistique Rivers in the Upper Peninsula are most often open, too.

Salmon's struggle often leaves tangled masses of leaders, attractors and lures.

Along Lake Superior, most of the fishing action continues offshore at the river mouths throughout the season. The better spots include (from east to west): Grand Marais (Sucker River), Munising (Ana River), Marquette (Chocolay), Big Huron Bay (Big Huron), Keweenaw Bay and Black River Harbor (Presque Isle).

Salmon seem little inclined to take artificial lures during spawning runs, so most anglers use such bait as spawn sacks (salmon eggs tied in small nylon bags), nightcrawlers and wigglers, all available in local bait stores. These are usually fished right on the bottom with enough split shots to keep them rolling on the bottom of holes where salmon rest in their passage upstream. Some fluorescent-orange or yellow lures work at times, but most fishermen finally resort to snagging. Where dams block upstream passage, snagging a limit of five salmon isn't hard.

If you'd like a crack at a really big chinook, your choices are still somewhat limited. Most big kings were taken last season at the south end of Manistee Lake where the Little Manistee River enters. There was literally a carpet of boats at the spot, nearly everyone still-fishing on the bottom with spawn or nightcrawlers. To actually land one of the 30-pounders in that maze was quite an experience.

The Muskegon River hosts plenty of big chinook, too, but after they pass through Muskegon Lake, most are taken by snaggers from holes along the way to Croton Dam upstream.

Up-to-date salmon fishing information is available seven days a week from the state's "hotline" number in Lansing. Call (517) 373-0908. The state's "Michigan Campground Directory" is a free pamphlet listing every public campground in the state (write Publications Room, Michigan Dept. of Natural Resources, Stephens T. Mason Bldg., Lansing).

Tourist accommodation information is available from the West Michigan Tourist Association (107 Pearl St. N.W., Grand Rapids, Mich. 49502) or the Upper Peninsula Tourist Association (Box 1188, Iron Mountain, Mich. 49801).

Michigan fishing licenses cost $3.10 for residents and $6.10 for non-residents annually. A trout and salmon stamp adds $2.10 for residents and $3.10 for non-residents. Seven-day permits are $3.10 and $5.10 respectively, and a one-day tag for all fishermen goes for $1.10. Take your pick.

Fairbanks unloads morning's catch of cohos taken off Manistee, Michigan.

BLACK BASS FISHING IS SUPERLATIVE SPORT ANY WAY YOU LOOK AT IT... BUT A BASS ANGLER'S EDUCATION IS NEVER COMPLETE UNTIL HE KNOWS

Largemouth comes out of hiding to inhale bug which is cast close to his lair.

HOW TO BUG BASS!

By Erwin A. Bauer

Typical bass bugging country with plenty of weedy edge and other targets for casting.

I suppose the story will sound fictional, but my forgetful friend Lew Baker learned about bass bugging by accident. Through his own mistakes he discovered a more exciting way to catch bass than he had ever known before.

It happened more than ten years ago and the occasion was Lew's annual summer trip to Michigan's Upper Peninsula to celebrate the opening of the state's bass season. Lew maintains a modest cabin on a lonely lake up there just for this one holiday alone. On this particular trip the weather was warm—practically perfect—and my friend looked forward to a week of complete escape from jangling telephones, from smog and traffic jams at home.

Only one thing was wrong; he forgot to take along his tackle. It was still piled neatly in his garage when he pulled away and he didn't realize it until he reached camp 650 miles northward.

But Lew is as ingenious as he is forgetful. There was an old flyrod and reel around camp and both had seen much better days. With dental floss, Lew managed to repair the windings on the rod, and simply by reversing ends of the cracked old flyline on the reel, he had a length of it long enough to cast.

Next Lew borrowed the cork from a bottle of bonded and inserted the shank of a rusty old hook through the middle of it. The pheasant feathers in his hat band were removed and tied to the hook as a tail. The finished product was as crude a bass bug as anyone ever presented to a Michigan largemouth . . . which is exactly what Lew did the next morning.

Actually it was the first time Lew had ever tried fly-rodding for anything except trout and panfish. It is under-statement to say that he had plenty of trouble keeping his improvised lure in one piece. In fact he spent the next evening making several new, sturdier models. But the whole affair was tremendous fun and it was a week Lew would never forget. As I stated before, the incident may seem fictional, but listen to what Lew himself has to say about it.

"Forgetting tackle," he admits, "Should happen to every-one—if it helps him to discover bugging for bass."

There isn't any doubt but that a suitable flyrod and reel, plus an assortment of bugs, are the means to the most fascinating of all bass fishing. Because it is strictly surface fishing, it does have its limitations on most bass waters. But when bass are in shallow water it is as deadly as it is exciting. And that goes for smallmouths as well as largemouth black bass.

Exactly what is bass bugging? It is using the long rod to cast a surface lure or bug of 1/16 ounce or less to likely bass targets. In other words it is dry fly fishing, but for bass instead of trout. And once you try it, it be-comes highly addictive.

Almost any flyrod can serve in a pinch, I suppose, but the ideal stick is a comparatively long and heavy one with sufficient power to toss large and wind resistant bugs. I personally use 8½ and 9 foot rods, not because the bass require them, but because my favorite bass bugs do.

Of course the line should match the rod and I know of no other specific type of flyrodding in which a level line will serve practically as well as some tapered line.

Maybe that is an unscientific viewpoint, but it *is* my experience. I should add that it is seldom necessary (or even practical) to make very long casts with bass bugs. I also use level leaders which test 8 or 10 pounds and which are about as long as the rod—or slightly less. Use lighter, tapered leader if you like, but I will explain this choice of heavy monofilament later on.

Except to say that it should be functional and only large enough to hold your flyline without backing, any fly reel is suitable for bugging. Sometimes when wading in weedy water, there is a good case for the automatic with which you can keep loose coils of line from looping around pads or bonnets. But my own preference is for a light single action reel, if only because it is uncomplicated.

There are too many exceptions to list here which disprove the rule, but generally the best bass bugging happens in springtime or early summer—before, during and just after bass have moved into shallow areas to spawn. Probably that is true because then the bugs can be easily seen, stalked and gobbled up by the bass. When the fish is in deeper water, a surface lure may be delivered overhead—and the bass either doesn't see it or is too lazy to

to pursue it. Water six feet deep is just about the maximum for effective bass bugging.

Although I travel widely in any year's time, most of my own bass fishing is done in Ohio where I live. It isn't the most productive in America because the fishing pressure is heavy the year around. The state is heavily populated, especially for the amount of water available. You seldom have even a portion of any lake to yourself very long. That means you work hard and carefully for your fish which often seem to know more about popular lures than the people who manufacture them. They know most plugs by their name and serial numbers, perhaps even the prices. It is in this heavily-pounded environment that bass bugging appears particularly effective.

Here is a theory I have often heard—and it sounds sensible enough to pass along. A bass is lurking along a shallow shoreline. He may be looking for a meal or his belly may be already full and he is simply killing time. Then suddenly a heavy surface plug falls practically on his noggin, startling him, and he darts away from the safety of cover or deeper water. He didn't even bother to take a second look at the lure.

String of fine bass, all fooled by popping bugs, taken on a springtime morning in Ohio.

The same bass is lurking again and this time a tiny bug falls overhead. But it falls so lightly that the bass is alerted rather than frightened—and so he gives it a closer look, maybe just as the angler twitches it slightly. On impulse or from hunger, the bass might grab it. If not immediately he could be tempted on the second or third casts.

Of course that is only theory—maybe even far-fetched theory—but bugs seem to work far better than bigger baits when the fishing pressure is high.

The best water for bugging, at least here in the Midwest, is either very weedy of full of obstacles. You look at it and your first impulse is to tie a weedless spoon onto a casting outfit and to start throwing it into the lettuce. Certainly that works—very, very well sometimes. (Read "How to Fish the Lettuce" by Dick Kotis elsewhere in the Digest.) But if it doesn't, try going back over the same area with bugs.

I realize there are problems with snagging when you cast a bug in weedy areas. But practice develops pinpoint accuracy and eventually any fisherman is surprised at how well he soon learns to drop his bug into the tinest bits of open water. It isn't even necessary to have open water for practice; you can spend spare moments developing casting accuracy right in your own back yard.

That brings us around again to the matter of using heavy level leaders. For one thing you have better control of a heavy bug casting. But more important than that, you can better horse a good bass right out of weedy spots, after it strikes. With the lighter leaders so necessary for trout, you would only lose most of the bass you hook.

Last summer I went fishing with my son Bob at one of the Muskingum chain lakes in eastern Ohio. We carried along a tent and pitched it as close to the lakeshore as the local camping rules permitted. Then we launched my square-ended cartop canoe and set out to catch our dinner.

But for dinner we had to settle for hamburger; nor could we catch anything for breakfast. If there was any consolation at all, it was that no other campers in the compound were doing any better. I thought about striking the tent and looking elsewhere—except that I have a stubborn streak a mile wide. So I went swimming and then sat in the sunshine to mull it over. Bob joined me.

"I have never seen this place so weedy," the lad said, "So early in the year."

"And I've never found the water quite so warm," I added.

"Then let's just forget about fishing," Bob continued, "Until well after dark for a change."

"You are reading my mind," I said.

"Maybe I'm just a chip off the old blockhead." Then Bob went swimming, too.

That evening we waited until all the campers were back in camp, boats pulled out on shore and steaks cooking on charcoal grills all around us. Somebody nearby started strumming a guitar. That's when we quietly launched our own boat, cranked up the small outboard and motored to the opposite side of the lake. There Bob began casting a weedless spoon. I had rigged a flyrod and began to toss a small popping bug. Bob didn't say anything, but I could practically "feel" him wondering how I would keep from snagging constantly.

In the beginning, before my eyes were fully accustomed to the darkness I did snag frequently. Sometimes I would retrieve long stringers of weeds and sometimes we would have to pry the bugs loose from lily stems by hand. To make it seem worse, Bob quickly hooked and boated a one-pounder with his spoon and casting outfit.

But suddenly things changed. By making shorter casts and with night vision improving, I had a couple of strikes

The light weight of the bug permits any bass to best show off his acrobatic talents.

which were missed. But the third bass hung himself and I horsed him right onto the stringer.

Ten minutes later there was another upheaval under my bug—only this bass wouldn't be horsed. I leaned into my outfit for all it would stand, but except to lurch upward and out of the water in a wild leap, the bass was too strong to be budged. While I just held on, Bob paddled back into the weeds and we were able to "dig" out my fish. The flashlight proved useless because it was knocked overboard early in the melee. But somehow we boated the bass which, on scales later on, didn't quite make four pounds.

The score up until about midnight was five bass to one in favor of the bug over the spoon. It is true that one inning does not constitute a ball game, but that was a dramatic example of the bug's effectiveness on a busy, weedy body of water.

One of the wildest nights of freshwater fishing I've ever known occurred on an alcohol-clear lake in central Ontario. This lake contained a fringe of vegetation around the shoreline, but mostly it was very thin as compared to Ohio or southern shorelines. Here again fishing had slowed down to almost nothing, except for a few smallmouths taken in deep water on nightcrawlers. That I went fishing at all must be blamed mostly on the unlucky trend of the poker game going on back in camp.

Fishing alone along the shore, I first tried tossing surface plugs with a spinning outfit. With these I had two strikes, landed one smallmouth and might have had much more action except that two sets of treble hooks were too much to get through the vegetation. Since my flyrod was already in the boat, I picked it up and knotted a popper to the leader.

That was like flipping a switch. Either the bass just started to strike at that moment—or the bug was the medicine they wanted. Take your choice. Before I gave it up, I had landed 11 bass, but kept only the five biggest. These weighed a total of 21 pounds and as you might suspect, broke up the poker game.

There are three basic kinds of bass bugs and many variations of all three. Best known and most frequently used today is the popper. These are solid-bodied (cork, wood or plastic) bugs with either flat or dished out faces which make popping or gurgling noises when twitched. The actual shape of the body varies greatly to imitate anything from frogs to grasshoppers, but mostly nothing natural at all. The tails and/or wings can be anything from rubber bands or bucktail to feathers and fur. My own favorite bugs are those with fluttering rubber skirt tails. I suppose you could call them miniskirts. Like the imports from jolly old England, they attract attention.

Another basic bug is the wounded minnow imitation which has a rounded or bullet-shaped face and which does not make a commotion or popping noise when retrieved. Instead it is quiet. Usually the tails are of deer hair or hackle. This type was far more popular in the earlier years of bass bugging than it is now.

A third type is that one fashioned wholly from deer hair, flared out by the tyer to make a very solid-feeling body. Some of these are made with fan wings and given an action similar to the dying flutter of a large insect on the water. Others are equipped with Z-shaped trailing legs to immitate a small frog. All were (and are) very, very effective. The main drawback is they ride high on the surface in the biginning, but gradually lose buoyancy and

this provokes shouldn't happen to anglers with weak hearts. I have been bass bugging for a quarter century now and still am not 100% prepared for the strike when it comes.

Experienced bass fishermen will already know the following, but probably this basic information should be included for any beginners interested in bass bugging. Stick to short casts at first—and only gradually extend the casts as you gain accuracy. In many waters containing vast shallow areas, wading is a good way to go bugging. It is a great technique for thoroughly covering water and the freedom from paddling or rowing enables the fisherman to concentrate on his fly casting alone.

Where wading isn't practical, a light maneuverable boat usually *is*. Most bugging will be confined to shallow, inshore

I land a largemouth which struck my popping bug near the fringe of bullrushes.

finally sink altogether. They are the hardest of all to cast. Not too many are available on tackle shelves anymore because they are expensive and time-consuming to make, as compared to the hard-bodied poppers.

All bugs should be fished very slowly. I have had bass rush crazily after bugs as they were hurriedly skittered or even being lifted from the water. But mostly the retrieve which kills is practically none at all. Cast out the bug to a likely spot and then let it work for you right there as long as possible—just by flipping the rod tip gently at intervals.

It is hard to resist making a popper pop—loudly as most can do. It's an exciting sound. But I have had far better luck when moving the bug just enough to broadcast circles all around it. Some of the surface strikes which

or protected waters and the need for a larger boat is small. A good accessory for bass flyrodding is a small electric motor for quietly maneuvering into tight places.

Good places for beginners to get a start in bass bugging are the numerous farm and ranch ponds which dot the American landscape. Most of these contain bass, in numbers if not in great size, and they are easy to fish. These small impoundments offer any angler good laboratories in which to test tackle and develop good techniques.

As my forgetful friend Lew Baker has always admitted, after that pioneer trip so long ago: "A fisherman hasn't really enjoyed bass fishing until he's done it with the light rod."

Lew ought to know; he learned the hard way.

Looking for high adventure with your fishing? Well, why not try a pack trip into the western mountains?

PUT YOURSELF IN THE SADDLE

by Bob Bauer

Casting for trout in any angler's promised land in the Alberta Rockies.

Spectacular scenery and solitude are the rewards for packtrippers into the western mountains. Scene here is approach to Fossil Lake, Montana.

Sparkplug, my dapple grey mare, pulled down on the reins and drank deeply from the cold water of Broad Creek. The other horses of the string followed suit and it was hard to get them moving again. The day was very warm and bright and the animals had traveled 14 miles across Yellowstone Park's Mirror Plateau under full loads. I guess those horses really deserved a breather.

After crossing the Creek and following it for a hundred yards or so, our outfitter, Gene Wade of Cooke City, Montana, announced that we would set up camp next to the creek. Then he also suggested that we could start fishing right beside the camp. But after all the commotion of splashing and drinking by the horses, I figured that every trout for a mile upstream and down would have been spooked.

But Gene seemed able to read my mind. "Don't worry about *these* trout," he said. "They haven't learned about horses and fishermen yet. I doubt if a handful of anglers have visited this whole stream this year."

After pitching camp, Gene proved his point by riding across a pool and then turning back around to cast a dry fly into it. As soon as the fly touched the water, a 1½-pound cutthroat trout rose to the surface and sucked in the fly. The battle that ensued, with Gene trying to control his mount and land the fish simultaneously, was one of the funniest antics that I have ever seen.

But that is only one of the beautiful things about pack trips. The fish in the back country just haven't learned about fishermen yet. If Gene Wade can ride across a pool and then catch a fish he almost trampled — well, an average fisherman using reasonable caution can catch all the fish he wants. Of course not all back country trout are as naive as the Broad Creek cutthroats. But they're a lot less

educated than the fish near the average fisherman's home.

The best way to reach these unsophisticated trout is by pack trip or trail ride. Pack trips are horseback expeditions into wilderness areas. Since the areas are unaccessible by road, all provisions must be packed in on horseback. The trips generally involve riding into a chosen area and making a base camp. Each day then, the fisherman rides out and fishes the surrounding lakes and streams. The advantage of pack trips is that by spending half a day or a day, the angler is able to fish waters which are out of reach for all other fishermen except possibly back-packers.

A pack trip into wilderness country can be one of the most rewarding trips an outdoorsman ever takes. But the excellent fishing is only part of the fun. The fishing itself is done amid some of America's most spectacular scenery. The lakes and streams are generally situated in verdant meadows or on the edges of cathedral-like woods. Snow-capped mountains offset the entire scene. After living eleven months of the year in the city, camp life in the mountains can be a perfect retreat and escape.

The pack trip is ideally suited for either family groups or fishing partners. During the summer the weather is usually mild enough for the women in the family to appreciate. The hardships are not so great that an active family cannot generally adapt to camp life. Furthermore, a wilderness pack trip provides the family with a great opportunity to be together. Pack trips can also provide fishing partners with an experience that they'll be talking about for a long time afterwards.

In order to have a successful pack trip, the fisherman must take certain personal items along with him. Every fisherman and every pack trip requires slightly different clothing but here is a general checklist of things the fisher-

Young rider in Utah's Uinta Mountains casts for trout without bothering to dismount.

man might consider: a pair of hiking boots, hip boots or waders, a couple pairs of durable pants, several changes of socks, wide brimmed hat, two warm shirts, jacket, and rain gear. I cannot over-emphasize the importance of having a good raincoat. Once it starts to rain in the mountains, it may last for days. The fisherman should always have a raincoat easily accessible in a saddle bag in case of such soggy conditions.

I once made a pack trip into the Beartooth Mountains of Montana with a family of Chicagoans who had been planning the trip for a long time. Unfortunately the man had never really "roughed it" before and he wasn't properly equipped for the trip. The whole family was very well dressed, however, only that is not enough. The father sported fancy riding pants, tooled alligator leather cowboy boots, Stetson hat and pearl-handled revolver hanging on his hip. In order to fully capture that "cowboy look," he even rolled his own cigarettes.

But among the gear he failed to bring were good quality sleeping bags for himself and his family. He bought the cheapest he could find. As a result the family was cold all night and they were the first ones sitting around the campfire in the morning. The father was also in poor physical condition and soon became miserable. Finally he demanded that a helicopter fly him out. It was necessary to take the man back to town several days sooner than the trip was scheduled to end. That ruined the adventure for everyone.

The outdoorsman's fishing gear should include both a spinning outfit and a fly fishing outfit. If you haven't fished too much before the trip, it is wise to work on your form and accuracy in the back yard before the trip begins.

A neighbor of mine practiced using his spinning and fly fishing tackle in the back yard every evening for about a month before his pack trip in Montana began. He practiced throwing a lure into his wife's clothes basket from all angles, including casting from spots directly beneath trees and shrubs. He also perfected such fly fishing techniques as the overhead cast, side cast, hook cast, roll cast, and reverse cast. After his pack trip was over, the pictures of the fish he caught were proof of the value of practice.

Besides the fishing outfits themselves, the fishermen should have a good selection of dry and wet flies and spinning lures. Favorite western flies include such patterns as the Muddler, Joe's Hopper, Adams and Blonde Wulff. The spinning lure assortment should include wobbling spoons and spinners of about ¼ ounce. The outfitter is usually acquainted with the likes and dislikes of the trout in his territory and can give good advice about your selection of lures.

The fisherman should bring along extra rods and reels in case any equipment is lost or damaged enroute to camp. The four-piece dual purpose rod which can be used with both fly reels and spinning reels makes an excellent spare. Other spare items which the angler should carry include fishing line, fly leaders, rod tips, and rod guides.

All of the camping equipment is generally supplied by the guide except for sleeping bag, mattress and personal items which the angler himself is expected to supply. However, it is necessary to contact the outfitter in order to get the most out of the pack trip. There are other items which the fisherman should take along. Mosquito repellent heads the list. Without it, the little demons can make the most beautiful day become unbearable. The fisherman should also take along other items that fit his own special interests. These might include a varmint rifle for hunting marmots, a tree or bird identification book, binoculars, a gold pan, rock chippers, and a good sharp sheath knife.

A camera, whether a simple snapshot camera or professional model, should be carried by every fisherman. The camera, like the raincoat and insect repellent should accompany the angler everywhere during the trip. While riding out, the fisherman should carry his camera and other important items such as his lunch and raincoat with him in his saddlebags.

The alert cameraman takes advantage of many photographic opportunities which will set his collection of pictures apart from the usual smug shots of an angler holding his catch. Try to catch that expression of genuine excitement in the angler's face. Shoot some landscapes of the fishing country. When out fishing, have your camera preset and ready to use. Using fast shutter speeds, try to get all the action of your buddy hooking a fish, playing fish, casting, netting fish, fish jumping and so forth. Take pictures of the guides doing camp chores. Pictures of the cook preparing a meal are different and interesting. Also try to take good pictures of your camp in the wilderness setting. You will always be glad you did.

A Western pack trip can be a wonderful experience but it can also be an expensive disaster. The final success of your pack trip depends a great deal upon the planning. Planning includes deciding where you want to go and who you will choose to guide you. Other smaller arrangements such as securing a fishing license must also be taken care of. In order to be reasonably sure of success, the fisherman should begin planning for his pack trip a year or more in advance. Start with these primary considerations.

Do you want really big fish or do you simply want a pleasant trip which doesn't involve riding long distances over rugged country? How much time and money can you afford? Are you an experienced enough outdoorsman to make the pack trip with minimum guidance or do you re-

Beautiful rainbow trout landed by Bill Browning (author of "Montana's Blue Ribbon Trout Rivers" elsewhere in this book) at Horseshoe Lake, Alberta Rockies.

quire the services of an outfitter? How many fishermen are in your party?

Write the state fish-and-game department of the state you are interested in and ask about seasons, licenses, prospects and best areas to fish. Many fish-and-game departments will send a list of the registered guides in their state.

The next step is to find a good outfitter in the area you plan to fish. The outfitter's advertising sections in outdoor publications are good places to find the names and addresses of outfitters. Possibly, you have a friend who made a pack trip previously with a reliable outfitter. Ask him about it. In any case, write several outfitters and tell them exactly what you would like to do, how far you want to ride, how many are going and so forth. Then ask the outfitter for references, recommendations, and a detailed estimate of costs. Before making a final commitment to a guide, check out all the references. Beware of guides who make extravagant promises. You will have to forward a deposit and agree to pay for a trip of a specified length

Author Bauer nets fat brook trout from icy waters of Fossil Lake, Beartooth Primitive Area on top of Montana.

Trail riders pause after long climb into the high country en route to Horseshoe Lake.

On pack trips, outfitters provide all camping gear, su the colorful tepee on a trip into Banff National Park, Ca

of time even though something may cause you to cut it short.

Costs of a pack trip can be cut if you can do the camp chores and handle horses yourself. This way an outfitter can pack you and your gear into a good area (where there is fishing), leave you there, and then pick you up later at a specified date. This can be the most adventurous type of all pack trips and it can generally save you more than one-half of ordinary costs.

Preparation for a pack trip has not ended as soon as you have decided what equipment that you are going to take. If you've been tied down in the office too long, you may need to do some physical training before your trip begins. Pack trips can be tailored somewhat to suit the individual's physical condition but you'll get more out of the trip if you're in good physical shape at the outset. Exercise before the pack trip can mean the difference between fishing an alpine lake that is inaccessible on horseback or doing camp chores without pulling a tender muscle.

Training for a pack trip may start months in advance for some fishermen while others may need only to ride Junior's bicycle a few times a week. If you notice a sagging around your waistline, begin training moderately and then work up from there. Try to find exercises that will keep your interest such as swimming, hiking, or golfing. It's often not necessary to search for activities. Walk to the drug store instead of driving. Avoid elevators by walking up and down the stairs. Push yourself away from the dinner table before dessert.

Horseback riding requires special attention. No fisherman, no matter what his condition, should take a pack trip without having previously done *some* riding. Riding long distances through the mountains exerts a strain on certain muscles that are otherwise neglected. Saddle soreness is a painful experience than can nearly immobilize a person for the duration of the trip. Spending some time training on the local riding trails before the trip begins is a good way to avoid misery later on.

A well prepared pack trip can offer you fishing memories that you will certainly cherish for a long time. You may enjoy it so much that you should not be surprised if your outfitter talks you into coming back out and hunting with him in the fall.

Pause to repair and rig tackle at half-way point on pack trip into Assiniboine Provincial Park, British Columbia.

WASHINGTON—A good area is the Strait of Juan de Fuca. Try bays like this one off Agate-Crescent Beach near Neah Bay and Sekiu.

CALIFORNIA—San Francisco Bay is a good salmon area. Charter boats can take you to action in the bay and in the ocean beyond the Golden Gate. East, salmon fishing is good in the Delta and rivers such as the Sacramento and Feather.

An Angler's Guide to

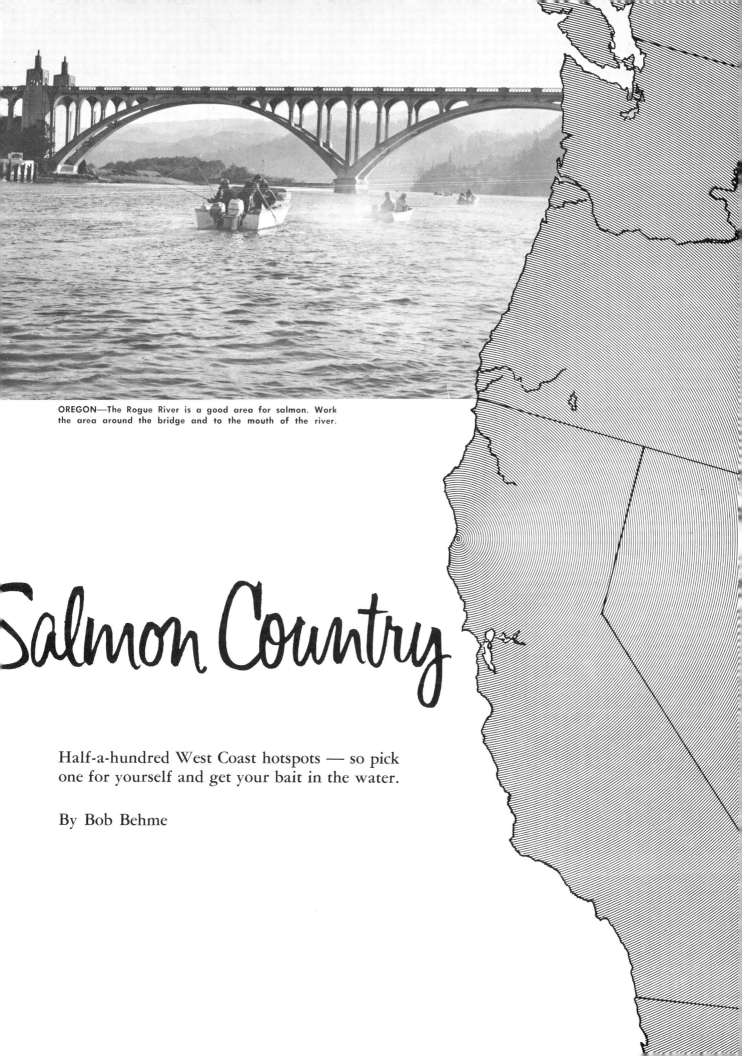

OREGON—The Rogue River is a good area for salmon. Work the area around the bridge and to the mouth of the river.

Salmon Country

Half-a-hundred West Coast hotspots — so pick one for yourself and get your bait in the water.

By Bob Behme

A "small" Chinook (it weighed but 14 pounds)—caught off the Oregon Coast. Chinooks average 15 to 30 pounds and can weigh as much as 100 pounds. Silvers are smaller and average 10 to 15 pounds.

To sportsmen from other areas the amazing abundance of Pacific Coast fish only compounds the headache of what to catch. But local fishermen solve the problem with characteristic simplicity. In the summer most of them concentrate on salmon. And why not? Salmon provide action from mid-California to Alaska.

If you want unforgettable fishing, come west for salmon. You can pick your battler from five species. Chances are that, like most westerners, you'll set your sights on two, chinooks and silver. These are the abundant salmon, the battlers, the famed fall run. They begin feeding off the coast as early as June and offer a season that runs hot through October. The chinook, larger of the two, is a bruising, stubborn bottom fighter. The silver, although half the size, is scrappier, a fancy, tail dancing surface fighter.

Tackle, baits and boats. Bring a medium-action rod. Short, "salmon" rods are popular and readily available, but not essential. A steelhead rod makes a good choice. Avoid stiff ocean-type rods. They are no fun.

Spinning tackle works nicely and if you prefer a bait or star drag reel, bring it. Any one is good and whatever your choice of reels, pack it with at least 15-pound line. Avoid light-weight tackle unless you plan to fish less popular areas. Silvers average 10 to 15 pounds, chinooks can top 40 and with light tackle you need plenty of room for either fish. In the popular salmon waters you don't have it.

Some fishermen prefer live bait. It is good, but it can be difficult to find. A few docks in Oregon and Washington carry it and I've found it in British Columbia but never in California. Frozen herring is ubiquitous and, when properly rigged, works well every time. You'll find it at docks from the Campbell River to Monterey so there is no reason to stock in advance. Buy only enough for a day's action.

Two-hook mooching rigs are standard in Washington and Oregon. They are fool-proof once you learn what to do with the hooks. Insert the rear hook (which can be a single or a treble) in the bait near the tail. The forward hook goes through the head. The line between the two slides and its tension controls the curve of the bait. The curve of the bait makes it roll when you troll and the tighter the line the more the bait rolls. Adjust this bend until you get just the right action, a slow, easy roll that imitates a wounded minnow.

Stick with trolling, since it takes the most fish. I generally run between three and five knots although spoons can be trolled faster for silvers. Troll deep, a foot or two off bottom for chinooks, and troll shallow, a foot or two below the surface for silvers.

When there is no action with bait alone, add a chrome attractor a foot before the herring. You can buy spoons and wobblers everywhere along the coast and it is wise to carry an assortment of four or more. Use them alone and as attractors with bait. When all else fails, I usually have luck with two lines. One holds bait, the other a fluorescent attractor.

Charter boats and launching ramps are no problem. If you bring your own boat you'll need at least a 14-footer for the ocean. County launching ramps are generally free, but may be little more than a cleared area. Commercial ramps, at a buck in and out, are usually paved and in good shape. In a few places (Whidby Island, Washington is one) hoists are common. Most moorages offer rentals, and the average coastal boat is a 14- or 16-footer. Rates range from $3 for a boat alone to $10 for boat and

motor. Several good publications list moorages, ramps and rentals. Two, from Standard and Mobil petroleum companies, are free.

The larger ports offer charter services. Ports I've tried and recommend include Westport and Ilwaco, Washington, Warrenton and Depoe Bay, Oregon and Smith River and San Francisco, California. Rates will vary from a low of $8 to a high of $16. The variation is explained by the differences in trip times. Some charters are further from good fishing than others and while most promise four hours of fishing a few are all-day-long.

Where to go. Western salmon country covers more than 2,000 miles of coastline. Obviously, you have a wide choice of places to fish. It is difficult to list all of the popular ports and hot areas, but these are my favorites:

Canada. You won't go wrong any place in British Columbia. Most salmon migrate south from Alaska by one of two routes. One swings west, around the Canadian Islands of Queen Charlotte and Vancouver to the Strait of Juan de Fuca and Washington, Oregon and Cali-

OREGON—Don Birely, seated, is the most famous guide on the Rogue River. He works the Rogue from the 101 Bridge to the mouth. Baits and attractors are common. Weights go from one to eight ounces, depending on the tides.

Six silvers displayed by a family on a short visit to the Washington coast. Salmon fishing is a man's sport, but it is geared to family action.

fornia coastal rivers. The other follows the mainland past Hecate Strait, Queen Charlotte Sound and the Strait of Georgia to the Canadian rivers and Puget Sound.

The ocean off Canada is prime salmon water. A Field and Stream contest winner — a 92 pound, 4-foot ten-inch chinook — was pulled from the Skeena River. You can do nearly as well in the south: the Strait of Georgia almost guarantees action.

One of my favorite mainland places is Powell River, north of Vancouver. If you want something different try Stuart Island. You can only reach it by plane or boat, but the fishing around Stuart is little short of fantastic. Try the water near Yucataw Rapids for big fish.

You can drive to the excellent waters off Vancouver Island and a lot of Americans do. My favorite place is Campbell River, an area made famous by Roderick Haig-Brown, the trout angler and author. Troll the sound to the east. Midway between Campbell River and Victoria is a stretch of water near Bowser, Qualicam Beach and Parksville that is hot with kings. At Parksville you can take the road west to Alberni, one of the most under-rated salmon areas in Canada. The last time I tried the fishing off Alberni Inlet and Barkley Sound I limited almost as fast as I could cast.

Washington. As with Canada, Washington has so much superb water you can't go wrong. There is action along the Pacific Ocean and in Puget Sound. Westport is the most popular charter town, and if you like ocean charters don't miss it.

I prefer the action in the Strait of Juan de Fuca, not because the fishing is better, but because the water suits me. Neah Bay and Sekiu are my favorite ports. Neah Bay is an Indian town on the Makah Reservation. I've never been treated better in any fishing resort. The charters are good and the facilities are more than adequate. Sekiu is another good pplace on the strait with good facilities. From either town you can troll to the ocean and beyond. Often the best fish are found off Agate-Crescent Beach. If you want to try the western end of the Strait try boats out of Port Angeles and Port Townsend.

Puget Sound offers a variety of choices and I never miss an opportunity to fish it. In the north take time to try the Skagit River. You'll have a chance for big chinook, silvers and, in alternate years, the humpback or pink salmon, a scrappy, barrel-chested battler. Work the river downstream from Mount Vernon. I usually stay at Phil's Landing because it is midway between Mount Vernon and the Sound. Here you will find log booms in the lower river. Moor near these and cast beneath and beside the logs.

Whidby and Camano Islands are good choices. Any of the salmon resorts will deliver action. A popular place is a stretch of water between the southern tip of Whidby and the mainland at Mukilteo. It is called "The Triangle" and trolling can deliver big fish. Last fall I trolled the area with an old friend, Louie Larsen. Louie hooked a chinook that shook his rod and ran and dove for twenty minutes before he could bring him to net. Later, when I weighed him at the dock, the fish topped 48 pounds.

Closer to Seattle you can find action trolling off Ballard and even in the waters near the Government Locks. Hoods Canal, from Hoodsport on the south to Port Gamble on the north, specializes in big chinooks. And in the south, the Columbia River is little short of great. On the Washington side you can get reliable charters at Ilwaco, Seaview and Long Beach.

WASHINGTON—A good Chinook caught off Sekiu. The fish scaled in at 25 pounds.

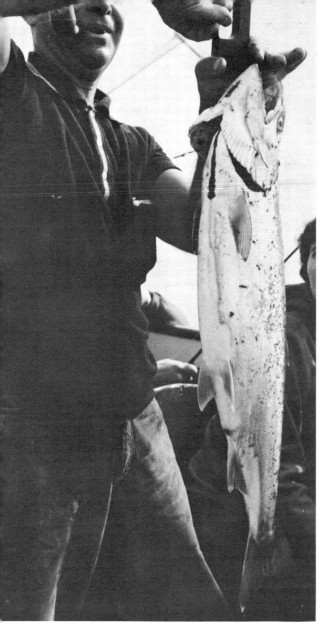

Oregon. There are salmon from the Columbia River south to the California border. You can find good fish and good action upstream as far as Bonneville, but I stick to the coast. In my opinion it offers some of the best salmon fishing in America.

If you like the Columbia, stick with charters out of Warrenton. The boats work to the mouth of the river and if there are any salmon in the northern waters, you can find them here. The Columbia offers several salmon runs; spring, fall and winter.

The first sizable salmon stream south of the Columbia, the Nehalem, is a favorite of mine. I usually work out of

OREGON—Rich Wisner's Tradewinds Trollers, out of Depoe Bay brought in this good looking Chinook.

WASHINGTON—a 21-pound Chinook caught by author's son, Erik, on the Sakgit.

OREGON—Nehalem River— writer's family with a typical salmon catch.

BAIT—Bait is the first choice for most salmon fishermen, but when it fails, bait can be used in combination with hardware—often larger chrome flashers and attractors—and hardware alone payed off. Shown here: wobblers, chrome flasher and red fluorescent spoons alone with the three common bait rigs—whole bait, filet and plug cut.

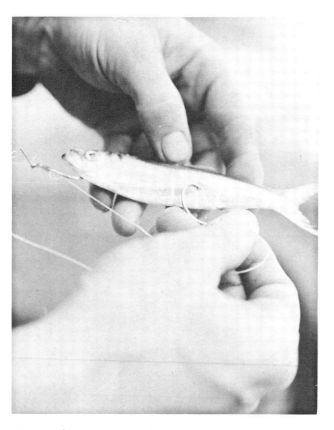

BAIT—Mooching rigs are standard but they vary in that some use single hooks, shown here, while others use a treble. The front hook is placed through the head, the rear through the body near the tail.

Easton's, at Brighton near the mouth of the river, and I've never been skunked. The bar can be tricky when the surf is high, but at these times work upstream. Last year I pulled two 20-pound chinooks from the river near Wheeler. The fish were as big and as scrappy as those I'd picked up in the ocean a month earlier.

Depoe Bay is a picturesque, snug harbor and if you like charter fishing try it out of this town. Some of the best charter action I've had has come from the Tradewinds Trollers here. Another port I can recommend highly is Salmon Harbor-Winchester south of Reedsport. Salmon Harbor has charters as well as excellent launching facilities. The day I fished this water I worked with Hobe Durbin who took me from the mouth of the Umpqua River to the buoys and back in a triangular troll that worked close to the breakers. We hooked two limits in less than two hours.

Coos Bay, one of the largest towns on the coast, offers good facilities. You'll find charters at Charleston Harbor and Empire.

Don't overlook the Rogue River, between Gold Beach and Wedderburn. The upper reaches were made famous by Zane Grey who loved the steelhead action there, but for salmon stick to the jaws of the river. I usually fish with Don Birely, a local motel owner and one of the best guides on the river. We troll between the bridge and the ocean.

If you have time check the Chetco River, at Brookings on the California-Oregon border. The Chetco is a sleeper with excellent facilities, good docks and a chance for fish that has barely been exploited.

California. The northern half of California's sunny coastline produces salmon. You can fish as far south as Monterey with guaranteed results. The Smith River, near Crescent City is the first hot spot in the north. The river is popular and probably crowded on weekends but you can usually find room on the boat lines that work close to the mouth. If you prefer calmer action work the river upstream as far as the Memorial Bridge.

Trinidad is another good possibility. I fish the area two or three times a year and almost always dock with good fish. Try the water near Trinidad Head. Humboldt Bay at Eureka is another good place. The fishing can run hot and cold, but on a good day you not only get action but big fish. South, try Noyo Harbor at Fort Bragg. The town, standing high on a bluff, offers a beautiful setting for the action that takes place below. Noyo has a good launching ramp and every facility you want.

California offers unusual "big city" action. From San Francisco you fish beyond the Golden Gate in ocean waters off the Faralones and you can fish the bay itself. I've caught good fish in both San Francisco and San Pablo bays. During the season charters can take you to the best action for less than ten bucks.

East, in the Delta, a famous area where three of the state's largest rivers meet, the action can run surprisingly hot once fall rains move the fish upstream. If you like river fishing you can choose between the Sacramento, Yuba, Feather and American rivers. I like the Sacramento and a favorite section is a stretch between Chico and Red Bluff. The river there is uncrowded. I can troll up or down stream without worry.

Alaska has not been included in this survey because it is the salmon state and a story in itself. (See Mike Miller's article "Fishing in Alaska Today.") But with three states and one province to choose from, you'll find it difficult to go wrong. Come west for salmon. I'll see you there. How do you find me? Easy enough! I'm always the guy with a broad smile on his face and a salmon on his line.

Handsome arctic char caught at Victoria Island, N.W.T. Fish at extreme left is a lake trout.

ON THE TRAIL OF THE ARCTIC CHAR

by Karl H. Maslowski

Angler at Bathurst Inlet, N.W.T., compares lake trout (left) with arctic char.

Mention "char" and someone may think you're discussing an unsuccessful attempt to broil a steak. But mention it to an angler and his eyes will light up instantly. He'll probably engage you in conversation that will touch not only fishing but also caribou, barren-ground grizzly bears, seals, Eskimos, chilled lakes, brawling streams, ptarmigan, Lapland longspurs, and a tundra landscape abloom with lavish scatter rugs of wild flowers.

The arctic char, closely related to the brook trout and Dolly Varden, is found in North America only in Arctic waters, and, depending on the season, in both fresh and salt waters. Some populations are landlocked, but most spend the spring and summer in the sea and return to ancestral streams and lakes to spawn and overwinter. It is when they first return to the streams in late summer or early fall that Arctic char are perhaps at their best. Then the fish may be an exceedingly colorful creature, cardinal red along the belly, with a dark median stripe, and a top-side somewhere between a sunset orange and a light tan. The pectoral, pelvic and anal fins are delicately outlined in creamy white, and splotches of white may appear around the head.

Any char over 15 pounds makes a good trophy, but exceptional individuals may weigh between 20 and 25 pounds. Most char average from six to ten pounds, and I've found myself supremely happy many, many times catching them at that weight.

The great thing about char fishing in the area I know best—the Northwest Territories and Arctic Quebec—is that you usually find the fish where you may also enjoy the solitude of vast places. Often when camped on the tundra my companions and I were the only people within 250 square miles, or more. When you consider that the Northwest Territories have a total population of only about 35,000 in an area spread over 1,300,000 square miles, you can understand why you are not likely to hear the squeal of brakes, jangling phones, the cacaphony of a jetport, or the strident rumble of a factory.

To get into char country, you must find a reliable camp operator and contract with him to pick you up via a charter plane at such northern hubs as Yellowknife, Baker Lake, or Fort Chimo. Individuals that come immediately to mind are Willie Imudluk, Illkalu Lodge, Box 2642, Ottawa 4, Ontario, Canada; Mrs. Glenn Warner, Bathurst Inlet Lodge, Box 820, Yellowknife, N.W.T., Canada; Don Hamilton, Arctic Outpost Camps, Ltd., P.O. Box 110, Edmonton 15, Alberta, Canada; Raymond "Pooch" Liesenfeld, Rainy Lake Airways, P.O. Box 790, Fort Francis, Ontario, Canada.

The first char I saw caught was a most unimpressive fish. Back in 1965 I was fishing on Victoria Island in the Northwest Territories with my long-time friend and neighbor, George Laycock. At the head of Minto Inlet our pilot, Don Hamilton, who was then stationed at Cambridge Bay, caught a specimen that weighed two pounds. While the size was far from spectacular, the taste of that fish on the dinner table made a most favorable impact on my palate, and I immediately wanted to catch more char.

The next day Don flew us to a fair-sized lake about four miles inland from Albert Edward Bay on the extreme southeastern edge of Victoria Island. It was late July, yet most of the bay still wore a heavy shield of rough ice. But close to shore where the outlet stream emptied toward the sea there was an open basin about 300 yards wide. As the plane passed over we could see a dark mass of thousands of fish in the shallows, which Don assured us were char, waiting perhaps to ascend the river for spawning.

We landed on the lake, and George and I hastily rigged up a rubber boat and rowed out from shore. On George's first cast with a silver-colored spoon he'd barely begun reeling when his rod arched and his 12-pound-test line began stripping off the spool at an alarming rate.

Ten minutes later an eight-pound silver-colored char with flaring red gills was thrashing about on the surface. In another moment George neatly led the fish into the landing net and I hefted it into the dinghy. Its body was as firm and well packed as a husky sausage and gleamed like metal in the bright Arctic sunshine.

George then suggested that I quit resisting temptation and let him row while I fished. A fellow doesn't argue with that kind of charitable logic, so I made my first cast and was rewarded with a heavy strike that eventually produced a twin to George's char.

It should be emphasized that biologists have found that once a char is hooked, fought and landed, its chances of survival are very slim if it is returned to the water. Inasmuch as the species grows very slowly, with an eight-pound specimen being fifteen to eighteen years of age, it is simply good conservation to keep the fish you catch and to catch only the number permitted by regulations. In the famous Tree River the current limit is two fish per day, but elsewhere it may range as high as ten per day.

It took just 45 minutes for George and I to catch four char apiece that morning, and doubtless we could have caught a hundred if we had wanted to. But eight char, though still several under our legal limit, were ample for our needs for the next several days. Besides, there were stone inuksuk to be examined, shorebirds to watch, Arctic ground squirrels to film, and tundra flowers to admire. Inuksuk are crude shafts of stones piled one atop the other which from afar look like figures of men. They were erected in bygone days by Eskimos, but no one seems to know exactly why. Perhaps they were guideposts, maybe they were used to help drive and herd caribou to waiting hunters, or possibly Eskimos felt lonely in the vast tundra land and simply erected the stonelike men for company.

Willie Imudluk is unique among my Eskimo friends. He's the only member of his tribe who operates a sportfishing

Author's son Pete admires char taken from Twin River, N.W.T.

Author fights char in swift water of Back River at Chantry Inlet.

camp. His is on Ford Island in the George River off Ungava Bay in Arctic Quebec. Just after his camp was opened, George Laycock and I arrived there in mid-August, 1967. Willie explained that in four more days, when the August high tide would occur, myriads of red-bellied Arctic char would ascend the nearby Hodalatuk River, and that we would have no trouble catching them in the pools below the falls. Meantime he suggested we spend a couple of days at his outpost camp on the Korak River about twenty miles away. And with two of Willie's Eskimo guides we did just that.

The Korak must be one of the prettiest of the raging Arctic streams which issue torrent-like from the Ungava Peninsula highlands. In two of the pools perhaps a mile below the outpost camp George and I had no trouble catching silver-colored char, including one 18-pounder and half a dozen more fish in the 12- to 15-pound range, all of them on big spinners and spoons.

Scene at Ilkalu Lodge on George River, Quebec, shows arctic char and lake trout taken by guests.

Only two pools produced char. Above and below these pools we could catch lake trout, but no char. This situation is typical of the species. When char move into a stream to spawn they school in vast hordes and then they must be searched for.

We returned to the base camp, and one night later the August high tide swept in (tides in that area are frequently 15 feet or more). The next morning, after a delectable—but almost stupefying—breakfast, Willie took us to the Hodalatuk in an outboard boat. There we followed a path through black spruce for about a mile which ended at the edge of a waterfall. Below was a pool not more than 75 feet in diameter. As I looked into the clear, frigid waters I had the uncanny feeling that the pool was nothing more than a big can packed almost solid with live fish! In the densely crowded mass I could easily discern flashes of bright red. The Arctic char, dressed in their most brilliant color, had come home to the Hodalatuk to spawn on the August high

tide, just as Willie had predicted they would.

My first cast with a red Stingsilda did not go unnoticed by the mob of fish. A scarlet-bellied eight-pounder struck, and once it felt the hook it charged downstream. But even with its weight and the benefit of the swift water, the fish couldn't win against the 12-pound-test line. Once it was turned back upstream it bored to the very bottom of the pool and then surged up under the waterfall. The other char jammed in the pool simply opened an avenue for the hooked fish as it fought to free itself. Ten minutes after the strike, George, Willie and I admired the spent char on the sloping granite shore.

We found we could catch about eight char from the pool before the fish became too wary. We had to stand right out in the open to cast. But a pool a hundred yards above could then be fished for perhaps an hour before the fish quit striking.

This same George River area is the only place I've caught

Author checks char near Ungava Bay, Quebec.

char in salt water. By casting fairly heavy spoons, spinners, and the Stingsilda near the mouth of the Hodalatuk we regularly hooked char weighing six to ten pounds. The Eskimos set nets in the same waters and caught hundreds of pounds of char during our brief stay. These fish were filleted and hung on racks to dry for winter use. Elsewhere in the Arctic I've often seen similar sights—hundreds of pounds of char hung like laundry to dry in the brief Arctic summer. Sad to say, some of these fish would be fed to the dogteams in wintertime.

I say "sad" because the flesh of the char is most delectable and even the poorest cook cannot ruin it. Char may be fried, baked, broiled, boiled, dried, or even eaten raw, and it always tastes good. Often I simply chunk the meat and drop it in a pot of boiling salt water for ten to twelve minutes. Then I fork off big pink flakes and dip them in drawn butter. I prefer them to lobster.

Eskimo Issac Akeetok enjoys
raw char at Chantry Inlet.▶

Anglers in lonely char country see variety of undisturbed wildlife: bull caribou swimming Burnside River, N.W.T.; arctic ground squirrel pausing while digging burrow; muskox, and willow ptarmigan.

I've had some especially exciting char fishing in the Baker Lake area and at Chantry Inlet. At Baker Lake in early August we caught fish up to 12 pounds at the mouth of the Twin River. A week earlier on that same trip my son Peter and I had flown to a tent camp at Chantry Inlet run by "Pooch" Liesenfeld. Here we caught only a few char, but we were assured that early in July there had been fair numbers taken, some up to 18 pounds in weight. And we were told that in late August there would be premium char fishing when the fish came back to the rivers to spawn. Here, too, an angler has the rare opportunity to see Eskimo women using both modern tackle and primitive fish spears with great skill. The fish spears have tips formed from caribou antlers that both grab and impale the fish.

If I had to pick my favorite char fishing hole it would be the Bathurst Inlet area near the Burnside River. Actually I've caught fewer than a dozen char there, the largest weighing about 15 pounds, but I really didn't fish very much. Nowhere else in the Arctic have I seen such scenic grandeur and concentrations of big game. Nearly every time I'd fish with guides Lyall Hawkins or John Naneroak we'd be distracted by ringed seals, tundra wolves, herds of caribou or muskoxen, barren ground grizzlies, weasels, yellow-billed loons, whistling swans, or oldsquaw ducks. Or we would discover a nest of peregrine falcons, golden eagles, Harris' sparrows, northern phalaropes, redpolls, or Lapland longspurs.

If you go on the trail of the Arctic char plan your trip for July or August. Take along clothes you'd wear hunting —say, in late October in the Upper Peninsula of Michigan. Equip yourself with good raingear (I found hip-boots unnecessary), a head net, and a can or two of insect repellent. Take along at least two fairly heavy spinning or casting rods and reels. One of the spinning outfits should have about six-pound-test line so you can fish for Arctic grayling. Other spools should contain ten- to twenty-pound-test lines. If you enjoy flyrod fishing, take an outfit along because it's possible to catch lake trout, char and grayling on flies. I'm not likely to forget the ten-pound char I caught on a big muddler fly in the Hodalatuk while angling for brook trout.

An assortment of spinners, spoons, and heavy plugs in various sizes—those you might use for bluegills, bass, and northern pike—are ideal. Take along a good supply because you'll lose lures and the nearest Hudson Bay post may be 350 miles away. Also take along a couple dozen nylon-coated wire leaders; char are not only toothsome, but toothy as well. For the same reason it's wise to take along a pair of needle-nose pliers to remove your lures.

Currently the accommodations in the best char fishing areas in the Northwest Territories and Arctic Quebec are very limited, so plan your trip at least six months in advance to assure yourself a reservation.

LAKERS
AND
LEAD HEADS

By George Laycock

Fishermen net heavy laker from deep waters of Lake Athapapuskow.

Anglers interested in catching lake trout — big ones and many of them — are hearing exciting reports out of the north. Fishermen are changing their trout fishing tactics. I first heard about this development some months ago in northern Manitoba and reported on it. Then readers began trying the idea and wrote to tell me the results.

"I have been fishing a lake in Canada for two years and it is loaded with lake trout," wrote one of these correspondents. "Not many are caught because trolling is a slow and not very rewarding business.

"A fellow fisherman and myself just got back from a week's fishing trip to Canada and we had a real bonanza. We followed your instructions.

"None of us had ever fished for or caught a lake trout in our lives, I caught my first one on my first cast, 8 lbs. We fished for trout for two days and easily caught our limits and gave fish away, plently of 12 and 16 pounders.

"We gave our supply of baits to the fishing guides at the camp, and they proceeded to bring in limit catches for their customers.

"Last year the largest trout caught in this camp weighed

13 pounds. In one day this year there must have been a dozen caught larger than that. The largest was 18 lbs. 3 oz. Before our week was out there were 132 trout caught on the baits we gave out. The old time wire line trolling group just couldn't believe it.

"This is probably the best fishing tip I'll ever have. If you have any more tips please send them along."

If I had any more fishing tips as good as the one which this correspondent put to use I would use it myself. The truth is, however, that this tip is still not widely known among anglers except on a handful of northern lakes.

This prescription for fish catching is one I learned first from Cap Anderson. Cap has spent most of his life around the settlement of Cranberry Portage in northern Manitoba. He has hunted and fished since he was old enough to walk, and he learned to know the big sprawling Lake Athapapuskow well enough to be a highly successful guide there. The lake, locally called "Athapap," incidentally, for many years held the record for lake trout. There are still numerous monster size trout taken from it every season.

Anywhere, even on the best of lake trout waters, fishing

Top left—Author (right) unloads heavy string of lake trout taken by deep jigging. Bottom left—Anglers weigh ten-pound laker caught in Lake Athapapuskow. Right—Here's jig-and-fish-strip combination the author uses.

may sometimes be in the doldrums. This unhappy time usually coincides with the hottest months of the year. The big trout have gone to the deep cool waters.

The most common method of putting a lure down where the fish live is to troll it for them.

Until recently trolling was the only method known to people in northern Manitoba and neighboring Saskatchewan. "We used to just sit in our boats all day running around the lake dragging a deep wire line," Cap explained. When the fish would not take a trolled bait, fishing was poor indeed.

Although jig fishing dates back to prehistoric times, it never seemed very effective for lake trout fishermen.

A few years ago on Lake Athapap, trout catches declined so much that the future of lake trout fishing in northern Manitoba looked bleak. Fishermen and lodge owners alike were moaning about the lost fishing. Then some creative fisherman decided that it was time to try jigging. The results were nothing short of spectacular. Said a news release from Manitoba in late 1963, "Lake Athapapuskow, traditional home of monster lake trout in northwestern Manitoba, has given sports fishermen their best season in 20 years."

The fishing method responsible for this development had anglers all around northern Manitoba highly excited. "You won't find anybody trolling around here anymore," Cap told me.

Cap's enthusiasm was catching. He explained that he had a million things to do as manager of Caribou Lodge and began outlining what they were. He was still listing them later when we put his boat on a trailer and headed for Lake Athapap.

After we reached the exact spot Cap wished to fish, he cut the motor. From his tackle box he took a large oval-shaped lead-headed two ounce jig. I seldom see one like it in tackle boxes of freshwater fishermen, although jigs this heavy and heavier are frequently used for saltwater species. Anyone who has fished jigs very much understands a little bit of their nature. They sink fast and go deep. Unlike most lures they have no built-in action. The action must come from the way in which the rod is handled and the retrieve made. But the jig in motion apparently resembles something edible to a wide variety of fish. In recent years it has moved inland from the salt water to become highly effective on such fish as walleyes and black bass.

The jig Cap chose was painted iridescent colors, and the hook was hidden in a bucktail skirt. It is important when using a jig, no matter what the species of fish, that the point of the hook be kept extremely sharp. The hook usually rides point up as the jig is retrieved, and sometimes, it is off balance as the fish strikes. Consequently it may not penetrate readily unless it is extremely sharp.

Cap tied the jig to his monofilament, then began adding decorations to the bottom of it. First there came a trailer hook. This, he explained was to circumvent the possibility of short strikes. Then he cut a three-inch long strip from the belly of a sucker. He hooked the strip of fish onto the lower hook of his lure. Now the whole affair was six or seven inches long. Cap held it up and let it turn in the sunlight as he admired his creation. "It's heavy," he said, "but it does the job."

In midsummer, even in these northern waters, the trout may go to depths of 100 feet or more. If you're going to jig

Many lake trout specialists in northern Canada now prefer deep jigging to trolling.

for them it is important to know where the deep holes are. Being a relative newcomer to Lake Athapap, I was fortunate in having Cap take me directly to what should be the most productive waters. Anyone wanting to try this method for the first time needs a guide or an electronic depth finder and thermometer. Once you locate the deep holes, you've made a good beginning.

On our first day the water was extremely quiet. Instead of anchoring his boat over the holes Cap let it drift gently. From time to time he would start the motor and move back upwind. A stiff breeze can move your fishing boat off of the fishing hole quickly. On days such as this — and Cap says it's better if there's a slight ripple — the anchor is the answer.

Why use the jig and the strip of fish together? The answer is simple. Neither one, as Cap explained to me, has produced as well by itself as the tested combination. There is no need to make long casts with an outfit such as this. In fact a long cast when using a light spinning outfit is difficult and definitely a risk to the rod because of the weight of the bait. You're aiming not for distance but for depth. My spin casting outfit was equipped with 20-pound test line. Following Cap's example, I lobbed the bait out to one side of the boat. It hit the water with a resounding smack, disappeared quickly and peeled line from the reel as it sank rapidly toward the bottom. I let the bait drop until the line went slack, then reeled up a foot or two of line to take the bait off the bottom. During the retrieve I jigged the bait up and down slowly.

Cap connected first and I quickly reeled in my bait and laid my rod aside to give him room to maneuver his fish. With the trolling rigs still used for lake trout in many places the ensuing episode would not have lasted long. After ten minutes of careful work he brought the nine-pounder to the boat.

At this moment there must have been 20 or 25 boats in view on Lake Athapap. Nowhere did I see a fisherman trolling.

Shortly after Cap released his fish, I had lobbed my bait out again and watched it sink from sight. It must have dropped a hundred feet or more before I felt the line go slack as the bait touched the bottom. I quickly lifted it off the floor of the lake and held it suspended there a few inches above the bottom. Then I brought it up as I had seen Cap do and stopped it quickly and let it drop a foot or two back toward the bottom. After a moment's waiting I repeated the process. This time, as I let the bait sink again, I felt the fish hit. He struck with a whallop and started home with

my conglomerate bait.

At that depth there is considerable stretch in a mono-filament line. This coupled with the willowy action of the spinning rod calls for a lot of force to set the hook in the hard jaws of a large lake trout.

He came with great reluctance. He sounded and made repeated runs first to one side and then the other. But against the relentless action of the rod there was not much that he could do in the long run and just as Cap's trout had, this one came to the edge of the boat. We photographed him and turned him free.

Time and again throughout the afternoon we sent those heavy jigs to the bottom of the lake and brought them back with big impressive trout attached. The biggest one weighed between 12 and 13 pounds. There were none under five pounds. There was no longer any question in my mind that jigging worked for lake trout.

Reports from other anglers since have verified these findings. This system seems to produce even when lake trout are not hitting trolled lures. I am confident that in the years ahead lake trout fishing is going to pick up in northern lakes wherever fishermen learn to jig for them.

More recently I put the method to test far to the north of Athapap. A small group of us were on an exploratory fishing trip in a lake on the Dubawnt River in the Northwest Territories. In this wild country in the heart of the tundra there is little need to fish deep for lake trout. They can be taken relatively close to the surface whenever the ice is out. I wanted, however, to see what would happen with my big two-ounce lead heads rigged as we had them in Lake Athapap. One afternoon I used my electronic fish locator to seek out the deep holes. Then, as the boat drifted, I dropped a jig to the bottom of the lake 50 to 60 feet below us. It fell rapidly and no fish took it on the descent. But scarcely had it touched the bottom of the lake, when it was hit so forcefully that the rod was nearly taken from my hands.

The trout weighed better than 20 pounds. I tried the idea again and promptly caught another lake trout. But because there is no need for jigging for lake trout out here, I removed the heavy lure and tied on one of the spoons which we had been casting. I had satisfied myself that jigging would work in these waters as well as where we had first tried it.

But, this system of jigging is at its best in waters and at times when other methods and lures fail. It frequently produces when nothing else will take the fish. The lesson learned on Lake Athapap is spreading.

It's evening on Michigan pond, and Bill Henderson strikes a bluegill on a popping bug . . .

Secrets of a Successful Panfisherman...

By Fred Steele

. . . and swings it aboard.

When Bill Henderson was maybe ten years old, he was already the best bluegill-catcher in Licking County. For several seasons he smuggled cane poles to the village park pond, and in time he graduated to a sort of patchwork fly rod. Finally he tried to convey the science of panfishing to me and other young incorrigibles, to the dismay of the local piano teacher.

Many years later — in fact, it was last spring — I fished with Bill at a backwoods Michigan pond. He was crouched tensely, carefully falsecasting to measure line, and at the last moment he shifted direction, shooting the fly over the water. When the bug plopped onto the surface, I stepped up for a closer look, and that move blew all the fishing. I clapped my hands over my ears, because, dammit, I knew not to throw my shadow on clear water, that bluegills weren't as dumb as I thought, ad infinitum. It was just like the old days (I never did learn piano, either).

I retreated to the far shore, where all the shallows were under the shadow line. On my first retrieve I whipped a bluegill back into the woods, then searched among the leaves, figuring to release it so I wouldn't have to apologize later for the size of my catch. When evening rolled around I found Henderson bellied up to the weathered pine slab that served as an outdoor cleaning table, with fish scales flying like snowflakes in the lantern light. His catch — a long string of bluegills and pumpkinseed sunfish—convinced me I'd better brush up on my panfishing. For a start I asked whether he'd found both species together, and here's what he told me:

39

Well, ichthyologists say the anatomy of all sunfishes adapts them for swimming in weeds, brushpiles, tight cover like that. With their flattened bodies they can turn sharply around obstacles. But I don't look for bluegills and pumpkinseeds in the weedbeds all the time. Most of the season, bluegills—at least the big ones—are in deeper, more open water. Pumpkinseeds stick a little closer to the weeds. Too many anglers think that all species of sunfishes are alike, the same way Ronald Reagan looks at redwoods.

Now today I found both species in the same spots, because they're spawning and there are only a few suitable nesting sites, shallow flats without any weeds. When sunfishes spawn together like that, they sometimes hybridize, and I have a couple here on the stringer that look like hybrids. I think conditions in this pond are especially favorable to hybridization. In the first place, these two sunfishes are closely related, in the same genus, *Lepomis*. The bluegill is *Lepomis machrochirus*, and the pumpkinseed is *Lepomis gibbosus*, I believe. Then you have the bluegills far outnumbering the others, maybe by 20 to one. That means the pumpkinseeds may have difficulty finding mates of their own species. Now consider that the spawners are crowded together, with the eggs fertilized externally, right in the water, and you see what can happen.

I asked Bill the easiest way to identify bluegills and pumpkinseeds, and how he spotted the hybrids.

Bluegills have a black "ear" on the gill flap. Pumpkinseeds have a black patch with a smaller red or bright orange spot at the edge of the ear. Usually that's enough for identification, but pumpkinseeds also have speckled bodies with orange stripes on the gill flap which radiate from the mouth, while bluegills usually have dark green bodies with a purple cast, sometimes with light blue coloration on the gill flap.

Hybrids are more difficult to distinguish. No two of them look exactly alike, and about all you can say is that the characteristics are intermediate. One fish I caught this afternoon had a green body with broken vertical stripes, orange stripes below the eye but no red spot on the "ear." And it was a big fish—a ten-incher—which is typical of hybrids, since they often grow faster than either parent species.

That brought up another question: whether both fishes eat the same foods. Later, with a fresh evening breeze blowing in the cabin door, the skillet warming, and fillets piled high on a platter, I asked Henderson about it.

The two have somewhat different feeding habits. Bluegills feed mostly on insects, both adult and nymph, and on fish. When forage is scarce, they may nibble on aquatic plants, including algae; and sometimes mollusks are in the diet.

For the pumpkinseed, though, mollusks are often the most important food. The fish has a set of grinding teeth in the throat which crush snail shells easily. I remember some experiments in which both species were fed small snails, but only the pumpkinseeds would smash the shells, eject them through the gill openings and swallow the soft animal. The bluegills would eat only soft parts from which the shells had already been removed.

Some biologists believe that pumpkinseeds also eat more small fish than bluegills do, perhaps making them better for pond stocking. By eating their own young, they may reduce the overpopulation problem common among sunfishes.

"As the seasons change, exactly how you go about finding the fish?"

Well, let's start with the spawning season, right now. That's when fishing is most productive and exciting and also when the fish are easiest to find. Ordinarily you can spot the beds just by cruising or wading through the shallows. The water should be cleared from the spring runoff by the time it's warm enough for spawning. The optimum water temperature for spawning—and here's where a pocket thermometer pays off—is 67°F., but I always expect some surface action even in the low 60's. Here in Upper Michigan that's in early June, but in Florida it might be in February. In Florida, of course, there aren't any pumpkinseeds, just bluegills.

Actually the spawning activity is spread over several weeks, sometimes even months. At least that's true everywhere I've fished. In this pond I've seen occasional spawners in late August. Not all female bluegills become ripe at the same time, and the eggs from a single fish may not all mature at once. I'd say, though, that 90 percent of the spawning occurs in the spring, in the first two weeks, unless disrupted by wind or cold weather.

I always look for the nests on a bottom of clean sand or fine gravel, where the eggs won't be smothered by silt or organic debris. Weedbeds usually aren't productive, because of the decaying vegetation settled on the bottom. In old ponds where there's soft muck everywhere, I look for an inlet stream where the current scours the bottom clean.

"What about the old-timers who claim to smell spawning beds?"

Well, I can't do it. But I know experts who insist they can smell bluegills or maybe crappies in the water, and they'll sit there smoking a pipe or cigar and still say they can smell them. And sometimes we catch fish then.

Here are sponge rubber spiders, tiny popper, dry fly and plastic cricket imitation—all effective for bluegills.

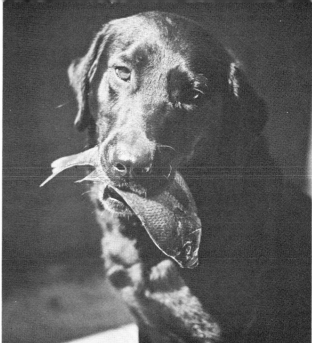

Henderson's Labrador retrieves everything from ducks to bluegills.

Bluegills and pumpkinseeds inhabit shallows during spring spawning, also on summer evenings and early mornings.

"What lures do you prefer for spawners?"

They'll attack anything that approaches the nest, but I use only flyrod surface bugs, because that's where the sport lies. I like a durable cork- or plastic-bodied popper, the smaller the better. A size 10 hook is good, though I use bigger ones if I expect a bass or two. Some anglers say a soft foam-rubber spider hooks more fish, because it's not spit out so quickly. Others prefer a bullet-nosed bug, which can't make loud splashes that might scare fish. But I stick with the dished-out face popper and just work it very gently. That way I can also make a bigger commotion if needed to wake up the fish. I think rubber "legs" make a popper more attractive, if they're short so fish can't nip the ends without being hooked.

Later in the season I switch to bushy dry flies which imitate natural insects more closely. But during spawning you need a durable popper that will catch fish after fish and still float like a bloated frog.

"You were going to describe, I think, how you find fish as the seasons advance."

As I mentioned, it's mainly water temperature that affects fish movements. When the shallows overheat in summer, the fish go deep—down to 20 feet, sometimes more. Last season I started using an electronic fishing thermometer, which can take a series of deep readings quickly, and I found that bluegills hang out in 65- to 75-degree water, with 70° to 72° ideal. The electronic gadget isn't really necessary; I used to get by with a simple mercury thermometer stuck in a bottle to trap the water. Either way temperature is a surprisingly reliable indicator, although other factors also influence fish distribution.

Once you locate the proper temperature level, you've still got a lot of water to explore. Usually, if I don't know the lake, I look for good feeding cover in the shallows—weeds, dock pilings and so on—and start fishing the depths nearby. Bluegills and pumpkinseeds don't roam far; generally they rest in deep water near a familiar feeding spot which they visit briefly at sunrise and twilight.

Black "ear" and purple or blue shading near edge of gill flap on bluegill (above) distinguish it from pumpkinseed sunfish, which has black "ear" patch with smaller red or bright orange dot on margin, also wavy orange streaks (which appear dark here) in region of mouth.

In some of these clear northern ponds you can see fish in the depths. Several years ago I would quit fishing after noon and just paddle around quietly, trying to spot fish below. I discovered bluegills in groups of ten or twenty, and they didn't conceal themselves in the sunken weedbeds as I had expected. Instead they rested on clear, sandy spots, often in open patches among the weeds. But the only fish actually in the vegetation were small ones.

Now I think pumpkinseeds, even the large individuals, usually stay right in the vegetation. They're difficult to spot but I have seen a few in the thick stuff. Also I believe they stay a little shallower than bluegills, even in hot weather.

"You mentioned that factors other than temperature can influence distribution. What are they?"

Oxygen content of the water is the most important one, but the angler really has no way to measure it. If he finds bluegills abandoning the deep, cool waters in midsummer, the reason is probably an oxygen shortage there.

Bluegills require more dissolved oxygen, more than northern pike, yellow perch or bullheads, for instance. That's why bluegills are among the first fish to die from winter kill in shallow lakes. Paradoxically, lakes subject to winter kill often provide better fishing because the bluegill population is held in check.

"When the fish are deep what lures do you use?"

One of the best is the weighted spinner—a very small one lighter than 1/8 ounce, usually about 1/10. The blade should be about one inch long and it should be slender so that the lure will stay deep. It also should be made of very thin metal so it will spin at the slightest pull. I let the spinner sink deep and then retrieve very slowly with a slight hopping motion. Sometimes it's more effective to attach a short thin strip of pork rind.

But even on summer afternoons you may get some surface fishing. Usually this happens only on windy days when terrestrial insects, such as grasshoppers, ants, leafhoppers, and so on are blown onto the water from trees or meadows. There are artificial flies tied to imitate all of these, and if you douse one in dry fly oil and cast it toward the rises you should get action.

"Can you describe the fly tackle you use?"

I like an 8½-foot slow-action rod with a WF-7-F line for casting bugs and bushy dry flies. When I'm using larger bugs, maybe hoping to catch a bass, I go to a 9-footer with a WF-8-F. It also should have a slow action to handle the wind-resistant bugs. When only short casts are needed and there are no obstructions in the water—as in certain farm ponds—it's more fun to use a light 7½- or 8-foot rod with a DT-4-F or DT-5-F line. Whatever the rod and line, I prefer a tapered leader with a 4-pound tippet.

About that time, Henderson's Labrador retriever showed up, and clamped in its jaws was a dried-up bluegill, which, suspiciously enough, was about as small as the one I'd lost earlier in the woods.

"Doggone, Blackie," Henderson grumbled, "that's the scrawniest fish you've ever caught."

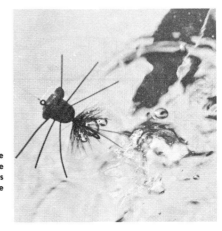

Here's bluegill's eye view of a surface popper. Rubber legs shown make lure more attractive.

OLD PRO USES A NEW THERMOMETER TO CATCH BASS

By Bill Rice

Bill Dance checks the water temperature at Irvine Lake on the new Lowrance Fish-N-Temp, a portable, battery-powered water thermometer. Couple the temperature reading with a depth finder reading, and Dance has instant knowledge of the conditions that first bass liked, and he'll find many more in similar conditions.

Pay off! The combination of electronics and angling talent is hard to beat. Dance shows a stringer of largemouth bass from Irvine Lake, topped by 7¼, 6¾ and 5½-pounders.

As every angler knows, the age of electronics has vastly changed the fishing waters of America and not always for the best. One small bright spot is that fishermen are getting to be much better anglers for it. At least such is the case of Bill Dance, the young bass "pro" from Memphis, Tenn. On a recent trip to California, he dazzled the local experts with his knowledge and use of both electronic fishing aids and his perfectly matched tackle. During recent years Dance has been by far the top money winner and bass catcher in a series of tournaments in the best southern bass waters. He has become a living legend among anglers in the Deep South.

But it was Bill's first trip ever to California and therefore was the classic challenge of fishing unknown waters. Even equipped with a depth finder and a new water thermometer from Lowrance Electronics, the task of catching bass immediately appeared relatively difficult. Dance's first test was Irvine Lake in Orange County, a 900-acre impoundment now noted for its supply of four- to seven-pound largemouths.

After checking the water temperature with the Fish-n-Temp electronic thermometer, we had determined that the water measured from 64 to 70 degrees at the surface down to about 30 feet, where the temperature dropped sharply. Since largemouth prefer the 64-70 degree range, we figured to find the best action in waters less than 30 feet deep, so next the Lo-k-Tor was put to use to "read" the bottom. As we moved to the east side of the lake looking for conditions he considered "right," Dance found a likely uneven bottom on the electronic dial. That was almost like seeing the fish because on the first cast, a scrappy 2-pound bass smacked Dance's blue jig-and-eel combination lure. It might have been pure luck but during that initial exposure, Bill finished up the day with bass weighing 7¼, 6¾ and 5½ pounds, in addition to more than a dozen two- and three-pounders which were released. He had beaten many of the best local anglers in their own backyard.

The next day Bill and I traveled to El Capitan Lake in San Diego County, one of the lakes featuring the imported Florida-strain of largemouth bass. Bass to 14 pounds have already been taken here, but on this day the best we could manage were several in the five-pound class. However the total catch, if we had kept them, would have been hard to believe. Again Dance had put the thermometer and depth finder to use and found the conditions similar to those at Irvine. The same combination will work anywhere.

Using a combination of the two devices, he discovered a long sloping point which ran from 10 feet out to 25 feet, then dropped sharply to 35 or 40 feet of water. The spot appeared ideal on the Lo-k-Tor and even better when we dropped our plastic worms down to the bottom and began to retrieve them slowly. That spot was loaded with fish of from two to four pounds. In an hour and a half, we boated over 35 largemouths, a score difficult to match anywhere, but made possible with a product of the electronic age.

Dance's ability as an agler is certainly unquestioned, but one must give much credit to his angling aids for instantly finding the perfect water temperature and right location.

The new Fish-n-Temp will become more and more important as serious anglers realize that water temperature has a very definite bearing on where fish are most likely to be. It will prove a handicap for anglers to go fishing without one.

Hand-held, the Fish-n-Temp is a compact, completely portable thermometer, battery-powered. The thermistor is lowered into the water by means of a wire calibrated at one foot intervals for easy depth reading. When the temperature most desirable to a species of fish is found on the dial, the depth can be checked by the reading on the wire. It is very simple to use.

The thermometer is most practical during the summer months for finding the deeper stratification of cooler water more suitable to many of game fishes. In the fall when the fish will briefly return to the shallows, the Fish-n-Temp will tell you when and at what depth to expect this prewinter feeding spree. In the winter, it is a valuable tool in discovering the warmer water where certain fish might congregate. During the spring, you may be able to pinpoint spawning areas and post-winter feeding grounds, as related to the ideal water temperature.

The new unit will read up to 100 feet on the easy-to-read dial scale. Effective in both fresh and salt water, the temperature range is from 30 to 90 degrees.

There's a compelling appeal to bright-light fishing for.....

CRAPPIES AT NIGHT

By Art Hutt

Photographs by the author

Half-mile bridge near Tavares is mecca for many central Florida crappie anglers. Time exposure caught several specialists plying their trade. On some nights, bridge is lit like a Miami causeway.

We huddled in the unseasonably cold Tennessee night, our exposed fingers frozen to our spinning rods, our breath forming white vapor in the damp spring air. The floating dock, with its powerful floodlight directed into the water, rode suspended between the black starless sky and the milky-blue translucent water below.

Other anglers, less hardy — or smarter — than we, had retreated to the comfort of their cabins.

Suddenly we warmed up. Our red-and-white floats, until now only agitated by the twitching of nervous minnows, dipped sharply under the surface. Within seconds we all hooked fish and scrambled to keep lines from tangling. We hauled in shiny slab-sided crappies, one after another, until we tired of the effort and went satisfied to bed.

That experience 15 years ago was my introduction to night-fishing for crappies — and it was more by accident than by design. Despite a threat of poor weather, Ed Howard and I, then both associated with the Fisherman magazine, had journeyed to Tennessee from our homes in Ohio to test the early spring bass fishing at Dale Hol-

low Lake.

We tested the bass fishing all right — or rather, it tested us. If you've ever tried to slap a lure into a bank in the face of a gusting, blinding storm of horizontally moving snowflakes, you'll know what I mean. My accuracy is poor enough in the sunshine!

But since we'd travelled many long miles for this week-end fishing trip, we stuck with it and caught a few bass despite the white stuff. Cold, numb, and wet, we quit early, hoping to save some energy for the night crappie fishing that our host, Dick Roberts, had been bragging about.

Happily, the snow and wind abated that evening. But the sky was still overcast and the temperature hung in the high 30's. We rigged our spinning gear in the warmth of the tackle shop, tying on No. 4 light-wire hooks with BB shot pinched on a foot up the line and with small red-and-white floats set up about five feet. For extra potential, we borrowed cane poles.

Roberts dipped up our minnows and directed us to a pair of choice but chilly spots under a floodlight — and quickly scurried off to the sanctuary of his restaurant up the hill.

One by one, the other fishermen were driven off the dock by the nippy air and the lack of fish. But hardly had the last angler left when the flurry started — not a snow flurry this time, but a flurry of crappies.

I'd been catching crappies for years but this after-hours technique was new to me. It was fishing under a different set of rules and conditions, and I was soon firmly hooked.

The deep-bodied, aristocratic-looking crappie needs little introduction to American anglers, but its variety of regional names can be confusing. I once listed over 70 of them. Actually there are two species, the white crappie *(Pomoxis annularis)* and the black crappie *(Pomoxis nigro-maculatus)*. Color alone is not always reliable for identification. To be absolutely accurate, count the stiff spines in the dorsal fin. If the count is six, it's a white crappie, while seven or eight means a black crappie. The white crappie tends to have a banded body; the black, speckled.

There seems to be some question why this fish in particular responds to a bright light hung over the water. Why don't bass or bluegills — or even gars and rough fish — build up in the same numbers?

Essentially a light over the water serves to attract plankton (minute organisms), insects, and minnows, or minnows alone. Some claim the insects hit the hot light and fall into the water, attracting the minnows, and the mass of minnows attracts the bigger fish. In Lake Erie this system has worked on walleyes but there's reason for a walleye grabbing a midnight snack since it has a set of eyes adapted to feeding in the dark.

But this still doesn't explain why, of all fish, a crappie, specifically, will tend to zero in on a bright light. One biologist suggested that it could be curiosity. But what makes a crappie "curioser" than other fish? Beats me!

Night-fishing techniques are basically the same throughout the crappie's range — which is rougly the eastern two-thirds of the country. After-dark angling is generally a winter and spring proposition although it could (and should) be a 12-month affair. The fish just don't disappear during the rest of the year. They're around and feeding somewhere and should be harvested the year around.

But no matter when you fish, you'll need several essentials for night angling. The first is a bright light. If you fish from a dock where there is electricity, you can dangle a flood or spotlight over the water. If you need a portable light you might consider a sealed-beam wet cell unit or a dry cell unit; for me, however, the wet cell is too heavy, the dry too short-lived.

The best choice is a gasoline or propane lantern. Either is lightweight and dependable, uses a minimum of fuel, and adapts to nearly any situation. From a bridge you can suspend your lantern from a stout cord just over the water's surface. From a boat, it will nestle securely in one of the several holders which fit into an oarlock. The holder I use on my single-mantle gasoline lantern is a stout wire gadget which clamps around the waist of the lantern and has two wire extensions which fit down into the oarlock, fastening the lantern securely in place. It takes a deliberate uplifting motion to dislodge it. If you want to move the lantern away from the boat, which is sometimes handy when you're using a long rod or casting artificials, a stout stick rigged across the thwarts and extending over the water is ideal.

Several years ago we watched nightly as a local live-bait dealer spread his string of lanterns across the waters of Lake Erie near Port Clinton, Ohio. He used inner tubes with the lanterns fastened onto cross-shaped platforms in the centers; then he'd come back to each one to dip up the minnows that gathered around the lights.

Hoping to catch walleyes by casting artificials, we made a single, similar rig, anchoring it about 30 feet from our boat. While it never produced for us, it might be worth a try for crappies, especially if you are an artificial buff.

For boat fishing, a reflector on your lantern is invaluable in keeping the glare out of your eyes. I've always used single-mantle lanterns and found they gave sufficient light, although the double versions are certainly brighter. And I always stick to gasoline or propane. Kerosene lanterns just lack the oomph to attract fish although they're handy as help-out lights, bright enough for impaling minnows on a hook, unhooking your catch, etc.

The classic crappie bait is the minnow. Drop one in front of one of the paper-mouthed hustlers and it will disappear as fast as a hotdog at a Cub Scout campout. While the species of minnow used varies from state to state, the crappie's appetite for them remains consistent. Try hooking your minnow through both eyes. Surprisingly, it will stay lively yet is much harder to yank off the hook than a mouth- or back-hooked minnow.

At times artificials will pay off, too. In Florida, for example, anglers use a cane pole or fly rod with a length of monofilament just shorter than the pole and a small jig-type lure in white or yellow. Whether the tail is of hair, feathers or nylon, it seems to make little difference. The lure is jigged upward, then allowed to spiral down again. Most experts believe it is this spiralling action that counts. Small spinners and streamers worked in the lantern's light also will outfish natural bait at times.

Monofilament line is ideal for crappies after dark, whether you use a cane pole or rod and reel. For fishing from a fairly high bridge my favorite rig is a standard bait-casting outfit loaded with 15-pound test monofilament. It's somehow satisfying to know that if a five-pound bass inhales the bait, the rig can probably hold him.

A split shot will hold the minnow down, but use a white-topped float that will stand out in the lantern's light. The red-and-white floats are fine. Use your favorite crappie hook; I prefer a thin-wire, gold-colored style in about size 4.

Since my chilly introduction to the sport in Tennessee, I've done most of my night crappie fishing in Florida — sometimes with a full moon glimmering on the rippled water and the scent of orange blossoms in the balmy air. Although any of the local crappie lakes would produce, a convenient hotspot near my home in Eustis, Florida, is the Rt. 19 bridge over Little Lake Harris between Tavares and Howey-in-the-Hills. While I'm not particularly timid about venturing out in a boat at night, many anglers like this half-mile long span (and other solid structures) for the extra safety not found in a boat. Traffic isn't too heavy, and there's protection in the four-foot-wide elevated sidewalks. On a warm weekend in late winter or spring the bridge is lit up like a Miami Causeway.

Our equipment for bridge fishing is rather spartan. We take a lantern tied to a ski rope or any light line, an ice chest for the refreshments and the fish, a kerosene lamp for light on the bridge, a flashlight, bait and tackle. Sometimes we use a wet burlap sack for the fish.

But anglers flock to this bridge from all over Central Florida, and many of them bring first-class accessories. For example, when you hang a lantern directly over the bridge to see your float about 20 feet down, you must do some fancy neck craning. And it gets tiresome. One enterprising specialist fashioned six-foot metal arms which clamp to the bridge railing. A pulley at the end of the arm lets the lantern down. The light and floats are easily visible from a stand-up or a sit-down position, and he avoids an aching back and neck.

Another angler prefers cane poles, so he ties loops of rope into the bridge railing to make a unique rod holder. He wraps a stout barbless hook onto the butt end of the pole, and hooks it into the railing loop. The pole dangles straight down but can be unfastened easily the minute a crappie bumps the minnow.

Another optimist made a no-handle net like those used at salt-water piers. The net hoop is tied into four short lines, then into a main line, ready to lower into the water to land that five-pounds-plus crappie that could set a new record.

Still another angler uses old garbage can lids as light reflectors after painting the undersides white. Add to these the children's wagons for hauling out the gear, the compact stoves or charcoal burners for fresh coffee (and fresh fried crappie), rod holders designed for the bridge, stools with heaters under them for cool nights; and you've got a specialized store of equipment that pays off in more fish and more comfort. As a result, many gimmick-laden anglers make a whole night of it.

The ultimate inventions for night crappie fishing are the barges widely used in Oklahoma and a few areas in other states. While not intended solely for night fishing, the barges are generally open year-round on a fee basis, and the night fishing really gets going full steam in the summer. Most of them are heated in winter, cooled in summer, and have a huge open hole in the deck where customers fish. Comfortable seats line the hole, and barge operators encourage fish to congregate by seeding the area with cottonseed cake, bales of alfalfa, Christmas trees, etc., working on the principle that these items attract the smaller organisms, which in turn attract minnows, which bring on the crappies. Of course bright lights help, too. Sometimes bass, catfish and white bass are icing on the crappie cake.

Oklahoma's Grand Lake has 68 of these barges, but two of the fanciest in the state are *Noah's Ark* at Arrowhead State Park and the *Unsinkable Molly Brown* at

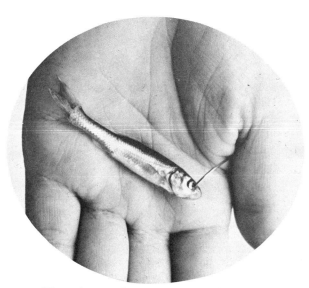

Minnow is top-ranking crappie bait. Hooked through eye, bait stays lively and on the hook more firmly. Type of minnows varies throughout the states but crappie appetite for them remains consistent.

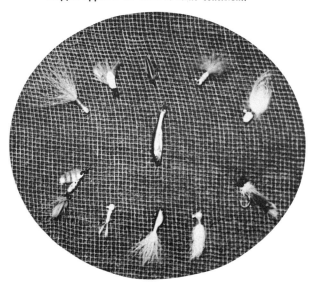

Minnows, jig, streamers, and spinners will all take crappies at night in lantern-lit waters. In some states, dry-flies work well during a mayfly hatch.

Four bridge fishermen at work. Floats in lantern's glare have hypnotic effect, quickly broken when a crappie makes off with the bait. Kids love this late-at-night style fishing. Rope-hung lantern is standard equipment for pier or bridge fishing. In boat, oar-lock-fitting commercial holders are a convenient accessory.

Fountainhead State Park, both at Lake Eufaula. A snack bar, lounge seats, carpeting, color TV and crappies are featured nightly!

It's well known that crappies are fond of brushpile areas. If you live on a lake as we do, you can build your own crappie reef for night (and day) fishing. We used Christmas trees weighted with broken tile, sunk them in a deep hole and had nearly instant fishing. Crappies came to the pile, as well as bass, bluegills, and catfish. Some anglers build these productive reefs as a club activity.

Whether you rough it with minimum equipment, or go first class with all the gadgets, give night fishing a try. With the exception of the lantern, no specialized equipment is really needed, and you can add a new dimension to your fishing. Here's a state-by-state list of nighttime crappie hotspots:

ALABAMA: June, July and August excursions to the T.V.A. impoundments in northern Alabama and the large power impoundments in central Alabama produce big crappies. Best fishing is from boats anchored in relatively deep water. Use lanterns, minnows.

ARKANSAS: Night fishing under lights in the larger, clear reservoirs seems more productive here than day fishing. Crappie action is in lakes Norfork, Bull Shoals, Ouachita, Hamilton, Greeson, and Sugar Loaf. Gas lanterns or sealed beam lights are used, and directed down into 20-to-60 foot deep water. Minnows are choice bait.

FLORIDA: The Lake Okeechobee Rim Canal (especially around the cuts through the spoil banks); the municipal pier at Pohokee; Lake Tohopakaliga's Shingle Creek, Goblet's Cove, and Friar's Cove, and the Rt. 19 bridge over Little Lake Harris are among Florida's most productive night-crappie fishing spots. Minnows are number one bait, but jigs pay off, too. Winter best, with spring and fall fishing fairly productive.

GEORGIA: Night fishing for crappies common in this state. Lakes Jackson, Allatoona, Lanier, Hartwell, Clark, Hill, Sinclair, and Burton most productive but many other areas hot, too. Anglers use light from boat, bank or bridge with minnows or small jigs in yellow or red-and-white second choice. One commercial dock (enclosed heated unit with theater seats ringing a fishing well) on Lake Allatoona near Cartersville.

ILLINOIS: Although crappies are abundant in many areas, night fishing for them has not yet become popular.

INDIANA: Markham Dam, Monroe Reservoir, Dogwood Lake, Lake Freeman, and Lake Schafer are the most popular crappie waters. Night anglers use jigs, minnows and streamers in lantern-lit waters.

IOWA: Crappie fishing peaks in late April and early May, with night fishing best from evening until about 11 o'clock. Minnows and artificials used extensively when crappies move into shallow water to spawn. After spawning, anglers use dry flies at night when mayflies are hatching. Best lakes include Geode, Wapello, Nine Eagles, Green Valley, MacBride and Viking.

OKLAHOMA: Grand, Fort Gibson, and Eufaula lakes are a few of the many excellent crappie holes in this state. Crappie fishing has developed to a sophisticated level here with enclosed barges heated in winter and air-conditioned in summer in which anglers sit in comfort facing an inner fishing well. Winter and summer are the most successful months on these fancy rigs. Boat, bank, and bridge fishing also are productive when crappies move into shallower waters to spawn in the spring. Minnows are best bait.

MICHIGAN: Limited activity here. In a few lakes, lanterns placed near ice-fishing holes sometimes seem to attract crappies. Ordinary ice-fishing tackle is used with minnows for bait.

MISSOURI: Lake of the Ozarks, Table Rock, Bull Shoals, Clearwater, and Wappapello lakes, plus a score of smaller impoundments are night-fished from docks or boats anchored over crappie beds. Spring and summer are best times with minnows and jigs the most productive baits. Many commercial docks here, too.

MINNESOTA: Only a few anglers try for crappies at night, mainly in summertime, with hotspots varying from year to year. Minnows and small spinners work best.

MISSISSIPPI: Ross Barnett Reservoir is the only spot where lantern fishing for crappies is very popular. Anglers fish from boats or tie their lanterns to tree limbs and fish from shore. Minnows are preferred baits; fishing is good in spring, summer and fall.

NEBRASKA: Crappie fishing peaks in April and May. For biggest crappies at night, try Harlan County Reservoir and Gavin's Point. Other spots include sand pits, small ponds, and larger rivers. Small minnows are used.

SOUTH CAROLINA: Some spring and summer night fishing at lakes Hartwell and Secession. Minnows best.

TENNESSEE: Top-producer Reelfoot has about 25 docks with permanent night lights. Crappie season peaks in May, continues through September. Wood Reservoir has night-crappie fishing from June through September. The Tennessee portion (100,000 acres or two-thirds) of Kentucky Reservoir is good from June through September also, especially the 40 mile stretch between Paris and Camden. Anglers use lanterns, cane poles or light spinning gear and small minnows. Hooks baited with mayflies also produce well in Kentucky Reservoir in June and July when these insects come to the bright lights.

They look bigger and pull harder in the dark. Florida angler Eddie Ratliff is happy with this one.

Go fishing almost anywhere anytime with this outfit assembled by the Digest editor.

DREAM OUTFIT FOR FISHING VAGABONDS

BY ERWIN A. BAUER

The road which climbed by switchbacks over a high, lonely ridge in the Beartooths was hardly a road at all. Often we had to stop to remove large boulders which blocked the way or to fill deep potholes. A couple of ice-cold creeks had to be forded. Time and again the faint track seemed to evaporate completely. In places the grade was so steep that only the four-wheel drive and low range assured our passage. But by late afternoon we reached the relatively flat meadow which surrounded a lonely, azure, alpine lake.

Judging from the lack of litter and beaten paths on shore, it wasn't a very accessible spot. Only the circle of charred rocks which was once a fisherman's fireplace revealed that anyone had been there before. We had the whole magnificent landscape to ourselves. In less than an hour our camper trailer had been unhitched and erected, our cartop boat had been unloaded and my son Bob was casting for trout just offshore. He needed about seven casts to hook his first cutthroat. A pot of coffee brewed on the stove.

"Surely," my wife Doris commented, "this is Paradise Found."

Paradise in this case happened to be a lake (which I will not name) on the edge of the Beartooth Primitive Area on the Montana-Wyoming border. It is only one of hundreds both within and outside of the Primitive Area. We had only to don backpacks and hiking shoes to reach other lakes, most of which contained trout. Paradise Found indeed!

But a few days later the Bauer family drove into — or rather beside — another Paradise. This time we entered

This is my basic outfit: Jeep Wagoneer with 4-wheel drive, Nimrod Americana trailer, Grumman Sport Canoe, plus other accessories.

Bear panhandles beside road in Yellowstone National Park as we pass.

How about this for an idyllic campground? A western wilderness? No, the site is a farm pond in Ohio. But it has all the comforts of home, plus nature's air conditioning.

the Lewis Lake Campground in Yellowstone National Park and backed the trailer into a designated campsite. We were surrounded by other campers, but not for long. Our ticket to do so was the same Golden Eagle Passport which had cost $7 and which permitted us to enter any federal recreation facility.

Soon after the trailer was opened, Bob and I launched the cartopper in Lewis Lake and affixed our six-horse outboard. With a light tent, grub and fishing tackle aboard, we motored the five miles across the Lake to the mouth of the Lewis River. At this point we cached the motor in brush nearby (no motors are permitted beyond this point) and began the one-mile paddle upstream to Shoshone Lake. Shoshone is a completely undisturbed wilderness body of water where it is difficult not to catch mackinaw (lake) trout. But it is not a particularly easy place to reach, except on foot, in which case the fishing is nearly impossible. And not many people carry along a suitable boat for such a trip.

Before last summer was finished, we discovered still other Paradises, and we plan to do the same thing again and again in the future. Fortunately I feel we now have the mechanical means to do it — a really versatile camping-traveling outfit. Without it, many of our paradises would not have been found. But first let me fill in some background.

I am a full-time, freelance, adventure writer-photogra-

pher. That means I write outdoor adventure stories and take pictures for a living. (My work goes into the outdoor or travel magazines and I have also written several books.) I am also the editor of this Digest. This means I spend a good deal of time the year around in traveling widely across North America; in the summertime this travel naturally includes my whole family of four. To give an example of my range, I have recently traveled by highway from Key West to Mt. McKinley and from home in Columbus, Ohio to Guatemala and Honduras on the Pan American Highway, hitting all points in between. During all this wandering, I have used or tried every manner of recreational vehicle from station wagon and tent to air-conditioned, self-contained motor home.

But it wasn't until a little more than a year ago that I assembled what I consider the ideal — absolutely ideal — outfit for my own needs. It might also prove perfect for sportsmen whose interests are similar to mine. I call it a "Dream Outfit For Fishing Vagabonds."

What I require is versatility — an outfit which will take me anywhere anytime, off and on the pavements. I have to travel often in rough or steep country, through snow, swamps or muck, in out-of-the-way places where hunting and fishing are best. But at the same time I need a combination which gets me quickly and safely from one place to another over the best interstate highways. It must be equally suitable in good and bad weather. I must be able

Here we're driving over Beartooth Highway in Montana to keep a date with some trout in a lonely mountain lake.

to carry along a great deal of equipment: fishing tackle, firearms, much photographic gear, such widely assorted items as hunting dogs and saddlebags. As a result of these requirements, I did plenty of searching and testing before I finally settled on my dream outfit.

My basic outfit consists of a Kaiser Jeep Wagoneer with 325-hp V-8 engine, a Nimrod Americana trailer, a Grumman Sport Canoe and a Johnson 6-hp outboard.

The Jeep station wagon with 4-wheel drive and low range was a necessity to take me into such places as the Beartooth Mountains, as well as to travel comfortably across country and to carry the mountain of outdoor gear. Some of the gear could be carried on the rooftop luggage carrier and under my boat which was good protection against weather. I installed fishing rod racks on the ceiling inside the Jeep for instant availability.

The trailer selection also requires explanation since I realize that other campers will naturally have other ideas. (See "Camp Coaches for Anglers" by Byron Dalrymple elsewhere in this book.) To begin, I wanted a station wagon and *some* kind of trailer, rather than a pickup-camper-coach combination, so that I could easily park my camp and be free to wander and explore in my vehicle. For my own particular needs, it is a nuisance to drag the whole camp everywhere I must go. And no pickup-camper yet designed can possibly take me where my Jeep alone will negotiate with ease.

I selected the fold-out trailer over the rigid sports trailer because of its lighter weight and lower silhouette. The latter is an important factor when traveling long distances across open plains country or in high winds anywhere. It also can be towed into "tighter" places than the high silhouette campers. The Nimrod Americana I do use has built-in stove, sink, cooler and dining table — all these features being concessions to my wife. We found we could store quite a bit of gear in the trailer and that purchase of spare wheels and tires is a good investment whenever much off-the-pavement travel is planned.

On many occasions, perhaps with rain pelting down on the roof, I have used the trailer as my office afield. My typewriter always goes along and more than one Fish 'n Camp column for Camping Journal magazine has been typed under canvas. Parts of my book "Outdoor Photography" were written outdoors. In a pinch, I could use the trailer for a mobile darkroom. My sons have used the place to repair reels and to tie flies.

A boat is also an absolute necessity for my work. And it must be a boat which can serve in the most possible situations. My Sport Canoe fills the bill fairly well. It is really a square-ended canoe which can be rowed or paddled (but not as handily as a regular canoe) or powered with outboards up to 9½ hp. Traveling speed is good with the 6-hp motor I selected for its compactness, fuel economy and light weight. The boat is excellent for float tripping rivers and fishing small lakes — and adequate for large lake and reservoir fishing, except in very rough weather. I have not yet had it in salt water. One man alone can load and unload it from the luggage rack, although two can handle the job easier. When not in use, the craft hangs from light cables, out of the way, from the roof of my garage.

My dream outfit also includes the following equipment, hopefully to cope with any outdoor situation a writer or other vagabond is likely to encounter: a light Drawtite tent and light sleeping bags with Trail Bed foam mattresses for "spike" camps; mountain pack boards; axe and shovel; a supply of rope; three-burner Coleman gasoline stove and two-burner Coleman gas lantern; camp heater; a broad selection of fishing tackle, including waders and landing net; spare fuel cans; Coleman water jug; electronic fish Lo-k-tor; a plug-in spotlight, all necessary cooking and dining gear; life saver boat cushions, whatever guns and ammo are required for the specific trip; bow saw; a portable grill; flashlight; aluminum folding chairs; first aid kit plus extra medicines; tool kit; clothing for various weather conditions; emergency food supplies; a small library containing maps, bird, rock and plant guides, etc. Other vagabonds with special interests might wish to add or subtract certain items from the list. For example, a screened patio attachment to the trailer, a portable shower and toilet would add considerable comfort to any camp. Either a manually operated or power take-off winch could prove valuable. And playthings for very small children could come in handy. On the other hand, some campers might have no desire to take fishing tackle or firearms along.

At this writing my dream outfit has survived severe testing. First came several weekend pilot trips to state parks in Ohio, mostly just to get acquainted. These were very valuable. Next came week-long fishing trips on magazine assignments during a spring which was uncommonly wet and dreary. But in spite of the weather my trailer was a comfortable place wherever I parked it from the Tennessee Smoky Mountain foothills to Michigan's Upper Peninsula. I began to develop a great fondness for it. Then in July we began our month-long, 6500-mile family search for outdoor Paradises in the West and Canada. None of us will ever forget that nearly idyllic experience which should happen to every family.

Then last fall my dream outfit became a mobile hunting camp for my friends and me. At first I suffered some doubts about the outfit's value in *really* cold weather, but I need not have given it a second thought. All winter long it was the headquarters for weekend grouse hunts in the southern Ohio hills and on one raw evening in December, while fresh liver fried in the skillet, Lew Baker described (over and over) how he outwitted the big largemouth bass earlier in the spring.

That deer hunt could have ended in deep trouble — or rather in deep snow — without the 4-wheel drive and low range power of the Jeep. We had set up camp near the end of a thin fire trail to escape as far as possible from other hunters. We also delayed striking camp when a wet snow began to fall because the whole adventure was proving so much fun.

"What the devil," Lew had laughed. "who cares if we get snowed in?"

Nobody. Snowing in is exactly what happened to many other hunters who had camped in the woods. And they had headaches aplenty. But we plowed out very neatly, camper trailer and all, and spent a good part of one afternoon in helping other hunters out of slightly snowy predicaments. At that particular time I wouldn't have traded my dream outfit for a working gold mine in the Klondike.

Does it have drawbacks? Deficiencies? There are a few, I suppose. For one thing it isn't as luxurious as some campers like their camping units today. But that is a very minor matter with me. I thoroughly enjoy the outdoors and I can wait until I return home again to revel in luxury.

And as I pointed out before, the boat is a bit small for turbulent water; it would increase my working "range" to have a larger craft with more power. But right now I can't see that this is possible as long as I'm pulling a camper trailer.

But all things considered, it's hard to visualize how I ever circulated around the outdoors without my versatile dream outfit. Those surely must have been the bad old days.

Ohio's Musky

In larger reservoirs around the state, Buckeye

Wear a muskie out before trying to land him. The safest way to land a muskie is to beach it, maybe. When in a boat, use a net or gaff.

Explosion

anglers are meeting a great new game fish

By Merrill C. Gilfillan

Every year Ohio anglers catch 200 to 300 muskies of trophy size according to Ohio Division of Wildlife records. All these muskies are over 30 inches long, and since only a portion of the fish caught are reported, this catch represents a much larger number of muskies taken each year.

It's remarkable that this happens in a small agricultural-industrial state with a high population density and comparatively little water area. The muskie success story is the result of a stocking program initiated and developed during the last 15 years. It also reflects the development of muskie fishing skill by the state's anglers, most of whom were new to muskie fishing.

Dr. L. G. Dunmire of Barnesville has boated 42 trophy muskies in the last six years, 21 of them in a single season. Muskie expert Neal Jackson caught 19 and his wife Edna took nine during the same period. And two Steubenville anglers, Jim and Lucky Wolfe, landed four muskies weighing over 20 pounds each in a single day. All these fish came from Piedmont Reservoir, one of the Muskingum Watershed Conservancy District reservoirs located in eastern Ohio and leased to the state for public fishing.

Almost 850 trophy muskies were reported in this six-year period by the Ohio Huskie Muskie Club, an organization founded to gather facts on the success of the management program and to encourage muskie angling. Admittedly the reporting is incomplete. But there's no doubt that Ohio anglers are enjoying good muskie fishing in a state where almost none existed before.

The Ohio fish technicians put a new twist on the Mahomet and the mountain story. They brought big muskies to the large angling population instead of making the anglers travel long distances northward to get to the muskies. And statistics suggest that the chances of hooking a big muskie in Ohio may be better than in any northern waters.

Still the odds of catching a muskie in Ohio are long, and only the dedicated angler will fish hard enough to assure success. Ohio anglers with knowhow catch a good muskie for every 100 hours of fishing, according to records of some of the better fishermen. Anglers who travel long distances to fish unfamiliar lakes experience lower success, and plenty of fishermen have fished at northern camps season after season without even hooking a muskie. Now their chances are greatly increased near home and at a greatly reduced cost.

Unquestionably the most successful muskie fisherman

Fish management supervisor Everett Ridge releases muskie fingerlings from an oxygenated polyethylene bag.

At right: Closeup of incubating eggs.

Fish management supervisor Ray Rieth-miller checks incubating muskie eggs in the Kinkaid Springs Fish Hatchery.

This bucketfull of small muskie finger-lings is being transferred to a rearing pond for added growth. Ohio's fish technicians now recommend stocking larger fingerlings in the 8- to 12-inch class for better survival.

in Ohio is Dr. Dunmire. He fishes Piedmont Reservoir at least two days a week during muskie season — and for him the season begins early in the spring and continues until snow falls again.

Dunmire has taken most of his muskies by trolling. "When I troll," he relates, "I like to cover all kinds of water. Generally I fish along the weed beds and shoreline in 8 to 12 feet of water. But in hot weather I also troll in deeper water — sometimes as deep as 25 feet. And when I fish during the summer, I troll all day long."

Dunmire thinks one of the important secrets is to keep fishing hour after hour. And he should know. Every trophy muskie he caught plus many others too small to meet Huskie Muskie Club requirements came hard. His wife Betty worked long, tiresome days for her eight trophy fish, too. Dunmire often takes other anglers with him, and many of Ohio's most successful muskie fishermen actually learned their craft from him. It's probably accurate to say this determined angler has helped account for more muskies on the stringer than any other Ohio fisherman.

During cool weather early and late in the season Dunmire hangs up his trolling tackle and goes casting for muskies. "When I cast," he says, "I fish the shallow water near weed beds and along the shoreline, since that's where muskies feed when the temperature is low. I use shallow-running lures, and I cast likely spots over and over. Sooner or later the muskie will be in the mood to strike, and then he'll hit almost any bait you throw at him."

Dunmire adds that he's spending more time casting every season, since he thinks it's a more sporting method than trolling. And Blanche Groh, who operates the boat house at Piedmont and keeps a close tab on muskies caught at the lake, also believes anglers could boat more fish by casting, except during the hottest months.

Leesville Reservoir, another Muskingum lake located near Carrollton, also produces plenty of big muskies. Ed Clow, operator of the Leesville Boat Landing, advises casting the bays and the mouths of small coves at Leesville. He reports that in the spring most muskies are caught on live bait in deep water, rather than in the shallows as you'd expect at this time of year. Soft craws, fished on or near the bottom are especially effective at Leesville.

In the early days of Ohio's muskie boom, largemouth bass fishermen plugging the shorelines often boated muskies, most of them at Leesville Reservoir. Their success encouraged many anglers to fish specifically for muskies and offered the first proof that stocked muskies could survive in Ohio's artificial lakes. Of course bass fishermen still take an occasional muskie.

According to Clayton Lakes, Ohio fish management supervisor, drift-casting is effective in lakes with logs, stumps, brush, rocks and weed beds. He recommends retrieving the lure rapidly and leaving it in the water a short time before picking it up for another cast, since muskies often follow the lure in and strike at the last moment. And Lakes always keeps casting to the same spot where a muskie hit but wasn't hooked to give the fish a second chance.

Ray Riethmiller, another fish management supervisor and a member of the Huskie Muskie Club (he caught a 25-pounder), put it this way: "The hardest thing to achieve in muskie fishing is to get the attention of the big fish. Once you get a rise, stay with it if you don't hook him the first time. You've found a hungry muskie, and he's ready to bite. Spend at least an hour fishing the vicinity with different lures and from all angles.

"Once you have him hooked," Reithmiller continues, "the first run is the most critical. Set the hooks hard and

keep a tight line, but give line when you have to. Try to direct the fish away from cover where he might tangle and break the line. Once he's tired net him tail first. The danger of netting head first is that the hooks might get tangled in the net, helping the fish to jerk free. The safest way of all to land a muskie is to beach him, but that's impossible when you're fishing from a boat."

Lakes and Reithmiller agree that the best way to take muskies in deep water during the hot summer months is to troll. They troll rapidly with deep-running plugs, spoons and Arbogasters along ledges, weed beds, brush and stumpy areas. When the water cools, a shallow running lure can be used, or trolling speed can be altered to keep the lure at the desired depth.

Some muskie anglers use live bait with good results, as the Leesville Reservoir report proves. The most productive baits are large chubs or stone-roller minnows and suckers 10 to 12 inches long. For stream fishing, live-bait fishermen use a float and drift it against a log jam or brush pile where the big muskies usually lie.

You can use the same technique in lakes too. Use a float to help prevent snags, and drop your bait alongside stumps, logs, brush piles and similar cover. Keep it there for about ten minutes before trying another spot, to give a muskie time to find it.

A few muskie experts know another trick with live bait: they tie a foot-long sucker to their boat to attract the fish within casting distance. And the best muskie fishermen don't cast far; instead they make many short accurate casts, keeping the lure in the water in the right places as much as possible.

Over the years commercial fishermen and trotliners in Ohio have reported muskies far bigger than the world record for hook-and-line. A 100-pound muskie taken from the Muskingum River was served at a Fourth of July celebration at Marietta in 1788. Since Civil War days buckeye anglers have made regular trips to southern Ohio streams for the giant fighters. It was even common prac-

Muskies should always be netted tail first to lessen the chance of the hooks catching on the net, allowing the muskie to jerk free.

tice on Sunfish Creek in Pike County for residents to set traps in the riffles to catch muskies for food.

Dr. J. Russell Finley of Zanesville has taken muskies in the Muskingum River drainage for 50 years, many of them at a time when few Ohio anglers even knew muskies existed. Herman Hartman of Duncan Falls caught 49 muskies in the same area from 1940 to 1945, and a Pike County farmer living on the banks of Sunfish Creek tacked several big muskie heads on his woodshed every year. All of this happened while most midwest anglers made long expeditions to northern muskie waters, often for nothing more than the exercise.

All these early muskies were taken in streams. But this was destined to change when Ohio's fish management men began working with muskies in the early 1950's. For years the technicians had captured them in test nets in southern Ohio streams, and gradually they built up a store of facts on the habits and distribution of muskies in the state.

Then in April, 1953, they removed spawning muskies from these nets, and Ohio's muskie propagation program was under way. They collected eggs from the female fish, artificially fertilized them with milt from netted males, and rushed them to the Kincaid Springs Hatchery. There the eggs hatched in 8 to 15 days, depending on the water temperature. And within three weeks, the tiny muskies were slurping up minnow fry provided for food.

Some of the muskies were stocked as fry; others were held until the fingerling stage (4 to 12 inches) before they were released. New lakes without an established fish population that would feed on the small muskies were stocked with muskie fry. The management experts quickly learned the secret to this stocking. Once the muskie fry were feeding on tiny minnows and adept at capturing their own food, they were ready for stocking. As soon as shad or other forage fish hatched and their fry were abundant in the lake, the young muskies were released.

With plenty of natural food available the muskies thrived. In fact the growth rate of Ohio muskies is said

Fishing Sunfish Creek in southern Ohio. Deep holes like this one yield muskies in the 12- to 14-pound class.

to be the highest known, probably due to this timing in stocking and the abundance of rough fish for food in Ohio lakes.

Lakes with established populations of fish large enough to eat small muskies were stocked with fingerlings big enough to take care of themselves. Both of these stocking methods worked, as today's yield of trophy muskies in Ohio proves.

In Rocky Fork Lake near Hillsboro technicians kept close tab on muskies in the early days of the program. In 1953, 10,000 muskie fry were stocked, and smaller numbers were added in following years. When anglers caught these fish a year later they averaged 19 inches in length, and at two years they averaged 30 inches. At three years their growth rate began to slow as they put on more weight, but muskies up to 37 inches long were caught. By 1957, when they were four years old, muskies 40 inches long weighing 20 pounds appeared in the catch.

Leesville Reservoir was also stocked with fingerlings in 1953, and like Rocky Fork provided excellent fishing in a short time. Piedmont Reservoir was stocked later but soon became the hottest muskie lake in Ohio. Other lakes were also stocked as the program expanded, and now anglers boast trophy muskies from many different waters scattered over the state.

For several years it was difficult to measure the success of the program because there was no systematic reporting of catches. In fact, many top muskie takers were reluctant to tell of their success. But in 1960 the state established the Ohio Huskie Muskie Club to gather information on the number and size of muskies caught, as well as to encourage trophy angling.

Anglers who catch an Ohio muskie weighing at least 20 pounds and measuring at least 40 inches in length are eligible for membership in the club. But anyone catching a smaller muskie that measures 30 inches or more in length receives an honorable mention citation. Thanks to the club, most anglers now are anxious to provide information on their muskie fishing success. As a result, Division of Wildlife officials have accumulated a vast amount of muskie lore useful in planning future fish management.

In six years of club activity (through 1967), 100 huskie muskies have been reported, and almost 750 honorable mentions are on record. And the state muskie record has been broken four times during this period. It was broken most recently in 1968 with a 39½ pounder from Leesville Lake.

The files indicate that 67 muskies (of the 850) were taken from rivers and creeks, most of them native fish. The rest of the fish came from lakes and reservoirs, reflecting the influence of the stocking program. The top muskie lakes are Piedmont, where 279 muskies were caught; Leesville, with 145; Dillon, 85; Rocky Fork, 75; Hargus, 43; Seneca, 31; and Lake White, 18. The most productive streams were Salt Creek with 16 muskies; Meigs Creek, 8; Wolf Creek and Olive Green Creek, 5 each.

In some cases a stream or lake ranks high because one or two dedicated, skillful muskie fishermen concentrate their efforts there. This suggests that there are other waters, especially streams, where muskies are available for the angler who will study the habitat and learn to outsmart the big fish lurking there.

That's the story of Ohio's muskie fishing success. In 15 years' time, muskies have become available to all anglers in public fishing waters through a sound muskie management program. The records of Ohio Huskie Muskie Club leave no doubt about that.

And it could be done in other states.

FISHING'S BIG in the

Waterfront area of Petersburg is full of great variety of sport and commercial fishing craft. Salmon angling is great here.

Sheefish caught in a tributary of the Kuskokwim near Sleetmute.

Brooks and young Bauer register their catch of silvers and chinooks with Fish & Game Dept officers.

BIG STATE

By Mike Miller

A report on the great sport and where to find it in Alaska today.

Maybe it all began on one of those Sunday television programs which show expert American sportsmen hunting and fishing around the world. Anyway it spawned the crazy notion among many fishermen that Alaska is the place to tackle *after* you've become an expert angler.

"I've wetted lines from Baja to the north woods of Maine," a Texas friend told me recently. "In thirty years of fishing I've filled my creel along rivers in Colorado, I've taken my limit along Gulf shores, and I've turned back pike in half the lakes of Minnesota.

"Now I'm ready," he concluded, "I'm really ready for Alaska."

But he needn't have waited. I submit that he was ready for Alaska three decades before when he plunked down the cash for his first casting outfit.

This isn't to advise the expert to stay home — not by a long shot. In Alaska as elsewhere an expert rod handler will land more and bigger fish and he will do it more consistently than the cheechako or the occasional angler. When salmon derby entries are tallied from Ketchikan to Juneau and from Seward to Sitka each year, it's usually the man — or gal — who knows a herring from a hooligan who pockets the $2,500 in cash for first prize. Or maybe he only drives away in a brand spanking new car for knowing his way around a tide rip.

But the average angler, too, and even the novice, can hook into more of more different kinds of fish in Alaskan waters than he considered possible. "Skunked" is a word seldom heard from Ketchikan to Kotzebue.

Following is a rundown, area by area and species by species, of the better fishing throughout the 49th State. Be advised, though, not to look for any single place to be labeled "best." There isn't one. The angling is just too good, too varied, and too dispersed across the great sprawling bigness of Alaska to justify a single, one-only top rating.

Working from bottom to top, the southeastern Alaska panhandle is the closest area to the "outside" — or original 48 states. It is therefore the fastest and least expensive to visit — via two major jet carriers, three summer cruise-ship lines, and the Alaska Marine Highway System of liner-like auto and passenger ferries.

The fishing: excellent.

King salmon is king in southeastern saltwaters. Although the species is generally available April through August the biggest lunkers (up to seventy pounds and beyond) are caught from mid-May through mid-June. Hot spots include Bell Island and Craig near Ketchikan; Greys Pass near Wrangell; Scow Bay at Petersburg; Saginaw Channel and Tee Harbor near Juneau; and Sitka Sound. Yakutat Bay at the very northern tip of the panhandle has begun to report some exceptional catches.

At most of these same points — and almost everywhere else in the region — silver salmon (cohos) arrive just about the time the kings move out. A leaping, sounding, splashing, hook-throwing acrobat, the silver is a small cousin to the king. And most Alaskans consider him a far, far better fighter. And so do I.

Also in these same salt waters are halibut, sea-run cut-throat trout and Dolly Varden trout. The latter two, available and in fighting trim June through September, show a healthy appetite for small spoons, flies, and eggs. Best bet for maximum catches of both: waters where creeks and streams enter the sea. There aren't more than several hundred such spots along the coast.

Freshwater angling hereabouts is as good, perhaps better, than saltwater but only a relatively small number of out-of-state sportsmen seem to take advantage of it. Nine-tenths of the outdoorsmen visiting the panhandle, in fact, overlook one of the world's great fishing bargains available only here: the rent-a-lake system of more than 100 cabins built and maintained at good fishing spots by the U.S. Forest Service. Incredibly, these cabins, located from one end of the panhandle to the other, on islands and mainland, can be reserved and used for the piddling price of $2 per party per night. You have the whole lake at your front door to yourself. Fish available: rainbow, eastern brook, cutthroat and Dolly Varden trout, plus a limited amount of grayling.

Although king salmon generally bypass southeastern freshwater streams, silver and pink salmon enter these waters to spawn by the thousands. A small bright lure furnishes fast, furious sport from July through August in the case of pinks, August to early November for silvers. Another line-stretching battler, the steelhead, migrates from sea to fresh water in this region. In the lower panhandle a fall run enters some lake-fed creeks in September and October while throughout the region a spring run enters larger creeks in April, peaking in May. Best bait is salmon eggs, although steelheads seldom ignore spoons or flies during the peaks of their runs.

Further north another great fishing region is the Copper River-Prince William Sound area where king salmon, silvers, halibut and Dolly Vardens provide the basic saltwater action. Access? You can drive here via the paved, scenic (some say Alaska's *most* scenic) Richardson Highway to Valdez, fly via scheduled air service to Valdez or Cordova, or drive and sail via auto and passenger ferry-liner to both points from the Kenai Peninsula.

Grayling and rainbows are probably the most sought-after species in fresh water here. The former (found in most streams around the more inland road system but not in the coastal watersheds) can usually be hooked throughout the summer in Mae West, Tolsona, Gillespie, Mud, Moose, Caribou, Elbow, Lost Cabin, Meirs and Big Twin lakes.

Make no mistake about it, Arctic grayling is one of the unique and abundant trophy fish of Alaska. Place a dark fly properly a few feet above him and you're in for a sight you will always recall and talk about for the rest of your life. Up from the depths darts a dark shadow, perhaps missing his target on the first pass. No matter. Without ever hesitating the grayling will try again, pop clear out of the water, bank to one side as a jet in a tight turn, and take your fly on the dive. Then the fun is just beginning. He's a beauty all right, this grayling, his most noticeable characteristics being a giant dorsal fin and iridescent coloring.

The Copper River-Prince William Sound area also pro-

Family fishing fun on a trip to Alaska, here at a scenic spot on Haines Highway at 11 Mile, is set against a background of cathedral peaks.

Examining a catch of lake trout, pilot and fisherman conclude a memorable fishing excursion in Katmai National Monument. Wien Consolidated Airlines operates fishing camps here.

duces sizeable stocks of lake trout, landlocked silver salmon, Dollies (try the Robe River near Valdez), and steelhead up to thirty inches arrive in late August or early September. If you're a fall fisherman, by the way, you can combine fishing hereabouts with some of the undisputed finest goose and duck hunting in North America.

The Upper Cook Inlet-Matanuska Valley area, with big city Anchorage as its jet-age hub, doesn't offer too much for the salt water sports fisherman. There's too much glacial silt entering the ocean here. But fresh water fishing . . . now there's something else again.

Silver salmon, quick to grab lures or egg clusters, strike most plentifully in late July and August when the migration peaks. Some of the hottest of the hot spots include the Deshka River, Little Susitna River, Chuit River, Alexander, Montana, Sheep, Caswell, Willow, Lake, Sunshine, Wasilla, Fish, and Little Willow creeks. You reach some by driving and charter float planes or air taxis into others.

Rainbow trout, quick to strike egg clusters or artificial spinning lures, run up to twenty inches in such selected stocked lakes as Bonnie, Echo, Wiener, Finger, and Ravine. If you like your water moving, good rainbow streams for the fly-in fisherman include the Deshka and Talachulitna (where grayling are also in abundance) while landbound motorists can frequently fill their creels in Montana, Sheep, Willow, and Little Willow creeks. Willow Creek has a great midsummer run of big dog salmon which strike spinners.

It's easier, by the way, to reach Anchorage than any other city in Alaska. In addition to excellent paved highway access, three major air carriers jet here from Seattle (as well as one from Chicago) while numerous intra-state carriers and bush lines fan out from the city to the interior, to the Arctic and other Alaska points. Also the Alaska railroad headquarters here, with tracks running north to Fairbanks and southwest to the Kenai Peninsula.

The Kenai Peninsula, incidentally, has been until recently Alaska's best kept outdoors secret. To be sure, Alaskans have gleefully fished and hunted "the Kenai" for decades. But until the state recently finished paving the highway which now runs the entire length of the peninsula, visiting sportsmen usually passed it by.

They shouldn't skip it anymore, particularly since anglers have learned that silver salmon seem to hold their annual national convention in Seward's Resurrection Bay. The fish first arrive during July, then peak their run in August. Kachemak Bay, at Homer, is another prime collection area for silvers and for large halibut as well.

In fresh water, only a few streams offer king salmon but a great number offer silvers (the Kenai River is especially good, especially west of Soldotna near Eagle Rock and the "Big Eddy"), red salmon (striking and fighting at their best June through mid-August in the Russian River and at the confluence of the Moose and Kenai Rivers), pink salmon (try Resurrection Creek near Hope) and steelhead. Among favorite steelhead waters are the Anchor River, Deep Creek, Ninilchik River, Stariski Creek and the Russian River during August through October.

The rainbow fisherman who wants to try near-virgin waters (and which fisherman doesn't?) can rent a canoe at half a dozen points along the peninsula highway system and paddle his way happily and productively through the Swan Lake Canoe System on the Kenai National Moose Range. Two additional strong possibilities for rainbow are the Russian River and Russian Lakes where the 'bows run to twenty-four inches.

Dollies are also present in large numbers on the Kenai, lake trout are present in all glacial lakes of the Kenai

These are steelhead trout, caught in the Karta River near Ketchikan.

Jim Brooks nets lively coho salmon for Bob Bauer near Admiralty Island in southeastern Alaska.

Here's a grayling, just ready for the net on the Delta-Clearwater near Fairbanks.

River system, and grayling are dependably present if you fly-in to Crescent Lake from June through September.

And here's a fresh twist. If you tire of fishing with a rod and reel and want the diversion of an hour or two with a dip net, try your luck with eulachon, a smelt commonly called "hooligan" or "candlefish." This tasty species can be taken by the buckets-full in Placer and Twenty-Mile Rivers near Portage during the May spawning run. Ditto the Resurrection River near Seward.

Bristol Bay and the adjacent Katmai National Monument is real tackle-bustin' country. Kings are at their best from early June through mid-July, especially along the Naknek River near the city of King Salmon and on the Nushagak River at Portage Creek. When the kings leave, the silvers come in (best spot: near the mouth of King Salmon Creek on the Naknek River). Grayling and "monster" rainbow angling deserve a superlative rating throughout the area, too, all through the summer. So do lake trout, Dolly Varden, and Arctic char.

Char fishing, incidentally, is at its hottest anywhere at the mouth of the Agulowak River in Lake Aleknagik during June and July. This is fast-paced, rod-bending, line-popping action, the kind you dream about but never really expect to find. Access to all of this region is solely by Wien Consolidated Airlines and, for the most part, once you get there it is necessary to charter bush flights

to reach most of the hottest hot spots. That isn't inexpensive, but if you have the resources it's worth it.

In the great rolling northerly region from Fairbanks to the Arctic Ocean the list of easily available fish starts with A (for Arctic char) and B (for burbot, a fresh water ling cod) and ends with V for a Varden named Dolly. Between are a variety including grayling (trophy size at Sinuk River near Nome), northern pike (natives consider them a nuisance), rainbows, lake trout, king salmon, chum salmon, silvers, and sheefish.

Two of these deserve special mention.

The sheefish, in particular, has become one of the great new "finds" in the realm of rod and tackle. A big brute (twenty pounds is average but he can range up to eighty-five and over), the sheefish appears like something of a cross between a salmon, a snook and a whitefish.

He (or shee, as the case may be) can be taken the year round in the Kobuk and Selawik Rivers. In the summer and fall exceptional angling is available in the Holitna and Hoholitna Rivers at Sleetmute and in such Yukon tributaries as the Koyokuk and Nowitna Rivers as well. A limited number can be found in the Tolovana and Chatanika Rivers near Fairbanks. With the exception of the Fairbanks waters, these are all Arctic or near-Arctic points. No roads or railroads presently run to such places. Two major air carriers, however, and a handful of hardy bush pilots offer dependable and convenient flight service to major airports, minor airstrips or, for float planes, lakes and streams.

The northern pike is something of an unsung hero among Alaska game fish. You seldom hear Alaskans or Alaska visitors make much of a fuss over the species. Yet, located throughout the interior of the state in shallow, weedy lakes and sloughs, Alaska's pike will range in weight to forty pounds or more and up to three feet in length. Although he'll strike most any bait you offer, spoons and plugs are the best producers in such waters as Quartz, Harding, Volkmar, Mineral, Minto, George, Healy, Sand, and Island lakes. Most of these waters are in the Fairbanks area.

That city, Alaska's second largest, can be reached on several flights daily via two airlines from Seattle. Intrastate flights by Alaskan carriers connect Fairbanks' modern jet airport with Anchorage, Juneau, the Arctic and other major destinations. In addition to serving as the present northern terminus of the Alaska Railroad the city serves also as the "last mile" of the 1,523-mile Alaska (Alcan) Highway from Dawson Creek, B.C.

As they are everywhere else in the 49th State, Alaskans in Fairbanks are happy, in fact frequently anxious, to share their local knowledge with fishermen from "the south 48." Bush pilots, state Fish and Game experts, resort people, even the-guy-on-the-street all know where the fishing's good. What's more, a great number of them will tell you. They know there's no need for "secret holes." They know there will be plenty of lunkers left for everyone.

That's the great thing about Alaska fishing. There is plenty of sport here for all — for the expert like my Texas friend and for a beginner such as my small daughter. And for everyone in between.

Want to try your luck fishing the Big State? OK. For specific pinpoint fishing maps and directions, write the Alaska Department of Fish and Game, Subport Building, Juneau 99801, for their excellent Alaska Sport Fishing Guide. Information and a map of the U.S. Forest Service rent-a-lake system can similarly be obtained free from the Regional Forester's Office, Box 1631, Juneau. More detailed travel info (as on the car ferry system) is yours for the asking from the Alaska Travel Division, Pouch E, Juneau.

For testimonials, though, you needn't write at all. Just ask the man who's been fishing in Alaska.

A 280-page book published annually, The MILEPOST, is the best and most complete reference for the fisherman traveling in Alaska. It includes a complete highway fishing guide. New editions are available each spring for $1.95 at Box 1271, Juneau, Alaska 99801.

For anglers camping their way to and through Alaska, a complete list of public campgrounds can be obtained from the Alaska Travel Division.

Proud fisherman holds a fair-sized lake trout from a lake near Fairbanks.

Fish by the bucketfull—When the eulachon are running near Portage, Alaska, fishermen don't even bother with rods, reels, or creels. They scoop them by the netfull and haul them home in buckets.

Upper Russian Lake, typical of the many scenic lakes on the Kenai Peninsula, is just 45-minutes from Anchorage by small plane.

MONTANA

A veteran trout fisherman
offers advice on America's
classic trout streams and on

BLUE RIBBON
TACKLE BUSTERS

By Bill Browning

Trophy trout of Montana's Blue Ribbon Missouri River are compared by dad and son on a memorable fishing trip.

Wilderness type clear Rock Creek is one of Montana's most productive and scenic trout waters with 50 miles of this.

If you are a serious angler in search of the best possible trout fishing in America, take a tip from the experts and try Montana's seven "blue ribbon" fishing streams.

Blue ribbon is no idle claim, and contrary to what you might think these aren't the remote, high country wilderness waters which are too difficult, too expensive or time consuming for the average angler to reach. Instead Montana's blue ribbon rivers include 452 miles of top-rated waters mostly within sight of paved highways or county roads. They are, specifically, the Big Hole, Yellowstone, Missouri, Madison, Rock Creek, Gallatin and Flathead.

All of these waters hold trout, most of which are of the wild (not hatchery) variety. Any three of these seven streams could offer more than enough fishing to fill one vacation with some exciting potentials. The chances of breaking up your tackle on some rough and tumble jumper is always possible and may, if contested, send you home a defeated but more experienced angler.

On one of my first visits to the blue ribbon Big Hole River in southwestern Montana, I was stung to defeat by a bruising rainbow which was just too much for my tackle and talents. Studying a stretch of likely looking water, I spotted a good run teeming with vigorous rises, indicating hungry fish.

With my first cast the buoyant Adams fly was viciously engulfed, and a hefty fish braced against the racing currents. Through flailing heartbeats I soon knew that it was a big whitefish. A sporting game fish, but what I wanted most was trout, any kind. After rapidly taking 7 or 8 more of these fine small-mouthed fighters, I was about to move out of the school of whitefish when the Adams again disappeared in the froth of rises.

Rather nonchalantly I struck and started to swing the fish out of the milling school. But no soap. Instead my rod doubled and it seemed the hook might well have been anchored to a mad bobcat.

From his first great splashing leap I knew I had tied into a magnificent rainbow. And on succeeding jumps I knew I had little chance of landing him in the swift currents because I had been using a 4X leader. But now that the deceptive work of the puny 4X leader was over, it would be of little help in the rough-and-tumble battle.

My hopes lifted a little as I fought the colorful trout into more quiet water near the bank. However, as its sweeping, broad tail was swept into tumbling currents just

Nymphing on Montana's Blue Ribbon Madison means matching the naturals. Note dried cases of large salmon flies (or stone fly).

Bill Browning, Helena, Mont. with a Flathead River Dolly Varden.

Good enough to make any angler smile are these two trout, a brown and 'bow, taken from Montana's Blue Ribbon Missouri River.

I decided then and there to check out every whitefish school for the odd lunker trout and never to leave a pool without giving it a good chance to produce. Persistence would be my new motto and it has since paid huge dividends. Fish, like gold, are where you find them in the blue ribbon streams. And they can be nearly everywhere, including mixed with whitefish.

ahead of shore, the fish easily broke off and darted downstream. It happened much more quickly than it takes to tell it. So I stood half stunned, fingering a shredded leader, a wiser and sadder angler.

The waters of these seven streams do offer the better potentials for the larger fish. They follow the adage, "big water, big fish." And big they are, posing a problem to some anglers who have never left the security of the small brooks. However, along their concourses will be numerous and more readable waters, breaking around islands, through channels, in pockets, around meanders, or over rocks and ledges, that will sooner or later lead a knowledgeable angler to a "glory hole."

After hearing local tales of huge trout running 15-18 pounds, you begin to think all trout in these Montana waters must be trophies. Nothing could be farther from the truth. Most common trout taken would be in a wide range of sizes from catchables to 2- or 3-pound browns and rainbows. The 4- to 7-pounders would be harder to come by and may take plenty of time and patience. From there upward the largest trout would be rarer, but possible to catch, given certain favorable conditions and a little Irish luck. But it's the challenge of the big ones that keeps me going back to the blue ribbon streams.

Montana waters are usually located in magnificent settings. Strikingly beautiful, all of these blue ribbon rivers rise in snow-fed forested mountains. Two of them drain to the Pacific Ocean and the others to the Atlantic. All have different characteristics, size, and beauty. And significantly, all are very accessible by auto, some tumbling through National Forests and spectacular canyons. But

Madison River rainbow lunker fell for muddler fly beneath shady bridge. (Montana Blue Ribbon stream)

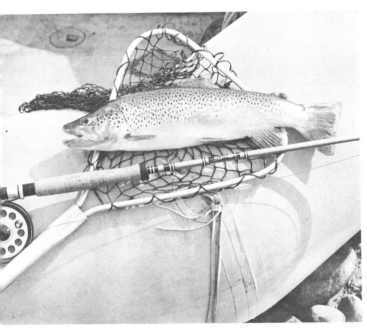

A hefty brown trout with vermillion spots grudgingly came to net on float trip on Blue Ribbon Yellowstone in Montana.

most flow through verdant valleys and ranchlands.

What gives these fisheries their top billing?

The blue ribbon streams are set apart as outstanding and of national interest because of their productivity, amount of use, availability, and aesthetics. Three scientific agencies conducted studies, creel census surveys, and on-the-spot samplings to determine their quality and their rating. Only certain sections of each stream are given top rating. Others are awarded red ribbon (only slightly less important), and yellow or gray ribbon ratings.

The Yellowstone River, with 103 miles of blue ribbon waters, offers three basic species of trout. Cutthroats are found mainly in the middle and upper reaches, along with rainbows and browns. The latter two occur throughout. Each of these fish inhabit certain sections more than others. The Yellowstone River rises in Yellowstone National Park, tumbles through Yankee Jim Canyon, and meanders through the ranchlands of Paradise Valley, at the foot of the rugged Absaroka mountains, past Living-

ston, and extends downstream to Big Timber.

The Gallatin River is basically rainbow and brown trout fishing, with brook trout in the upper sections and tributaries. The river flows past several western dude ranches, and seldom leaves sight or walking distance of the road along the 45 miles of canyon section from Yellowstone Park to Gallatin Gateway.

Lower on the stream the waters slow up somewhat, providing deeper pools where the trout become heavier and quite wary. Numerous campsites dot the drive-in wilderness landscape.

The world famous Madison River, flowing north for 72 miles from Hebgen Reservoir, is a brown and rainbow fishery with some brook and a few grayling in its upper reaches. Brook trout live in many of its tributaries. Although several other streams have salmon fly hatches (large stone flies), during the May-June-July periods, the Madison annually seems to have the greatest, most spectacular hatch of all. And occasionally anglers are nearly as thick as the hatches.

The Big Hole River was once tagged by a renowned outdoor sports writer, Joe Brooks, as the nation's best trout stream. Today, after 18 years, he still spends a large portion of his annual Montana visit exploring new challenges of this river. Rainbow and brown trout prevail, but grayling and brook trout are common in its upper reaches. The blue ribbon section of 51 miles runs entirely through ranchland from Divide to the mouth where it joins the Jefferson River. Access is easy with permission.

The Missouri River rises near Three Forks, Montana, as one of the world's greatest trout streams, being formed by the blue ribbon Gallatin and Madison, and the red ribbon Jefferson. It is a superb fishery. The 86 miles of the Missouri can produce abundantly at times, but can be uniquely temperamental, yielding reluctantly for only brief moments at dawn and dusk.

Of course rainbow and brown trout are the most sought after, but walleye fishermen can also find some interesting fishing. Much of the fishing is close by the highways, but some is in remote canyons. Three power dams between Toston Dam and the town of Ulm offer the troller some excellent boat fishing.

Rock Creek, near Missoula, is a wilderness type river, flowing swiftly out of mountains and forests for 50 miles to the Clarks Fork of the Columbia. Here a spin fisherman can easily cast to the other side of the river but to many it is a classic fly fishing stream. Rainbow and brown trout make up the main species, while cutthroat and Dolly Vardens add variety to the creel.

Rock Creek Inn at the mouth is considered fishing headquarters where expert guides and information are available. National Forest campsites are numerous along its forest road, and access is quite easy.

The only blue ribbon stream in Montana's northwest is the unique main Flathead River. Here is a broad stream made up of three other famous wilderness forks. Together they form a migratory run from Flathead Lake to their headwaters for the big Dolly Vardens each spring and fall.

The rough fighting Dolly is king of the river during his spawning runs, and may be taken upwards of 20 pounds or more. According to regulations they must be at least 18 inches to keep, which starts you out with a big fish.

Cutthroats are the Flathead mainstays with some running up to 5 or 6 pounds and more. However, the average is much smaller, say a pound and a half.

Running the Flathead also are the kokanee salmon, providing excellent fall snagging which is then legal. On several adjoining sloughs is some of Montana's best bass fishing. Other top bass fishing can be found in nearby lakes and ponds.

The Flathead River forms at Glacier National Park where you can take an excellent side trip in matchless mountain scenery, and enjoy wilderness fishing in superb back country.

The big Dolly Vardens of the Flathead present an unusual challenge to the angler. As tackle busters they rank high on anybody's list. Called "bull trout" locally, they present bull-like tendencies whether they are simply resting, or feeding, or on the prod, darting after a sizeable cutthroat trout. Their very features befit their bull-like character. They have big heads and jaws, unlike the more delicate profile of the cutthroat trout.

I remember one Dolly Varden that gave me plenty of problems until I finally beached him. We were on a float trip down the Flathead, fishing from a McKenzie River boat, and the guide was pointing out Dollies hovering over the white sand bars we were passing.

Using heavy spin tackle with 12-pound mono and a half-ounce red and white spoon, I had just succeeded in retrieving my lure from a hangup on overhanging brush along the shore. The spoon wobbled freely in the water while the guide pointed out a couple of extra large Dollies below. Then the spoon sank quickly in a backwater and hung up again on the bottom. Or so I thought.

The swift downstream float stripped off my nylon line despite the two-handed hauling and reeling I was doing, hoping to break off the spoon. All at once I was free of the bottom, only to find my line singing out across the river toward a deep hole. I knew now that there was a big Dolly on the line, and felt him slap on the brakes against the whirling eddy as he reached his defensive position. Again it felt like the bottom, only this time the trout came out fighting, a yard at a time and shaking the spoon like a bull dog. The hydraulic force seemed to double his weight.

Gradually the Dolly gave way and turned down river with us as I began to gain back some of my line. For ten minutes or more we ran a floating duel. Finally tiring, the bull-trout was hauled behind us to a still pool by a sandy beach. There after several more stiff runs, bottom scraping, and vicious head shaking did he reluctantly allow me to beach him. Still he thrashed and fought the sandy beach until I held him up by the gill covers. What a great moment that was!

I had landed an eleven-pound Dolly that felt like a 20-

Floating anglers pass scenic cliffs and fine trout pools along Blue Ribbon Yellowstone River. Southwest Montana.

CHICO LODGE

pound fish. He was a genuine beauty, with bright vermillion spots and silvery sides. Yes, he was bullish looking but to me he was a real trophy. It was the largest fish I had ever caught up to that time. He fought me every inch of the way, and that's what I call spirit and good sport.

Dollies will take bait, big streamer flies, spoons and spinners, or huge salmon plugs, depending on how they feel. Generally they're simply mad at the world. On their spawning runs they seldom feed, but do not depend on it. At other times they are voracious feeders. I saw one Dolly take a darting lure and when landed we found several cutthroat in its stomach, with the tail of one still sticking out of its mouth.

In all the other blue ribbon streams the sophisticated browns and rainbows head the list with cutthroat trailing just behind. The flamboyant rainbow has its great admirers but it seems that most of the visiting experts seek out the durable and wary brown trout. The brown is to some extent similar to the Dolly in dogged fighting, but will, like the rainbow, often make great leaps when pricked with even the smallest of flies.

In western waters trout will often take larger offerings than usual, and sometimes a big heavily dressed fly splashed down on the surface or skittered will tempt a big 'bow or brown out of his pool or pocket.

Normally in wading, you hunt your quarry and cast to the rises, unless you are fishing wet. In this case you often fish the center parts of the stream, forgetting the shore sections. A revelation on how close to the shore trout will lie will come on a typical float fishing trip. In fact this is perhaps the quickest way to learn about western trout fishing.

A first-time visitor to Montana's blue ribbon streams would do well to stop in at some local tackle shops and engage a river guide. The cost ranges from $25 to $40 per day for two and the guide furnishes the boat and does the work. This makes for a cheap lesson in local fishing techniques.

The guide will put you in the best fishing waters as he keeps the boat just good casting distance from shore. Under his direction you will soon begin to pick out likely pockets, holes, and runs, and make your casts as you float along. With the river traveling from about 3 to 7 miles an hour you usually get only one cast at each hole and it had better be good. You learn quickly to anticipate the best trout lies.

Fishing with a number eight Wolly Worm fly, for example, the guide will tell you to lay it on the shore. Some guides mean just that! Put it at the very edge, within inches, or pull it off of bare ground or grass into the water. Often as the fly is dragged out of the pocket a big trout will flash out after the fly and hook himself before you know what has happened.

One day, floating past a brush pile on the bank of the blue ribbon Yellowstone, I tossed my small Muddler fly into the white foam swirling at the bank's edge. Before the fly sank clear under the suds a beaver-like slap hit the water and I was tied to a 3½-pound brown trout. He had been lying in the shade of the foam, pouncing on grasshoppers which dropped off the bank's edge.

Sometimes a cast 3 to 4 feet from shore will draw a blank while a tight one just at the edge will get a vicious strike. The guide will travel from one side of the river to the other and occasionally stop at riffles and holes to fish the likely looking spots. For the most part, however, he will hug the deeper shorelines.

It doesn't take much more than a day or two of this rapid-fire instruction and practice until you feel like a veteran fisherman. Often the knowledge you gain from one float will save a vacation for you when the trout fishing is in the doldrums.

All the blue ribbon rivers are floatable, but few floats are made on the upper Gallatin and Rock Creek.

Another type of float fishing for fast action is to use a power boat, drift fishing below the several dams on the blue ribbon Missouri River, letting your weighted fly, bait, or lure trail behind the boat. You can bob it over rocks and the bottom, or make short jerks with the lure just off the bottom. Often this accounts for surprising catches while fishless shore anglers stare unbelievingly. Once in a while you may tie into a lunker that simply walks off with your outfit and you can't do anything but cry.

The blue ribbon Yellowstone and Missouri are open for trout fishing the year around while the season for the others is from the third weekend of May through November 30th. Rainbows are the first to spawn in the spring and early fishing can be excellent, running from April into June.

July and August are good but have hot-weather ups and downs. Later, the browns spawn in the fall. September and October are ideal for fishing the blue ribbon streams, as the waters are usually lower and steady. With frosty nights and Indian Summer days, fishing is often better as the day progresses and some guides do not start out until ten in the morning.

Winter fishing is usually deep fishing and will turn up some surprising catches. Almost every fall, in November and December, lunker browns and some rainbows in the 10- to 14-pound class are taken below the Missouri dams and on the other two open rivers.

Even the avid dry fly purist could get in some unusual fishing during the winter and early spring, using tiny "snow" flies, size 17-20. Warm sunshine will often bring out tiny naturals around the rocks and shore where trout lay gobbling them up.

Many anglers like to fish the blue ribbon streams of southwestern Montana during the spectacular salmon-fly hatch. These large stone flies start hatching in late May or June in the lower reaches of the rivers and progress upriver during the month. At their peak they are as thick as flies at a summer picnic and leave behind split cases on willows and protruding rocks along the shore. Using a large squirrel-tail fly, called "Sofa Pillow," you can often take lunker trout fishing wet or dry. The flies are tied locally as a specialty and inquiries at tackle shops will help you locate the hatches from day to day. Some anglers have made a science of this fishing and seldom fail to produce.

A wet fly fisherman will find hellgrammite lures or nymphs to be excellent producers. The bait fisherman will collect a can full of the long black naturals, found under the river boulders.

Trout of the blue ribbon streams are much like trout of other areas with a few exceptions. Generally they will take the same time-tested flies and lures. On occasion a lunker will take a tiny fly or small lure. However, for the real tackle busters. I like to gear up with a little heavier leader tippet, bend on a large Muddler, Spruce Fly, or Honey Blonde streamer and have a go at it. I would rather catch fewer fish while looking for a big one than to catch a limit of small friers.

For quality fishing that will please an expert and make a believer out of a beginner, I feel Montana's blue ribbon waters offer the best trout fishing in America and often the biggest trout. But there is one danger in offering this "secret" information: fishing the blue ribbon rivers can be addictive. A man can easily get "hooked" and fishing elsewhere will never seem the same again.   🐟

If there's one thing about fishing I'm hooked on, it's just that I like pike

By LOU KLEWER

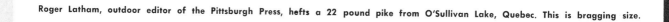

Roger Latham, outdoor editor of the Pittsburgh Press, hefts a 22 pound pike from O'Sullivan Lake, Quebec. This is bragging size.

There are times, albeit much too rare, when an angler can use an extra pair of hands. One such time occurred on a fishing trip to Manitoba with Jack Ackerman. We had found a bay full of northern pike and the action was almost too fast to handle. The pike, in fact, were going wild.

"Jack," I yelled, "I've just hooked the high-jumping champ."

"Look yourself," he answered, "mine thinks he's a kangaroo."

I took a quick glance at Jack who had a deathgrip on the rod with one hand while the other clutched his reel. His problem was to keep both from going overboard. His rod bent nearly double and the tip was in the water under the boat.

That was all I could see because I had a battle of my own. Before it was finished, my arms felt like worn-out rubber bands because we had been tied to fish constantly for more than an hour. Those fish just loved to eat our spoons — or at least to chew on them. Then one of us, I forget who, came up with a bright idea — or at least we thought it was at first — to see which lures would *not* catch these hungry northerns. It seemed like the best way to give both of us a rest. Only it didn't work out that way.

Jack Ackerman, the Toledo (Ohio) Blade outdoors photographer, and I (the outdoor editor) were fishing in Manitoba at Barney Lamm's God's Lake camp. We had started out early that morning for the Wesatchewan River where it empties into George Andrews Bay, a spot Joe Yellowback, one of Barney's Cree Indian guides, said would give us plenty of action.

Joe was ultra-conservative. All morning long we had tied into walleyes, but nary a northern pike. We had been fishing perhaps a quarter of a mile the Wesatchewan from the lonely place where it pours into the Bay. None of our walleyes ran more than four pounds but we had taken about a dozen in that category and possibly two or three dozen smaller.

At lunchtime we had headed back for the mouth of the stream. While Joe was preparing a shore lunch, I made movies of the campfire and of frying fish. I also tried to get shots of Canada jays and chickadees as they came close to us for handouts. That's when Jack made an idle cast or two from shore.

On his second throw he let out a yell which could be heard back in Toledo. "Hey, I gotta northern pike!"

He did and then some. Before he could be lured from the water by a platter of walleye filets, crisp and delicious, he had taken five more good northerns. Even then he wolfed down a delicious shore dinner so he could get back to the fishing. But soon we caught so many northerns on our regular pike spoons that it became monotonous. And that's when we decided to change.

Our plan was to keep changing each time we caught two pike before we discarded a lure since catching one northern might be an accident.

First I snapped a new red and orange lure to my leader. This bait hadn't caught a thing for me during a trip a month before to Quebec. Now I barely started to retrieve it the first time and socko! Next thing I knew a northern lurched out of the water — twice — and fought all the way in.

I tried another cast of the red and orange bait and right away six pounds of fighting pike caught up to my retrieve. That lure would certainly take pike so I had to change. Next I went to a surface lure, the well known Jitterbug, which I have found to be tops for largemouth black bass and rock bass. But I had never taken a pike on it.

The Jitterbug landed near the bullrushes and I let it sit there quietly. I gave it just one light twitch and out of nowhere came a northern pike, arched like a rainbow trout, and he hit that lure coming down. I had never seen that trick before. Also like a rainbow, the pike continued his aerial tactics. This one jumped three times before I played him back to the boat.

From that point I used every surface lure in my tackle box and results were almost the same. Those pike hit one floater — the Sputterbug — as if it were the last meal on earth. Occasionally we missed a strike or a pike missed the lure when it struck, but at least one more pike made a pass at the lure before we got it back to the canoe.

Only two casts with that Jitterbug meant two pike. Then I shifted to still other lures and used some I'd forgotten I had in my tackle box. One was a large saltwater lure I bought for chinook salmon years before at Ketchikan, Alaska, which had a most unusual action in the water.

It was a large wooden plug with detachable hooks. I mean that the hooks pull away from the body of the lure whenever a fish strikes, much as the line pulls away from the outrigger when a billfish smacks the bait.

That salmon lure hadn't been retrieved two feet in the water when the biggest pike of the day hit it. It was a 12-pounder which went frantic a split second after it felt the hooks. We couldn't understand why it smashed that lure so hard, because it couldn't have been too hungry. When we removed the hook from its jaw, we saw the tail of a small hammerhandle-size pike it had just swallowed extending from its throat.

Fishing for pike hasn't always been so sensational. I've known my share of slow days, too. But that fishing at Wesatchewan reminded me of another time Erwin Bauer and I were fishing in Manitoba, this time at Molson Lake northeast of Lake Winnepeg. The pike and the rocks had taken a heavy toll on our lures that trip until all I had left was a trick bottle opener with two sets of gang hooks fastened to it.

The bottle opener had been sent out by a brewing company some years before more as a gag than anything else. I had never used it, but with no more spoons left in the tackle box, I gave it a try.

It paid off. Bauer, in another canoe, watched me haul in northern after northern and yelled, "What the heck you using?"

All I could yell back was, "a bottle opener."

Before we called it a day, that bottle opener had taken 36 pike with the largest weighing 17 pounds. Most of them ran in the six- to eight-pound class and it was the brand of fishing I had never experienced before, until Ackerman and I hit that bonanza on the Wesatchewan River.

I have fished for northern pike for many years. It is a great fish and a good eating fish, as is almost any species taken out of those crystal clear and pure waters of Canada and the northern states. They are even good eating when taken out of Lake Erie or the streams and quarries of northwestern Ohio.

How big do pike grow? There's an argument about that. Dr. H. H. MacKay, in his book entitled "Fishes of Ontario," says the world record pike weighed 53 pounds and was caught in Lough Conn, Ireland, by I. Garvin in July, 1920.

Another big northern pike, a 53-pounder, was shot by Joe Devlin, a County Tyrone sportsman in Lough Neagh in February of 1950. That huge Irish northern pike was reported to have a six-pound pig inside but what wasn't explained was how a pike ever got a chance to swallow a pig. Maybe angler Delvin had been sipping too much

Irish Fogcutter. Little pigs seldom go swimming and pike are seldom found in hog wallows, but the pike and pig story were reported in a number of Irish and English papers.

Field and Stream, custodian of the world's freshwater fishing records, lists a 46-pound two-ounce northern pike as the largest ever taken with rod and reel. That one was caught Sept. 15, 1940, in Sacandaga Reservoir, New York, by Peter Dubuc. It was 52½ inches long with a girth of 25 inches.

While pike aren't always regarded as excellent eating by everyone these days, it hasn't always been that way. In the closing days of the 13th Century, Edward I of England set the value of pike higher than that of fresh salmon and about ten times that of the best turbot and cod. In Henry VIII's time, it was reported that one large pike sold for twice the price of a lamb. Just how much that pike weighed is unknown, but it is hard to imagine pike filets being more expensive than fresh lamb chops.

The northern pike has many aliases ranging from just pike to great northern to great northern pike. In many places it is called jackfish and the small ones, 12 to 16 inches or so in length, are generally termed hammer-handles. Cree Indians call the pike "kenoshi," but scientists and biologists around the world know this lean and always-hungry fish by its Latin name, *Esox lucius*.

Here the guide displays a hefty one.

Gods Lake is one of many excellent pike waters in northern Manitoba.

Pike spawn in shallow, marshy areas almost as soon as the ice goes out in the spring. In the Great Lakes region, they move up into the small streams, going as far as possible and sometimes even spawning in grass-covered drainage ditches. The landowner may not even realize that spawning takes place. But here also they are frequent victims to spears, pitchforks or any other implement that will take them. Spring spearing, however, is illegal in most states and provinces.

A large female northern pike can lay up to one-half million eggs. Hatching occurs about two weeks later. Then, after feeding on microscopic aquatic life, the pike become ardent fish eaters before they are two inches long. Those which grow fastest may devour their own brothers and sisters. Under normal conditions, they can gain a pound or more of weight in a year.

In some places pike eat ravenously during two periods of the year and do not eat much at other times. In northwestern Ohio, for instance, they do not actively feed from about the second week in June until the second week in September.

While curator at the Toledo Zoo aquarium, Harold Wascko conducted a survey on the small streams west of To-

Some northerns jump; others do not. But every jump is a breathtaking experience for the fisherman.

Author Klewer (with beard) points to pike which has partially swallowed smaller pike—but still struck a lure.

Northern pike of this size—about 23 pounds—are splendid game fish. But look for them in the lonely waters of the northern wilderness.

Author here has trouble landing a reluctant pike at Molson Lake, Manitoba.

ledo and of 110 northern pike taken out of Swan Creek during the summer. He found not an ounce of food in all of them.

Not only that, but several pike kept in tanks inside the aquarium also quit eating at that time, according to Wascko. Minnows were placed in the tank along with these pike, but the northerns paid no attention to them. Then suddenly during the second week of September, the minnows disappeared and from that point the pike were again ready to eat anything.

There are just as many legends, myths, and wild theories circulated about northern pike as about some other creatures of the wild. The chief one, of course, claims that northern pike annually shed their teeth in August and that is why they do not eat.

It is true that northern pike may have a tooth or two missing just about any month of the year, but they do not shed *all* their teeth anytime. August just isn't an active eating period. In some parts of the country, they will not feed at all during dog days, and the few taken are often snagged. There is an old saying that "even a blind pig will find a few acorns," so at times northern pike may be irritated enough to strike a lure even when not feeding.

While not considered in the same class with muskelunge, there is very little difference in the fighting abilities of the two fish or in their eating qualities. Pike will break water as often as muskies and the payoff in number of fish caught is a great deal better. Creel census statistics compiled by a number of fish management bureaus give the general average of one muskie caught for every 50 to 100 hours of fishing in the best musky waters. If there weren't some recompense in the form of walleyes, black bass or northern pike, there soon wouldn't be many fishermen out after muskies today. Few modern anglers are willing to put in more than a full work week to catch one muskie. In most places, pike are caught far more frequently.

While northern pike may get to be a nuisance to some anglers, there are some lakes where bluegills and sunfish tend to over-populate the waters and to become stunted. The introduction of northern pike has helped to equalize these conditions. Pike, at times, feed voraciously on small bluegills and as a result will keep down the quantity of bluegills. This gives the panfish more chance to grow to adequate size under less crowded conditions.

Northern pike will feed on just about any other fish sharing their waters, including smaller pike. They are hungry cannibals, and many sportsmen have had them hit lures or try for other fish before they have completed swallowing the last fish grabbed.

When is the best time to go pike fishing? Pike enthusiasts can argue all day and not come to any definite conclusions. Spring and fall are always good times, yet in some areas, especially in Canadian waters, they can usually be taken all summer. As we've pointed out, August is the slowest period. Winter ice fishing also finds large numbers of northerns taken, but most of these seem to be speared from a shanty while the pike is nosing up to the wooden decoys or the big chub minnows which are used to attract them.

Pike do not hit in the wintertime as well as during the spring and fall, but then not all species do. As springtime right after spawning is the best time for walleyes, perch, white bass and for black bass, so is it best for pike. It is the period to catch the biggest northerns as well as the greater number. I've found it almost impossible to go through an early spring day without catching exceptional fish, both in quality and quantity. But remember that this can also be a time of bad weather, cold spells and when mosquitoes are active in the North.

Where is the best place for a northern pike fishing trip? Generally it is Canada and the northern section of the United States from Quebec to the Yukon and from Michigan and the Great Lakes area to beyond the Arctic circle. And in that same general latitude, you'll find 'em around the world. But specifically the lakes of northern Manitoba and Saskatchewan are by far the best. Ontario also offers excellent pike fishing in its northern fly-in country. So does Quebec.

Last spring, I watched Dr. Roger Latham, Pittsburgh Press outdoor editor, haul a 22-pounder out of O'Sullivan Lake north of Maniwaki in central Quebec. That is a bragging size fish anywhere. Then a month later over the Fourth of July, Jack Ackerman and I enjoyed that field day in the God's Lake area of Manitoba when the northerns hit anything. And I *do* mean anything.

Those great days aren't too common however; even a springtime trip doesn't guarantee them. But the most consistent lures are the spoons, the daredevils, red-eyes, silver minnows, and various spinning lures, followed by the Hula Pike, Hustler and other underwater plugs. But for most excitement when the pike are in shallow water, a fisherman should also have a number of such surface lures as the Sputterbug and Jitterbug just to make the northerns behave like leaping tarpon or snook.

Trout fishermen may look down their noses at northerns, and pike are often avoided by smallmouth bass enthusiasts. Stalkers after bonefish or many of the flyrod tarpon fans never even hear of this species. But I've caught 'em all, from Arctic char to rainbows in Tierra Del Fuego and from Costa Rican sailfish to snook in the Florida mangroves. Fishing for anything is fun.

But I still like pike. And so will you.

Klewer wolfs down a shore dinner of walleye filets so that he can go back to casting for pike.

SNOOK ARE PSYCHOS

By Jim Martenhoff

That Famous Florida Fish Is Mean And Maybe A Little Mixed-Up Too!

Any seasoned angler will probably find virtue in the observation that fish, like people, have distinctive personalities, although there might well be some difference of opinion in interpretation of the traits displayed. One man's fool may be another man's friend.

A writer I know, for example, once insisted publicly that bonefish were boneheads, and this possibly hasty asseveration forced him into a temporary withdrawal from a segment of society that would have nothing to do with him.

With some slight trepidation, therefore, I'd like to suggest that snook are essentially psychopathic. If I sound bitter, blame the snook. This fish is a mean, short-tempered, violent, arrogant, disreputable, infamous, opprobrious, nasty brute. It is the only fish I know that would spit in your eye if it knew how to spit. Lacking this social accomplishment, it knocks your plug out of the water instead, showering spray, and you get the message: It's spitting contemptuously at you in the only way it knows.

It is probably, for all those reasons listed above, more sheer fun to fish for than almost anything else that swims. True snook fishermen know this, and you can spot a genuine snook-chaser by the way he describes his day:

"I got my limit," he will assert with quiet pride. Since the limit in Florida is only four fish, it doesn't adequately describe the achievement to announce the number that you capture. "Four" just doesn't sound like much of a bag. "Limit" does. And when you get your limit, you've done something: climbed the Mt. Everest of piscatorial challenge.

Pursuit of legal limit bags drives snook anglers mad. I once spent a day baking to a crisp under Florida's summer sun, chasing snook in a remote mangrove area with indifferent success, and heard next morning that a youngster playing with a new fly rod captured a 30-pounder on six-pound test tippet. It didn't help a bit to also hear that (a) he used a live shrimp for bait on the fly rod and (b) caught the big 'un in a former rockpit, open to salt water. I said the snook is psycho. Maybe it's plain nuts. That fish must have been swimming around with an unfulfilled death wish, looking for a place to commit suicide, in as spectacular a manner as possible. Bridge jumper at heart.

The true snook, *centropomus undecimalis*, is a tropical species — which may explain its cockeyed personality. All that heat can bake a brain, even in a fish. It occurs from Florida to Brazil, and can be found in any type of water: brackish, almost drinkable stuff well upstream; river mouths, passes and inlets; around jetties and breakwaters, fishing piers and even in the surf. At times snook fishermen land in Paradise when they fish the turbulent water below dams, whether it be a salinity control structure on a South Florida canal, or the locks of the Panama Canal. In Florida Bay, it is now even becoming common on the flats, and it is not impossible to pursue snook the same way you hunt bonefish. Lots o' luck, buddy.

Best snook fishing in Florida is from late spring to early fall. Highlight of the year for snook anglers is the early summer run on the lower west coast, headquartered around Marco and Everglades City at the northern edge of the wild Ten Thousand Islands. The spawning run begins with the full moon in late May or June, and the angling world's version of the moccasin telegraph goes into full operation. Within hours, workers have literally walked off their jobs, taking anything from sick leave to brief vacations, to camp, trailer-camp, or otherwise congregate where the action is.

It slowly tails off until fall, by which time snook fishing becomes a bit more work.

Meantime, the ubiquitous snook roams the mangrove shorelines, which appears to be a preferred habitat. They lurk about oyster bars and bank edges on selected tide stages, and lucky is the man who learns the combination. If there is a combination.

When the snook is in a feeding mood, he'll take anything — and I mean anything. Choicest baits include finger mullet, shiners, pinfish, shrimp, small needlefish. The needlefish, a surface swimmer of the inshore shallows, is captured by shooting with a 22 rifle. This idea is to stun the bait, by shooting next to it — not hitting it. So the ardent snook angler who really goes to work in pursuit of his chosen quarry begins by hunting for his bait with a rifle.

On artificials, the snook is geographically choosy. What works on one coast of Florida bombs on the other. In the Everglades National Park waters that lie at the southern edge of the Ten Thousand Islands, a floating wood plug that is a shallow runner on the retrieve drives snook into a fury. It is ignored to the north, and on the Atlantic side. Around Marco snook prefer a wobbling, medium to deep runner with a built-in action. I tried it one day — grimly — 50 miles away and they turned up their elongated snouts at it, smashing happily into the plugs offered by my companions. On the eastern side, they go for a medium runner with flashy sides and very little action. Almost anywhere, when in a good mood, they'll take a variety of jig, yellow or white. And at Marco, I've seen them caught on cardboard, torn into the shape of a fish and hung on a hook. Nuts, that's what they are.

Fly fishermen take them on streamers, which they seem to prefer to popping bugs, also tried with some success.

Snook are night people, and those who know this manage to do well. Work almost any coastal bridge in Florida after dark, and you may come up with snook. Look for signs, however. So many snook-seekers (as well as other fishermen, to be honest about it) crowd bridges that some are off-limits. Others have catwalks, provided by the government on the theory that if you can't lick 'em, join 'em.

Snook specialists will rig a cane pole with wire line, attach a plug known to attract snook in that particular locality, and walk the bridge while dappling the plug along the surface of the water, imitating a frightened, skittering baitfish. The canepole is the only way to handle a husky snook from a bridge. The big bully, when hooked, normally heads for the nearest object around which he can wrap your line and break you off. Stout cane and wire line often, but not always, stop the snook short. Some come too big to be stopped easily; 30-pounders aren't exactly rare, and the record is a fat 52 pounds, although most run from 10 to 20.

Casters normally do best early and late in the day. Snook like noontime siestas, although if you disturb one

Bill Barnes unhooks another snook.

Bill removes snook, Boyd keeps trying . . .

Heading west in Everglades National Park at dawn.

Finally Perry lands a good one . . .

while he's in a sleepy mood he turns savage and will bust up your tackle to a fare-thee-well. Snook strike at the surface, and slash into bait fish, within an unmistakeable "popping" sound that once heard is never forgotten. It makes a snook fisherman's pulse skip a beat when he hears it and knows a feeding snook is nearby, for at times like this the fish will hit almost any offering.

If I had to point out a prime area for those who would fish for this bass-like species, it has to be the wild coastal region from Flamingo, in the Everglades National Park, westward and northward to Marco. This doesn't fault snook fishing in the Florida Keys, nor at the Stuart-Jensen Beach area where they run to nice sizes, nor even along the Miami Beach Causeways where snook can be taken at night in the reflected neon glow of Go-go joints, almost within sight of the undulating go-go girls. But snook seem thickest in the mangrove wilderness far from civilization, and perhaps a bit more willing to tangle with an angler. They can be aggravatingly uncooperative and downright surly closer to the cities. But who isn't?

Fishing mangrove edges in creeks that are sometimes pretty narrow calls for special techniques. I have two friends who developed a bounce-cast ability that drives snook even further out of their already unbalanced minds.

Mangroves, you see, grow well out into the water. Snook and other fish lie back beneath the overhanging branches, in the cooler, shady waters (they may be psychopathic, but they aren't totally stupid). You can drop plugs or streamer flies all day at the outer edge of the mangroves, and go away convinced there isn't a snook for miles. Actually, the brutes are glaring at your proferred lures but refuse to swim out to get them. To attract a snook's serious attention, it is sometimes necessary to virtually knock them over the noggin.

Perry Boyd and Bill Barnes, both of Homestead, Florida, found the answer to this. I fished the Upper Shark River area with them one day in a two-boat expedition. (This remote region is almost 40 miles by boat from the nearest anyplace, and it's smart to travel in company — just in case.)

Benny Martins and his two fellow fishermen in the other boat wandered down Rookery Branch on their own, and we cast the mangroves.

Both Boyd and Barnes, using wooden plugs that floated, but were shallow runners on the retrieve, began bouncing their plugs back underneath the mangrove branches. Distance isn't important in creek casting; accuracy is. They used a short arm motion, mostly wrist, shooting the plug downward in a straight line and aiming at the edge of the mangroves.

Almost every cast the plugs would bounce back beneath the overhanging branches for several feet, where they would be twitched once or twice and then retrived fairly fast, as if a bait fish had suddenly discovered a reason for fear and was taking to flight.

Snook would smash into those plugs in an absolute fury, sometimes before they had traveled a foot. They ignored the medium runner I was using.

The battle is always interesting. Snook resemble bass in many ways. They will jump as well as fight doggedly just beneath the surface. And they love to try and drag your plug back under the mangrove roots, where they can snap it off and sneer at you. It takes husky tackle and a lot of pressure. Barnes broke one rod that day.

But those crazy snook can fill your day before you know it. Action in the mangrove islands kept us so contentedly occupied with our psycho snook that mid-afternoon arrived with unaccustomed speed, and we had to

Barnes gets strike, Perry Boyd retrieves plug out of way.

start the long voyage home. Those crazy snook probably were sorry to see us leave. They seem to LIKE fishing as much as people do, making a game out of it.

I know one time I was fishing the mouth of Lostman's River, a remote stream that must be 60 miles from the nearest settlement. Two of us had thrown everything in the tackle box at the snook we knew were there, but those crazy fish didn't want to play.

In desperation I rigged up a wiggling-type bonefish jig on eight-pound test spinning with a monofilament leader. This was insanity to begin with, for the snook has knife-sharp gill covers, and a wire trace is considered *de rigeur*. (Keep your fingers away from those gill covers, too!)

I tried dragging and bumping it over an oyster bar. The tiny bonefish jig was designed to ride with the hook upright, so the stunt worked.

And a 20-pounder gulped that tiny jig like a drunk downing a shot of hooch. Fortunately there were no nearby mangroves to which he could retreat, popping the light line; and after a furious battle we were able to boat the prize. My friend was totally dismayed.

"Anyone crazy enough to go after snook with a bonefish rig deserves to catch one," he commented, and perhaps thereby summed up Florida snook fishing. The fish are crazy. We know that.

And while you don't have to be crazy to catch snook, it certainly helps.

Fishing above Shark River in narrow mangrove creek.

Don't CUSS CARP... CATCH 'EM Instead!

By Bob Bauer

Almost no angler is happy to have the unhandsome carp in our waters. But it's a good fish to catch anytime.

If a popularity poll is ever taken on our fishes, it is doubtful that the carp will accumulate many votes from sportsmen. Yet this fish is accessible to more fishermen than any other fish. Since their introduction into America in 1877, they have spread completely across the country.

Carp are stubbornly strong fighters when taken on sport fishing tackle. Specimens of 50 pounds and more have been taken. They are comparatively easy to catch and abundant within a short drive of almost anybody's home. Then why do so many people cuss carp rather than fish for them?

The reason is probably that fishermen are unwilling to discard the common prejudice that carp are fish of polluted waters, low in food value, and completely nongame fish. But nothing could be farther from the truth. Carp do thrive in pure water, they are good food fish (and nutritious, too) and far more exciting when hooked than some so-called game species. Let me explain.

The Olentangy River in central Ohio was once heralded among the greatest smallmouth bass rivers in the country. Unfortunately flood control and farming practices have helped to change all that. Consequently, few anglers still fish that stream. But a few years ago, the scarcity of fishermen on the stream attracted me to it. My first visit to the stream didn't produce many bass, but I noticed a lot of carp milling about in some larger pools.

Several days later I returned to the stream with doughball baits and an ultra-light fishing outfit. I had long believed the usual carp-are-not-sport-fish theory and I didn't have great expectations when a carp began to mouth my doughball. But once I set the hook, line began to peel off my reel with amazing speed. All I could do was to hang on and try to play it cool. I was sure that the carp weighed at least fifteen pounds. So I couldn't believe my eyes when I finally grounded the fish about ten minutes later. It weighed only about four pounds.

I hooked five more carp and landed three of them that day before I had to leave. I managed the largest one, a nine pounder, only after chasing it far downstream and maneuvering it around the roots of several streamside sycamores. I've gone back fishing there many times since then and have shown many former sceptics how thrilling carp actually can be. Since the river is only about a fifteen minute drive from my home, that's where I'm likely to be found on any summer or spring evening.

Pond-raised carp had become an important part of the national diets in China and Japan for more than 2000 years and were introduced into Europe before the year 600 A.D. But the origin of the carp in America dates back less than a century when Rudolph Hessel, a fish culturist for the United States Government, successfully shipped by boat 345 carp from Hochst, Germany to New York Harbor. These fish were first stocked in ponds in Boston's Druid Hill. The fish soon became overcrowded in Boston and 113 carp were transferred to Babcock Lake in Washington, D.C.

Soon Americans everywhere demanded breeding stock of this fish which they knew nothing about. Government fisheries "experts" made glowing promises to outdoorsmen about the species' great qualities. So in 1883, 260,000 carp were divided among 298 congressional districts leaving only three left without carp. Naturally the politicians had to get into the act. The ancestors of those original 345 carp have now spread and dominated many American waters from coast to coast. Furthermore, scientific studies all indicate that they're here to stay and fishermen might as well start paying some attention to them.

Light spinning tackle enables a fisherman to detect soft strike of carp in situations like this one.

Now that the carp are here, what kind of tackle is required to catch them? Carp, of course, aren't very particular about it. The same tackle that you use for bass and other fish is also fine for carp. Casting, fly, and spinning rods are all used. Many youngsters and oldsters alike have caught respectable strings of carp on cane poles. However, a casting outfit is often a necessity in order to reach schools of carp which lie some distance from shore.

An ultra-light spinning outfit provides the greatest carp fishing sport of all but don't underestimate the power of ten pounds of carp. If you ever do catch a big carp on ultra-light tackle, you may never want to use heavier tackle again. But remember, some of the largest carp hooked every year are lost because of line breakage. The stamina and power of a big carp have been responsible for breaking up many an unsuspecting panfisherman's tackle.

Baits used for carp are as numerous as carp fishermen themselves. The doughball, however, is probably the all-time favorite. Many carp fishermen like to brag about having their own secret recipes. Most recipes involve boiling flour with certain other ingredients such as sugar, corn syrup, molasses, licorice root, and aniseed. A friend of mine reports good catches of carp using doughballs made from bread which he kneads in his hands. He insists that spitting on the bread not only helps greatly in holding it on the hook but also helps increase his luck. Kneading a little corn meal into the bread can also be helpful. After the water has time to wash the bread off his hook twice and there is no action, he moves to a new spot.

In any case, the doughball should not cover the hook completely. The bait which is usually best covers only the bend in the point of the hook. When carp become gorged as they often do in mid-summer, the fish merely mouth the bait a few seconds and then spit it back out again. If you suspect that this is happening, cover just the point of the hook and strike as soon as you feel the fish inspecting the bait. This is the only effective method I know for catching carp that are seemingly curious but not hungry.

Other popular carp baits include such naturals as night crawlers, minnows, and crawfish. Many kinds of vegetables such as tomatoes, beans, potatoes and peas are particularly good carp baits. I have caught carp in Lake Erie on spinners when fishing for bass and walleyes. However, these carp were exceptions to the normal feeding patterns of carp.

My favorite bait for carp is canned sweet corn. First I throw a handful of kernels in a pool of water where the carp are likely to be feeding. (I guess this can be called baiting or chumming.) Then I string enough kernels on a size 8 hook to cover the point and bend. I use a light spinning outfit so that split shot will not be necessary to cast the corn. Carp with their unusually tender mouths sometimes spit the bait back out when they feel the weight of the split shot. After the hook is baited, I cast my bait into the middle of the scattered kernels and wait. It isn't too long afterward before a carp begins to sample the bait. I immediately flip over the bail (of the open face spinning reel) so the carp can strip line off the spool when he begins to run with the bait. After the carp has run with the corn for about ten to twenty feet, I set the hook and prepare to start chasing him downstream.

After the springtime spawning season, carp may be taken in early morning by stalking along a riverbank and watching for the fish to roll in the weeds and mud. Be alert, because only a fin or a tail may be visible. When you spot a carp, cast your bait beyond the fish so as not to

frighten it. Then slowly reel it back in. If the water is clear enough, you may be able to see the carp mouth the bait, suck it in, and then start to run with it. After the carp begins its run, drive the hook home. Hard.

A friend of mine who specializes in catching big twenty pounders and even heavier carp recommends fresh water clams. He opens up some clams and when they get a strong enough smell to suit him, he cuts them up in the evening and baits a place in the river where he's seen some of the jumbos splashing. The next morning, he goes back and fishes the spot with another piece of clam on his hook. He has also caught bragging size catfish this way.

It surprises many anglers to learn that Izaak Walton was an avid carp fisherman. In *The Compleat Angler* he commends the meadow worm and paste made with honey as being the best baits. Walton was greatly handicapped, however, because there were no reels and his line was then necessarily tied directly to the rod. When he hooked a big carp, he'd throw his rod in the water to save his tapered horsehair line. Then later with the fish still on, he'd dredge up his rod and finish the fight after the fish was weakened.

Izaak Walton believed that the table qualities of carp make him worth the labor of catching the fish. However, few Americans agree with Mr. Walton. If you would like to try carp, here is one of the many recipes to either enhance or subdue its flavor.

Broiled Carp
2 lbs. carp filets
3 tbls. bacon drippings
½ tsp. salt
¼ tsp. pepper
1 medium sized onion
paprika

Wipe with damp cloth and place on a rack of broiler pan. Brush top of fish with fat, season with salt and pepper. Sprinkle with chopped onions and paprika. Place fish in pre-heated broiler and broil two inches from the heat for 15 minutes. Turn fish over. Brush with fat and season as previously. Broil for another 15 minutes or until done.

If this recipe isn't to your liking, try smoking some filets. If the fish doesn't taste good to you after either treatment, it probably never will. But whether you like to eat it or not, the odds are stacked that the "wonder fish from Asia" likes it here and is going to stay. So if you have't tried fishing for carp, it is high time you investigated this much neglected fishing pastime.

Garden vegetables—canned or fresh corn or peas—are great baits for river carp in summertime.

THE FUNDAMENTALS OF OFFSHORE TROLLING

You own a boat and now you yearn for fishing adventure.
Read on how to catch the blue water species.

by Milt Rosko

There is something exhilarating about pointing the bow of your boat to the horizon, pushing the throttles ahead to flank speed and watching a beautiful, high squirreltail form as your propellers push you forward. With your boat throwing showers of spray as you slice through the swells, land soon disappears off your stern and the water turns a deep blue, a color seldom found close to shore.

This is blue water country and you'll find it off our Atlantic, Pacific and Gulf Coasts. It's where you're most apt to encounter the game pelagic species that roam our offshore waters in search of a meal. These waters are also the stomping grounds of boatmen who thrill to the sight of gamefish chasing lures trolled in their wake, and of the battle that ensues once a fine blue water gamefish is hooked.

It is surprising, however, the relatively small number of boat owners who have experienced the thrilling fishing that is available beyond sight of land. For contrary to popular belief, blue water trolling isn't difficult to master. If anything, it's often less difficult catching offshore gamefish than it is those species that live in close to the beach where boat traffic and fishing pressure is heavy.

One prerequisite, before even thinking about catching blue water gamefish, is having a seaworthy boat in the 20-foot or larger class. You must also have a thorough knowledge of seamanship and be able to handle the boat safely in any type of weather you may encounter while on the grounds far from shore. The type of fishing I'll discuss here is for boatmen with craft suited to traveling many miles to sea in search of their sport. It is not my intent to encourage owners of small boats to venture beyond their intended range, for in doing so you flirt with disaster.

During the past couple of years I've done a great deal of offshore trolling on all three of our coasts; off Mexico's offshore islands as well as many islands and cays that comprise the Bahamas and the waters of Bermuda. I have found with few minor exceptions that tackle was remarkably similar in all of the spots I fished. So were the terminal rigging and the basic trolling techniques used by both private and charter boatmen.

At the time I was writing a book, "Fishing From Boats," and I wanted to prove that certain basic tackle combinations would well serve a small boatman on his own craft just as if he had traveled to a distant angling paradise on a charter boat. So I began with a great variety of tackle and in the course of my travels eliminated what I felt was unsuitable. Also I finally settled on what I believed to be the ideal equipment for all medium-sized offshore gamefish.

So it happened that my choice narrowed down to a combination most often called "a regulation 20-pound

You'll enjoy maximum sport while trolling offshore when you use light tackle. The author employed light regulation class tackle to subdue this 26 pound African pompano while trolling in the Bahamas at the tip of the Tongue of the Ocean. It took over a half hour to bring the tough adversary to gaff.

class rod." I chose this rod because it has a limber tip, yet it is powerful enough in the butt section to subdue gamefish which may approach the hundred pound mark.

While the rod is rated for 20-pound test line, I've found that by using 30-pound test line instead, I have fifty percent more line strength and do not have to worry when I hook the occasional very big fish. Once the fish is tired I do not have to handle it with kid gloves. Instead I can "lean" on it and boat it without incident. I load 300 yards of 30-pound test nonfilament on a regulation 3/0 trolling reel. This gives me 900 feet of strong line, which is more than most gamefish up to 100 pounds are capable of running from a reel, providing that the boat is handled properly.

Although I prefer the 20-pound class rod, I might note that for a beginner or a boatman who sails with inexperienced friends, the 30-pound class rod would be better suited for general offshore trolling, thus giving a perfect balance of a 30-pound class rod, 30-pound test monofilament line and a 3/0 reel.

While there are different styles of swivels which may be used as connections between line and leader, I've found the ball bearing type of swivel with a coastlock snap to be ideal. This one has positive swiveling action and will prevent a line from twisting no matter how much the bait or lure spins. The coastlock snap that is attached to it also facilitates changing leaders.

While many anglers use a double line, for most medium-sized gamefish it is not necessary. Simply attach the ball bearing swivel to your line by using a strong clinch knot.

With respect to leaders, I most often use either #8 or #9 stainless steel leader wire, or 50 to 75 pound test monofilament. The reason for the heavy test of the monofilament is that it is less apt to be cut by the fins, scales or sharp gill covers of many offshore gamefish.

To stay within International Game Fish Association regulations a leader can be no longer than 15 feet. But for practical trolling for most medium-sized gamefish, a leader ten feet long is perfect. By using a leader that isn't too long, there is a minimum amount of leader to handle when a fish is led to gaff.

Although some trollers use a stainless steel snap at the end of their leaders to facilitate changing lures, I've found it better to make direct connections, either by twisting the wire leader to the lure, or by attaching it (via a clinch knot) to monofilament leaders. Keep in mind that the less hardware you use the less conspicuous is the connection, with fewer parts to fail at a crucial moment.

It is good to have several torpedo-shaped trolling sinkers in your kit ranging in weight from one to four ounces for those occasions when you want your lures to work just beneath the surface. Most quality trolling sinkers come equipped with stainless steel hardware and are attached between line and leader.

There are a great many lures and natural baits which are suitable for offshore trolling. There are so many, in fact, that an entire article could not cover all of them. So here we will cover only the few lures which produce the best results no matter where they are trolled.

Tops on my list and a lure on which I've caught more different species of gamefish than any other lure by far, is the Japanese trolling feather. Depending on where you live, you'll hear it called feather, just plain trolling feather, feathered jig or trolling jig. Basically it is nothing more than a lead head which is chrome- or nickel-plated with a pair of bead, plastic or pearl eyes and a full, feathered skirt tied to the head. It is rigged by passing a leader through the hole in its head, after which a hook is attached and then pulled up tight to be concealed in the feathers.

The Japanese trolling feathers (also made in the U. S., but still called Japanese feathers because most of them are manufactured there) come in a wide variety of head weights and in practically every color in the spectrum. If you keep a selection on board that includes ½, 1, 2 and 3 ounce heads, with red and white, plain white, black and white, green and yellow and solid blue feathers you'll be able to catch practically any of the gamefish you'll encounter on blue water.

There are several variations of the Japanese trolling feathers; some are equipped with plastic streamer skirts, while others have two-part heads that enhance the lure's action as it is drawn through the water. All work well, for they closely resemble any one of the many dozens of varieties of baitfish that frequent offshore waters.

Years ago the bone squid was a lure that found extensive use on the offshore grounds. Today you don't see too many made of bone any more because hard plastic is more durable and available in a wider variety of colors. The lure ranges in length from 5 to 7 inches and is equipped with either a single or double hook. The bone squid in design resembles the hull of a boat, either round or V-shaped on the bottom, flat at the stern and tapered to a point at the head, with a flat top.

The true bone squids are white in color, but the plastic models come in a wide range of colors to suit the fancy of offshore sport fishermen.

Spoons are still another type of lure that should be included in any kit since they account for a lot of fish on all coasts. Most favored by experienced blue water fishermen are either chrome-plated or stainless steel spoons that measure from 5 to 7 inches in length. There are dozens of models on the market, but basically most have the same type of flashing action. It is this bright flash as the blade sweeps from side to side when trolled that brings the strikes.

There are also a number of other lures that find favor on the offshore grounds, including surgical tube lures, cedar jigs, soft plastic baits, bucktail jigs, plus a host of others which find regional favor. But in the main, you will find that if you use a basic starter set which includes trolling feathers, bone or plastic squids and spoons, you will enjoy consistent results.

With all of these lures a 7/0 forged O'Shaughnessy hook is best, although on occasion some of the spoons or bone squids will be equipped with an 8/0 hook.

In addition to lures, trolled natural baits account for many fine catches. Among the most popular skip baits are strips of either squid, pork rind or fish belly that is cut to the shape of a small fish. Balao (called ballyhoo), mullet, eels, sardines, flying fish and mackerel also account for many offshore gamefish and are generally rigged as skip baits, i.e., to skip across the surface of the water as they are trolled, thus resembling a frightened baitfish skipping across the water.

One of the best bits of advice I can offer a private boatman new to offshore trolling is to keep a good distance from the professional charter and party boat skippers who are fishing the offshore grounds for a livelihood. But at the same time you keep your distance, watch what they do. These men are on the water every day and they know precisely where the bait concentrations are. And most often the gamefish are there too.

You can easily observe the charter boatman's trolling patterns and speed and be guided accordingly. While this may sound like copycat tactics, it's also good horse sense. Most casual fishermen just aren't on the water frequently enough to know day-by-day what is going on.

John Mason just gaffed this 33 pound albacore for Milt Rosko as they trolled over 60 miles out in the Pacific off San Diego, California. The big albacore struck a Japanese trolling feather, which can be seen extending from its jaw.

The dolphin is caught off all three of our coasts. It's a fine light tackle adversary that will readily swat most any lure or skip bait. They have a habit of taking up residence around flotsam and along weedbeds far from shore, so never pass one by while trolling.

The Pacific bonito is a fine light tackle fish that puts up an excellent scrap. This beauty weighed 8 pounds and walloped a Japanese trolling feather fished right in the wake, as the lucky angler trolled near the Los Coronados Islands off Mexico in the Pacific. Bonito prefer a fast moving bait and, because of their inquisitive nature, will often move right up close to the stern, where they'll hit lures on short lines.

Captain George Seemann of the Mitchell I is about to deposit a hefty king mackerel in the fishbox, while Bob Stankus fights another tough king. Note the light action in Bob's 20-pound class rod, thus offering maximum sport with tough offshore gamefish. Kings such as this are available to the offshore troller in the Bahamas, on Florida's East Coast and along the entire Gulf coast across to Texas.

Most gamefish are best gaffed. Here's Herb Schoenberg about to put the gaff to a husky school bluefin tuna hooked while trolling off the middle Atlantic coast.

For a moment Herb Schoenberg thought he could hold onto the leader wire and get this tough gamefish being fought by Bill Perry within range. It just wasn't ready though, and Herb had to let go of the wire and the fish made another run. Scene is typical of the exciting scenes you'll find when fishing blue water, many miles from the sight of land.

The strip bait is a favorite of trollers everywhere. This bait was cut from the silvery belly of a bonito. When trolled on the surface it flutters in a lifelike manner that all gamefish find irresistible.

The little tuna is a husky fighter that provides fast action for Atlantic and Gulf coast anglers. This one swallowed a Jap trolling feather fished along the edge of the Gulf Stream off Stuart, Florida. It's an excellent light tackle fish, ideally suited to 20- and 30-pound regulation class tackle.

southeast Florida and the Bahamas, we caught wahoo, dolphin, amberjack, African pompano and blackfin tuna. In the Gulf of Mexico a pattern such as outlined here brought strikes from king mackerel, little tuna and oceanic bonito. On the broad expanse of Pacific it was albacore, Pacific bonito and school bluefin tuna which succumbed to our lures. So essentially the same trolling patterns prevail everywhere.

It is always wise to start off the day with a good selection of lures. A pair of spoons, one up close and the other far back, plus a pair of feathers or bone squids is a good starter. Keep alternating until you find a combination that brings strikes. Sometimes the gamefish you run into will want everything right up close, almost at the transom. On other occasions the only way you will get strikes is to let the lures well out until they reach the water where the wake is flattening out.

All of the species mentioned earlier will take a fast moving lure or bait much quicker than a slow moving one. It has been my observation that most beginners troll much too slowly on the offshore grounds. Move the throttles ahead until your boat is churning up a nice wake. If you're not sure of the proper speed, watch someone who is catching fish and adjust your speed accordingly. Bear in mind that in such an article as this it is difficult to tell the exact speed you should troll. Each boat trolls best at a different engine speed.

There are other variables that must be taken into consideration. Even far offshore there are ocean currents, and when you're trolling *with* the current you've got to move your throttles ahead, whereas when you're going against it you can slow down somewhat. Wind often plays a role in the speed you use, depending on whether you're bucking it or running with it.

It has been my experience that constant circling movements of the boat will result in far more strikes than just a steady, straight troll. Try figure-eights, "S" turns, zigzags, or long, slow circles.

When you spot fish "working" bait on top, first troll along the edges of the school so that you do not drive the fish down. Usually the lures just skirting along the edge of the feeding fish will draw gamefish away from the main school to strike your lures.

Once a fish is hooked, continue trolling slowly, and have the anglers in the cockpit work their rods with a jiggling motion because often other fish will follow the hooked one. When they spot your lures darting and faltering as you slowly move forward you will often be rewarded with several more strikes. Sometimes it is possible to keep a school milling about for an hour or more,

Proof positive that light tackle can lick big fish. This wahoo is almost as big as June Rosko, who landed it on regulation 30-pound class tackle while standing up and wearing a belt socket. Herb Schoenberg did the gaffing honors while fishing from the Mitchell I.

Most small boats can comfortably fish either three or four lines. If you have no outriggers, three lines are about the maximum you should troll, all of which would be trolled flat off the stern. If your craft is equipped with outriggers, then it's wise to fish one line from each outrigger and a pair of flat lines from the stern.

A good pattern is to fish a couple of lines right up close in the wake, preferably at the top of the first or second wave that your propellers throw up. The outside lines, or the outrigger lines, as the case may be, should be fished farther back, in the range of 100 to 125 feet from the stern. This gives you a pattern of a couple of lures tossing about in the churning wake and two more way back where the wake flattens out.

I've fished aboard boats using this exact pattern on all three coasts and have caught an immense variety of gamefish. Along the northeast Atlantic coast, the school bluefin tuna and Atlantic bonito were the quarry, while in

Here's a light trolling outfit and four fine trolling lures, from left to right; Jap trolling feather, plastic imitation squid, cedar jig and aluminum headed trolling jig with plastic skirt.

Anything can happen at a moment like this. Here's the author leading a big albacore to the gaff of John Mason. The tough fighter was hooked while trolling over 60 miles at sea off San Diego, California.

so long as at least one hooked fish is kept in the water at all times. We've had this happen with albacore, bonito, bluefin tuna, king mackerel and dolphin, to name but a few of the curious species which follow a hooked fish.

It is worth noting that even when steadily trolling it is wise to "work' (jig) your lures. Most trollers relinquish all of their rods to rod holders as they troll along. Frequently fish will dart through the wake and after giving the lures a quick once over will continue on, showing no interest.

If, instead of moving at the constant trolling speed, these lures were instead darting ahead and then faltering, you can bet that they would get strikes as soon as a gamefish spotted them. This takes work, however, for you have to hold the rod and constantly keep working the tip.

A good way to prove to yourself that this system works, especially with Japanese trolling feathers, bone squids and cedar jigs, is to have one angler working his tip all day while a second rod is relinquished to the rod holder. At day's end the jigged rod will have accounted for twice as many strikes as the rod in the holder. Admittedly, the angler doing the jigging will be a little arm weary, for it is hard work, but it does put more fish in the box.

It is wise to always keep alert for any surface activity when offshore. Look for feeding fish. If you don't spot them, watch for signs of bait. Often a school of baitfish will appear as only a patch of slightly discolored water, with a slight shimmer to it. But sometimes you can spot the baitfish leaping out of the water, which often indicates they're nervous or have just recently been assaulted by gamefish.

You can be sure that sometime during a day's fishing a school of gamefish will meet up with a school of baitfish.

I've been offshore many times when we trolled for hours without a strike, although there was a lot of bait in the area. Then suddenly the baitfish would start nervously, fluttering on the surface, after which the schools would be literally ripped apart as schools of hungry heavyweights waded into them.

Another thing to keep alert for, especially in tropical climes, is flotsam. This can be anything that is floating on the surface: a log, hatch cover, garbage from a passing steamer, lumber, or what have you. Baitfish tend to congregate around flotsam, seeking what little protection it offers. Gamefish know this and often cruise around in search of flotsam, knowing an easy meal is usually close at hand.

A heavy weedline offshore holds plenty of natural bait too, and there is almost always an abundance of gamefish in the shadows beneath the weeds. So make it a point to troll close to the weeds and flotsam.

It is wise to take a few moments before sailing to the offshore grounds to check a Coast and Geodetic Survey Chart. Often the chart will indicate high patches of bottom, underwater plateaus, canyons and gullies. This irregular bottom causes unusual offshore currents in many areas and frequently such spots harbor large schools of small fish that prove to be easy prey for roving gamefish. It is always worth a little time to investigate them.

So if you've tired of fishing in close to the beach for small fish, and of competing with crowds of boats on your favorite inshore fishing grounds, consider pointing your bow to the horizon and giving offshore trolling a whirl. It's packed with thrills galore. Out in blue water country live those wandering gamefish which will test your skill and tackle to the utmost. It is a challenge I always find difficult to resist.

The Trout of America

by Parker Bauer

First you need a warm night in midsummer when the north-country bush glows like quicksilver in the moonlight. You're out near the stars, crossing an open lake in a small outboard. Camp isn't far ahead, your stringer is full, and chances are you're thinking of an overwhelming dinner and a pleasant hour at the fireside.

A few mosquitoes slap your face as you slide up to the dock, where the rest of the boats have already been carefully tied. Your guide lugs the fish off to the icehouse, and you climb wearily toward the bright windows of the lodge. Probably the shark is up there methodically cleaning the rest of the group in a quiet game of five-card.

But as you trudge nearer, it's soon obvious that there's a spirited debate going on about a very old subject . . . about the game qualities of the various species of trout. You hear one advocate claim that the brown trout is superior for his intelligence, wariness, and his propensity to feed on flies. Another voice insists that the brown, when hooked, fights about like a bloated mud turtle, while the rainbow is a spectacular long-running, high-jumping battler.

And then a third participant, in his finest moment, allows that his opponents bear more than passing resemblance to the south end of a horse heading north, since for great size and sheer power the lake trout can't be beat. Someone else argues for the brookie, someone for the cutthroat, and still another for the Dolly Varden.

Probably your wisest move in such a situation is to slip quietly past the dining room and head straight for bed. But there's really no avoiding the controversy, since American anglers have discussed the relative merits of the trout family for decades — in fact, ever since men first moved west coast trout to the East, eastern trout to the West, and imported a European trout, making a greater variety of species available to greater numbers of anglers. In some states conservation departments have even sent questionnaires asking anglers which species they wanted stocked.

Exactly which trout you think is the best game fish depends on what qualities you believe constitute "gameness." Certainly you'd have to consider brains, brawn, beauty, size, willingness to strike lures (and flies in particular) perhaps the type of country where the fish lives, and any of a dozen other qualities. If you enjoy shore dinners as much as I do, then the flavor of the fish will probably be important. I have my own favorite trout, but let's take a look at all the species and rate them as game fish.

For his size alone the lake trout would rank high. Not long ago a commercial fisherman hauled a 102-pounder from Lake Athabasca in Saskatchewan, and none of the other trouts are known to reach even half that size. While the sportfishing record rests at 63 pounds, it's possible some angler whose star spins the right way might take a 120-pound fish from Athabasca, Great Bear, or Great Slave Lake. But even the average weight of 5 to 12 pounds would be trophy class for any other species of trout.

Lakers are essentially fish of deep, transparent, cold-water lakes of the North. Most anglers fish for them along the southern limits of their range, which stretches from upper New England through the Great Lakes west to Vancouver Island. In these waters the lake trout's appeal lies mainly in his great size, since the fishing is generally a matter of trolling deep with heavy wobbling spoons or live shiner baits on a copper or Monel wire line. Many of the most successful anglers use depth finders to locate the slopes which lakers inhabit and thermometers to find the thermocline, that narrow band of cold water favored by trout which may be 25 or 75 feet down.

But farther north, in Alaska, Labrador, Quebec and the upper sections of other provinces, the laker is a different critter and fishing for him is a far more sporting game. He's generally big and lives in shallow water, making it possible for anglers to cast for him from boats or even from the shoreline. Where the waters are cold enough, he even thrives in fast rivers and streams alongside land-

▲ Typical black-spotted cutthroat taken from outlet of Yellowstone Lake. Cuts furnish vast amount of sport to western trout anglers.

Ontario angler holds up typical north country brook trout from Yesterday River. ▼

locked salmon and brook trout, and frequently hybridizes with the latter. If you make long casts in these frigid lakes and streams with light spinning tackle using wobblers or diving plugs to cover the 10- to 20-foot zone, you'll have some of the greatest sport in trouting. But to see the laker at his best try a fly rod with any of the standard New England streamer patterns, or when there are good concentrations of fish use nymphs and dry flies. This same shallow water fishing, incidentally, occurs all across the southern parts of laker territory in the autumn when the surface cools and in the early spring after the ice breaks up.

An additional dividend from lake trout fishing is in the eating. Certainly none of the other trouts can match the delicate flavor of this fish. In fact this has made the laker the only freshwater game fish whose commercial value perhaps exceeds its sporting value, with over ten million pounds taken annually by commercial fishermen. In the Great Lakes this intense commercial fishing probably accounts for the disappearance of the huge lakers of the past.

You may know that lake trout are not true trout at all, but are chars. Brook trout and Dolly Vardens are also chars, a distinction based primarily on the arrangement of the bones and teeth of the mouth which actually makes little difference to fishermen. Chars require colder water, live farther north, and spawn in the fall unlike most true trouts (except browns), which spawn in the spring. In general appearance, all true trout have black spots, while chars instead have lighter markings against a darker body color.

The rainbow is a true trout, and even though he's not as big as the laker, he's a far more spectacular fighter. And he enhances his excellent reputation every time he's

Casting excellent trout water of the Firehole River, Yellowstone Park, at daybreak. Both rainbows and browns live here.

hooked. A large one will make long, hard runs that melt the line from your reel, and rainbows of any size are wild jumpers that can send the spray flying like bits of cereal exploding from Gabby Hayes' cannon. That's why countless anglers consider them the gamest of all the trouts.

The rainbow is everyman's trout, the trout of thundering canyons, or of tiny brooks you can step across, of remote mountain lakes and city park ponds. Small boys tease him with worms at fishing derbies, and wealthy men chase him around the globe. Almost everywhere that there are anglers and fast water that's cold and clear, there are rainbows.

Their native waters were limited to our Pacific coast from California north into Alaska, but they've been exported to Africa, South America, India, New Zealand and Australia. In the United States, rainbows, most of them from California, were transplanted to the Ozarks, the Alleghenies, Great Smokies and Michigan as early as 1880. Today they're by far the most abundant trout in the East, occupying streams once inhabited by the native brook trout, which could not compete where the water was slightly warm or other marginal conditions existed. Certainly the ability of the rainbow to live where other trout can't is another point in his favor.

In fertile waters rainbows grow to impressive size. The record is a 37-pounder taken in 1947 from Lake Pend Oreille, Idaho, where great numbers of fish over 30 pounds have been caught. This lake is still an excellent bet for a once-in-a-lifetime trout — it might easily contain 50-pound fish. At Pend Oreille the biggest trout are caught by trolling with wobbling spoons and salmon plugs, with late May, June, late September, October, and November the most productive months.

Of course in most other lakes and streams where rainbows live, trolling is not necessary, and anglers use light fly or spinning tackle. Almost everywhere these trout are insect-feeders which will rise readily to either dry or wet flies, but will strike a small spinner or other flashy minnow imitation just as willingly. And wherever found the rainbow is the most spectacular fighter of all the trouts, as well as one of the most beautiful in appearance.

Probably no fish was ever more appropriately named, since most adult rainbows have a colorful pink stripe along the body and sometimes have a bluish tint on the back. Some species of trout have nearly as many local names as there are fishermen, but all anglers everywhere call the rainbow a rainbow. While over the years ichthyologists have given the species a dozen or more different Latin names, fishermen use just one.

If keeping the fish hooked is the biggest part of the battle with a rainbow, with a brown trout it's getting him hooked in the first place. There's no doubt he's the most discriminating and challenging of them all, requiring your most cautious approach and the most careful selection and delicate presentation of the fly—and even then he'll pass up your offering for some obscure reason you'll never understand. Eventually you'll decide he's smart enough to read the label on your rod, and you'll walk away muttering to yourself. Surely he's shattered more nerves than all the king's horses and men could ever reassemble.

Of course, the brown's shy, sophisticated ways are precisely what makes him the prized angler's trophy he is. He knows how to take care of himself. He's wise enough to live and reproduce under the heaviest fishing pressure, providing interesting angling in waters where rainbows and other trout could be maintained only by put-and-take hatchery programs. What's more the brown can hold his own in streams too sluggish for his more delicate cousins and can withstand even warmer water than the rainbow can take. Naturally all this has made the brown an important and highly desirable sport fish in the crowded northeastern states where once-pristine streams are beaten

Large lake trout caught from pontoon of a float plane in shallow water of an unnamed river in Quebec.

Hook jaw of huge 12-lb male brown trout. Few browns of this size are taken anywhere in any season's time.

by anglers and beleaguered by bulldozers.

Like the rainbow, the brown has made himself at home in congenial waters all across the continent. But unlike the rainbow, the brown is an imported fish, native to Europe and part of Asia. The first shipment of brown trout eggs reached our shores from Germany in 1883, and the fish which hatched were planted in the East, where they were named German browns or von Behr trout, in recognition of the importer.

Two years later browns from Scotland set up housekeeping in California and later in other sections of the West, where anglers called them Loch Leven trout. According to the literature, the Loch was a distant strain of trout, generally smaller, more slender, and less inclined to have red or a combination of red-and-black spots than other browns. Nowadays through widespread transplanting and interbreeding the differences have virtually disappeared, and fishermen almost everywhere simply call the brown a brown.

The long-standing world record is a 39½-pounder taken in Scotland in 1866. But the American record — a monster hauled from Utah's Logan River by a 16-year-old boy — falls only two pounds short of this mark. Almost everywhere browns are found there are a few oversize individuals which apparently become so sophisticated over the years that they're virtually impossible for anglers to catch. Due to their propensity to eat small trout these lunkers are usually labelled "cannibals" and considered detrimental to a stream. But the truth is that any large trout — brown or not — will eat small fish, and he can probably catch bullheads, darters, chubs and suckers easier than small trout, so he actually may help to keep the water clean of these competitive species.

Occasionally a skilled fisherman brings one of these old settlers to net — and it's the possibility of nailing one with fly tackle that fires the boilers of many brown trout enthusiasts. But probably a far greater number of anglers care not so much for trophies as for the sheer challenge of catching browns of any size. It's said that a young angler measures his fish in quantity; then with more experience only size becomes important. But soon even record fish lose their significance unless they are a particular

species, and finally the size doesn't matter provided they are difficult to catch. Presumably that's why many fishermen would rather net just one small brown than a creelful of any other trout of any size. But even considering this the brown is still not my own choice as the gamest of the trouts.

Neither is it the cutthroat, although I've spent many of my most pleasant fishing hours matching wits with him on remote mountain waters where he and I were absolutely alone. I remember particularly one golden afternoon on Slough Creek in Montana, when the sunlight filtered through the aspens along the bank and the cutthroats inhaled my dry flies hour after hour. Never before or since have I seen trout of any kind continue to rise for so long a period. By evening my casting arm felt like a worn-out rubber band.

While most of the trouts have expanded their ranges as a result of man's activities, the cutthroat has disappeared from countless waters where it could not compete with introduced trout of other species. His original range was the most extensive of all the trouts, stretching from Mexico to Alaska mostly west of the Continental Divide, and after a gap of several thousand miles he's found again in the western Aleutians and along the northern Asiatic coast. Still the cutthroat is fairly abundant across most of this range, particularly where other species have not been stocked.

Cutthroats are not spectacular fighters, nor even strong ones, except for large individuals. Neither do they seem very wary or wise. But they do grow to tremendous size in some areas, with the world record a 41-pounder taken from Pyramid Lake, Nevada, in 1925. Of course the average in most waters is closer to one or two pounds, but oversize individuals are common nearly everywhere.

The Dolly Varden is another large trout of the West native to the Pacific coast from northern California to Alaska and east to Idaho and Montana. As with the cutthroat, the Dolly's size is probably the characteristic that most intrigues anglers. While the record of 32 pounds from Lake Pend Orielle can't match the cutthroat record, Dollies on the average are much larger. In most large streams and lakes where they're found, four- and five-

mbo Dolly Vardon trout fell for a cast into the Saskatchewan River of a, near Jasper.

Angler Jim LaValley extracts fly from good brown taken on Yellowstone River near Livingston.

String of speckles—brook trout—from a lake near White River, Ontario.

pound Dolly Vardens are common, and even ten-pound fish are often caught.

Unfortunately the Dolly is no longer abundant in many of its home waters, since in the past every effort was made to eliminate him and almost nothing done to preserve him. As with the brown trout, sportsmen called him a "cannibal," and when commercial fishermen discovered he ate the eggs and young of salmon, a bounty was slapped on him in some areas. Trout tails were strung on a wire, and forty tails brought one dollar in Alaska. The bounty didn't last long, but it helped establish a prejudice against the fish that still exists.

The buckskin-colored Dolly is a strong fighter, but certainly not an acrobatic one. He usually stays deep, which makes it necessary to use spoons, spinners, and wet flies to catch him most of the time. He's a very willing striker — perhaps too willing for some anglers who like a great deal of challenge in their fishing. While the Dolly certainly deserves more attention from fishermen, at the present probably very few anglers would vote for him as their favorite trout.

All of which brings us around to the trout I consider the best game fish. You may have a low opinion of the eastern brook trout if you've fished for him in some lake high in the Rockies, where the fish are overcrowded and all of them dwarfed, with the biggest brookie you caught a half-pounder. And you may say that no matter where brookies are found and however large they may be, they're still not exciting fighters. And they're not at all selective; if they're in a feeding mood and you don't spook them, they'll slam any bait or fly you throw at them. If you'd say any of these things, you'd be absolutely right.

But there's no denying that brookies are tough. Although they were long ago squeezed out of most of their native streams in the eastern United States by introduced trout that could withstand warmer waters and the advance of civilization, they still hold their own stubbornly in tiny headwater streams from Georgia to our northern border. It's in these little trickles that many a young boy, willow wand in hand, has made his first acquaintance wtih the brook trout — indeed, his first meeting with fish and fishing of any kind.

Catching brookies that hang on in such backwoods hideaways, whether with willow or fancy fly rod, is for me a gentle reminder of the past, of days already slipped away. In the brookie there's a suggestion of more abundant fishing and more abundant times gone by, a hint of things I never knew but would like to have known. I wasn't around to see the bandstand in the city park on Sunday afternoon, to ride the streetcar to the edge of town for a picnic, to see the air circus land in a pasture and scare the pants off an unwitting farmer. When I was very young the steam locomotive was already in its death throes, but sometimes when I'm casting for brook trout I think of pounding drivers, billowing coal smoke and vapor blowing out a safety valve.

Often it seems the brookie has a personality all his own. He's painfully shy and retiring like the brown trout yet he's not at all particular about what he eats, unlike the brown. If you can avoid spooking him, and assuming he's in a feeding mood, he'll inhale almost any bait or fly you give him with complete abandon. In fact his innocence on the subject of fishermen can make you hesitate to put him in your creel; sometimes keeping a brookie seems almost like a trust violated.

Brook trout are generally much smaller than other members of the clan. An adult from a tiny mountain creek may be only eight or nine inches long, and the world record weighed in at only 14½ pounds. But most lakes and streams in the northern part of brook trout range — as well as some waters in our western states where they've been stocked — hold big fish in considerable numbers. In parts of Quebec and Labrador especially, four- and five-pound trout are common, and even fish over seven pounds could not be called too rare.

In the big, brawling rivers of the north country brookies are exceptionally strong fish — at least as powerful as any other trout. They usually battle underwater, but frequently they'll roll and writhe on the surface, and perhaps once in a season you'll hook one that even jumps.

Certainly the brookie is the most beautiful of all the trouts. Sometimes I crawl cautiously along a stream bank and peek over into a deep, shady hole to see if a brook trout is there. From above his flaming red belly is hidden, and the olive brown wormlike mottlings on his back blend perfectly with the stream bottom. But the white edgings on his pectoral fins betray his presence like electric signs, and in his innocence he doesn't know it.

I think how he's escaped the onslaught of civilization, and it's a good thought. After all, it's the reason I go fishing. 🐟

Rare albino rainbow trout from Beartooth Primitive Area lake in Montana. Albinos occur in several species of trout.

Take a flyrod and head for the Far North to enjoy the —

Return of the LAKE TROUT

BY KEN BOURBON

When Archie Boy came around to the tent to awaken us at midnight, it wasn't simply to show us the strange Arctic sunset. Instead he pointed to a spot about two hundred yards offshore where an orange surf seemed to be breaking over a rocky reef.

"Trout," the young Cree said simply, "trout feeding on top."

Through binoculars the surf we saw quickly became a vast school of fish churning the surface of Black Lake to a froth. And even as we watched, the school kept advancing parallel to shore, feeding on smaller fish as it moved. It was a spectacle which anglers seldom see outside of salt water.

For a minute we were too fascinated to do anything but follow the school through the glasses. Then all at once Frank Sanderson and I were grabbing rods and following Archie at a dead run for the freighter canoe pulled up along the shore. Without pausing we slid the canoe into the water and Archie somehow started his reluctant old outboard. What happened after that should happen to every serious fisherman some day.

As soon as we approached the school of chopping, milling fish, Archie cut the motor and we drifted into casting range. "You fish," the guide suggested, "I paddle."

Almost in the same motion Frank and I tossed silver spoons into the mass of motion and immediately both of the rods were dancing. In addition, the line which peeled from my reel was burning my thumb. The look on Frank's face was intense.

These fish we hooked weren't crazy jumpers. In fact they deserted the surface the moment they tasted our hooks. But they surely knew how to cavort in deep water and there wasn't much to do about it except hold on and hope for the best. A few minutes later we managed to horse a couple of five-pound lake trout to the surface, but that's only half the picture. Following closely on the tails of both of them were twelve or fifteen other lakers of similar size. It wasn't until we hoisted the hooked fish aboard that the followers disappeared.

"That alone," Frank said, "was worth the whole trip here."

We were fishing on top of Saskatchewan, near the 60th Parallel, in a lake which then was practically virgin as far as visiting sport fishermen are concerned. We had traveled half way across North America to check a report, or rather a rumor, of giant northern pike. But in several days of hard fishing we caught only a few of them and these were no bigger than axe handles. But in the next wild and wooly hour, all the disappointment over the pike was forgotten.

"Now we go to follow trout," Archie said after we'd unhooked the first pair. Only a few seconds and one cast later, both Frank and I were in business again.

What had been merely a strange spectacle from shore became a savage sight at close range. As we played the hooked fish, the entire school surged and swirled around us feeding on fingerling ciscoes. Hundreds of the small forage fish would squirt out almost from under the boat and in the next instant several trout would slash into them. And to make the scene even more primitive and unreal,

With midnight sun low on horizon, fisherman plays out laker at Nueltin Lake, Manitoba.

Large lake trout taken by John Moxley at Reindeer Lake, Manitoba. The fish was hooked early in the season near the surface.

the midnight sun was hanging just above the horizon, from where it bathed everything in a weird orange-olive glow. It made me think of the eye of a hurricane.

Before the feeding binge ended about an hour later, which was just about the time my arms wouldn't take the punishment any more, we had 16 lakers from three to six pounds apiece in the canoe. For the first time since we'd met him, Archie Boy was actually smiling.

"Good fishing," he grinned, "plenty eat for sled dogs."

"Plenty eat for Frank, too," Frank added.

In the past decade, with numerous small airways and many modern float planes opening up Canada's remote northern frontiers, the spectacle of surface feeding lakers is becoming more familiar to more of America's wandering sportsmen. It wasn't too long ago that lake trout fishing meant trolling in Lake Superior (mostly around the Apostle Islands) in Ontario's Rainy or Nipissing Lakes with heavy tackle and nothing more. It was super-heavy tackle, in fact, because during summertime in these "southern" lakes, the trout would search for the cold water they need to survive — and this cold water was always somewhere near the bottom. Only the few pioneering fishermen who happened to be around when the ice went out ever had a chance at the lakers with light tackle.

When taken on metal lines and wound on reels as big as bass drums, lakers aren't very game. Nor is anything else. But catch them in shallow water or on the surface and they are at least as stout as any brown or brook trout of similar size. And they do grow much bigger than either. But best of all the lakers remain on or fairly near the surface all summer long in most of the "new," far northern waters.

In recent years the writer has joined the great search for "new" lake trout waters and some of the best of them are in Saskatchewan and Manitoba. Black Lake is a good example and so is Wollaston not far away. Nueltin Lake on the northern boundary of Manitoba may be the best of all. You reach all these and hundreds of others by airplane since no roads penetrate this still unbroken wilderness.

Lake Athabasca (in extreme northern Saskatchewan) is a spot where a fisherman can not only catch as many lakers as he wants, but where he also stands a good chance of breaking some records. Lakers of almost 100 pounds have been taken here in nets and 30-pounders on hook and line seldom raise any local eyebrows. The Crees around Stony Rapids and Uranium City have seen plenty that size.

Stony Rapids, where the wild and noisy Fond du Lac River pours into Athabasca Lake, is the scene of another extraordinary lake trout spectacle. Both in early spring and late fall, lakers migrate from Athabasca and into the lower reaches of the River. And while they're there, catching them is as complicated as getting a bit of glittering hardware into the water.

Lake trout wherever they exist are among the most accommodating (or stupid or unsophisticated — depending on how you look at it) game fish on earth. The secret to catching them, usually, is finding them. After that, you simply deliver a lure where the trout can see or "feel" it. At Reindeer Lake, also in northern Saskatchewan's primeval bush, John Moxley and I found there is nothing better than the flyrod for lakers near the top.

We were camped in June on an island. Like the hundreds of other islands in Reindeer Lake in June, this one was alive with mosquitoes. The only thing that made it bearable at all was that surrounding waters were alive with lakers, plus a few fat grayling which were active every evening. We could catch the lakers, which averaged

Northern Canada lake trout country looks like this to a sportsman hurrying northward by float plane.

four or five pounds, just about any time by trolling or casting spoons along the rocky reefs and bars, but after a time the novelty wore off.

"Let's pull out of here tomorrow," John suggested, "and look for bigger fish somewhere."

At daybreak we were striking the tent when John spotted the familiar disturbance far out on the otherwise calm, open lake. For a minute we watched and then we hit the canoe on the run, a reaction which had become almost ritual when we saw rising fish. But when we almost reached the feeding school, I made an unhappy discovery.

"The casting rods are back on shore," I said, "all we have are a couple of flyrods." These were still rigged from grayling fishing the evening before.

"OK," John answered, "then this is our chance to see if lakers will eat fur and feathers."

Well, it's understatement to say that trout will take flies. Not only will they attack streamers, but we also hooked a pair of them on bass bugs. We could have filled the canoe with trout on any kind of flies, I'm certain, if John hadn't tied into one trout which was almost too much to handle on a 4½-ounce bamboo stick.

Even though his green and white marabou streamer was almost chewed down to bare hook shank, John placed it on the edge of the furiously feeding school. Then before he could catch a coil of loose line, a trout nailed the fly and was headed toward the Arctic Ocean. John's single action reel sounded like a mixmaster as fly line evaporated into backing line. Luckily the knot between them was small or it would have stripped all the guides from the frail rod.

"We're really in business this time," John said weakly.

It wasn't an especially exciting duel which followed because I did most of the work. While the fish bored down, down, down and away, I paddled to try to stay on top of it. John just tried to keep from reaching the end of his backing. Nobody checked a watch, but 30 minutes must have passed before John could regain as much as a yard

Much of best laker water in the far North is accessible only by float plane.

Sometimes it's possible to catch lakers from the plane's pontoon.

of line. After that it was a tedious and ticklish task working the fish to the surface inches at a time.

Several times John would maneuver the gray, spotted laker within sight, but then it would lunge for the bottom again. After we saw it the first time, the contest became tense as well as tedious because this was no average trout. A really big one, it would have weighed 20 or 25 pounds.

But unhappily we'll never really know. The trout made another run, much weaker than the others, but at the end of it John's hook pulled out. Probably it had worn a big hole in the laker's mouth during the long fight. In any case the feeding school had disappeared by that time and never did appear again.

"At least we know about lake trout and flies," John said in consolation.

I learned another trick that will take lakers from the landlock salmon fishermen of New Brunswick. This is a trolling technique, but it involves a flyrod, rather than a stiff boat rod and is meant for mid-depths rather than extremely deep waters.

The place was Blackfish Lake, Ontario, which we reached after a river trip on the Michipicoten and then by portaging through a series of smaller lakes. The time was June and although we calculated that the lake trout would still be close enough to the surface for casting, John Moxley and I found that wasn't the case. But John wasn't dismayed.

"We'll just go down where they live," he said, "like we do after landlocks."

To his 8½-foot flyrod, John clamped a fly reel full of soft, leadcore line. To the end of the line he knotted about ten feet of 6-pound nylon leader. On the business end of that was a tiny brass spoon.

"Now," he continued, "we'll just troll slowly along those steep rocky shores and see what happens."

What happened wasn't nearly as spectacular as the bonanza at Black Lake or an Reindeer, but it wasn't too long before John's rod began to bounce and I had to cut the motor. A few minutes later we netted a four-pounder and shortly after that a three-pounder. Altogether the flyrod-leadcore-line combination accounted for six fine lakers where shallow casting had produced nothing.

Of course it isn't as lively or as interesting as casting, spinning or fly casting, but other trials have proved it deadly during that period when the lakers are gradually moving from the shallows to the depths — or back again in late fall. I've also hooked many walleyes, whitefish and northern pike while trolling or drifting for lakers this way. Incidentally it *is* possible to drift rather than troll if a fairly stiff breeze is blowing.

But today's fisherman doesn't need to go very deep for his lake trout if he has the time and means to travel as far as Great Slave and Great Bear Lakes, both far up in the Northwest Territory and both red-hot at the moment. There the trout stay near the top 12 months a year. Fishermen who visit the several new camps on these lakes are pretty certain to average 50 good lakers a day, if their muscles hold out that long, and perhaps to tie into something 30 pounds or better. In both of these huge sub-Arctic lakes, Indians have netted many lakers larger than 50 or 60 pounds.

Too often by-passed in the rush to the far North are the fine lake trout waters in Manitoba. At one time the world's record came from Lake Athapapuskow which lies between The Pas and Flin Flon. Unlike many of the best laker waters, this one is accessible by auto road. So are Atikameg and Clearwater Lakes. Gods Lake is another great one, but so far it isn't approached by any highways, which is

Laker comes only reluctantly to the surface at Black Lake, Saskatchewan.

good.

All of the best laker country isn't confined to western Canada. There are a number of hotspots as far east as Labrador, in fact, and one of them is in the cool and misty Lake Ashuanipi region. Here a laker fisherman can enjoy a bit of variety with his fishing because the lakers occasionally inter-breed with the jumbo brooks, which share the same waters. The result is a robust, white-finned hybrid called a "splake" or "splaker."

This Ashuanipi cross-breed isn't to be confused with the hatchery splake which have been released in several places in the eastern United States and Canada. Instead it's a natural hybrid which probably gave biologists the idea of cross-breeding in the first place. But in any case, it's game and perhaps a bit more exciting than its pure-blooded cousins.

Guide Abe Lessard and I had a ball with mixed lakers and splake one morning where Ashuanipi Lake drains out into the Ashuanipi River. The magic spot where they were concentrated, we found, was at the point where the current began to gather speed, but where the water was still from 15 to 20 feet deep.

"Cast up and across the current," Lessard advised me, "and let your spoon flutter downward before you retrieve slowly."

I followed the instructions and needed only four casts to be in business.

My fish, which proved to be a 7-pound splake, knew which way to go to give me the most trouble. That was downstream, of course, and as soon as I set the hooks he swapped ends and pointed his nose into the current. There was little else to do — except hope that the drag on my spinning reel was working smoothly. I don't remember exactly how long it required to land that one, but I do recall that a sizeable rain squall came and then passed on before the splake was safely in the boat.

Often all the lake trout (and/or splake) in a given area or school are of similar size and weight. Probably they're also of the same age group. At least that's the way we found them at this Ashuanipi outlet — running from 6 or 6½ pounds to a maximum of 8 pounds. Some of the lakers showed more characteristics of brook trout (such as faint spots on the flanks, a more rosy hue and whiter fin tips), but the size varied very little.

Many guides around Ashuanipi use a technique which will seem unique to any experienced lake trout fishermen. Perhaps the method will work well elsewhere. First they try to obtain a supply of bait fish about 5″ or 6″ each in size. These can be whitefish, suckers, smelt or whatever is available locally. The bait then is cast and allowed to work its way to the bottom of known laker or splake holes. What usually follows is a jolting strike, a pause and . . . then the typical deep, strong fight of a lake trout.

If live bait runs out or somehow isn't easily available, a bit of cut bait — say a belly strip from a laker — is just as good. I watched one Montagnais guide using belly strips in the Ashuanipi and by raising and lowering his rod tip at intervals, he had a strike on practically every cast. But for some reason he didn't seem able to hook his fish until suddenly all hell broke and he eventually wrestled a 20 pounder into his boat.

Until recently the fortunes of lake trout seemed on the wane. Lampreys had virtually eliminated the species from the Great Lakes. Pollution hadn't helped in many other lakes in the southern part of their range. But as new country opens up in Canada's north, so is new lake trout water discovered every year. A word to the wise fisherman should be sufficient.

Florida's Tarpon

Here's a simple recipe for pulsating action: Take one Florida west coast fisherman and add huge schools of tarpon which appear annually from late spring to fall.

The result? Aching muscles, occasional broken tackle, and enough tall tales to last through the winter months.

Relatively few anglers fish Florida's west coast for tarpon, perhaps due to the bigger fanfare over tarpon in the Keys. But during the warmer months along Gulf shores the fish are abundant — and big.

Generally the silver kings arrive along the Gulf of Mexico beaches in April or May, depending on when water temperatures climb into the 70's. Then from June through September or October, they'll be rolling in the bays, passes and rivers and cruising the beaches. With cooler weather in autumn they head into the Florida Keys and points farther south or migrate into warm, brackish rivers where they winter in the deeper holes. Most of the larger fish — those from 125 to 175 pounds — are caught in May, June and July, while the smaller and more abundant schoolers of 50 to 100 pounds take over from July through October and sometimes even later.

One of the best-known tarpon hotspots anywhere is Boca Grande Pass, located between Gasparilla and LaCosta Islands northwest of Ft. Myers, or south of Sarasota. Although the *sabalo* (Spanish for "tarpon") are caught year-around in the pass, the greatest numbers gather to spawn from April through early August. Sometimes they churn the water's surface literally by the thousands. A school boiling within a short cast of your boat is a sight you'll never forget.

The tarpon hole in Boca Grande Pass dips to 90 feet in depth and is roughly 250 yards wide and 500 yards long. During tide changes, when most of the activity takes place, there may be 50 to 100 boats drifting the area. When big fish are hooked, you'll see some frantic maneuvering.

Skilled anglers drift across the hole and fish deep with live bait. Crabs about the size of silver dollars, pinfish, squirrelfish, mutton minnows, and small ladyfish are the favorite offerings. At this spot heavy tackle is preferred, with line testing between 50 and 90 pounds, steel leaders, heavy cast-off sinkers and hooks from 3/0 to 5/0.

Because of the depth in which they're hooked, Boca Grande tarpon don't leap as spectacularly as shallow-water fish. Three to six jumps are average with most of the battle occurring beneath the surface. Except for trophies to be mounted, the fish are usually released.

While Boca Grande enjoys the best "press," there are other hotspots nearby which are far less crowded. Slightly to the north are Gasparilla and Bocilla Passes, and to the south Captiva Pass is productive.

All along the network of islands which separate Charlotte

Left—Here's typical tarpon action along Florida's Gulf coast. Right—Big Tarpon are abundant along Florida's west coast during the warmer months.

Coast BY BOB COOK

Harbor from the Gulf, anglers find rolling tarpon just off the beaches, in waters ranging from 6 to 20 feet deep. Employing light tackle, either casting or spinning, with 20- to 30-pound-test monofilament, a short wire leader and artificial lures, boatmen cruise the shorelines hunting schools of surfacing tarpon. Many times the fish are sighted within 100 yards of the beach.

The angler must move ahead of the school silently to avoid spooking it and toss his lure ahead of and beyond a fish. Then he retrieves the bait directly across its nose. Many fishermen use jigs, but most prefer medium-running plugs, particularly the Mirrolure.

Following a strike — and provided the hooks hold in the hard, bony mouth — the angler is treated to one of the most spectacular of all saltwater sights, a silver-sided bundle of energy twisting out of the shallow water 10, 20, 30 times in a frantic drive for freedom. You have to wear a tarpon down before attempting to boat it. Usually that means hanging on until the fish rolls weakly on its side.

North of Boca Grande a favorite tarpon spot is the Tampa Bay area. Here I'm reminded of a television feature in which a reporter claimed that "tarpon hit on everything from live bait to plugs to dry flies. But," he concluded, "they never take dead bait of any kind." Tarpon enthusiasts around Tampa Bay never got this message. Probably nine of ten tarpon caught there hit dead, cut pinfish, grunts or small ladyfish.

Tarpon anglers cruise slowly and silently through productive areas and watch for rollers. Favorite places in the bay are the Alafia Spoils, Alafia River, Apollo Beach, the Estuary, Catfish Point, Gadsden Point, the Middlegrounds or MacDill Pocket, to name a few.

After spotting surfacing fish the angler drops anchor, casts several baits and arranges his rods about the boat like spokes on a wheel. The reel is set on free-spool and the fisherman simply sits back and awaits a run. When a tarpon hits he must reel the remaining rigs hurriedly and clear the decks for action. Then he lets the tarpon mouth the bait and swallow it before tightening the line and setting the hook.

Another popular method in the Tampa area is bridge fishing. It's most effective at night, and two local experts, Roger Cavallo and Fred Skettini, offer these tips: give the fish a little slack after it hits and before you set the hook so it'll move away from the barnacle-encrusted pilings. "If you'll not apply too mnch pressure at the beginning," says Cavallo, "the fish will tire itself with three or four jumps and be easier to hold off the pilings."

Tarpon anglers here cruise the interior waters—the mangrove-lined channels which seem to stretch endlessly.

Right—Tarpon fishermen work shallows near Boca Grande Pass.

The best time to fish, they say, is at the end of an incoming tide, when the bait is most active. From a catwalk ten feet above the water, Skettini watches for bait concentrations under the lights. "Tarpon usually hang nearby in the shadows," he emphasizes. If a tarpon is spotted in the shadows both men suggest placing the bait about six feet from it. "If you drop it too close," they warn, "it'll probably spook."

Unlike many boat fishermen, these bridge anglers prefer live — and lively — baits. They use greenback minnows, small ladyfish, mullet, pinfish (with the sharp dorsal fin spines trimmed) and angelfish. They also "troll" strip baits and artificial plugs by walking the bridge catwalk.

Bridge buffs must use heavier gear than boatmen. Cavallo recommends a 10-foot rod and 117-pound-test line with a 90-pound Sevenstrand leader. His favorite reel is a 4/0 Senator. Either a 6/0 or 7/0 hook will do.

It's particularly important to hook the minnow properly. During a fast tide, hook it through the lips, but on a slow flow place the hook through the back about a quarter-inch below the first dorsal fin. The minnow should be allowed to swim on a free line. "When casting," suggests Skettini, "watch the direction your bait moves. If it swims under the bridge, cast in another direction and hopes it swims freely."

Although bridge fishermen usually jump more tarpon than other anglers — sometimes 15 or 20 during an evening — their landing percentage is lower. In spite of this, Cavallo once landed and released 53 tarpon in eight weeks.

Boatmen also work the bridges, particularly the Howard Frankland and the Gandy. They fish at night with both live and artifcial baits, and a few have discovered that a fly rod and streamers can raise havoc with the tarpon population. Even popping bugs designed for largemouth bass get strikes.

Another Tampa-area hotspot is the water around Anna Maria Island. The tarpon there are found both on the Gulf and on the inside and they may hit live, dead or artificial baits.

North of Tampa, in the Clearwater-Dunedin area, there's a productive spot at the north tip of Hurricane Pass where Harold LeMaster, owner of the L & S Bait Company (makers of the Mirrolure), Bill Roy, Doc Harmon and perhaps a dozen others are seen at daybreak nearly every morning from June until August casting to a steady stream of tarpon entering the Gulf from the bay. From Hurricane Pass boatmen often follow the schools down the beach to the hole off Mandalay Shores at Clearwater Beach.

The north end of Honeymoon Island off Ozona — both

Night fishing produces tarpon in the mangroves and along the coastal rivers—the Crystal, Suwanee, Homosassa and others.

Angler checks tarpon taken on surface plug in Ten Thousand Islands region.

inside and outside — often produces tarpon when things are dull elsewhere. And in Clearwater Bay, on the north side of the Dunedin Causeway, there's one special place where silver kings are taken in August and early September. After you pass the first bridge on the causeway, slow down and anchor about 100 yards off the fourth little pine tree you'll see on shore. For some reason a school hangs around there every year at the same time, and you've got to admit, folks, that's really pin-pointing them.

Many tarpon are caught each year in the Homosassa, Crystal and Suwanee Rivers by the mere handful of anglers who go after them. An unusual tarpon method was developed several years ago by Crystal River's Tom Bonsall who can tell you almost to the second when to expect a strike. Bonsall fishes only at night from about five days before to five days after a full moon, and spots the fish in deep holes with a flashing depth finder. Except for returning shrimp boats, Tom has the river almost to himself while trolling a pair of jointed red-and-white plugs. When he passes above the fish, the face of the recorder begins flashing like a pinball machine. "Get ready," Tom will say, "we'll have a hit in 10 seconds." And sure enough, all hell breaks loose.

Early in Tom's fishing career two or three big tarpon jumped into the boat with him. As a result he learned the hard way to get out of the way after a hook-up. Evidently the Crystal River tarpon, when hooked at night, make a run directly at the boat and often make the first jump near the stern. Nowadays when he hooks a fish he guns the engines and shoots off at right angles.

An unpublicized area containing hordes of "virgin" tarpon is in Apalchee Bay at the bend of the Florida panhandle, south of Tallahassee. With Jim Bagley, who manufactures fishing lures in Winter Haven, I was working the lush trout (weakfish) flats at Apalchee last summer using ultra-light equipment and Salty Dog plugs when Jimmy jumped a tarpon of perhaps 75 pounds. It made three leaps before snapping his four-pound-test leaderless line.

Later, while traveling back up river to the Shell Island Fish Camp docks, we noticed several fish rolling. Later the dock owner told us that on account of the excellent trout fishing no one bothered with the tarpon. He said the tarpon show up in mid-June and hang around offshore until August when they move into the rivers and inlets. I'm making plans right now to "bother" with them.

Another great tarpon area on Florida's west coast — not to mention the Peace River, Sanibel Island and Wiggins Pass, which are good also — is the famed Ten Thousand Islands south of Ft. Myers. For big tarpon, guides here generally work the outside waters with dead bait — a trick they admit stealing from Tampa Bay anglers. Smaller fish ranging from 5 to 40 or 50 pounds are abundant in the vast, mangrove-lined interior and will bust almost any artificial or live bait.

A fringe benefit of Gulf-coast fishing is that the action is fastest during the summer and early fall months, long after the winter visitors have gone home, leaving the waters relatively uncrowded. What more could any tarpon angler ask?

Live baits, cut baits and artificials all take thrashing tarpon along the Gulf.

The author fly casts for stripers at Race Point, Provincetown.

Revolution in the surf

BY FRANK WOOLNER

Since this is an age of rapid change, one shouldn't be amazed by spectacular development in any field, including that of salt water sport fishing. Sometimes those of us who are greying at the temples overlook progress by the inevitable Young Turks and then one day we find the wave of the future over our boot tops!

For example, I once associated surf casting with big, powerful squidding outfits and lonesome beaches. You know the picture: a lean, hip-booted hombre battling furious breakers and throwing heavy metal lures with a 10-foot rod. Prior to World War II, and for some time thereafter, nobody toted any other tackle combination to the sea beach. It just wasn't done.

Brother, times have changed!

On Cape Cod, where I hunt stripers, enthusiasts wage total war. A regular's equipment invariably includes one beach buggy, and often two — for reasons which will be examined. He covets an outboard powered surf boat which is transported on a specially adapted trailer, and his fishing tackle runs from ultra-light to the grunt-and-groan category.

I think it necessary to credit inland anglers for this revolution in the surf. Classicists resist change, unless it arises within the confines of an accepted group, but newcomers — throughout history — have been hungry men who progressed by discarding outworn traditions and blazing new trails.

When in the immediate post-war years, inlanders began migrating seaward, it was probably enough for them to gaze wide-eyed, to take snapshots and to think — beyond that horizon lies Spain. The seas are so vast that they boggle the mind of man, particularly the mind of a human being attuned to blue mountain lakes and trout streams.

Initially, devotees of the high surf chuckled at Pilgrims who marched into the wash with light spinning and bait casting rods. At that time flies were for optimists who delighted in beating their heads against figurative brick walls. In the surf, it was reasoned, one needed a big stick, a big lure — and lots of stout line.

Almost immediately strange things began to happen. Ancient mariners grumbled about luck when some of the amateurs came in with eyebrow-raising catches. Gradually, skepticism was succeeded by interest and the classicists glumly reviewed their own tactics.

If, under certain conditions, light spinning or fly casting tackle paid off, it seemed stupid to rely on a single big rig.

If a motor vehicle could be converted to soft sand use, why walk?

If a surf boat could reach fish just beyond the cast of a shore-based angler, why remain shore-bound?

Small boat recovery at full throttle.

Pete Kissell with his 55 pound bass caught on light tackle.

Curt Gowdy and Frank Woolner with a chase car on Cape Cod.

Coach campers and small boats please many Cape Cod surfmen.

Launching an aluminum boat in gentle surf is easy. But in a rough surf . . . WOW!

Thanks to a new and flexible approach, Cape Cod surf fishing has enjoyed an astonishing boom during the past couple of decades. On open beaches where striped bass, bluefish and a host of other inshore battlers are taken, the most successful of modern surf casters are very erudite characters. They "match the hatch" by using a wide variety of tackle combinations and they swear by almost complete mechanization.

Fold-away helicopters are still in the future, but a few of the top hands currently rely on air spotting from light planes which carry them from inland cities to coastal areas. Having reconnoitered the quarry, these specialists employ beach buggies and small boats to score on the actual fishing grounds.

Cape Cod is home port for America's most elaborate over-sand vehicles. While the sportsmen of other coastal areas boast occasional big rigs, only here on Massachusetts' "narrow land" will you find concentrations of custom-built machines. This is probably the only ground where enthusiasts consider it necessary to use two buggies.

One, and most important, is the basic camp on wheels. It's a big, rugged job, often a four-by-four, fitted with bunks, a propane gas range, refrigerator and chemical toilet. This rig will boast a great deal of cabinet space for tackle and, almost always, it will be equipped with CB radio. Many feature portable TV for entertainment between tides.

Second and almost indispensable to Cape Cod anglers is a much smaller four-by-four which is used as a general work horse and chase car. Universal Jeeps, Jeepsters or Jeep Wagoneers are favored. They are used to push surf boats into the suds and to recover them after a landing, for transportation into town when provisions are needed, and for running the beaches at all hours of the day and night. A chase car is just that — it is a small, mobile vehicle used to chase fish that are feeding and moving along the shore.

Second only to a beach buggy, Cape Cod's surfers consider a small boat essential. Usually these are 14-foot aluminum utilities powered by 20-horse outboard motors. Aluminum is favored because that metal can take the beating administered by successive full throttle landings and because a tin hull is light enough to be manhandled or hauled around by a Jeep.

Actually the term "surf boat" is misleading, for these skiffs are seldom launched when heavy breakers are pounding the shore. They are employed in gentle surf — although they can be brought ashore in any sea condition short of lethal, hurricane-pushed combers. That's because a light planing boat of this type rides the waves. In the hands of a skilled helmsman, such a craft jockeys ashore right on the slope of a rolling ground swell. As the wave slams in and explodes, the skipper guns his motor and hits the beach at full throttle. Well done, this is a safe, albeit spectacular operation. Botched, it can lead to broaching and trouble.

However, a practical surf boat assures seven league boots for any angler. At the helm of a responsive little craft, a sportsman can reconnoiter the offshore bars and rips, or ghost into quiet bays. He can stand and cast or troll a productive ground. Light, easily handled skiffs have extended the operational range of the enthusiastic surfman.

A majority of tin boats used on Cape Cod grounds are equipped with live bait tanks and duffel compartments, rod racks for various outfits, and — of course — extension-operating handles on outboard motors so that helmsmen can stand while they cruise and search for fish.

A few mechanized anglers still transport their skiffs on cartop racks, but an increasing number rely on trailers fitted with over-sized tires and wheels. The average trailer wheel is much too small for soft sand operation because it fails to provide enough clearance. For this reason dune jockeys prefer 13 to 15 inch automobile wheels mounting four-ply tires in the 800 to 820 size range. Air pressure on the beach may go as low as five pounds.

Standard automobile wheels which match trailer studs are hard to come by. Some models of Studebaker and compact Ford cars featured such wheels, but they are far from plentiful in the nation's junk yards. Therefore sand trailer wheels often are custom-built by local welders.

Tackle needs are more easily satisfied, All you need is that magic ingredient, money, or the skill to build rods in a home workshop. Nowadays there is a necessity for a variety of rigs, and each enjoys a definite sphere of efficiency. Today's one-rod man gets that way because he delights in a single technique to the virtual exclusion of all others. However, versatile fishermen catch more fish.

Taken from the top, you will find that the time-honored squidding stick is still well represented, and will continue to fill a need because there is nothing to replace it. For certain well recognized tasks, the high surf rod reigns supreme.

It should be fully understood, however, that any 10 to 12-foot heavy surf rod, whether it mounts a conventional or spinning reel, is a casting — and not a fish-playing — tool. Its job is to heave a big lure or a chunk of bait together with an adequate sinker the greatest possible distance. Once a fish is hooked, any long, stiff rod works to the advantage of the angler.

So long as it remains necessary to heave a bait or lure anywhere from 80 to 100 yards, these heroic weapons will endure, together with the classic 36-pound test braided line that compliments them. This line test is favored less to contain the runs of a heavy fish than to absorb the tremendous pressures generated in casting.

The advent of surf boats, which can place fishermen within easy casting range of available game fish, has generated the development of shorter and more limber rods. On Cape Cod, these are similar to the Jersey jetty jockey's stick — a tool developed for shorter casts with lighter lures for a maximum of sport.

There is no slavish dedication to the big production rod on Cape Cod. Indeed enthusiasts have found that many occasions demand a change in pace. Often game fish are within the practical range of lighter tackle and are patsies for small, light lures. Then it is time to break out spinning — and even fly casting — combinations.

Perhaps the two-handed, medium weight spinning outfit is today's most practical rig. It will cast lures in the light to medium weight range, say 1 to 2½ ounces, and its 15- to 18-pound test monofilament line is adequate under normal circumstances. Where lure weight is ideal, the spinning rig gives no quarter to any other outfit: it fails only where the long cast and the heavy tempter is a necessity.

Similarly a one-handed spinning combination can be big poison on school stripers. During the course of any given year, I probably catch more bass on a seven-foot rod and 10-pound monofilament line than on any other outfit.The little fixed spool rig which is calibrated to handle lures weighing ¼ to 1½ ounces is a deadly weapon. School stripers dote on featherweight plugs and jigs. Trophy bass sometimes muscle in on the act.

A one-handed 10 pound test spin-casting outfit is not recommended for the conquest of record-breakers, yet some monsters have fallen to its wiles. In 1967 Pete Kissell

Jerry Kissell with Cape Cod stripers taken on a squidding rod.

Jack Woolner uses CB radio in his four-wheel-drive beach buggy.

Joe Pol of Woonsocket, Rhode Island, racks rods on the side of his custom-built beach buggy.

of Worcester, Massachusetts came up with a 55-pound striper on such an outfit. Pete was fishing for schoolies when he hooked the heavyweight from shore. Careful drag adjustment insured against a break-off, and the steady pressure from that tiny, buggy-whip rod licked the big bass.

However, it is folly to conclude that one catch of this magnitude proves the all-purpose worth of such an outfit. Light one-handed spinning rods are effective because they can handle very small lures. If trophy stripers are gobbling midget tempters, then the featherweight rod and line earns its keep. A one-handed spinning rig is close to useless when it is necessary to heave a three-ounce metal squid to the edge of a rip 100 yards from the beach.

By the same token, any herring-head who thinks he can use a fly rod to compete with a surf caster in rough water is out of his cotton picking mind. I have seen feather merchants industriously dropping streamers and popping bugs 60 feet from shore — when the bass were grabbing eight-inch plugs at the 60-yard mark. In this case the tackle was not job-rated.

On the other hand, most of my Cape Cod friends now carry big, salt water fly rods for special occasions. These are broken out when bass are walloping surface bait and can be reached with a relatively short cast. The fly casting outfit is best used from a boat, but it can be deadly in the surf as well — under certain conditions.

Sometimes stripers chase bait right into the wash. At this time they are difficult to tempt with plugs and metal squids, for the simple reason that such lures are difficult to control when they are worked right at the edge of the shingle. A streamer fly or popping bug then becomes a winning ticket, for either will float on anything approaching 100 per cent of humidity!

Let me burst another bubble and ruin the dispositions of precious types who invest themselves with the Medal of Honor for sportsmanship because they use a fly in the surf. Once hooked, a flyrod bass has less chance than he would enjoy at the business end of a treble-barbed plug. When I use a salt water fly rod, I use it because it is a very deadly weapon. Consider the facts.

You have a powerful, yet limber rod which measures approximately nine feet from butt to tip. The leader tapers down to about 12-pound test, and often higher. There is something like 180 to 200 yards of 20-pound test backing spliced to 35 feet of forward tapered fly line.

This may well be the ultimate in a "fighting rod," an outfit more lethal than any spinning combination ever devised. Indeed, because the rod is limber, you probably have less chance of breaking-off than the high surf squidder with his stiff stick and 36-pound test braid.

Where stripers are concerned, fly rod problems boil down to limited casting range and equally obvious limitations of lure size and weight. There are other handicaps, such as speed of retrieve. Sometimes a fly cannot be stripped in fast enough to interest feeding stripers. Happily, when circumstances mesh to provide ideal conditions, the fly rod is a productive weapon.

Now go to the other extreme. There are periods when striped bass will take nothing but trolled baits which are presented right on, or close to, bottom. It would be pleasant to say that a surf caster, spinning addict or feather merchant possessing sufficient skill could rack up catches comparable to those of trollers, but such is not the case. There are times when deep trolling is the only way to turn the trick — and tackle must be job-rated.

Granted, you may use sinking lines, lead sinkers, planers and all of the other aids. You can fool with lead-cored line, which is a blessing to the amateur because it requires

Charley Whitney and L. Page Brown land their fish.

little control. Or, you can sit on the beach, drink beer and curse the Law of General Cussedness.

If you want to catch fish, you go out there with a wire line outfit, and you dredge. This means single-strand wire, which is the most miserable stuff in the world to control. It is stubborn and springy, it tangles if you relax for a split second, it tends to kink (and a kink means a quick break). Terrible stuff!

But it slices down into payoff territory and it catches stripers like there's no tomorrow. Moreover, because there is no appreciable stretch in single-strand wire, each strike is a jolt like none you've felt in the past and each battle is memorable. These's a wonderful niche for wire in our marine fishing world.

Now you'll want a boatrod with roller guides. Granted, you can get by with a roller tiptop and rings, but a complete set of rollers is preferable. The rod will be somewhat stiffer than you'd like, because it must take the beating of weight (the wire), and the reel will be larger, heavier and metal-spooled — again to accommodate that cursed wire.

So you'll catch fish and you'll have fun! Isn't that reason enough to tote another outfit?

On the striper coast no weapon is all-purpose, and none is ultimate. Today's bass fisherman lugs an arsenal of equipment to the seacoast. His beach buggy is a camp on wheels, designed to carry a wide range of rods, reels, lines and lures. If he plans to cash in on every opportunity he will stock and use all of the various outfits, from ultra-light to heavy. He will find it necessary to master the techniques associated with each rig, and he will know when and where to use each to best advantage. Luck is a minor ingredient. Skill is most important.

It has been said that 10 per cent of the fishermen catch 90 per cent of the fish. There is no doubt about it in the surf.

Sometimes, after an unproductive weekend, I wonder whether I'll ever move into that magic 10 per cent bracket!

IF YOU VALUE YOUR SURFACE BAITS BE CAREFUL WHERE—AND AT WHAT YOU THROW THEM TOP WATER TROPHY BASS FISHING

By Dick Kotis

Surface plugging is never more productive than late in the day in weedy waters as here.

There's probably no more exciting experience in freshwater fishing than a lunker largemouth bass smashing, grabbing or just daintily slurping a surface bait. I've had cautious five-pounders gently nip the tail hooks of a floating bait bobbing in a breeze-rippled pond. And I've known hair-raising moments after dark when the rhythmic gurgling of the same bait was obliterated by a noise like a cow falling from a bridge. How any bass can make that much splash I'll never know.

But no matter how a bass takes a surface lure, once hooked he'll usually fight it out on the surface. Almost always a surface-hooked fish puts on a more spectacular battle than one hooked on a medium- or deep-running lure.

It's been my experience in top-water bass fishing that different methods are needed for day and night times. I also change angling techniques according to water temperature, color of water, time of year, and local weather conditions.

I've found, for example, that water temperatures must be 60 degrees or higher before bass will strike top-water baits with much enthusiasm. When it's colder than that, you'd be wise just to settle for deep fishing. Murky water, on the other hand, often makes surface baits — especially dark-colored ones — more effective than underwater lures. Bass can often spot a surface disturbance in muddy water even when they can't see a deep lure more than a few inches from their noses. Clear water usually calls for different lure colors and may make bass more wary, especially during the day.

BAIT COLORS

On cloudy days or in dark or choppy water, a dark-colored surface lure is my first choice. With poor visibility bass evidently see dark objects better than light ones, especially against a sky background. At night dark-finished baits are almost always the best producers. But bright days and clear water normally call for red-and-white, yellow and frog-finish surface lures.

Naturally, anytime you spot bass feeding on or near the surface your best bet is a lure colored to resemble the food they're after. One memorable day on the dark, murky waters of the lower St. Johns River in northern Florida, I spotted a school of bigmouths feeding. They were chopping into what I thought was a school of minnows, although I couldn't actually see any skittering bait fish. The bass completely ignored all the minnow-finish baits I offered but kept boiling on the surface at something I couldn't see in the brown water.

Finally, my fishing partner accidentally snagged a 3-pound bass in the back and managed to boat him after an unusually wild fight. We immediately opened his bulging stomach and found it stuffed with young saltwater blue crabs about the size of quarters and colored dark brown. Evidently they were migrating from their hatching grounds in the river down to salt water.

We broke out our flyrods and offered the crab eaters some tiny black Hula Poppers with rubber legs and skirted tails that resembled the swimming crabs. For one wild hour we had strikes from largemouths up to four pounds on nearly every cast.

No matter where you fish, incidentally, it's often a big

help to check the first bass big enough to keep to see what he's been eating. At times bass can be incredibly selective, but the odds favor you if your lure closely resembles the natural food in color and action.

HOW TO FISH—DAYTIME

When fishing surface baits during midday, especially in the clear water of midsummer, look for shady areas under overhanging brush or trees, alongside docks and stumps, and in lily pads, surfacing weed beds, and floating rafts or duckweed. In early morning and late evening or on cloudy, windy days, watch for fish cruising open water for an easy meal. Look for leaping or darting bait fish and the wakes and swirls of large bass chasing them. Once you have located feeding bass the rest is easy.

On cloudy days with fairly rough water, feeding bass tend to lose their normal daytime caution and often move into shallow water on lee shores. At such times I like to use a dark-finish Sputterbug or Sputterfuss and reel it fairly fast with the rod held high and with little or no line in the water. I cast the bait downwind and retrieve so it skips from wave to wave. A fast-moving Sputerfuss has also taken many large bass for me when the males are guarding

their nests during the spawning season, especially in the South.

On bright days try a light-colored or frog-finish Jitterbug. Cast it as softly as possible into shaded bassy areas and let it rest until the ripples disappear. Then twitch it forward a few feet and again wait for the water to smooth. When the bait is about 25 feet from the boat, I speed up the retrieve. This trick often brings a hard strike if a bass has been following the lure. Maybe the fish thinks his prey has spotted him and is making a frantic dash to escape.

Quite often during the day you'll see a surface bulge traveling behind your surface bait. Even though you don't get a strike that V-shaped hump is pushed up by a bass following close. Rest the water a few minutes, change your bait for one with a different color and try again. Once you have a follow you know where the fish is and eventually a particular combination of lure, color, and method of retrieve may make him hit.

HOW TO FISH—NIGHTTIME

I'm sure more lunker bass are taken on the surface after dark during the summer months then during any other period of the year. It's true there's a brief period in early spring when water temperatures reach 50 degrees and winter-weary largemouths school and move into shallow water to feed. But spring bass don't feed much on the surface even though they're in the shallows, so I'll stick to summer nights for most of my top-water fishing.

I try to pick a moonless night and start with a brown or black Jitterbug. On still nights I listen carefully since

Author Kotis duels surface-hooked bass on Ontario lake. That's Bob Bauer, youthful author of "Put Yourself in the Saddle" watching from the bow.

Author Kotis plays big bass hooked on topwater plugs at Lake Murvaul, Texas.

Surface plugs are even deadly south of the border. Here Carl Lowrance holds string of lunkers taken in Lago Novillo, Mexico.

the disturbance made by a feeding lunker can often be heard for 75 yards or more over calm water. If I can't pinpoint any surface activity, I just work the sand bars, underwater weed beds, swimming beaches, and other shallow areas where large bass often move after daytime activities like power boating and swimming have ended.

On dark nights with no moon, black or brown Jitterbugs or Sputterbugs are my favorites. Soft casts with little splash and slow, erratic retrieves with frequest pauses will get big bass action if you're where the fish are.

At night it's especially important to keep a tight line between rod and bait. Usually there's no warning of an impending bass hit at night and you must strike immediately when a splash occurs near your bait. A wise old largemouth can spit a surface lure on a slack line in a wink.

Since it's difficult to cast accurately after dark, my favorite method of fishing surface lures at night is to move quietly to the shore and cast parallel to it rather than using the usual in-and-out procedure. That way I can cover more good water, snag fewer baits and consequently avoid spooking fish.

I use flash lights and lanterns as little as possible while fishing. Lights definitely will spook bass, beside blinding the angler for a few moments after they are doused. Once your eyes have become accommodated to the dark it's surprising how well you can see even on the blackest nights.

Author Kotis holds up his prizes.

A perfect place, besides a deadfall on shore, to toss a top-water plug. Surely a bass waits somewhere beneath.

Fooled by floating plug, largemouth leaps clear of water and tries to shake free of the hooks.

The author with other lunker.

Surface popping plug is cast to edge of pond lilies and . . . a bass strikes it and is hooked.

Starlight and light reflected by clouds always furnish some illumination. A good trick to use at night is to cast toward a distant light on a house, street light, or even a lantern. On the retrieve you can see your bait all the way back to the boat in the faint path of light.

My favorite boat for night fishing is painted flat black. I'm convinced that even educated fish often don't notice flat black or camouflaged boats. Many times I've hooked bass right at the side of the boat as I lifted my bait from the water. I also prefer dark or inconspicuous clothing and hats when fishing, especially at night.

One of my fishing friends — an enthusiastic angler but not experienced at fishing after dark — had a five-pounder grab a Jitterbug just as it reached his rod tip one dark night. In the excitement he forgot to release his thumb from the casting reel spool, and the green fish thrashed himself into a frenzy alongside the boat. Results: two very wet fishermen and a largemouth rudely derricked into my lap on 20-pound-test line and a very stout rod.

MORE TOP-WATER TIPS

Most surface baits are delicately balanced and carefully designed to ride at certain angles when retrieved at various speeds. I tie the line directly to the lure with an improved clinch knot, since a large snap swivel ahead of a bait can ruin part of the action. If you must use a swivel, make it a small one.

For the ultimate thrills in surface fishing for big bass try wading after dark. Fish apparently ignore a wading angler since I've had smashing strikes right at my feet. Bass have even bumped into my legs underwater as they chased darting minnows or crawfish. Sand or gravel bars and beaches are ideal for night wading. I should mention that surface

For most explosive results, surface plug should remain motionless before beginning stop-and-go retrieve.

lures moving toward the beach seem to interest wise old largemouths more than those cast from a boat and heading for deep water. When fishing in obstructions like rocks, brush piles, and weed pockets it's a good idea to toss a surface plug very gently at the nearest target first. That way you'll avoid spooking other bass that might be lurking in similar cover nearby. Pulling a thrashing bass over a long distance will scare potential customers all the way back.

The most exciting surface fishing for big bass I ever experienced happened one February on Florida's St. Johns River. I was cruising slowly upriver when what seemed an entire acre of the coffee-colored water exploded with skittering hickory shad and berserk bass.

My partner and I tossed silver Sputterbugs into the mael-

strom and were both fast immediately to bruiser bass. It took perhaps 10 minutes to land our fish, which weighed 5 and 7 pounds each, and by that time the river had quieted again. We anchored the boat there and waited for the next flurry, which started in about 20 minutes. This time we were right in the middle of the action. Hickory shad a foot long bounced off the sides of our boat and huge mouths engulfed them right at our rod tips. These striking bass were all lunkers. I'm sure a two-pound bass would have been afraid to join the fun since there were plenty of bass almost big enough to gulp him in the confusion.

We wound up the day with nine bass weighing from four to eight pounds. But the fish would hit only fast-moving Sputterbugs and then only when the school was striking on top. When we tried jigs and deep-running plugs during the lulls, we were skunked. The bass were schooled on what the Florida crackers called a striking ground. When a mass of the spawning-run hickories were rounded up, the frenzied bass tore into them from all directions. Each feeding flurry lasted only a few minutes but the fishing was fast as long as the shad run continued, which was about ten days.

Evidently nearly all of the large bass in that stretch of the river (and probably many more from nearby Lake Jessup and Lake Harney) gathered there every February to smash the shad as they moved thru. They completely inhaled the silver Sputterbugs and I presume they would have hit almost any fast-moving minnow-like lure during the orgies. You have to see one of these mad striking sprees to believe it, and if your breath doesn't come faster and your hands don't shake a little when you cast the splashes, better take up something like motorcycle racing for kicks.

SURFACE SURPRISES

Some pretty awful things can happen to an enticing surface lure, especially after dark. One balmy spring night I cast a black Jitterbug to a surface disturbance evidently made by a feeding bass. While the bait was floating motionless in the water something tugged it, and I struck back. There came a loud splash and a strange, steady pull unusual for a bass. After a short struggle I netted what must have been the most unhappy muskrat on earth. He was thoroughly tangled in the net, snagged on the Jitterbug, and wrapped in about 10 yards of line. In an instant he chewed at least ten holes in the landing net. More through luck than skill I was able to unhook him, get him back into the water, and remain unbitten.

On another night a mixed-up screech owl apparently mistook my frog-finish Jitterbug for the real thing and wound up hooked in a talon. This strange catch gave up easily. He staggered up into the bow of the boat and after drying out a while was able to get airborne once more. I suspect his appetite for frogs was never again quite the same.

But I've made more rewarding catches on surface lures when big snapping turtles have surfaced within casting range. By casting beyond and swimming my bait past a turtle's head, I can usually provoke a vicious strike. And I usually wind up with a badly creased lure.

Turtles are strong swimmers but unless they can get to the bottom or some obstruction where their powerful claws can dig in, it's possible to boat them. I work a turtle to the boat, grab him by the tail and hoist him into the boat. They're delicious eating either fried or stewed — but they're pretty hard on surface lures.

The moral to all this seems to be: if you value your surface baits be careful where - and at what - you throw them.

WHERE THE

Most bass anglers know all the largemouth hotspots—Toledo Bend and Sam Rayburn Reservoirs in Texas; Florida's Kissimmee, Okeechobee and the rest—a list as long as your favorite casting rod. But few have fished or even heard of the best smallmouth places, except perhaps for Dale Hollow Lake (where the world record's from, or is it?, and oh, yes, there's that spot up in Minnesota somewhere, the one that Harry's uncle told us about).

Of course there are many hotspots that produce smallmouths in unusual size and numbers. Though we often think of bronzebacks as stream fish, most of the highly productive waters are cool, rock- or sand-bottomed lakes. One of my favorites—and I'll mention several others later—is Ontario's Crow Duck Lake, which is a short portage west by canoe from the famous Winnipeg River. It's ideal bass habitat with long, flat sand and gravel bars where the fish spawn in the spring and steep, rocky shorelines where they feed on crayfish and minnows.

It was at Crow Duck that I first learned how wary smallmouths can be. The time, I remember, was early spring. I was fishing with a bait-casting outfit while my companion Chuck Danforth was using an ultralight spinning rod and reel. We were dredging the deep water with Busy Body spinners and Arbogaster plugs, and we hadn't been fishing 15 minutes before he caught his first smallmouth, and quickly his second, third and fourth. I switched lures, as most anglers will, feeling that might make the difference.

But soon Chuck started to fill my stringer, his ten snaps already full, and by then my face was a bit red. I used the same lure color and the same retrieve, and finally I noticed our lines. Danforth's four-pound monofilament was scarcely visible in the clear water, but my 12-pound looked like the Trans-Atlantic cable. I picked up my spinning rod, tied on the same lure I'd been using and within five casts caught my first smallmouth. Of course I should have seen the solution sooner. I know how perceptive smallmouths can be, particularly when the water is cold and they're just not busting every bait you throw.

Our week at Crow Duck and at nearby Echo Lake seemed to pass almost overnight. We kept our tackle light and our casting delicate and we caught fish. It's a spot I'd recommend to any smallmouth angler. Crow Duck is in the Whiteshell Provincial Park of Ontario. To reach it you first drive to Pinawa or Pointe Dubois on Route 11 and then take a boat up the Winnipeg River to the Pine Island Lodge, which is operated by Vic Burgess. It's also possible to fly to Pine Island by float plane. From Pine Island it's another hour's boat trip upriver to the Crow Duck outlet stream. To finally reach Crow Duck you have to portage around a waterfall. You can also drive directly to Crow Duck on an unnumbered, unpaved forest trail or fly directly by charter float plane.

I've often fished at the Crow Duck falls by throwing a surface lure such as the Sputterbug into the turbulent water. The lure pops to the surface, and the small bubbles and particles of floating foam explode as the smallmouth, perhaps thinking the bait's a small creature washed over the falls, gobbles it up.

One afternoon Chuck and I spent an hour or so watching smallmouths trying to hurdle the falls, only to be washed back down into the big pool. With that going on — and I am not sure what the fish were trying to do — Chuck and I

Smallmouths in Lake St. Clair, though abundant, have shown mercury contamination.

SMALLMOUTHS ARE

By Dick Kotis

Author plays bass at falls below Ontario's Crow Duck Lake. Canoeists must portage here to reach lake.

Chuck Danforth works productive tributary of Winnipeg River in Ontario for smallmouths.

started to discuss our favorite smallmouth spots. What popped into my mind was Basswood Lake in the Minnesota border country. There's no better early season fishing anywhere than in Basswood's Wind Bay area west of Prairie Portage. There an angler can have as much sport as he has time for, surface fishing with a Sputterbug or Hula Popper.

Chuck interrupted my spiel on Basswood to ask if I ever used snaps or snap swivels on surface lures. "I certainly don't," I told him. "I think the delicately-balanced surface action can be completely ruined by them." That discussion might have continued indefinitely if Chuck hadn't mentioned his own favorite smallmouth spot in northern Minnesota — Rose Lake. It's on the maps of that region, and Chuck said the quickest way to reach it, the way that saved him a long drive, is by way of the Minnesota entry, where there's a portage stairway with 150 steps.

When Chuck mentioned Rose Lake I immediately thought of a classic in that border region — Rainy Lake. It's large and the angler making his first trip shouldn't pass up Swell Bay, Red Gut and Seine Bay. I like to fish Rainy early in

121

the morning — in fact, before breakfast — and again in the evening after dinner. During the day I cast for walleyes or northern pike, but my mornings and evenings are spent tossing Sputterbugs, Hula Poppers and Jitterbugs for smallmouths, waiting for the quiet morning or still evening to explode.

Another smallmouth hotspot in Ontario, one that's not even in the wilderness, is Lake St. Clair. For a brief period after the Ontario bass season opens, smallmouth fishing in the northeastern section of St. Clair may compare with the best anywhere. All during May the bass migrate into shallow, hard-bottomed bays to spawn, and normally they remain in good numbers until the water's warm enough to drive them to deeper places.

The best of the fishing occurs on the Walpole Island Indian Reservation. Go there by way of I-94 and Michigan 29 eastward to the ferry crossing (over the St. Clair River) at Algonac — or launch your own boat at public facilities in Algonac. It's necessary to clear Canadian customs on Walpole Island and also to obtain a special $5 license to fish on the reservation. Because the Island is really a complicated maze of channels, bays and smaller islands, it is wise to hire an Indian guide (many are available in the community at the ferry crossing) until you become acquainted with the geography.

There is a sad note to this excellent smallmouth fishing; because of high levels of mercury found in the bass, they are unsafe for human consumption. This is fishing for fun only. The smallmouths run to four and occasionally to five pounds. Two-pounders are the average. Light spinning tackle works best, and among the most effective lures are the Swimmerspoon, Lau Lure and Busybody.

Author checks day's catch of smallmouths from Crow Duck Lake.

Smallmouths are acrobatic where they're found—from deep reservoirs of the South to remote Ontario waters. Author recommends light-colored lures for smallmouths on bright days and darker ones for overcast periods.

Left—Great Lakes guide Glenn Lau and party made this haul at Walpole Island on Lake St. Clair. Above—Minnesota's Rainy Lake produces heavy bass like this four-pounder.

Too many anglers overlook the excellent smallmouth fishing in the southern U.S. One time I bragged to a Tennessee fisherman about the 4-pound smallmouths I'd often caught on Rainy. He listened politely, then showed me a mounted eight-pounder he'd taken at Center Hill Reservoir in his home state. Needless to say, my sails were deflated.

Center Hill has been a consistent producer of big, heavy-bodied smallmouths, and don't let anyone tell you there's a difference — other than size — between southern and northern smallmouths. The rebel bass jump, they hit surface lures when the season is right, and they grow big. I usually fish from the Sligo boat dock. A call to Junior Hays at Cove Hollow will get you the latest fishing information.

Of course Dale Hollow Lake in Kentucky offers outstanding smallmouth fishing. No one can dispute a lake that gave up the world record smallmouth. The best fishing period in Dale Hollow — and in other southern lakes as well — is during the colder months — say, from mid-February to early April. Of course bad weather can disrupt the fishing, and it's wise to call ahead for information on the temperature, color and level of the water. Usually the best method is to cast or troll very close to a steep shoreline with a jig-and-pork-strip combination or a deep-diving plug.

I told Chuck about two other hotspots he surely must fish next year — Pickwick Lake and Wilson Lake, both in the northwest corner of Alabama. They're both TVA reservoirs on the Tennessee River near Florence, Alabama, and the angler who visits them should be prepared to handle heavy fish. I particularly recommend the tailwaters of Pickwick Dam, and the bays on the north side of Wilson Lake where Shoal Creek and the Elk River enter.

After that discussion Chuck asked about the best colors for smallmouth lures, and I think when the campfire sputtered out that evening we still hadn't settled our differences. When I fish a deep-running fast-swimming lure I like a light color, usually yellow with some red or white in it; but for sinking, slow-action lures I like dark shades such as black, blue or dusky brown. When fishing the surface on a bright sunny day, usually at dusk or dawn, I like light colors; on cloudy days, dark ones. Of course there are expert anglers who will disagree. If you're of a different opinion, drop me a note at Akron, Ohio.

Jim Boone checks string of saugers, which are small relatives of the walleye.

NEW WAY FOR saugers

By Larry Rankin

I know the whole thing sounds ridiculous. This fellow in Kentucky named Boone (I'm sure that'll seem contrived) has a sure-fire method (honest!) of catching saugers, if you know what they are. He fishes with a reel, but no rod. Maybe I should have said the whole thing sounds fishy.

Jim Boone catches his saugers in the tailrace of Kentucky Dam, and he fishes for nothing else. The waters there are big, silty and turbulent—factors characteristic of good sauger habitat everywhere. The species actually ranges throughout the north-central U. S. and south-central Canada, but it's found only in the largest rivers and lakes where it can wander for great distances—primarily in the Great Lakes, Lake of the Woods, and the Mississippi, Missouri, Ohio and Tennessee Rivers and the vast artificial reservoirs along their courses. Repeated stocking in smaller lakes and rivers has failed, for unknown reasons.

Of course the sauger, *Stizostedion canadense*, is closely related to the walleye and is similar in appearance and habit. Like the walleye, it has an elongated body that's nearly round in cross-section, a forked tail, spines in the anal and first dorsal fins, glassy eyes, and a mouthful of sharp-pointed teeth. Unlike the walleye it has irregular dark blotches on the body, and rows of dark spots on the spinous dorsal. It also has a rather pronounced black spot at the base of the pectoral fin, and lacks the dusky blotch at the rear of the spinous dorsal characteristic of walleyes.

Saugers are typically small, usually running from ¾ to 1½ pounds. The maximum size is 3 to 5 pounds, except for Missouri River fish, which sometimes reach 8 pounds and may be a distinct subspecies. Most saugers are caught during migrations in late fall or winter, particularly below dams, where they concentrate.

Jim Boone fishes from mid-August through October and almost always catches his limit of these fine-flavored fish in less than two hours. He launches his boat below Kentucky Dam on the Tennessee River about 20 miles by road east of Paducah. His only tackle is an unusual trolling reel, which looks like an oversize automatic fly reel about nine inches in diameter. It's loaded with approximately 200 feet of 100-pound-test nylon-coated wire line. Attached to the line's end with a heavy snap swivel is a yard-long length of 40-pound-test nylon monofilament, which in turn is attached with a heavy swivel to a two-pound homebuilt sinker made from an eight-inch-long lead-filled copper pipe of one-inch diameter. To each of the two swivels Boone ties a length of 30-pound mono, one twenty feet long and the other, forty. Finally, to these two lines are fastened floating gold-and-black balsa-minnow lures. With all this gear ready, Jim attaches the reel to the middle seat of his 14-foot outboard boat with a C-clamp. And that's when the action starts.

Maneuvering the outboard with his left hand, Boone pays out about 150 feet of line and trolls slowly over the turbu-

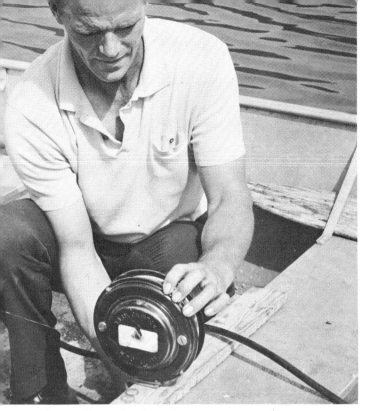

Large trolling reel is clamped onto forward boat seat.

Tackle and target: Balsa-minnow and heavy pipe sinker took this average-sized sauger.

While trolling, Boone hand-holds line to detect strikes and lures bumping along bottom.

Sauger comes aboard from tailwaters of Kentucky Dam.

lent waters. He holds the line with his bare hand to feel the heavy sinker bumping along the rocky bottom. With the sinker just scraping, the floating plugs swim barely above the snags. When a sauger strikes Boone simply brings the line in hand over hand, taking up the slack with the auto reel as fast as it accumulates. There's a lot more sport to this maneuver than you might think. Without a rod flexing to maintain tension, the fish can wriggle loose quite easily.

Boone learned early that it's not advisable to handle sharp-toothed, finned, and spined saugers with his bare hands. Once the fish is aboard, he seizes it with a heavy cloth and extracts the hooks with a pair of pliers.

The afternoon I fished with Jim he caught three saugers in about half an hour and then lost his sinker and baits on one of the numerous snags in the riverbed. He thought he'd have to quit fishing because he had only one more of his lures along. But I recalled that I had a somewhat similar lure, a gold-and-white AC Shiner, which was made locally, in my tackle kit back on shore. Though Jim doubted it would work, we went after it and he reluctantly decided to give it a try. After re-rigging he had a strike almost immediately—and it was on the new lure! In fact, the next three fish hit it, so it's possible that many different floating baits might produce with Boone's deep hand-lining method.

In slightly over two hours Jim caught his limit of ten saugers, all 1½- to 2-pounders. The largest he ever caught was a 4 lb., 1 oz. fish taken in 1968 that is currently the Kentucky state record.

Actually, the fish can't put up a great fight due to the swift water and heavy tackle, but once in the boat they're as lively as a frog on a hot griddle. Boone's method appears the only effective way to fish for that species in that particular stretch of water. Conventional rod-and-reel methods just don't seem to work. The truth is that Jim Boone has shown a lot of ingenuity in devising this method. Early frontiersmen like Daniel Boone—to whom he's distantly related—certainly would have admired that kind of genius and skill!

How to catch a walleye

THE LAKE COUNTRY'S GOLDEN BOY

BY HANK BRADSHAW

Frank Lucien shows off a beautiful walleye we caught in Crooked Lake on the Minnesota-Ontario border. This fish brings more anglers to the North Woods than any other.

Slowly, carefully, our Cree Indian guide maneuvered our canoe among the rocks, edging in close to shore and alongside the swift, white-topped current that roared from the long, sloping waterfall pounding its way out of the Saskatchewan woods. Over and around huge boulders it flowed, into a lake section of the historically famous Churchill River. The sky was overcast, but the air was light, almost fluffy, as the low pressure system moved out. It was a day made for walleye fishing.

My wife Vera fastened a small, heavy spoon to her spinning tackle, cast into the torrent, watched the line swing and suddenly snap tight. She jerked, and was fast to a tugging fish—the fish we had driven 1600 miles to catch in new country. A couple of minutes later, a golden-black walleye was splashing its way to our guide's net.

This fish was followed quickly by others—we caught 16 almost as fast as we could cast. Since we wanted only enough for a shore dinner, we released most of them. Each of the fish weighed from 1½ to 2 pounds. Since the chance of catching a whopper at the base of a waterfall is somewhat slim, we eventually tired of the fast action and moved on to deeper water in search of larger fish. As we pulled into a bay sided by high rock cliffs, and our guide indicated that we could start fishing anytime, Vera and I cast, this time baited with yellow and orange jigs, felt the rocky bottom, bounced the lures a couple of times, twitched them off, and Vera had a smashing strike. Her rod arched beautifully when she set the hook. The fish didn't move. "This is a good one!" grunted Vera, as she tussled. "He's just laying there."

Sign of a big fish—and sure enough, following a vicious, bull-dogging battle, Vera worked a 5½-pounder to the net, a tremendous walleye for that far north.

The foregoing points up two of the many methods of catching walleyes, the fish that draws more anglers to the great North Woods than any other. The states of Minnesota, Wisconsin, Michigan, the Dakotas, Iowa, and the provinces in central Canada would be missing a whale of a lot of fishermen if it weren't for the beautiful, tasty, argumentative walleye. Resort owners throughout this north-central section of the continent continually clamor to their fisheries departments for more stockings of walleyes, and the resorters in areas that have plenty from natural reproduction, loudly proclaim the fact to the fishing public. The walleye is the real Golden Boy of the lake country.

With a great many anglers, this is the first fish they try to catch when they go north. Given the proper instruction, almost anyone can learn to catch walleyes quickly—and therein lies the secret of an initial happy vacation and the promise of many more.

For those of you who have never fished for walleyes, let's start from scratch with some of the rudiments, and perhaps we'll mention something that even the expert can consider a good tip.

Walleyes are usually found in five places: (1) at the foot of waterfalls; (2) in currents; (3) on the rough side of a fairly shallow lake; (4) in deep holes with rocky or sandy bottoms; (5) along underwater sandbars or rocky

Walleyes like to gather at the foot of a waterfall to feed on what the rushing water brings. Casting with a rapidly sinking lure and retrieving it along the bottom is a good way to catch these choice fish. This picture taken at Curtain Falls on the Minnesota-Ontario border. The fisherman is Frank Lucien of Ely.

Another good spot is at the edge of a current such as this. Note that the two fishermen are using oars instead of a motor and are working the eddy alongside the current, a fine place, usually deep, for walleyes. The angler is Bill Zup, owner of Zup's Lac La Croix Fishing Camp. (Ontario)

reefs. You'll find them elsewhere, it's true, but you'll almost never go wrong in these five places if you are fishing a lake or river that contains walleyes.

Walleyes are bottom feeders. Occasionally they come up on reefs or into sandy shallows at night, where you can catch them with surface plugs, but for reliable fishing, I go to the bottom. Night is the most active period for walleyes, but, since most anglers prefer daylight fishing, the walleye wouldn't be much good if it couldn't also be caught then.

I've already mentioned how we angled at the base of a waterfall where walleyes like to gather to feed on what the falls bring. Good lures here are heavy little spoons, jigs, or deep-running plugs, especially those that vibrate or wriggle sharply on retrieve. Small minnows, hooked as if for trolling (through the gill then through the sides) and used with a spinner and enough weight to take the lure down, are frequently successful when cast, allowed to settle, then retrieved slowly. I like to use a light, limber rod and a 6-pound line for this, "feeling" along the bottom —sort of pulling then winding up the slack. When a walleye takes hold, I feed him the minnow for a few seconds,

letting the rod drift toward the fish, then set the hook with a snap. You can develop a touch with this gear and method that is so sensitive that you can feel every bump.

Currents are good places for walleyes, especially the tail ends. Usually, such water develops an eddy. Walleyes like to lie in the eddy and dart into the current for food. So we give it to them that way. These eddies are also ready-made for still-fishing from a boat, lowering a minnow or frog to about a foot off the bottom. Or using an artificial jig (preferably—for me—one with yellow, orange or white pliable feathers or marabou) and bouncing it off the bottom. Frequently, this eddy covers a deep hole.

I've had success standing on shore or a dock on the rough side of a lake and casting into the waves a rapidly sinking lure, such as a small heavy spoon, perhaps with a few wisps of hair tied over the hook. Walleyes seek the rough shores for the same reasons they seek the base of a waterfall.

Deep holes in rivers at spots other than eddies are sometimes walleye holes. The fish lie in the coolest water they can find, and on the bottom, so still-fishing or casting with deep retrieves are the order.

The writer motoring home with some big walleyes, including an 8-pounder.

Here Vera hands our rods to Guide Billy Zup, Jr., at Zup's Lac La Croix Lodge in southwestern Ontario. It pays to take plenty of fishing tackle when angling for walleyes. Ways to catch this fish are so varied, you may need to try several types of equipment.

Probably the most rewarding technique may be employed when fishing where both lunkers and pan-size walleyes prefer to hang out. This is in deep water along underwater sandbars or reefs in a lake. Try jigs bounced off the bottom while still-fishing, casting, or as you move very slowly along in a boat, preferably by using oars rather than a motor. It is difficult to slow a motor enough to handle a jig properly, although it can be done if you know the lake bottom well.

The difficulty lies in keeping your lure at a specific depth, following the bar, while moving at motor-rate. (I've seen fishermen blithely trolling in 80 feet of water, not realizing that the bar had turned and now lay fifty yards from where they were fishing.) An electronic depth finder would be helpful here.

When rowing slowly—holding the boat back when necessary if windy—you can keep your line nearly perpendicular. By also using a sounding line, you can constantly feel the bottom and follow every indentation of the bar. This method keeps the lure constantly at the depth where fish are feeding. The most successful fishermen use their motors to get to the bar—then use oars to fish. It is harder

work, but it pays dividends.

Walleyes are creatures of habit and should be fished for by understanding these habits. For example, if walleyes are feeding on the bottom in 30 feet of water, you rarely will catch anything—except perhaps a fiddler or two—in 25 feet. They also are school fish and seldom roam alone as do northern pike and muskellunge. When you catch one, throw out a spotter can with a weight going to the bottom to anchor it, then fish the same area at the same depth until you catch all you want, or until the school moves.

Gauging the proper depth will vary with the season. At the spring opening, walleyes probably will have recently finished spawning and be in shallow water, from 8 to 15 feet. As the water warms, they move deeper, usually spending the summer at about 30 feet. As dog days come on—and on into fall—walleyes frequently go as deep as 40 to 45 feet, then move back up shallower as water cools. But even under ice they seldom seem to feed in less than 20 feet of water. Until the ice goes out, that is—then they move up quickly.

Tackle, in these days of small lures, may be kept fairly

light, although the rod should have enough backbone to set the hook with the lure down 30 feet. This takes a healthy sock. Most successful anglers use transparent leaders of three feet or so, just heavy enough to stand the shock of the sock. Sinkers, heavy enough only to take the line straight to the bottom, should be attached just above the leader; then the line reeled up until the lure rides a foot or a bit more off the bottom. A reel with a good drag system is a decided assist, and the line should be heavy enough—8-10 pounds or more—to land a big fish if you're lucky enough to entice one. Anglers who rig for small fish usually lose the picture size.

If you prefer live bait—and many walleye anglers find it especially effective—the guides of the north will prove that the way you bait your hook is important. First, the hook must be comparable in size to the bait—with a large minnow (suckers, shiners, chubs), a large hook, and vice versa. For still-fishing, the hook may be run under the skin alongside the dorsal fin with the barb barely out. The minnow should hang in a natural swimming position. Too, this keeps him alive, which usually is essential. Hooking for casting is the same as trolling, aforementioned—and it makes no difference whether the minnow is alive or dead.

If you prefer nightcrawlers, try wadding them on the end of the hook, although some anglers like to leave a bit of both ends trailing (and wriggling). For a frog, hook it through the lips. With the latter, it helps to occasionally lower it to the bottom and bounce it along gently.

Frequently, a spinner or a jig used with the live bait helps. These flash even when still-fishing. Vera catches more fish than anyone by continually working her line lightly with a finger to be sure of the flash.

To successfully hook a walleye while using live bait, the payoff comes from an accurate mental measurement of the amount of time the fish needs to get the bait well into his mouth before setting the hook. With a large minnow or a frog, allow more time. Usually a hungry walleye will run a short way with a bait, stop to chew it or twist it so he can get it head first. The zero hour—time to jerk—comes when he starts off again. The deeper the water, the harder the jerk.

Sometimes, however, a big walleye five pounds or more will just "lay" on the bait, grab it and not move. Then you need to guess the amount of time he needs to get the bait in the proper position so the hook will catch. With artificial lures, though, you may sock him as soon as you feel him.

Once hooked, a walleye will almost continuously shake his head, trying to rid himself of the lure. With a big fish, it is essential to let him run when he wants to run, but its wise to maintain a tight line, for a walleye can shake loose from a slack line almost as easily as a bass. Once he begins to come toward the boat, keep him coming. If you are using a thumb-type reel, wind until the fish makes you stop by the strength of his lunges. With a spinning or spin-cast reel sporting a properly set drag, it is unnecessary to stop reeling. Wherever the fish wants to run, he'll run, but you will retain control with a tight line.

When the fish is no longer "green" and is apparently tired out (turns on side or belly-up), slip the net over his head—not his tail—and in one continuous motion lift him into the boat or onto shore. You will have earned the Golden Boy of the North Country and can follow the same science to enjoy many more thrilling days fishing walleyes.

To net a walleye, slip the net over his head, not his tail. If his tail gets a bearing on the net, he is apt to tear loose from the hook and escape.

Walleye fishermen congregate at the mouth of the Tamarac River where it empties into Upper Red Lake at Washkish, Minnesota. In the spring, this is one of the finest walleye fishing spots in the North Woods. Here anglers anchor and still fish as the walleyes collect to feed on what the river carries. The bottom is rocky. Walleyes spawn in the river then move out in May and June.

THOSE TERRIFIC LANDLOCKED SALMON!

Many consider the landlock the greatest fish on earth. Read here where and how to catch one.

BY KEN BOURBON

The guide gaffs a 4-pound landlock for spin fisherman on Lac de la Robenaire.

Nothing stirred this gray and gloomy day in early June that I'll always remember. Not even a summer breeze or the rain, which constantly threatened, disturbed the lifeless surface of the water.

The place was Palfrey Lake on the Maine-New Brunswick border and we were trolling for landlocked salmon. Fact is we'd trolled for several days in water which seemed completely dead, completely barren. Then late, this afternoon, a school of smelt skipped on the surface. Minutes later another school skipped and skittered. Then still another. Quickly smelt were surfacing everywhere. Then suddenly two flyrods were dancing and far behind the canoe a pair of landlocks were up and high out of the water.

It's hard to describe exactly what happens when you hook a landlock. You just hold on and try to keep a tight line . . . and you wonder if your knots were well-tied. For five, maybe ten minutes, Don Ray and I just held on and hoped while our section of Palfrey Lake came alive with smelt and with landlocks attacking them in every direction. It was a savage scene. We lost both of those first

two salmon right away, but no matter because we quickly hooked two more. An even dozen jumps later we netted both of them. Then Don hooked another fish, lost it on a wild leap and the excitement was over. The smelt vanished and the salmon followed them. That's landlock fishing. Fast and furious and finished all too soon. Still it's dangerously contagious.

At one time or another almost every fish on earth — from bluegills to blue marlin — has been called the gamest species that swims. Bit virtually every angler who ever tangled with the remarkable landlocked salmon quickly agrees that here is the greatest of all, at least in fresh water.

The landlock is a mysterious, relatively rare fish. It's only an Atlantic salmon, some biologists say, that was isolated from the sea and the salt by sudden geologic changes during some distant earlier age. The species simply changed its habits and became accustomed to a new, landlocked environment. But other biologists disagree. Some say it *is* the Atlantic salmon, isolated or not. Still others insist it's a separate member of the trout and sal-

Late expert angler, Larry Koller, nets landlock in New Brunswick. Fish was taken by trolling a streamer fly.

Landlocks seldom fail to give fishermen plenty of acrobatics out of the water.

mon clan — and it *always* was. But that's only the beginning.

Many icthyologists believe there are *two* kinds of land-locks — the Sebago and the ouananiche (pronounced wah-nah-neesh). Others say no; both are the same. But all of this makes little difference to fishermen, for no matter what the origin or the family tree, this is an incredibly swift and exciting fish that must be hooked to be believed.

The original range of both landlocks was very limited. Those called Sebago were confined to a few waters in Maine — notably Sebago, Sebec, Green and Branch Lakes — and perhaps to a few lakes in New Brunswick. The ouananiche was found only in the Lake St. John region of Quebec (notably in Lake St. John itself and in the Saguenay, Peribonca, Mistossini Rivers) and in scattered waters through Labrador and Newfoundland. It isn't hard to find an icthyologist, however, who will say the Newfoundland landlock is an entirely different species. But that's splitting hairs again because all have been transplanted elsewhere. Nowadays they're naturalized and maybe even hybridized in many other northeastern waters from upper New York to northern Ontario.

Far less is known of the life pattern of landlocks than of most sweet water fishes, but it does go something like this. As soon as the ice is out—and no landlocks exist in lakes that do not freeze tight every winter—they follow smelt and other forage fish into tributary streams or onto the shallow beaches where the small fish spawn. Then they'll stay in these same shallows a long as the living is easy and the water remains cool, perhaps to fifty degrees. When the temperature passes that point they retire to deep water for the summer. Even then they may come to the surface for brief feeding binges, but that happens all too seldom. In fall, they run upstream again to spawn.

The landlock is a handsome one. It's a sleek and stream-lined, silvery fish with black spots most numerous on the upper half. Its tail, fins and eyes are over-sized, larger than a sea-run Atlantic salmon. A five pounder is a trophy fish. A ten pounder is barroom-betting size anywhere in America.

The best time to fish in most salmon country is from ice-out until mid or late June. At best it's a tense unpredictable sport, but after that early spring-summer period, the odds in an angler's favor fall fast. But the best bet anytime is to troll a streamer fly that resembles a smelt or other small fish fairly fast and close in the turbulent wake of the outboard motor. A slow troll, as for lake trout or walleyes, seldom scores. Very early in the season, the fly should be trolled near the surface; later it is necessary to go down much deeper.

The type of tackle isn't too important because trolling is possible with any gear. But to get the most action, I like to use a flyrod with a large-capacity reel. For the shallow fishing, the reel is simply filled with at least 100 yards of 12-pound monofilament line. For deeper trolling the reel contains 100 yards of lead-core line that tests about 20 pounds. The all-metal or wire lines are entirely unsatisfactory for landlock fishing. They not only kill the fish too quickly, but they're difficult and unpleasant to troll at the high speeds necessary. The lead-core line is "softer," will not kink or "spring" off the reel spool and it handles almost as easily as a level fly line.

Landlocks are sophisticated fish. They will strike long, thin lures (usually spoons) that resemble smelts, ciscoes, candlefish or emerald shiners occasionally — and they will take live smelt, too — but nothing beats a heavily-dressed, tandem streamer fly in a few of the proven patterns. The Barnes Special, Gray Ghost, Green Ghost,

This shot was made at Lake Traful in southern Argentina.

Argentina landlocks often run twice the size of the species in North American waters. This one was taken in Traful Lake near Bariloche.

Highlander, Nine Three, Smelt Marabou and Mickey Finn are among the best.

One of the finest landlock waters in Canada is Trout Lake near North Bay, Ontario, thanks to the late and colorful pioneer outfitter, Len Hughes. More than twenty-five years ago he urged the Ontario government to obtain ouananiche from Quebec and to try them in local waters. Although many of the transplants were unsuccessful the salmon caught on quickly in Trout Lake and today they grow much bigger than their forebears in Lake St. John from which the original stock was obtained. The top Trout Lake fish to date is an almost incredible 11¾ pounder.

Like muskies, landlocks are not really abundant anywhere — so Charles Groetzinger of Pittsburgh must have set some sort of record at Trout Lake when he once landed five in one day from four to 8½ pounds. He added a 9½ pounder the next day! A Toronto angler, Lee Miller, once caught 14 ouananiche in less than a week's fishing — which might also be a record.

Outfitter Len Hughes went a step farther, though. Besides introducing a new fish, he also developed a new and deadly fly to take them; nearly all of the trophy fish from Trout Lake nowadays were taken on Hughes' Champlain. It's a tinsel-ribbed, yellow-bodied tandem streamer with yellow, white (must be Polar bear hair) and peacock herl wings, a jungle cock eye and red throat. Naturally the Champlain has invaded other landlock waters farther east.

Good landlock water in eastern Quebec, near Mingan.

Another big one taken from Lake Traful, Argentina.

Fishermen's Digest editor catches seven pound landlock on flyrod and streamer fly.

Don Ray with Spednic salmon taken during frantic feeding spree.

Probably Maine has more topnotch landlock water than any other state or province. Every large lake drainage contains the species. Starting from the northern tip of the state, some of the major fishing waters include: the Fish River Chain of Lakes, Moosehead Lake, the East Grand and Grand Lake areas of Washington County, the Rangeley Lake area and the region around Sebago Lake. Also there is excellent fishing in the coastal lakes of Hancock and Waldo Counties. More research and management work has been done on landlocks in Maine than in any other state because of its extreme importance as a game fish thereabouts.

The best waters in neighboring New Brunswick are the Spednic chain of lakes and the St. Croix River. Spednic Lake probably has the largest fish.

Early in the spring of 1960 landlocks weighing 16 lbs. 14 oz. and 16 lbs. 9 oz. were taken in New York's Lake George to set a new New York State record. Both catches were all the more amazing because salmon are not native to this lake, nor to any New York waters. It's just a case of intelligent and aggressive fish management by the State's Conservation Department which has actually introduced Atlantic salmon into many waters. It's entirely possible that even larger landlocks will eventually be taken in Lake George and it will be no great surprise if the 23-pound world record from Sebago Lake, Maine, is eventually passed.

Besides Lake George, New York's best salmon waters are Schroon Lake, Clear Pond (Essex County) and the Schroon River. A decade ago many good fish were being taken in Cayuga Lake. Other places where persistent salmon stocking have paid off are the Fulton Chain, Sara-toga Lake, Paradox Lake, Raquette Lake, and Upper Saranac Lake.

Last fall a party of caribou hunters pushed deep into the back country of Newfoundland to look for trophy heads. They saw plenty of game but only one hunter fired a shot. Instead the others became so occupied with the unbelievable fishing for landlocked salmon they found in the waters all around them that shooting was practically forgotten.

It's hard to believe that an extraordinary species like the landlock could long go all but unknown, but that's pretty much the case in Labrador and Newfoundland where they're quite abundant but where few have ever been taken by sport fishermen. Many of the waters have been too remote or too inaccessible to reach easily.

Newfoundland especially may develop into a promised land for fishermen with landlocks (locally called "winnish") only in mind. The best known waters now are Lake St. John, Deer Pond and the Exploits River. The Salmon River and Bay d'Espoir contain big fish. In many waters on the Avalon Peninsula, landlocks are numerous but relatively small. As more roads are pushed into the interior of this wilderness island, it may reveal the finest, fastest landlock fishing in the world.

But not quite. Landlocks have also been exported to Argentina. There in Lake Traful, the Traful River and adjacent waters they reach twice the average size of the species in any North American waters. Visiting anglers, in fact, find it impossible to describe the salmon fishing they find on the other side of the globe.

But landlocks anywhere are worth an angler's time. They're splendid game fish any way you look at it.

Fast action with large northern pike in Northern Manitoba. This province is a great destination for anglers who are making the first big trip.

SO YOU'RE PLANNING THE

BIG TRIP

By
Erwin A. Bauer

Every angler embarking on a long trip is wise to check every item of tackle until all is in perfect working order.

Dan Stewart is not the real name of this unfortunate angler. Nor is Big Deer the correct name of the lake where he went fishing. But the sad story of both is commonplace enough that it bears describing here.

Stewart might be called a typical outdoorsman in that he spends as much time hunting and fishing as family commitments and his budget will permit. He is reasonably skilled in shooting, casting and camping—and hasn't missed an opening day of the local deer or trout season for many years. A partner in a modest television repair service, Stewart had always dreamed about traveling farther away to fish—to some day make the *really* big trip to one of the great, distant fishing holes he'd read so much about.

Last summer that became a reality; Stewart had finally saved enough to get away for a couple of weeks. Because of sudden illness, a friend had to cancel out on a trip to Big Deer in northern Canada and on the spur of the moment, Stewart agreed to take his place. The deposit he made was large enough to make him shudder. But he had heard a good deal about the Big Deer area on a TV program and in fact had long poured over the colorful brochure of one of the camps on that lake. Hopefully the stiff price tag was only an indication of how spectacular the fishing would be.

But what followed, Stewart revealed to the writer, was among the greatest disappointments of his life.

There is no point in describing all the unhappy details, but Stewart did not find much to match what he had dreamed about. The accommodations were crude and unlike those pictured in the brochure. The guides were inexperienced, often unwilling, and both boats and outboard motors were old enough to be a constant source of trouble and delay. But worst of all by far, the fishing was very, very slow. Stewart had assumed he would be able to cast for lake trout on the surface and catch fairly big ones wholesale. The brochure had said so. But the biggest he caught might have weighed eight pounds and like the few other smaller ones, it was taken by deep trolling.

"Maybe," Stewart concluded, "the kind of fishing I've dreamed about just doesn't exist. Traveling long distances seems to be a mistake."

Of course he is wrong on both counts. There is no reason that Dan Stewart's money—or any other angler's—should have been squandered on such a bad trip. Countless fine fishing opportunities *do* exist in every corner of our continent and today it is possible for sportsmen of even modest means to enjoy many of them. It is simply a matter of planning and selecting the right places to go—both factors largely ignored when Stewart suddenly decided to make his trip. The following is designed to help FISHERMEN'S DIGEST readers to avoid making the same mistake.

The best advice is to begin planning thoroughly and far ahead; a year ahead is not too far. Assume you know the

Dolphin gives fisherman plenty of fight in waters off Panama's Pinas Bay before it is swung aboard.

A tarpon hooked on light tackle comes aboard near Isla Aguada, Mexico, a top saltwater fishing area.

Typical group of anglers heading northward to waters in Canada's north.

type of fishing you prefer—northern freshwater, southern saltwater or whatever—and you want to discover the best possible place for this which is within your budget. Unless you have close friends, whose advice and experience is entirely reliable, to suggest the spot, the place to begin your search is in the where-to-go section of the national outdoor magazines — *Sports Afield, Outdoor Life* and *Field & Stream*. Next, select several (rather than just one) places and write to all for details. Ask all for references from previous customers, particularly anglers in your own area. When all answers arrive you will have a good basis for comparison, but still that is not sufficient. You must also contact all the references and be very specific in the questions you ask about accommodations, the guides, the country and especially about the fishing. Do not rely on any individual's word, but rather consult several. You may find great variation in their reports.

Keep in mind that no resort or fishing camp operator has any control over the weather. There will be times when very unseasonable rains, bitter cold or prolonged flood waters can seriously affect the fishing. Nothing can be done about this except to grin and bear it—figuring, as any good sportsman does, that bad comes along with the good.

But a sportsman planning a trip *does* have a right to expect an outfitter to advise him about which times are best

Angler has lively time landing large lake trout on trip to faraway lake in Northwest Territory, Canada.

The bonefish is among the gamest of all fish — and is worth traveling far to catch.

141

Pair of trophy eastern brook trout from Yesterday River, Ontario. Trips to catch trout like these should be thoroughly planned far ahead.

Large halibut is reward for angler on trip to Alaska's southeast coast.

for which kinds of fishing. That should be one specific question which the angler always asks. (In the case of Dan Stewart, for example, he might very well have caught lake trout by casting on the surface either earlier or later in the season. But he did not realize this.) Also there will be occasions when a camp owner can well call to cancel a trip because the prolonged or unexpected bad weather in his area has spoiled the fishing. It may cost him income for the present, but it may also establish him as a very reliable, honest operator far into the future.

Many states and Canadian provinces either grade or regulate their fishing camps and it is a wise precaution to check

with the proper state tourist or travel bureaus about the matter. For the most part, however, they are mostly concerned with the quality of the accommodations, which is more important to some anglers than to others. In Manitoba, for instance, fishing camps must meet certain high standards before they are permitted to operate. This eliminates one possible headache of the sportsmen who travel there.

Understandably a number of commercial airlines promote fishing areas and facilities which they serve. Some also act in various degrees as travel agents or advisors for fishermen. But with the exception of Air Canada's Fur, Fin and Feather Club, which acts as agent for a number of specially selected fishing facilities across the far north, a fisherman is better off making his own contacts, even though more time, paper work and phone calls will be involved.

There are some truly spectacular fishing opportunities— for making the big trip of a lifetime—in the Latin American countries. Some notable examples are the great reef and flats fishing at Roatan Island, Honduras (Reef House Resort, Oakridge Harbor); the remarkable tarpon fishing in Costa Rica (Parismina Tarpon Rancho); big game angling at Pinas Bay, Panama (Tropic Star Lodge); and mixed bag fishing all along Baja California, Mexico. But there are drawbacks in heading southward for the uninitiated sportsmen as well. Too many of the well-advertised package trips to catch exotic South American species do not work out as planned and there is also the growing social unrest in some countries. Recently (as this is written in early 1971) fishermen in Chile and Peru have reported much unfriendliness toward visiting Americans. This sentiment appears to be spreading.

Perhaps Canada and Alaska are the most suitable destinations for the average fisherman making his first fishing trip. For one thing, no complicated or sophisticated tackle is necessary. You can use what you already own. Besides, there is no language barrier, no entrance requirements, and the natives are friendly.

Probably because it is so far away for many American sportsmen, Alaska has been largely ignored as an angler's destination. But nowadays there is excellent air service from several points in the Lower 48 and there are many good facilities for visiting anglers. Among the best are Tikchik Narrows Lodge (in the Tikchik-Wood River Wilder-

Heavy string of walleyes taken on fly-in fishing trip to Molson Lake in northern Manitoba.

Drifting across warm, shallow, saltwater flats for bonefish is an old dream come true for many fishermen.

ness) near Dillingham; Battle River Wilderness, Brooks River and Kulik camps at Katmai National Monument (c/o Wien Consolidated Airlines, Anchorage); Bell Island Resort near Ketchikan.

Planning the big trip anywhere should also include acquiring the proper equipment and getting it ready for use. An inquiry about the expected weather will dictate what kinds of clothing to carry along. Remember also that there are few places where it is safe or advisable to venture without foul weather (rain) gear and insect repellent. Such insects as mosquitoes may seem small and insignificant when contemplated from far away in a cozy living room. But their abundance has probably ruined more fishing trips than inadequate plumbing and bad guides put together.

Tackle should be thoroughly checked to be certain that

Sailfish is top prize for many anglers making the big fishing trip. The species is plentiful off both Atlantic and Pacific coasts.

it is in 100 per cent working order. Lubricate reels, check reel drags, replace worn or frayed windings on rod guides and ferrules, replace old line on all reels, sharpen hooks on lures, check waders for leaks. It is really tragic to undertake a long expensive expedition, only to have tackle fail right in the middle of it. Replacement tackle you need is seldom available in the faraway places.

If it is a trip south of the border, you will need a valid U.S. passport to enter some countries, a tourist card for others, or a visa stamped in your passport before arrival to enter still others. A smallpox vaccination, certified and often proof of other innoculations are necessary to visit many countries, as well as to return home. Cameras, binoculars and expensive fishing tackle manufactured in Europe or Japan should be registered with U.S. Customs before leaving the U.S. so that there is no difficulty in bringing it back.

For more adventuresome anglers, the big trip may be striking out alone into unknown situations—into distant unexplored country—rather than depending a great deal on established fishing camps and facilities. For these, even more planning and research is advisable before starting out. Be sure to have all the topo maps or navigation charts which are available and in the case of extreme wilderness travel, be acquainted with survival techniques and materials. It may also be necessary to repair beforehand such items as tents and camping gear, canoes, paddles, compasses and such.

Even the best anglers often find it difficult to catch fish in a wilderness lake—even if the region is nearly virgin and the fish unused to humans. But much time can be saved and more action guaranteed by carrying along such inventions of the electronic age as the Lo-k-tor and Fish-n-Temp. The first is a light, compact fish finder and depth locator invaluable in exploring the underwater geography of any body of water. The latter is a pocket size device which instantly gives the water temperature at any depth down to 100 feet. Both are available from the Lowrance Electronics Corp. in Tulsa and can be worth their weight in pure gold when in unfamiliar surroundings.

As the waters nearest to where most fishermen live become more degraded—tragically—by "progress" and pollution, it becomes necessary to travel farther and farther in search of good sport. And when you travel, be sure to make the most of it.

Author Kotis boats bass hooked in very thick lettuce.

LARGEMOUTH
BASS LIKE
THE DARKEST
PLACES...SO
LEARN......

HOW TO FISH
THE LETTUCE

BY DICK KOTIS

Near my home in northeastern Ohio there's a secret little lake which is nameless and which I hope will stay unnamed for a long time to come. It's a natural bog pond, clogged with weeds, lily pads, floating mats of duckweed and, near the shore, flooded stumps, logs and brushpiles. It's a caster's nightmare and a lure manufacturer's dream come true—but it's also loaded with lunker bass that take advantage of the abundant cover.

Not long ago I took an enthusiastic bass fisherman to this pond and pointed out some spots in the thick snags where I'd taken good bass before. He listened but didn't believe a word I said. Like most bass anglers he was accustomed to fishing *around* the tangles but never right in them.

"You can't fish in that garbage," he insisted. "The chances are ten to one you'll get snagged. And even if you don't, and then if you're lucky enough to hook a bass, you'd never be able to pull him out of that mess."

It's true that you can't get many fish out of heavy cover using standard bass fishing procedures. But there are ways, and many anglers—including the fellow I took fishing, who wound up with a stringerful—have discovered how it can be done.

There's an old saying about artificial lures: "If it's weedless, it's fishless". But new lures and techniques of using them have pretty well discredited that one. I've proven to myself that weedless wigglers and spoons and plastic worms and eels can catch bass—and big ones—right in the garbage. Let's take a look at some of the best methods of fishing heavy cover.

Fishing Duckweed
Many springtime hot spots become completely covered with green carpets of duckweed during the midsummer months. This tiny free-floating, round weed drifts into sheltered coves and bays where it reproduces rapidly until the entire area becomes covered with what looks like a stagnant scum. Actually the water beneath is usually weed free and considerably cooler than nearby open water. And big bass appreciate that cool shade in hot weather.

While a few of the small duckweed plants may stick to a spoon or worm, they're not large enough to affect the action or appearance, and most bass don't seem to mind small amounts of salad with their meat. Cast into the duckweed carpet as if it were open water. Use a silver or red-and-white Hawiian Spoon with pork chunks or rind hung on the single weedless hook. Reel the spoon fast across the surface or let it sink and retrieve it erratically along the bottom. Either method may produce strikes, and the duckweed is no problem in either hooking a fish or fighting him to the boat.

What a fast-moving spoon and frog-colored pork chunk slithering across the duckweed looks like from a bass-eye view I don't know. Bass possibly strike at the movement rather than at something they recognize as being edible. I miss many short strikes when fishing in this manner, but once I have located a good fish under the greenery I keep dragging the spoon and chunk across the spot where he struck. Eventually he will correct his lead and connect. The rod should be held high and the line kept out of water during the retrieve. I set the hook immediately upon seeing or hearing a strike.

Fishing the Tree Tops
High water during early spring in most of our man-made reservoirs floods acres of willows, alders, and often larger trees. When the surface water temperature reaches 50 degrees most of the bass in the lake will be prowling and feeding in the warmer water among the tree tops.

Bass in the tree tops call for some rather special baits and techniques. Plastic worms or bottom-bumping jigs with

black worm or eel tails are deadly. In fact, more big bass are probably being taken today throughout the U. S. on artificial worms and eels than on any other lures.

I cast them into the worst possible tangles of underwater brush and let them settle to the bottom—this may take 10 to 20 seconds for an unweighted worm. Twitch them back slowly with frequent pauses—it should take 2 or 3 minutes to retrieve an 80 foot cast. Keep a tight line and when you feel a tug, don't strike back but let him run with your reel in free spool, or with the bail open if you are spinning. After he stops he will mouth the worm and gulp it down. When he starts his second run strike hard.

If the tree tops are in deep water try vertical jigging right beside the boat. Raise the worm-tipped jig a few feet and drop it back to the bottom. Here again the fish must be allowed to mouth the bait before you strike.

Spoons and wigglers with pork chunks or rinds are also great fish-getters among the trees. They should be fished slowly just off the bottom and allowed to climb over the limbs gently to prevent snagging. Twitching the rod tip will add a lot of action to a spoon and chunk combination. I split the chunks almost back to the hook with a sharp knife, making longer legs with wilder action than the standard factory-cut chunks. You must strike immediately when a fish hits a spoon and chunk. A bass will mouth a pork chunk but if he feels the metal spoon he'll spit it out in an instant.

Tree-top fishing calls for stout tackle. Twelve- to 20-pound test line and fairly stout rods are in order unless you don't mind loosing lots of lures and big bass. A hooked bass just has to be horsed out of the branches. If he does wrap around a limb or if the weedless baits do snag as they sometimes will, a 20-pound test line will often pull the fish or lure free.

A trick that often frees a snagged bait is to move directly over the spot and, keeping the line tight with the reel, extend the rod tip down the line until it touches the swivel or bait. A spearing motion with the rod will then reverse the direction of the hook point and the bait will be freed nearly every time. If you are hung up too deep to reach with the rod tip try hand-lining the lure out.

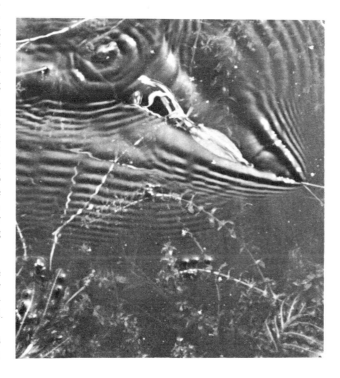

Other emergent vegetation which attracts big bass includes potamogeton, elodea, coontail, lily pads, and water hyacinth. Fishermen should learn to identify them. Nearly all weed tangles have open pockets and many of these serve as homes for large bass. Of course the outer edges of any weed bed are always likely bass hot-spots. During early morning and in the evenings, fish the edges of surface beds with medium-running or top-water baits. During the day most big bass retreat into the weed patches and that's when the plastic worms and eels produce best. I like to cast the worm beyond an open pocket and let it sink to the bottom when it reaches the far side. I rest it in the pocket for about a minute and then slowly climb it up the near wall of weeds.

Worms or eels also get many strikes when crawled across the top of a matted weed bed. Many fish miss when they strike at a worm on top, but it provides action and you at least have them located. If missed bass won't hit again, try the spoon and pork chunk on him. Reel it fast and chances are you'll slice off a load of weeds with your line after he chomps down on the chunk.

Fishing Rock Piles

Keep in mind that largemouths on underwater rocks are probably feeding on crawfish, and you must keep your lure as near the bottom as possible. A long-lipped lure such as the Arbogaster will trip as it hits rocks and avoid snags. A lure in the rocks should either dart rapidly or move very slowly right on the rock tops.

Weighted jigs which ride with the hook up are also productive in the rocks. Allow the jig to sink until slack line tells you the lure has touched bottom. Crawl the jig across the rocks and occasionally lift the rod tip to make the bait hop. After hooking a bass, fish the area thoroughly. Bass seem to school more around rock piles than in other types of cover.

Since contact with gravel and rocks will soon dull hook points, it pays to touch them up frequently with a pocket stone. Dull hooks can easily cost you a trophy fish.

Fishing Hyacinth and Lily Pads

Thick mats of water hyacinth—the curse of many southern waters— probably present the toughest garbage challenge of all. A Florida bream fisherman showed me a trick which we later tried on largemouths with good success.

First, we worked the boat about 30 feet into the green and purple floating mass, then thoroughly beat the surrounding hyacinth with flattened oars. Next we backed the boat out and repeated the weed beating several times at 100 foot intervals down the lake. By this time the first temporary boat-made channel and beaten area was ready to fish. We moved back to it and flipped black eel jigs into the slowly closing hole in the hyacinth.

We usually managed to dredge out at least one good bass per hole, along with some panfish. Shiners, bream speckled perch (crappies) and bass evidently move in and feed on a smorgasbord of aquatic larvae, minnows, bugs, and other food knocked out of the floating jungle of hyacinth by the oars. Ordinarily bass under hyacinths don't spook easily and the commotion caused by the beating seems to attract them.

This method of fishing is time-consuming but when fish are far back in the hyacinths, it's just about the only way to reach them. Even weighted jigs will not ordinarily drop through a mat of water hyacinth. Thrashing the vegetation is merely a method of freshwater chumming. The smaller fish attract larger ones which eventually bring in the lunkers.

An easier way to start activity around hyacinth rafts and lily pads is to zig-zag an outboard along the edges. The prop wash will swirl under the plants and dislodge swarms of aquatic critters. It's best to rest the area a few minutes before starting to fish again. Then work medium depth lures parallel and close to the edges.

Locating Bass

One of the easiest ways to pinpoint active largemouths in early summer is to drift near a bed of weeds whose tips break the surface. Deer-tongue potamogeton is one of the best. A quivering in the weeds is usually the first sign that a bass is on the prowl. Chances are he's after freshly-hatched dragonflies which have to spend an hour or so drying their wings before they can fly. The adult dragonfly emerges from an ugly larva sometimes called a water cricket. In order to split its skin and crawl out as a mature adult, the larva must first climb a weed stalk, leaf or reed and remain above water.

It's during the emerging and wing-drying stages that the bass slurp them down as fast as they can find them. One hot June day in Ohio I observed at least a dozen bass lunching on emerging dragonflies in a single large weed bed. If you can quietly flip a small popper to the spot where a bass has just taken a dragonfly he'll grab it almost every time. There's no need to retrieve the popper—just wiggle it slightly by twitching the rod tip. The strike, when it comes, will be gentle and the only problem is to work the fish out of the jungle.

An important advantage of fishing in heavy cover is that water-skiers and pleasure boaters, who can make fishing tough on busy lakes, give clogged waters a wide berth. You can usually fish such areas with very little competition even from other fishermen.

And remember the keys to successful fishing in the rough stuff: use lots of patience, strong line and weedless lures, and fish where the cover is most abundant. Trophy bass probably spend three-fourths of their lives in the garbage. He's a wise angler who spends most of his time there, too.

Fishing in lettuce ponds like this one is tough. But bass are hiding in the shade underneath.

Fisherman on Ontario lakes retrieves weedless spoon through pond lilies and bullrushes.

Bass fisherman tosses lure into aquatic salad bowl and fish strikes.

Fishing Stumps and Logs

Stumps and logs are usually found in fairly shallow water and the bass using them for shade or warmth, depending on the time of year, are likely to spook easily. Present the bait on the water with as little splash as possible. Cast to the shady side or cast beyond, and then bring the lure back alongside the object.

On sunny days in early spring the surface water temperature near a stump or log will be several degrees warmer than the rest of the lake. This is due to absorption of the sun's heat by the dark objects which in turn warms the surrounding water. Spring bass look for warm spots and often every stump in a lake seems to harbor a hungry bass.

Fishing Emergent Weed Beds

Cattails, wild rice, and reeds usually grow in water less than 3 feet deep. Jitterbugs fished along the edges are often deadly, but when the fish are back in the grass a weedless Hawaiian spoon with pork rind or chunk is probably the most effective. In Florida's Lake Okeechobee where reed beds often extend for miles, silver spoons and pork rinds are the favorite baits, although weedless black eels and worms grow more popular every year.

I prefer to fish a spoon rig fairly fast in the grass. Again stout lines are a must since a hooked bass nearly always manages to wrap himself up. Once a bass has weeds draped over his head, he invariably stops fighting but the mass of "lettuce" can badly strain the line.

Largemouth hooked on weedless spoon comes into the boat enmeshed in lettuce.

When fishing it's important to avoid all contacts between tree branches and your boat. Vibrations and noise from a boat will usually spook nearby bass, and if they don't scatter at once they'll at least refuse to hit for a while.

If the tree tops are in shallow water, I believe the most deadly approach is to wade, since shorter and more accurate casts can be made. Also there are no problems with a drifting boat, and the bass evidently think you are a slow moving tree. I once caught a half dozen big largemouths without moving 10 feet while wading the willows. On that day I used a silver Hawaiian Spoon with a long-legged pork chunk, and the bass were under some dense alders in about 3 feet of water. As soon as one struck I horsed him from the brush and we fought it out in more open water. After every three or four casts another lunker would grab the spoon and chunk. It seemed there were dozens of them ready for action until an overly eager boat fisherman moved in and banged around in some tree trunks. That ended the action.

Weedless lure slithers through and over dense vegetation. Of course it will snag up occasionally, but it will also catch bass.

Plastic worms and eels must be fished very slowly and it takes lots of patience. When I first started using them I'm sure I missed more strikes than I hooked. After you have hooked a few dozen bass on plastics, knowing when to strike becomes almost instinctive, and your average will improve rapidly.

One of the deadliest tricks I know is to cast a worm over a branch and reel until it hangs with the tail touching the water. Jiggling the rod tip will cause the worm to writhe and squirm just above the surface. If nothing happens within a minute you can bet there are no bass underneath that tree. I once saw a four-pounder jump at least a foot out of water to grab a dangling worm. A word of caution—be sure the branch where you hang the worm is limber enough to bend and release the lure when a fish strikes. If not, you may look pretty silly trying to drag a maddened mossback three or four feet over the limb.

Fishing Brush Piles

Try fishing bottom-bumping jigs or glowing worms right in the pile and deep running baits or spoons near the bottom around obstructions. A weedless plastic worm slowly wriggling its way over the top of a brush pile is deadly. But be sure to use heavy line since a bass will normally take a worm back under before swallowing it, and you may have to lift part of the brush pile along with the bass after he's hooked.

When the signboards look like this in the lake country, it's time to think about frostbite fishing.

Angler Dick Kotis cooks and smokes the Lake Erie perch as quickly as he catches them. The result is a gourmet's dream.

THEY ALMOST FREEZE TO FISH

For many outdoorsmen, winter is no excuse to put tackle away and to huddle beside the fireplace at home. Ignoring the ice and snow,

BY TOMMY B. ANDERSON

All day long Al Zelinsky sat motionless in the dark dreary interior of his shanty, peering through the hole in the ice at his feet. Except for a few passing suckers he saw nothing to interest him. Now mid-winter's dusk was approaching the Lake Winnebago country of central Wisconsin and visibility was rapidly disappearing. Zelinsky decided to hang up his spear for the day and walk home across a mile of ice.

But suddenly things began to happen. At first Zelinsky couldn't believe his eyes as a dark shadow glided past in the darkness below and paused beside the wooden decoy fish suspended on a line in mid-depth. That was just long enough to aim the five-tined spear and to thrust it downward for all his might.

There is no recalling — or describing — exactly what followed. The spear connected and it was all a strong man could do to hang onto the handle without breaking an arm or being dragged into the water. But somehow, by bracing his feet against the edges of the ice hole, Zelinsky wrestled the huge fish out of the water and into the shanty. There it started to fight all over again and was finally subdued by a wallop on the head with an empty coke bottle.

Zelinsky's prize was a lake sturgeon of truly bragging proportions. It weighed 89 pounds, but still wasn't the largest of twenty-odd other sturgeon speared on Winnebago that bitter February day. But the "catch" does help explain why thousands upon thousands of other anglers across northern United States and Canada annually almost freeze to catch fish.

At Mogadore Reservoir, Ohio, other anglers head out with great variety of sleds, shelters and fishing gear.

Ice auger comes in handy to cut fishing holes through the ice. A small power saw is even faster.

Question: what's this man doing?

Answer: he's using a home-made gaff to capture large carp through the ice in Sturgeon Bay, Wisconsin. It's fast, exciting sport. Huge "catches" are possible.

There is no way to tell exactly how many Americans go fishing through the ice, and few of them can hope to tangle with a sturgeon. But the number grows every year and so do the rewards. It is scientific fact that winter fishermen enjoy far greater success per hour spent fishing through the ice than do summertime anglers in the very same waters. And they "harvest" everything from smelt and foot-long yellow perch to jumbo lake trout and northern pike as long as any fisherman's arm. Some days the fishing is so good that it isn't necessary to lie about it later.

Ice fishing varies, across the land, from spearing, gaffing and gigging (where it is legal) to the more standard rod and reel or hook and handline. But mostly the technique everywhere is to cut or chip a hole in the ice and then to dunk a bait, hoping a school of fish will come along and find it. This isn't a great deal different from summer fishing, except that it is done in sub-freezing weather. Nor is it a great deal different than the way grandpa went ice fishing more than a generation ago. But recently, as in other sports, there have been some radical changes. And all of them favor the fisherman who risks frostbite to have fun.

Up around the Great Lakes in the last year or so, somebody started using electronics to find fish. It was discovered that a small portable sonic device called a Lo-k-tor (actually a miniature of the instrument that detects submarines for the Navy) would spot fish under the ice. This meant a fisherman no longer needed to sit and wait for fish to come along. Instead the fishermen went exploring until the red blips on the instrument face indicated perch or walleyes or some other species below him. The result was that around Lake Erie, whole platoons of fishermen would follow a man with a fish finder. And usually all of them scored.

Naturally there were other developments. Instead of relying on semi-permanent ice shanties (which are usually heated and quite cozy) ice fishermen have become more mobile as well as less comfortable. They carry all the gear they need on their backs or in a small sled which might have been built in a home workshop for the purpose. Besides tackle and bait, the gear could include a collapsible shanty or windbreak for use on the coldest days or when a wild wind threatens to sweep everyone off the ice.

What else might a wandering ice angler carry in his sled? Dick Kotis of Akron, Ohio, who is among the most hopelessly addicted to the sport, carries a small one-burner Coleman stove and a mini-fish-smoker. That way he can enjoy hot snacks, or even cook his lunch at the same time he's fishing. He figures it beats munching on cold sandwiches.

"Perch filets," Kotis insists, "could never taste better than when deep-fried only a minute or two after leaving the water." All of his deep-freeze fishing friends agree with him

Ice fishermen have always had a tendency to be gadgeteers. They have devised more different kinds of fishing rigs, such as X-shaped tip-ups with red flags to signal a biting fish, than anybody has been able to count. There are also tip-ups with buzzers and flashing red lights. At least one spring-operated device has been made to set the hook and save the fisherman the trouble.

Ice anglers also have been very clever in their designs of collapsible shelters and windbreaks. Some which are prefabricated of aluminum sheeting and are mounted on sled runners require a few minutes to erect. But some other shelters made of canvas with fiberglass "ribs," practically pop into place in the same manner as today's splendid camping tents.

But until the past few winters, ice fishermen had never really, adequately solved the chore of opening holes in the ice. Their crosscut saws, hand-operated iron spuds and augurs did the job well enough, but it became a long, tedious job in places where the ice might reach a thickness of almost three feet. Then one cold day on Lake Michigan, an enterprising outdoorsman discovered that his gasoline chain saw was perfect for the task. With it he could open a dozen holes while a man drilled only one with an augur. Naturally he went in business cutting holes for 25 cents apiece. However he never had much time for fishing himself.

Another more gradual change which is occurring in ice fishing everywhere is from the use of live or natural bait to artificial lures. Bait is not always easy to obtain in winter and it may be even harder to keep alive — or unfrozen. But that is no great handicap to the fishermen who have experimented with ice flies, ice spoons and jigs and found that these will catch many species. Of course the angler must give them life-like action in the water by jiggling them up and down.

Even when the fishing is good, staying warm enough to be able to concentrate on fishing can be a problem. Of course, it is necessary to wear very warm clothes and these are available in stores all over ice fishing latitudes. The new insulated boots are especially good for this sport. Caps with ear muffs are essential and so are fur-lined mittens. Most ice fishermen carry one or two spare pairs of gloves because it is difficult to keep one pair dry very long.

Hand warmers in side pockets are worth their weight in gold to revive hands immersed in water or after baiting hooks. Special "hot seats" have been designed particularly with ice fishermen in mind. Heat is radiated upward when the angler sits down on these beside his ice hole. A regular gasoline lantern placed beneath a collapsible or folding stool will accomplish practically the same thing. It is also a source of light if the fisherman decides to stay out after dark, at which period fishing often is best, To walk safely across ice, in daylight or dark without slipping and falling, ice cleats can be fastened or clamped onto boots. There are manufactured models of these, but they can also be made in home workshops. Some simple ones can be made of leather straps with golf spikes or old pop bottle caps.

Another new development in ice fishing takes advantage of the enormous number of carp which infest too many American waters. Since laws have been liberalized almost everywhere to capture them by any means, except with chemicals or explosives, the door has been opened to one of the most exciting, action-packed of all winter sports. When carp congregate just under the ice or in very shallow water, fishermen go after them with everything from spears and pitchforks to gaffs and snag hooks.

A common tactic is to cut a line of holes in the ice, perhaps across the entrance of a shallow bay. While several fishermen crouch over the holes, with spears or gaffs held ready, other sportsmen stomp or beat the ice all around with clubs to "drive" or start the carp milling about. Then fishermen at the holes try to connect with the fast moving targets. It's a great way to quickly get cold and wet, but there are no dull moments to think about it.

Perhaps these carp gaffers come the nearest of all ice fishermen to freezing — just to catch a mess of fish. But somehow they never seem to mind it. The number of frostbite fans gets bigger and bigger every year.

Winter whitefish angler walks snowbank along Montana's Yellowstone River.

It's often difficult to distinguish the strike and struggle of whitefish from those of grayling.

The angler was tired and hot, and the placid river seemed devoid of trout. He had fished long and hard and tried every dry fly in his book without even a "looker."

Sitting beneath a friendly cottonwood the angler decided to wait until the sun tipped behind the rim of the colorful rocky ridge, before fishing in earnest. The place was the Bitterroot River valley of southwestern Montana, with the majestic Rocky Mountains etched in the western sky. The angler was a visitor, and the scene reminded him of a calendar photo he'd seen somewhere.

Mopping his brow, the angler noticed a tiny squirt of water along the dancing run, near the edge of the shade, about ten feet from shore. He replaced his glasses, and his heart leaped as he spotted another boiling squirt, then another, and another. Before long there were swirls of feeding fish everywhere. But somehow the rises weren't typical of trout. Since the swirls were delicate, the angler removed his Royal Wulff and tied a size 18 eggsac Adams to the 4X tippet. Then he carefully waded in below the fish and began cautiously casting upstream.

At first the fly slid by the dimples without a taker. *Maybe there was a little drag,* the fisherman thought. But after several more tries, perhaps on the fourth cast, the surface broke apart and the hit was solid. And then came the action! The fish was off to the right, then the left, boring downstream in the fast water. Then it darted across some white water, showing a glimpse of brownish side, to a pool where it hung tight.

Careful to not snap the frail leader or straighten the hook, the angler retrieved line and followed the fish into a quieter pool where he wedged it into shore. He beached it with a mighty splashing kick. It thrashed wildly on the dry rocks, but it wasn't a trout at all. The angler didn't know what to think; was this a "good" fish?

That's the way with whitefishing. You make a perfect cast, you catch a strong 1½-pound fighter, but you hesitate to tell anyone about it. That's a strange paradox because the whitefish belongs to the salmon family—the aristocracy of angling history. It's a good trophy and a great table fish that goes without recognition.

mountain whitefish
THE UNKNOWN ARISTOCRAT
by Bill Browning

Mountain whitefish, excellent dry-fly fish, are more abundant than trout in many western rivers.

This is typical whitefish water—which also produces trout—along Montana's Madison River.

The mountain whitefish *Prosopium williamsoni,* not to be confused with the Great Lakes whitefish, is native to the northern Rocky Mountains from British Columbia eastward to Alberta and southward into the Colorado River drainage. In Montana the mountain whitefish is one of the most abundant game fishes, with very large populations in the Yellowstone, upper Missouri, Flathead (all forks) and Clark Fork (of the Columbia) drainages. Almost none of the cold-water valley streams is without them, says Dr. C.J.D. Brown of Montana State University, but they're not usually found in the small mountain tributaries.

The whitefish has a rounded and elongated body, with a large adipose fin and a deeply forked tail. It might fool some anglers into thinking it's a grayling, which share some of the same waters, but the whitefish's tiny rounded mouth and much shorter dorsal fin are distinctive. Also the whitefish lacks black spots on the sides typical of grayling. Coloration is grayish blue or green above, silvery on the sides and white on the belly. Often the whitefish appears yellowish-brown underwater, so it might be confused with the brown trout. The presence of the adipose fin (a fleshy protuberance between the dorsal and tail) will distinguish it from the sucker and chub, and the small mouth and large scales separate it from the trouts.

Most whitefish you catch will run from 9 to 15 inches. The fish mature at three to four years of age, weighing about ½ pound, and measuring 10 to 11 inches. It's not uncommon to catch three-pounders, but the maximum weight is only about four pounds. Occasionally you will hear of five-pound whitefish from well-meaning anglers, but a biologist I know is still looking for even a four-pounder.

When speaking of whitefish abundance we Montanans sound like Texans. A fisheries study on one mile of the famous Madison River by the Montana Fish and Game Department indicated 350 pounds of whitefish (yearlings and older) per acre, but only 130 to 150 pounds of brown and rainbow trout. The number of whitefish per stream mile was estimated at over 15,000, with a total weight over 8500 pounds.

Whitefish spawn in the fall—from mid-October to mid-November in Montana. They move into riffles near their home pools to scatter eggs on the gravel bed. There's no apparent nesting activity, and they spawn in 5 inches to 4 feet of water and aren't particular about current speed. Apparently a water temperature of about 42°F. triggers egg-laying, which occurs at twilight or soon after dark.

Scientists have often observed the spawning fish holding in the current. At intervals, fish from a small group move close together for 2 to 4 seconds and then drift apart, showing no rapid or violent body movement. These maneuvers leave 5000 to 10,000 eggs per pound of female on the stream bottom. In natural waters of about 35° the eggs incubate from four to five months, the first ones hatching in March. By June the fingerlings disperse into the pools.

The adults recover quickly from spawning and become very active during the winter. Many anglers who pass up whitefish during trout season delight in catching them throughout the cold months.

As early as 1875, thousands of whitefish were captured annually (presumably by seining) from the Provo River in Utah, and sent to Salt Lake City markets as "mountain herring." No license was needed and no creel limit was set.

But in Wyoming in 1936, the legislature declared whitefish a game species, though permitting some seining for several years as a concession to residents depending upon it. In 1951 the sportsmen of Jackson Hole, Wyoming, obtained a winter angling season. The catch that year averaged about ten fish per man, at a rate of four per hour. The short experimental seasons were lengthened when it appeared the angling pressure had not reduced the whitefish populations.

Rocky mountain whitefish hit flies readily, are relatives of trout and salmon

Whitefish have a varied diet, but with decided preferences. It consists primarily of the larvae, pupae, and adults of aquatic and terrestrial insects, plus fish eggs. The most important insects are the midges, Dipterid (true) flies, mosquitoes, stone flies, mayflies and caddis. Studies indicate that midge larvae are the most important of all, with the midge pupae next.

Biologists have learned that whitefish feed primarily during twilight or night and on the bottom, though they occasionally school to surface-feed. But I have also observed them feeding throughout the day, particularly during the summer. Unlike trout, they feed actively the year around.

When there are hatches of insects, the exact weather conditions don't seem to affect feeding. I've caught whitefish before, during, and after thunderstorms and on bright, hot days. I remember one day on the Yellowstone, which is known for occasional lunker whitefish, when the sky was quite threatening, turning quickly into heavy rain. I worked a good school of whitefish throughout the downpour, and the fish hit practically any fly I tied on. I ran from large Grizzly Wulffs to tiny Cahills. One of the best that day (good for trout too) is the Adams fly with the egg sac. When a fly became plastered with fish slime I'd change to another, and I kept catching whitefish.

I've taken whitefish on every kind of tackle and lure, from dry fly to bait to hardware. But what I enjoy best is the dry fly fishing. Usually a small fly is best, but often when fishing for trout I've hooked good whitefish on a size 10 Joe's Hopper or other big fly. I've also taken them on big red-and-white or brass spoons with spinning gear.

When I'm fishing for whitefish specifically, I'm always careful to tie on a delicate leader and lures. Flies in sizes 14 to 18 are most successful, perhaps because they hook into the whitefish's tiny mouth better than the larger flies. When I get lots of strikes but few catches, I always tie on a smaller fly.

Since whitefish feed heavily on trout foods, any of the smaller well-known trout flies will work. The various quill patterns, mosquitoes, Adams, Gray Hackle, Cahills, Hendrickson, gnats, and even small Wulff flies are excellent. It's worth noting here that whitefish under study have been shown to prefer red.

Whitefish strike similarly to the trouts. In fact, unless you're experienced and see the fish when it hits it's tough to distinguish the strike from a trout hit. Generally whitefish are bottom fighters like the brown trout, but they sometimes thrash wildly on the surface. When you hang a good whitefish—say, a 2-pounder—you'd better be prepared for a good fight. Normally whitefish prefer fast water, which adds force to the size, strength, and endurance of the fish itself.

To find whitefish I generally watch for a small boiling hit on the surface with a sidewise fling of water. They feed in many types of water but perhaps prefer the shoreline glides. In a large river I generally find them in knee-deep water, some 5 to 20 feet from the bank. Often I hook them at the tails of long pools or in the intermediate depth of a dimpled run or choppy current. Though they're supposed to prefer the deep pools, I seldom fish for them here.

I remember one bright, beautiful summer day on the

Angler works spectacular whitefish water along Montana's Dearborn River.

Tiny flies are most effective for whitefish. Size 18 "snow flies" shown here are favorites for winter fishing.

Fly-rodder casts for whitefish beneath irrigation flume on upper Missouri River.

Bighole River when I was midstream in thigh-deep water fishing for trout. I wanted a big fish for photos and was working hard in a river alive with feeding trout. But I just couldn't help catching whitefish, because the water was ideal for both species. I'd hook a whitefish and try to horse it from the run to avoid downing any trout. Some seven or eight whitefish later, I suddenly hit a big rainbow trout of perhaps four pounds, which gave me fits until my hook bent and I lost the fish downstream in some fast water. Since then I've never passed up a good whitefish run when fishing for trout.

The best whitefish rivers in Montana are the Yellowstone, Missouri, Gallatin (both east and west forks), Jefferson, Madison, Smith, Shields, Stillwater, Boulder, Bitterroot, Clark Fork of the Columbia, Thompson, Kootenai, Bull, Yaak, Fisher, the Flathead and its forks, the Swan, Jocko, and the Bighole. All these also offer outstanding trout fishing.

Sportsmen in several areas are finally taking note of the great potential of whitefishing. In the Bitterroot Valley they have asked the Fish and Game Commission for a closure of fishing from October 1 through November each year, to correspond with the spawning period—this despite the trout season which runs through the end of November. Some progress has been made too on setting creel limits on whitefish, but in most areas these are very liberal. Montana Fish and Game men are interested in any management policies the sportsmen will support to improve the image and following of the species. The winter season for whitefish is opened from December through the following year.

Winter fishing sees lots of activity, and with high limits of 30 or more whitefish many anglers prefer them to trout, winter whitefish are delicious eating, especially when smoked. During the cold months bottom fishing is most productive, with maggots a popular bait.

If the whitefish is neglected and is so abundant, you might wonder why there are seasons to protect and manage them. Fish management men and sportsmen actually are trying to encourage whitefishing, and they believe there's a natural urge to fish for anything on which there are certain restrictions. Perhaps that's good for the future of fishing. Should trout angling deteriorate we may still have an abundance of whitefish to supply sport and fine food for anglers of the future.

For more information write the Montana Chamber of Commerce, Box 1730, Helena, Montana 59601. Ask for a general fishing bulletin I've prepared titled *Big Sky Fishing*. The organization will answer general travel queries and send road maps and copies of fishing regulations.

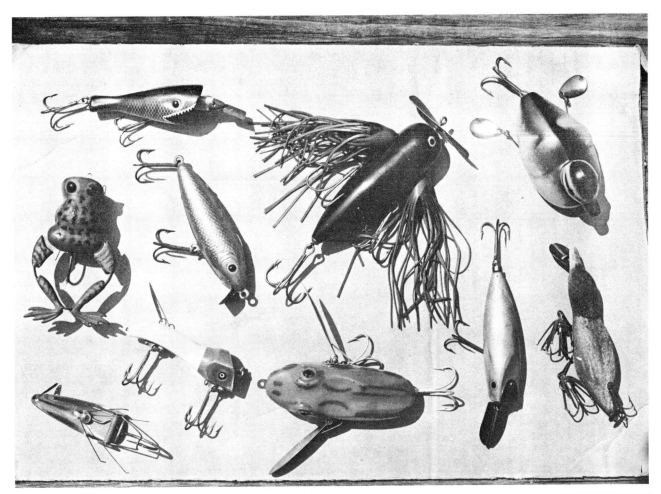

This lure selection, mostly meant for bass or northern pike, contains two imitation plastic ducklings, a redwing blackbird fallen on the water, a kicking frog and a fish eating a smaller fish.

..... speaking of

CRAZY

Fishing lures!

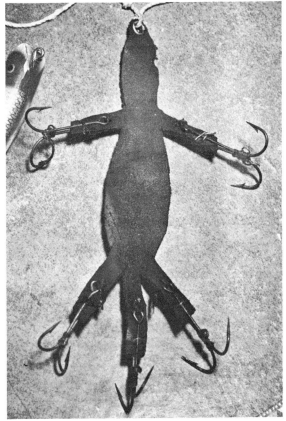

This unique bait, evidently intended to imitate a hellbender, was cut from an old innertube.

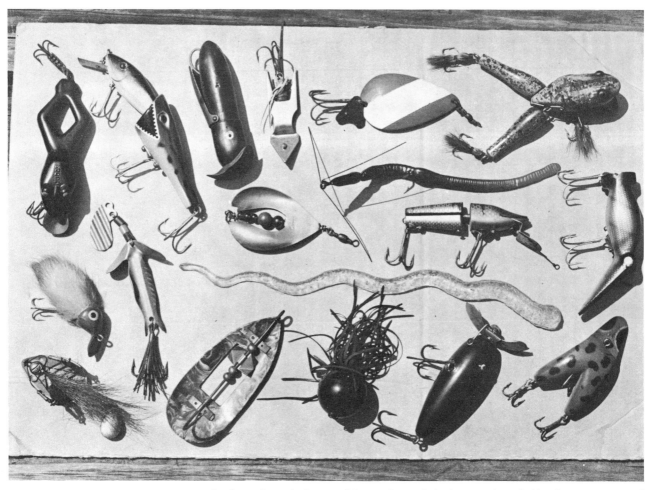

Another curious selection containing a scissor-tailed minnow, spinner inside of a spoon, assorted frog imitations, a rabbit's foot, half of a beer can opener and others.

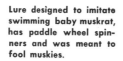

Lure designed to imitate swimming baby muskrat, has paddle wheel spinners and was meant to fool muskies.

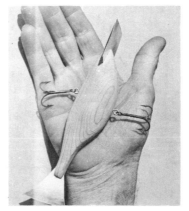

Weighted wooden plug for ice fishing. The plug hangs down straight from the hole and is activated by jigging up and down.

Muskies and northern pike are known to eat ducklings in the spring— so this designer offered them a genuine mounted duckling with treble hooks attached.

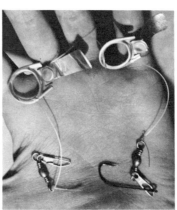

Openers from new self-open beer cans have been used successfully to catch cutthroat trout in Yellowstone Lake.

The Turneffe camp offers complete tropical island escape as well as the finest saltwater game fishing.

GOOD FISHING IS HIS LIFE WORK

By George Laycock

Meet a man who has built two great fishing camps and is always looking for others.

Below us the matted palms and tangled vines of the Yucatan jungles blanketed the hills and valleys in endless deep green. Here the ancient Mayans once grew their corn and squash and now and then paused in their labors long enough to offer up a human sacrifice. But the creeping jungle had pulled a blanket over even their tallest temples and left these jungles to jaguars and roving bands of lurking *banditos*.

Then the plane droned in over Belize, capitol city of British Honduras. With its back to the jungle and its face to the blue Caribbean, this port town, once an infamous slave trading center, dozes in the sub-tropical sun.

Who would think of migrating to this place to create a plush resort for traveling outdoorsmen? I knew the answer to this one, and the chances were good that he would be waiting for us outside the dingy little customs office at the airport.

He looked much the same as he had the last time I saw him, except that now this professional fishing camp manager wore a sport shirt and shorts, and his skin looked as if someone had dipped him in brown shoe polish. Of medium height and build, Bill Haerr, then in his early forties, seemed to be everywhere at once, soft-speaking and calm but highly efficient.

"I think I have things figured out now the way I want them." We were rumbling down the narrow, rutted road toward the center of town where Bill's boat rode gently at anchor. "I can winter here on my little island in the sun. We've got soft sea breezes and fresh coconuts drop off the trees right in the front yard. Then I can go back to the Arctic for the summer, and both places we've got the world's best fishing. That's living."

Beneath the blazing tropical sun, my mind flashed back 3,500 miles to the distant Arctic where I first met Bill. It seemed another world. On that trip several years earlier, I had flown north beyond the Arctic Circle, following reports of fantastic lake trout fishing. Bill had greeted us at the shore of Great Bear Lake. Later Bill and I met several times, but always it was in that cold country toward the top of the earth. Recent word that he had migrated to the Caribbean reached me when the north was locked in its mid-winter ice. And, knowing that Bill has a habit of showing up in some of the world's most exciting locations, I started south with Bob Hart of Cincinnati, to track the restless Bill Haerr down in his new fishing camp.

In town I talked with the driver who had brought us from the airport. "Are there any Mayan ruins," I asked, "within easy driving distance?"

Bill and Dolly Haerr, native Minnesotans who have built luxurious fishing camps on opposite sides of the globe.

"Good ones," he said in his excellent English. "They're just uncovering one now. When you come back from fishing — just ask for me. Ask for Smitty at the hotel."

Bill's camp in the sun-washed, palm-fringed Turneffe Islands is a 25-mile run across the open Caribbean from the port of Belize. Down past the Turneffe Islands, along the east coast of the Yucatan Peninsula, runs one of the world's largest barrier reefs. The reef extends through the Caribbean for 190 miles and harbors so many species of sport fish that few fishermen can ever hope to catch a good sampling of all of them.

Lonely little sail boats manned by lobster fishermen sometimes move around the islands, their crews out of touch with the world until they have their pay load salted down and start back for port. Few other people can be found through much of this wild seascape. This vast, open, lonely expanse of sea, sand, sunshine, and mangrove flats, is populated by pelicans, terns, man-o-war birds and countless fish and shellfish. Bill first learned about the Turneffe Islands from Vic Barothy.

I had met Vic some years ago in Cuba, about the time Fidel crawled out of the mountains to take over in Havana. Vic, originally from Michigan by way of Islamorada, Florida, operated a fleet of houseboats from which visiting fishermen caught uncounted tarpon and snook.

He knew that he was destined to be tossed out of Cuba and have his property confiscated by Castro. But Vic had quietly made a few trips to other sections of the Caribbean. One of these took him to British Honduras.

Then one dark night three of his houseboats putted away from the dock on the Isle of Pines, and like the Nina, Pinta, and the Santa Maria, set off rocking gently across the blue waves of the Caribbean. They came eventually to Belize where Vic built a cozy new fishing camp on the river.

But soon Vic heard tales about the fishing out around the Turneffe Islands. Eventually, he established a camp there and set up a few buildings from which fishermen could explore the barrier reef. It was the only sport fishing camp anywhere in those lonely islands.

Meanwhile the restless Bill Haerr, who had long had his eye on the Caribbean, learned during the spring of 1966 that Vic Barothy was thinking of selling the island portion of his British Honduras operation to concentrate on his mainland camp.

Bill is driven by a beaver complex. He looks at a wild little island and sees a vision of a fine big fishing camp. "Then," says his wife and partner Dolly, "nothing will do until he has built it."

He had already built a second lodge in the Arctic. That was now finished and running smoothly, and for Bill much of the challenge had been met.

Flying south across Canada, the states, and the Caribbean, Bill turned over in his mind the sheer beauty of his plan. Fishing in the Arctic lasts only for a couple of ice-free months in mid-summer. This leaves the winter open for running a fishing camp in the land of coconut palms. The way he had it plotted, Bill and Dolly could migrate like the shorebirds and follow the seasons from one wonderful extreme to the other.

He took a quick look at Vic's camp and began immediately to visualize additions. He flew back to the states, hurriedly lined up his stockholders and closed the deal.

With a brand new fishing camp on their hands Bill and Dolly began enlarging and changing the Turneffe Island operation. Bill had a barge load of supplies shipped in from New Orleans, everything from 20 new fishing boats and outboard motors to a generator for the electric plant. He added to the camp until the capacity was doubled. And when the building was well under way, Bill and his crew hacked away at the tangled vegetation, pushed back the jungle and enlarged the size of the camp clearing.

What makes Bill willing to gamble on such a dream in a distant wilderness? Dolly sometimes thinks he belongs to an earlier age. "He's a pioneer," she says, "always looking for new challenges." This search goes back into his high school days, when he went to Florida and worked for a year as a commercial fisherman.

Then he returned to Minnesota and married Dolly. They headed for Florida again in their Model A. But always in the back of Bill's mind was that restlessness, driving dissatisfaction with crowds and the settled places. He dreamed of lonely distant landscapes where a man might still fashion the wilderness to his needs.

In the summer of 1953 Bill traveled to Northern Manitoba to take a job managing a fishing lodge on Cormorant Lake. He had found what he really wanted to do, and during the years afterward he continued to manage fishing lodges until he landed on the shores of Great Bear. Within a few years Bill became one of the most widely known operators of successful wilderness fishing lodges in the western hemisphere.

Shortly after taking over the Turneffe Island camp he began assembling a crew of local helpers. Some of his guides worked previously with Vic. All are youthful men who have always lived around the sea and loved it with a love that won't let them leave. My guide explained one day that before coming with Bill, he had worked on one of the little sailboats we saw occasionally around the islands. His specialty was diving for lobsters, sometimes to surprising depths. The equipment was a face mask and a pair of flippers. He had spent much of his life staring sharks in the eye. One evening three years ago, he came into Vic's camp and Vic asked him if he wanted a job. That evening he left the lobster boat. He has been guiding fishermen ever since, first for Vic then for Bill.

When we docked the Sea Fair at Bill's camp several hours of sunlight remained. We had come a long way to fish, so Bob and I made a fast change into fishing clothes and were soon trolling heavy feathered jigs along the deep water.

Before long we began to feel the "bumps." Something down there was alive — and hungry. A fish picked up my bait and gave it a gentle tug, then began moving away.

Visiting anglers catch lake trout like these at Bill Haerr's camp on Great Bear Lake, 3500 miles from Br. Honduras.

Ohioan Bob Hart with a bonefish taken wading within sight of the Turneffe Island camp.

Haerr's newest camp on Turneffe Island, British Honduras. The camp is surrounded with bonefish, permit and a hundred other species of game fish.

I heaved back and brought the rod tip up fast and high.

Under such a circumstance, I chose to give him all the tackle would stand from the first, and pumped and cranked as fast as he would come. Part way up the bends hit him, and he was dead when he came to the boat, a big, fat, red grouper, 20 pounds of fine table fare for the camp dinner.

During the following days four of us staying in the same cabin fished together, with two men to each boat. One morning I was fishing with Gil Vandermail of Grand Rapids, Michigan when some monster suddenly picked up Gil's bait and started off with it. It was the opening round of a battle that lasted more than two hours.

Gil's 30-pound test line was strained to the limit. He pumped and cranked. Time after time, the fish pulled off great lengths of line and Gil had to go through the whole fight again. But he handled the fish with skill born of long experience, hoping he was tied to a huge sea bass.

Late in the morning, peering down through the deep blue water, we could make out the flash of a white belly. Our guide, Joel Westby, spoke softly. "Shark."

"Damn," Gil said. "I've got a notion to cut him off." But he brought the fish on up to the boat, and Joel picked up a club stored in the boat for such moments. He began beating the shark around the head as if venting an age-old hatred.

Other times we concentrated on tarpon around the narrow mangrove-bordered channels between the islands. Or, when the tide was right, we waded the shallow flats seeking the elusive bonefish. This is one of the best bonefishing spots in the Caribbean.

Behind the big barrier reef lie miles of bonefish flats where the bones cruise when the tide is right. Pole a boat quietly across the flats, stop often to study the waters, and you will see their dark forms as they travel in schools. The bonefish is a magnificent fish to have on the loose end of your line. Few fish in the ocean can match it for dash and strength. Hook one and your line sings and whines off the reel. With luck, you may have a few feet of line left when he slows down.

But then he's off in the other direction. The race continues until he breaks the line or is worn out. Most bone-fishermen gently release their catch because the bonefish is not considered edible for humans. A three or four pounder is a good one but during the week bonefish weighing more than seven pounds came into camp.

Bill has a two-way radio which keeps him in contact with the mainland. The commercial radio station in Belize frequently broadcasts personal emergency messages to people in the jungles or out on the islands. Such a call came one evening for Joel Westby, our guide.

Joel's father was seriously ill and Joel was wanted in town. It was already dark. Instead of sending the big boat in, Bill sent Joel and another guide in one of the faster skiffs across 25 miles of open water with a 20-horse outboard. Joel's cousin, who had run him into town, returned the following morning in time to take over as our guide. That's the way it goes.

After a week of fishing we loaded our duffle aboard the Sea Fair again. Waiting at the dock in Belize was Smitty, the cab driver.

British Honduras is only 75 miles wide and stretches for 175 miles along the Caribbean coast. It borders Mexico and Guatemala and is the last remaining British Crown Colony in Central America. In 1964 it took its first step toward independence. The major language is English and the unit of money is the B.H. dollar.

This is the sub-tropical world Bill and Dolly migrate to during those winter months when the Far North is locked in its deep freeze. The problems of running a fishing camp are much the same in either place. Often their familiar northern guests show up at Turneffe Island too. Every year when they arrive they find that Bill and Dolly have added some new feature to their camp operation.

Even in the unlikely event that Bill grew rich at his business, he would always be driven by that restless spirit that keeps him working on improvements until he exhausts his ideas for fashioning a better fishing camp. Characteristically, the Haerrs have seldom settled down long in any one place, although their home address is St. Paul, Minnesota where both of them grew up and went to school.

A fishing camp manager anywhere will testify to the importance of a well-managed kitchen and dining room, and this part of the operation falls to Dolly. Just as Bill does, she likes the changing scene and the challenge of running a comfortable lodge in some remote wild setting. And when Bill has to be away on business, Dolly calmly takes over his duties as well as her own.

Recently Bill bought a large, sea-going boat on which fishermen who want to vary their days of fishing the nearby reefs and flats can stay out at sea for days at a time for the big off-shore species, especially the billfish. The new boat also speeded up the trip from the mainland in Belize city out to his remote Turneffe Island fishing lodge.

When I last saw Bill he was on the flying bridge of the Sea Fair. He had returned us to Belize to meet our plane. He double-checked to see that his guests were taken care of to the time their plane would depart. Then, with Joel at the wheel, he climbed nimbly aboard and the boat eased away from the dock into the current where Belize River fans out into the Yucatan Basin.

Bill had things the way he wanted them. Although the rest of us were headed back for the cities and the crowds, he was moving off again in the opposite direction. As usual he was headed away from the crowds and toward the fish. And, in spite of the fact that his camp was already luxurious, he was probably thinking all the way out to his island of ways to improve it. Or his mind may already have turned to some other wild frontier where he might go with Dolly to build one more fishing lodge.

A pair of beauties from Great Bear Lake.

Sunlight can be very damaging to the eyes unless protected by the proper sunglasses.

A COMPLETE GUIDE AND TODAY'S BEST MEDICAL ADVICE ON HOW TO BE A HEALTHY FISHERMAN

BY C. JOSEPH CROSS, M.D. F.A.C.P.

Unfortunately almost every angler will some day be forced to administer first aid—to himself or a partner—and he should be prepared for it. This article (which might wisely be carried in a tackle box) suggests how to prevent trouble as much as how to care for it.

There is an old medical maxim which every medical student learns at about the same time he hears of the Hippocrates Oath. It is "First of all, do no harm." The basic truth of this statement is such that it should be tattooed on the inside of the skull of anyone, professional or amateur, who attempts to administer aid and comfort to an ailing individual. Many tragedies have occurred from well intentioned but overzealous activity which converts minor injuries to irreparable damage. Yet there are other circumstances in which prompt and proper action can be life-saving. More often than not, the best treatment is the least treatment. Fishing is fun, so let's have fun fishing and if certain problems do occur, let's take care of them properly.

This fisherman could get in trouble landing this large musky—by hooking himself in the hand.

Double trouble here from barracuda's teeth and the hooks. This fish must be handled with care.

CUTS AND BRUISES

The average fisherman's tackle box is full of potential hazards. The sharp edge of a cleaning knife, the serrated edge of a scaler, or the needle-sharp barb of a fish-hook when improperly or carelessly used can lacerate, puncture, abraid, or contuse the skin. Blood usually follows in various colors and rates of flow according to the depth and location of the injury. Bright red spurting blood comes from an artery, dull red blood flows smoothly from a vein, and medium red blood oozes from shallow capillary cuts and abrasions.

A cut deep enough to produce spurting or copiously flowing blood is fortunately rare in the average fisherman's experience, but it may occur with the unwise use of an axe or sheath knife. This represents a medical emergency and the victim should be speeded to the closest doctor or hospital. But first of all the bleeding must be controlled. Direct pressure over the laceration itself must be the number one first-aid measure. A sterile gauze pad is preferable, but as infection is not the problem it once was, and as the bleeding must be slowed at all costs, any cloth will do—a folded handkerchief, a folded undershirt, anything!

The cloth may be held in place by the flat palm of the hand until gauze or other material can be applied as a wrapping. Added pressure may be applied to the pressure points between the wound and the heart if necessary to control the bleeding. The best pressure wrapping is an elastic bandage of the type used to support a sprained ankle, but gauze or cloth strips of any kind will do.

The key word is pressure, but not so much as to cut off the circulation to the rest of the limb. This brings up the hazards in the use of a tourniquet. A tourniquet is rarely necessary, and its overzealous use can cause much more damage to the limb than the cut on which it is used. The only time it should even be considered is when the limb is severed or so badly cut as to be beyond repair. Bleeding from any other type of injury can almost always be controlled by a pressure bandage, and unless one has had fairly extensive first-aid training, the use of a tourniquet hould be discouraged.

The important things to remember here are pressure and speed—pressure applied to the site of the wound and speed in getting the injured person to the closest medical aid.

For the average cut or abrasion, the most important medicine, the most important surgical procedure, is plenty of soap and water. Cleanliness is all important; a clean wound will heal. The first ingredients of any first-aid kit should be a small bottle of liquid medicated soap and a box of sterile cotton. The bleeding area should be washed with water and thoroughly cleaned with liberal applications of soapy cotton. If still bleeding, the application of pressure through a sterile gauze pad will usually suffice. A dry sterile dressing may be applied and the area bandaged. Sterile dressings come individually packaged in all sizes and shapes, from tiny adhesive bands to large 'four by fours,' and a selection of these together with a roll of gauze and adhesive, should be included in your emergency kit.

Sutures and suturing should be left to the experts and the so-called butterfly bandage—adhesive tape designed to hold the edge of a wound together—should also be discouraged. I have never seen these do more than hold dirt in a contaminated wound and the key to healing is cleanliness. Leave the iodine and other antiseptics at home; there has never yet been a better method of immediate cleaning than soap and water.

A special type of injury peculiar to the fishermen's fraternity is the imbedded fishhook. The sharp barbed hook designed to prevent the fish from shaking loose is equally effective in resisting removal from the human epidermis.

The time honored method of correcting this predicament is the simple one of pushing the barb through the skin, and with the wire cutting edge of the usual fisherman's pliers, cutting either the shaft or the barb so the remainder can be easily pulled through. Before attempting this maneuver, be sure to remember that the skin is a rather tough material and the shaft of the hook must be firmly grasped in the pliers. Then firm, fast pressure must be used. It is well to wash both hook and skin with soap and water before attempting removal and sterilize with alcohol (or whiskey) if available. After the hook is removed, encourage bleeding and again wash and clean thoroughly. A closed wound of this type must be considered as potentially infected, especially tetanus-prone, so your physician should be seen promptly to administer the injection to prevent tetanus.

Incidentally, this is a good time to remind you of the importance of being up to date on your tetanus shots. Outdoorsmen are especially susceptible to the type of injuries which promote this dreadful but preventable disease.

From Australia comes another method which, my son Doug tells me from practical experience, is completely painless. Thomas Cook, M.B.B.S., of Carramulka, South Australia described this technique as used by the fishermen in the St. Vincents Gulf area.

The barb is depressed and freed from the skin by depressing the shank of the hook, and a loop of string is placed around the curve of the hook. The patient's finger is placed on a firm surface and the eye of the hook is firmly grasped by the thumb and forefinger of the operator's left hand. The loop of string is securely wrapped around the operator's right index finger. Steadying the loop against the curve of the hook with the middle finger of the left hand, the operator suddenly jerks with the right hand, keeping the pull parallel with the shank with the barb still depressed. The barb should come out painlessly and the same cleaning and preventative precautions should be observed as described above.

SPRAINS AND STRAINS

The rocky bottom of a fast moving stream is not the most stable of footing; an ankle joint loosely encased in a flexible rubber boot is not the most stable of supports, and this combination often produces damage to ligaments, tendons, muscles and blood vessels which have been stretched too far. These are notoriously painful injuries causing much limitation of motion, swelling, bruising, and frequent discoloration of the involved joint.

Treatment is fairly simple—cold, heat, and support. For the first twenty-four hours heat should not be used because of the injured blood vessels and the possibility of increasing bleeding. As soon as possible after the injury apply ice packs or cold compresses to the area, keeping them up for twenty minutes at a time, three times during the first day. A portable ice chest is a handy first-aid measure here, and in many areas the icy water of the stream itself may be utilized.

After twenty-four hours, hot packs or hot soaks should be used two or three times daily.

Support, preferably in the form of an elastic bandage, should be applied to the involved joint, and early use is encouraged. With a sprained ankle, bear weight on it as soon as endurable; with a sprained wrist, move it as soon as possible.

A few points to remember! A severe sprain may mask a fracture and if the discomfort is too great or recovery too slow, an x-ray should be obtained. If adhesive rather than an elastic bandage has been used to provide support, be very careful in the use of heat because of the danger of burns beneath the tape. Finally, if walking unassisted is too difficult, a cane or even a crutch can be easily improvised from some sturdy stream-side timber.

Obvious fractures, of course, require prompt medical attention, and first-aid measures should be limited to improvising splints which will keep the injured limb as immobile as possible. Any rigid object—lumber, broom stick, tent pole, or peeled branch which is long enough to extend above and below the fracture site may be used. The splint should be padded if at all possible, and the bindings should not be so tight as to cut off the circulation.

Slings may be used to keep the arm and shoulder area quiet, and if a leg or back is involved, a stretcher can be made from two long poles and a blanket or sleeping bag. If the injury is serious and medical attention reasonably available, it is best to let the victim rest where he is until more skilled help is available to move him. The important thing is to keep the fracture area as quiet and stable as possible until proper orthopoedic treatment can be obtained.

BURNS

Brushing the hot edge of a grill during a shore lunch or chomping on the wrong end of a cigar in the excitement of pulling in a lunker bass exposes one to another of the minor hazards of outdoor activity, namely burns. When a hot object comes into contact with a cool skin several things happen: the blood vessels dilate, fluids leak into the area, the protein material in the cells coagulate like the white of a fried egg, and it hurts! Medically we classify burns into three types.

First degree burns are the mild ones, involving only the outer layer of skin. These produce redness and swelling but no blisters.

Second degree burns involve all the layers of skin, outer and inner, producing blistering but not deep enough damage to prevent the growth of new skin.

Third degree burns are deeper, more serious burns which destroy the tissues underlying the skin. These are beyond the limits of first aid and require skilled medical attention.

First and second degree burns usually heal well within two weeks, but certain "do's" and "don't" should be followed. The number one problem complicating burns of the more serious type is infection, and even for relatively minor ones the first principle is cleanliness. Here again the bottle of liquid medicated soap and the cotton should be used and the involved area cleaned with gentle thoroughness. I put this question to one of my colleagues who specializes in the treatment of severe burn cases. "What kind of first-aid do you prefer to see in those patients who come into your office with burn injuries?" His immediate answer was "soap and water."

After the area is thoroughly clean there are several things that can be done. There is increasing evidence that

Cooking around an open fire exposes an angler to burns. Know what to do when this occurs?

the use of cold water will favorably affect the progress and healing of a burned area and it certainly helps ease the pain. If your portable ice box and a bucket are available, make a chilled pail of ice water and immerse the burned area in it. If it is an area that cannot comfortably be submerged, use cold wet packs and change them frequently.

If the skin is unblistered, a light application of one of the many anesthetic-antibiotic ointments may be spread over the involved area. A tube of this medicine may be obtained from your pharmacist and should be a part of your emergency medical kit. A sterile dry gauze dressing should then be applied and no complications need be expected.

With blistered second degree burns, one of the most important DONT'S is to leave blisters alone. Do not open them because this is a job for your doctor. An open blister is an open door for wound infection, and this operation should be carried out under sterile conditions not likely to be available in the field. Should the blisters break spontaneously, leave it intact, do not (as many first-aid books recommend) attempt to trim it. The skin of the blister is in itself an excellent dressing material.

in itself an excellent dressing material.

Another DON'T—never use a greasy or oily material on a second or third degree burn. Cleanse them thoroughly as soon as possible and use a dry sterile dressing until more specific measures can be taken. Leave the ointment in the first-aid kit.

DO—Clean thoroughly with liquid soap and water. Immerse in cold water, or use cold wet packs to the area. Use light application of an anesthetic antibiotic ointment to first degree burns. Cover with dry, sterile dressing.

DON'T—Open a blister. Cover a blister with an oily or greasy material (including butter).

SUNBURN

Each year there are enough people who develop an incapacitating sunburn which ruins many days of good vacation time that we should emphasize a better understanding of the perils of too much sunlight. Solar radiation, the fancy name for the rays of the sun, reaches the earth in three basic forms; ultra-violet, visible light and infra-red. These are separated by different wave lengths for each type of radiation, the shortest being ultra-violet and progressing through the visible colors of the spectrum. The longest are the infra-red. The trouble comes in the short wave lengths, the ultra-violet rays, which penetrate through clear skies or cloud cover and produce the reddened, inflamed and blistered skin which is all too familiar to the incautious fisherman. It is the ability of ultra-violet radiation to penetrate through a cloudy sky which produces sunburns on days when the visible light of the sun never appears.

Prevention is far better than cure and in this respect there are several points which should be remembered. First if you are sandy-haired, fair-skinned, and blue-eyed, be doubly careful since you are much more susceptible to sunlight than your brown-eyed friends. The time of day is important, the peak of the burning time usually occurs between 10:00 A.M. and 2:00 P.M. (fortunately not the best time for fishing activities),but in warmer climates and higher altitudes the critical time may be extended to 5:00 P.M. Reflected light can burn just as effectively as direct rays and reflection from a sandy beach or a light-colored boat deck can sometimes almost double the risk of sunburn. If you are taking any kind of medication, be sure to check with your personal physician as to any sun sensitizing effects it might have. Certain medications, including some sulfa's, antibiotics, diabetic tablets, fluid pills, and tranquilizers are known to produce an increased reaction to sunlight.

One additional factor has been well expressed by the Committee on Cosmetics of the American Medical Association. "The threat of malignancy is not a concern of the occasional sun bather, but the evidence is clear that chronic exposure to sunlight can be one of the major factors in the production of pre-cancerous and cancerous conditions of the skin. This is as pertinent to the health of the ardent outdoor sportsman and sun enthusiast as it is to the farmer, the sailor, the sheepherder or the cowboy who follow vocations in which chronic solar exposure has long been recognized as an occupational hazard." And it is the same ultraviolet rays which cause sunburn that with repeated exposures over long periods of time may cause skin cancer.

Obviously some sort of protection is in order. The best protection is a broad-brimmed hat and long sleeved, closely woven clothing, preferably in red, brown or orange colors. These have been shown to be the most impervious to the sun rays. White is satisfactory but when damp it loses its protective effect. The length of time of exposure to the sun should be increased gradually day by day, and twenty minutes is usually long enough for the first day. A good suntan lotion or sun screen will enable the pallid fisherman to stay out longer. There are many of these preparations on the market and their efficiency depends on the type and concentration of the sun-screening ingredient, how thickly it is applied and how frequently it is re-applied, especially when sweating or swimming.

Always check the labels: those listing benzophenone, paraaminobenzoic acid (PABA), tannic acid and red veterinary petroleum probably work best. For the feminine angler, a simple solution is the use of pancake make-up, and its effectiveness as a sun screen also depends upon the thickness and frequency of application.

If the mid-day fishing has been too lively or if you haven't been able to leave the fighting chair on a tropic afternoon, what should be done to relieve the resulting rosy glow? Cold compresses and aspirin will help as much as anything. The old fashioned remedies such as butter, vinegar, and baby oil should be avoided, although warm baths with oatmeal or corn starch and baking soda may be comforting. A light application of an anesthetic-antibiotic ointment may be used for one or two times, but continued use should be avoided since these can sometimes cause an allergic rash which will slow down the healing process.

If more than thirty percent of the body surface is involved, and if blistering is extensive, it is best to seek medical attention.

In Summary:

Stay out of the mid-day sun.

Increase exposure gradually.

Wear protective clothing, preferably brown, red or orange.

Use a good sun screen.

Check any medication for possible sun sensitivity.

If mildly burned, use aspirin and cold compresses.

If uncomfortably or severely burned, see your doctor.

Sunglasses are an absolute necessity for bright days out on open water.

OTHER HEAT PROBLEMS

The natural environment in which the fisherman prefers to find himself usually prevents the sort of illness which fell so many people during heat waves in the city. However, too long an exposure in an open boat or along a beach in mid-day may lead to some untoward symptoms.

Heat stroke and heat exhaustion are the most serious of these; produced by the failure of the heat regulating system of the body. This system fails when it has been working too hard, when the vaporization which normally enables the body to lose heat no longer is operating. The individual stops sweating—always a danger sign—and the skin becomes hot and dry. The temperature rises rapidly and collapse occurs.

Since the mortality rate of this condition in its full blown state ranges from 20 to 80 percent, roughly paralleling the age of the patient, prevention is most important. Get to a cool location at the first sign of trouble, which may start with a headache, restlessness, avid thirst, lack of perspiration or increase in heart rate. If serious faintness or unconsciousness occurs, speed is essential in lowering body temperature. A cold water bath or spray is the most effective method for total body cooling. Wet sheets may be wrapped around the victim and evaporation accelerated by the use of fans. Medical aid should be summoned as quickly as possible but do not wait for it. Untreated heat stroke is fatal!

The salt loss which occurs with excessive sweating can cause symptoms, especially in people who perform heavy physical activity and drink a lot of fluid without replacing the salt. Severe muscle cramps, especially in the limbs and abdomen, are the usual complaint and can be treated or prevented by an adequate salt intake. Salty foods and the liberal use of the shaker at meal time are usually sufficient to meet the needs of the body, but salt tablets may be used during periods of heavy sweating.

Prickly heat is an uncomfortable, itching skin eruption due to the blocking of the pores of the sweat glands during hot weather. This occurs most frequently at the neck, wrist, armpits and elbows and is best prevented by wearing loose, well ventilated clothes and bathing or showering with a limited use of soap. Cool baths will give prompt but temporary relief. A heavy salt intake may increase the symptoms as it puts a heavier load on the already clogged up sweat glands.

SUN GLASSES

Sunlight can be even more damaging to the eyes than to the skin. The short waved ultra-violet rays can damage the outer part of the eyeball while the longer waved infra-red rays can penetrate through the lens and burn the retina, the working part of the eye where visual images are made. Ultra-violet injuries produce the irritation known as snow blindness, while infra-red damage occurs when looking directly at the sun, and is most often seen as "eclipse blindness."

Sunglasses are the answer. The primary purpose of this important bit of equipment is to reduce excessive brightness while still allowing the wearer to see clearly. They will also absorb some of the harmful infra-red and ultra-violet rays which can damage the eye. Sunglass lenses are recorded as having transmission or density values representing the amount of light which reaches the eye; a measurement of 10 to 20 percent is best for beach or snow, while 20 to 30 percent is satisfactory for daylight driving and similar activities. At more than 30 percent transmission a lens is not especially protective. Both lenses should be equally dark—look *at* them as well as through them—and they should be made of unbreakable case-hardened glass or a high quality plastic.

Polarized lenses are frequently helpful, permitting light rays to hit the eye from one direction only. Their light transmission values range from 12 to 16 percent and may be particularly useful in decreasing the glare from a watery surface. Finally, choose neutral grey or greenish tints, as the others—orange, yellow, blue or rose—distort natural colors. The world does not look better this way.

Florida Keys guides give themselves extra protection by mounting home-made sun shields on the sides of their sunglasses.

SNAKES

This year approximately 7,000 people will be bitten by poisonous snakes in the United States and this will result in 14 or 15 deaths and many days of serious and incapacitating illness. About 10% of these bites will occur during hunting and fishing activities, and the angler may expect to get the worst of it as he will be out when the snakes are most active. They will be more sluggish or in hibernation during the fall hunting season in many areas.

Lest this information discourages anyone from going afield, remember that the average danger of being bitten is very slight and that the mortality rate in adequately treated cases is as low as 3%. There is usually far more danger in driving your car to the fishing area. However reassuring these statistics may be, there is still a great latent fear in most people and one of the best protective measures is to know your snakes and know their habits.

In this country about 98% of these poisonous bites are inflicted by pit vipers, the remaining 2% being caused by coral snakes and foreign captive venomous snakes. The pit vipers *(Crotalidae)* include the rattlesnake, copperhead and cottonmouth moccasin, at least one of which is found in every state except Maine, Alaska and Hawaii. The name comes from the presence of a pit located between the eye and nostril on either side of the head. Other features aiding in identification include a flat triangular head, elliptical pupils, well-developed fangs which spring from the upper jaw when their mouths are open, the rattle, and the single sub-caudal plates (the flat plaque-like skin plates beneath the tail.)

Harmless snakes do not have facial pits, the pupils are round, the subcaudal plates are double, and the teeth are small and shaped in a U-pattern with no fangs.

The coral snake is a small, colorful, relatively placid and retiring reptile with an extremely poisonous venom. It is easily recognized by its red and black bands, separated by yellow or cream colored stripes: "red next to yellow will kill a fellow."

There is still a good deal of controversy about the proper method of first aid treatment and even the most knowledgeable of medical authorities are often in disagreement. Before doing *anything,* be sure to determine if a significant amount of venom was introduced into the system as the snake will often strike a glancing blow or be deflected by clothing, and no poison will penetrate the skin. The four signs which indicate significant venom injection are as follows:

1—Visible puncture wounds.
2—Burning pain.
3—Swelling.
4—Redness and discoloration.

If any of these four are present, first aid measures should be started immediately.

Do not panic! This advice is as important for the companions as for the victim. A snake bite is an emotional experience for all concerned and excitement and hysteria have no place in the proper handling of this (or any other) emergency.

Move the bitten area as little as possible, as any movement will speed the spread of the venom. If walking is necessary, walk slowly and leisurely—don't hurry.

A light constricting band or tourniquet should be applied above the bite site to prevent diffusion of the poison. This should be tight enough only to block the superficial veins and the lymph flow. It should be moved ahead of the area of swelling and released for one or two minutes out of every fifteen. A good rule of thumb is to keep it loose enough that a finger can be pushed beneath it without too much force or about as tight as a neat necktie.

In spite of the vast folk-lore to the contrary, it is *not* a good policy to use whiskey or other alcoholic beverages in snakebite. It might improve the morale, but any stimulant will increase the spread of the poison and in addition, alcohol acts as a central nervous system depressant. Coffee or tea may be used if available, but it is not worth the trouble to prepare a pot at this time. There are more important things to do!

We now come to the more controversial part of snake-bite first aid, the question of incision and suction. One group of doctors (Leopold and Huber) have demonstrated that the use of tourniquets and suction does not increase the survival of immobilized experimental animals after injection of snake venom. But another group (Snyder and Knowles) indicate that these procedures do aid in removing a significant amount of venom. I personally believe that the best scientific evidence supports the latter belief, and that unless medical help and an adequate supply of antivenom is available within one hour, incision should be

the next step. This should be through the fang marks, along the long axis of the limb, about ½ inch long and not more than ¼ inch deep. This will get into the lymph spaces just beneath the skin where the venom is spread.

The sooner suction is applied the more venom is removed. Snake bite kits usually come equipped with suction cups, but your mouth can be used if you have no cuts or sores. Don't worry if you accidentally swallow some because the poison is inactivated by the gastric juices. Suction should be kept up until antivenom is available.

Finally, prompt but not hurried removal to the nearest hospital should be carried out, and the three A's of definitive treatment started:

Antivenom—the specific neutralizing injection for pit vipers.

Antibiotics—a snake bite, like any other animal bite, is potentially infected.

Antitetanus—as with any other puncture wound, tetanus must be considered a possibility and properly treated.

A number of small efficient snake-bite kits are on the market which will greatly ease the prompt administration of these first aid measures. One of these should be in the pocket of anyone venturing into snake country.

Summary:

Move as little as possible.

Use a constricting band, not too tight.

Avoid alcohol.

Incision and Suction.

Go to nearest hospital, '3A' treatment (antivenom, antibiotic, antitetanus).

BITES AND STINGS

When we look at the over-all death rate from venomous bites and stings in this country, we find that the number one killer is not the poisonous snake, the usually accused villain, but rather the honey-bee. Out of 460 victims of poisoned wounds from 1950 to 1960, 50% of the deaths were due to bees and wasps, 30% to snakes, 14% to spiders and the remaining 6% to scorpions, sting-rays, jelly-fish and assorted unidentified animals. It is interesting to note that during this period there were no deaths due to Gila monsters, copperheads, millipedes, centipedes or tarantulas.

Bee and wasp stings are extremely painful, and in susceptible individuals may be deadly. Whereas in snake-bite there may be several hours before the full effect of the poison is reached, in bee or wasp stings there is usually less than one hour from sting to death. The problem here is one of allergy; first aid measures must be prompt and the long term problem should be handled by a medical specialist in this field. There are methods of desensitizing individuals who are known to be susceptible, and anyone who has had a severe reaction to stings should carry certain drugs to be used immediately upon being stung again. The basic drug is epinephrine or adrenalin, which in this instance can be life saving.

Whether one is allergic or not, it is well to avoid stings if at all possible. Knowing nesting habits of these insects is helpful. Honey bees are usually encountered around fields of clover or banks of nectar-containing blooms. Bumble bees nest in the ground. The small honeycomb mud nests of the wasp are found in protected areas around buildings, the yellow-jackets nest under logs or rocks, and the large paper mache hornets nests are found in bushes or trees. So:

—Avoid any known nesting areas. Bees and wasps usually sting only when their nest is threatened or when they are actually touched.

—Never flail at a flying bee or wasp. Walk gently away. Stinging insects are more likely to attack a fast moving object.

—Avoid the use of perfumes, hair spray, hair tonic, sun-tan lotion or other cosmetics containing floral odors attractive to insects.

—Wear long trousers and long sleeved shirts at all times when out-of-doors, and be careful with your colors. Bees seem to be angered by dark clothing, bright colors or flower prints. It is best to wear light colors; tan, khaki, green or white.

The honey-bee will leave his stinger behind imbedded in the skin, literally disemboweling himself. Remove it since the attached muscles may continue to pump venom for as long as 20 minutes. Scrape it off with the edge of a knife blade or finger-nail, being careful not to squeeze the venom sac.

Local discomfort can be relieved by prompt application of a fairly strong solution of household ammonia, or by liberal application of a typical anesthetic ointment.

There are only two kinds of spiders which may cause serious problems to fishermen in this country. One is the widespread Black Widow and the other is the aptly named Brown Recluse. The ferocious looking tarantulas and wolf spiders are amazingly docile and may be gently handled without fear of biting. The Black Widow female, and this is the only sex that bites, has a characteristic red or orange hour glass marking on her under-surface, while the Brown Recluse has a nondescript violin-shaped marking on its back. Both have a predilection for dark spaces; i.e. shoes, bed-rolls, tent crevices; and will bite only if disturbed.

Local treatment does little good, although pain is a prominent symptom. Ice packs and cortisone-containing creams may be applied locally, but early and specific medical attention is necessary. Calcium and anti-venom injections will help with the Black Widow bite, while good results from intensive treatment of a cortisone-type drug have been reported with Brown Recluse poisoning.

Blood-sucking insects include mosquitoes, sand flies, horse flies and deer flies, as well as assorted kinds of lice and bedbugs. Of this unwholesome company the most universal annoyance is undoubtedly the mosquito. Recent research has uncovered some interesting facts about these abundant bugs.

—Dark complexioned individuals are more attractive to mosquitoes than the lighter-skinned and healthy individuals are bitten more than ailing ones.

—Excessive perspiration seems to attract them, as does the carbon dioxide of exhaled air.

—Any cologne or after shave lotion with a noticeable fragrance will pull them in like a homing beacon.

—Clothing has a great influence, the darker the more attractive it is.

To put these facts to a practical purpose we can dress in light clothing, bathe frequently, cut down on strenuous activity which produces excessive perspiration, and avoid lotions or colognes.

There is no venom in a mosquito bite; the saliva which she injects (like spiders, only the female bites) contains a protein which stimulates the formation of a reactive material which is called an anti-body. This anti-body combines with the saliva in an explosive reaction which releases a substance called histamine, and it is this substance which raises the welts and produces the intense itching.

When this happens, avoid scratching, wash with soap and water and use any substance which will soothe an itchy sensation. Household ammonia water, alcohol, baking soda, calomine or anesthetic lotions will help for short periods of time.

The best solution is the use of a good repellent and use it liberally. In recent years a number of extremely good repellents have been developed and are marketed under various trade names (Off, 6-12). Apply to both skin and clothing, and reapply liberally.

With the coming of springtime and the warming waters of streams and lakes the big trout and bass are most likely to bite. So is the tick, hungry after a winter's fast and anxious to go after warm, red blood. He will hang onto a long blade of grass or low lying shrub, and as man or animal brushes by, will grab on and work his way to the skin.

For defense against these tiny invaders, wear high boots, a hat and a tight collar while walking in the woods and use a tick repellent (benzene hexachloride, dimethylphthalate) on exposed skin. Check your clothes and your own hide carefully while dressing or undressing.

In removing any ticks which have managed to make their way through these protective barriers, the most effective method is to pull it from the skin with tweezers and wash the area with soap and water. The use of the burning end of a cigarette, turpentine, gasoline, kerosene or tobacco juice may very well kill the bug, but the cure may be worse than the ailment. Do not "unscrew" the jaws. The tick bites much like a mosquito and should be pulled out directly.

The same local applications can be used as with mosquitoes, but it should be remembered that these animals can carry a myriad of diseases and if any unusual symptoms occur in five to seven days, waste no time in calling your doctor.

SEASICKNESS

This unpleasant malady, properly called motion sickness, is an unpredictable and often severe ailment well known to any charter boat captain. Any pitching, rolling, rotating, or up-and-down movement may precipitate the symptoms, which begin with excessive salivation, sweating and pallor, and end with the head over the side or close to a bucket until the harbor is reached. The cause is not completely understood, even by the experts, but it involves the balance apparatus within the skull, the labyrinth of the inner ear. However, there is no doubt that psychic factors play an important part in starting the symptoms; I have observed healthy young soldiers become violently ill on first boarding a troop transport while the ship was still in dock. Apprehension and unpleasant odors may also provoke an attack.

There are a number of drugs developed for the Armed Forces which will modify or prevent this disease. Dramamine and Bonamine are two such pills. It is well to take one of these about an hour before starting on your trips, and repeat as often as necessary according to the prescription directions.

If you are without pills, at the first sign of queeziness when aboard ship, sit down in the coolest spot available, press your head firmly against a head rest, concentrate on a fixed point or close your eyes, and breathe deeply. This will often prevent the attack. If not, tough it out. The only infallible cure is stepping (or staggering) onto the dock.

POISON PLANTS

There are more than 60 plants which can react on the human epidermis to cause itching and erupting rashes, but the big three are poison ivy, poison oak and poison sumac. Poison ivy with its characteristic cluster of three leaflets per stem is found generally distributed adjacent to streams and lakes throughout the eastern and central states. Poison oak, a low bush with a leaf similar to that of the oak family, is found in the western states, sumac is found in swamps and wet areas in the south-east and south.

The poisonous potion in all of these is a complicated chemical substance with the unpronounceable name of urushiol. This is an irritant of the first order, but more than one exposure is necessary to start the itch. The rash is allergic (no one is susceptible the first time he comes in contact with the plants) but after that the irritating ability builds up rapidly in most people. It is not contagious from one person to the next, but it can spread from one part of the body to another. A susceptible individual may not need to come in contact directly with the ivy plant to acquire the rash. A brush against a pet who has been running in the woods, the smoke from burning ivy leaves or vines and even mosquitoes have been incriminated.

Much misinformation exists about what happens after the skin is touched with this toxic substance and about what should be done to prevent it. Washing with a strong alkali soap and cleansing with alcohol as soon as possible after contact is the traditional and probably still the best method. But the results are dubious. The reason is that the toxin as it touches the skin forms a binding combination and there it remains anchored until the disease runs its natural course. The best prevention is avoidance; "leaves three, let it be." The effectiveness of injectible extracts of poison ivy as an immunization procedure is variable, but in most cases it will decrease the severity of the attack and perhaps prevent its spread to other parts of the body.

Once the rash is in full bloom there is a plethora of remedies which supposedly help in healing. In true fact most of these take credit for what nature is already doing without help. The simplest treatment is the use of cold compresses of Burrows solution, calomine or other astringent lotions or sprays. These help the skin to heal itself by promoting a clean and healthy environment. Cortisone type drugs, provided by your doctor, will shorten the course of the disease and provide prompt relief to the itching.

DROWNING

This melancholy subject must be mentioned since it is the fourth leading cause of accidental death in the U. S., claiming about 7000 lives each year. An alert bystander, perhaps a fisherman, may be able to sustain life if equipped with the specialized knowledge of modern resuscitation techniques.

The primary concern of the rescuer must be to restore respiration and to do it immediately. Mouth to mouth breathing, the most efficient method of maintaining a basal oxygen supply, may be started as soon as shallow water is reached. Attempts to empty the lungs of water are a waste of time and time is precious. The head must be held fully extended, that is tilted backward, and the operator must be sure that the airway is not blocked by any debris in the mouth. Older methods of artificial respiration are not nearly as effective, and the proper use of this new technique can be developed by contacting your local Heart Association or Red Cross for specialized instruction.

If the heart has apparently stopped, external cardiac massage may be started, and this technique may also be taught in your community. It should, however, be used only by individuals with proper training.

Never give up and keep going until professional help is available, even while the patient is being transported to the hospital. Some phenomenal recoveries have been observed, especially in children. One Norwegian boy of 5 years recovered after being submerged for 20 minutes.

Detailed instruction on how to deal with drowning victims cannot be given in a short article of this type. But classes are available within the reach of nearly everyone, and the results of this teaching might save a life, perhaps your partner's. Why not attend one of them?

When fishing the Florida Keys flats for bone-fish and permit, exposed skin and eyes must be protected from extended exposure to sun.

Even on some dull or hazy days, as here at Cape Hatteras, the sun can blister an angler's skin.

WHEN WHERE (and HOW) TO CATCH ALBACORE ON THE WEST COAST

BY HARRY BONNER

A hand-balancing scale is used to determine the largest tuna.

Albacore are very powerful, providing memorable battles. The lady anglers also hold their own ground at the tuna banks.

Like Lake Michigan's new coho fishermen, Southern California's anglers flock *en masse* to the offshore tuna grounds from July through September, all bent for albacore: a dynamic, highly palatable, bullet-shaped member of the tuna family with a steel-blue back, silvery sides, and elongated pectoral fins, occasionally exceeding 40 pounds.

Annually, countless tons of albacore migrate from Japan's waters to the Eastern Pacific, usually arriving in Baja's offshore waters during June, often in the vicinity of Guadalupe Island, which is located approximately 220 southerly miles from the border city of San Diego, California. Following a brief sojourn, the dragonflies commence a northward migration, ranging as far as Oregon, or even Alaska, traveling from roughly twelve to more than 80 miles offshore. The trip is one of Nature's great wonders.

These very temperamental tuna prefer a clean, open, blue sea with a temperature range of 60 to 65 degrees Fahr-

enheit. When the sea temperatures of Baja's offshore waters are unfavorable, the *greater*, initial influx may range as far north as Washington, or Oregon, or wherever the ideal sea temperatures prevail. For example, approximately 63,670 albacore were caught during '67, which was a lean season with unfavorable sea temperatures. Conversely, the sea temperatures off Washington and Oregon during the same season were ideal, providing very rewarding catches for the predominant commercial fishery. During '64, approximately 112,358 albacore were caught from the waters of Southern California and Baja, while ideal sea temperatures reigned. Obviously, the varying sea temperatures of the eastern Pacific play a major role during the brief albacore season.

Normally, anglers aboard San Diego's open-party, charter, and privately-owned craft reap the first, *major* sport fishing catches during July, intercepting the longfins on Baja's offshore waters, normally at least 60 southerly miles from San Diego, often on a southwesterly, magnetic course of 182 degrees. Catches of ten albacore per angler are not uncommon, ranging from 14 to 40 pounds, often supplemented with bluefin tuna to 40 pounds, skipjack to 15 pounds, bullet mackerel (frigate mackerel) to two pounds, and yellowfin tuna to 40 pounds, although yellowfin weighing 100 pounds are not rare (several of the regal lunkers were docked at San Diego during the '67 run, plus hundreds of the much smaller, 16- to 25-pounders).

Strategically located, San Diego's anglers normally enjoy torrid albacore fishing from July through September, chasing the variously located schools daily on southerly, westerly, and northerly courses as the schools trek northward from Baja's waters at a normal rate of five or six miles daily.

During August, the schools of albacore are generally within range of craft sailing from the staggered coastal harbors between San Diego and northerly San Pedro (roughly 80 nautical miles), including Oceanside, Newport Beach, Balboa Beach, and Long Beach. The multitude of boats departing from these harbors often fish for albacore near the east end of San Clemente Island, located roughly 50 equidistant miles from all these harbors, including San Diego. As the albacore continue their northward trek, or as other schools infiltrate from the west and northwest, the albacore eventually abound within range of the Santa Monica Bay area, plus the several harbors which range northward to Point Conception (near Santa Barbara), dividing southern and central California.

During September or early October, the schools customarily invade the offshore and inshore waters of Morro Bay (near Point Conception) and Monterey (near San Francisco), occasionally abounding in great numbers until December: the last battlegrounds for California's anglers. Weatherwise, October is *the* month for Morro Bay and Monterey, often providing torrid angling, plus albacore of the 30 and 40 pound class. Unfortunately, November and December often usher strong winds and storms, interfering with the excellent fishing from one to several days. Assuredly, the waters of Morro Bay and Monterey can be very rough.

When the albacore depart from California's waters, they normally trek to the afar offshore, rough, wintry grounds of Washington and Oregon, even as far as Alaska. Thence they return swiftly to Japan, capable of traveling at least 500 miles per day with ease, traversing the deep, swift currents during the transoceanic crossing, like riding an express subway. It is an amazing, punctual trek, similar to the swallows which return annually to southern California's San Juan Capistrano, and to the great gray whales which trek annually from the Bering Sea to Baja's sheltered bays for calving.

When the longfins are within range, California's large fleet of open-party and charter sport fishing boats are scheduled for daily albacore trips, departing from all of the harbors, plus several of the public fishing piers which dot the coastline. The boats range from 45 feet lengthwise to deluxe, completely equipped 85-footers with complete galley service, modern navigational and communications equipment, bunks, heads (rest rooms), and a plentiful supply of lively anchovy baitfish which are maintained within stern live-bait tanks. The boats normally depart between midnight and 2:00 a.m., allowing for arrival at the distant banks by the prime, magical hour of daybreak. The cost ranges from $15 including live bait. A complete array of tackle, rod rentals, canning and smoking facilities, motels, restaurants, ample parking, and other accommodations are available at or near all the many landings.

Likewise, complete marina and other accommodations are available within the many harbors for privately-owned craft. Like the open-party and charter boats, the sportfishermen also depart early, returning between late afternoon and midnight, refueling, replenishing, unloading tuna, scurrying to get underway on schedule for another trek to the albacore banks for a carbon copy of torrid action! Assuredly, when albacore arrive in southern California's waters, it's like a gold rush! The vendors of live-bait and fuel remain open almost continuously during the season, advising the changing magnetic courses and distances upon request, though many yachtsmen prefer to follow the albacore fleet, forming an illuminated chain, extending to the horizon and all bent for albacore.

Prior to getting underway, experienced yachtsmen ensure that their craft are shipshape for the long trip with running lights, sufficient fuel, repair tools, safety equipment, first-aid kit, empty bilges, and operational navigational and communications equipment. They must be pre-pared for fog, heavy sea or any arising emergencies. As in marlin fishing, an automatic radio direction finder is worth its weight in gold, pinpointing the course for albacore during the radio-telephone transmissions from yachtsmen at rewarding grounds, especially when one area is "dry" and other banks are exploding with the blazing rockets, striking with unrestrained abandon, driving the yachtsmen and anglers to a frenzy, etching nostalgic memories.

Normally, albacore are located by strikes on trolled feather, Nylon, or plastic-skirted jigs, while chumming sparingly with live or dead anchovies, forming a continuous "chum-line" in the trailing wake. The average trolling speed is five or six knots, but varies according to the prevailing sea conditions. A faster trolling speed will often trigger strikes when a flat, glassy sea predominates; a rough sea usually requires reduced speed, especially while heading into a strong wind and oncoming swells. Although albacore feed randomly throughout the day, the early morning and late afternoon hours are consistently rewarding.

When a strike on one or more of the towed jigs is realized, the boat is stopped, and lively anchovies are chummed sparingly to leeward as the jig-striking tuna are retrieved, often followed by the trailing school of tuna which may foray from seconds to several hours, while anglers entice them with live-bait on weightless lines. When the tuna disappear, trolling is resumed.

While underway, veteran skippers usually maneuver to pass the towed jigs near floating masses of kelp and other flotsam, chumming simultaneously. The flotsam attracts saury and other pelagic forage, plus the schools of tuna which may remain near the flotsam for several hours, or days, foraying at random. The various species attracted by flotsam include the tunas, yellowtail, occasional dolphin, mola mola (sunfish), skipjack, mackerel, bonito, striped marlin, and swordfish to mention but a few. Accordingly, the gamesters will abound near or beneath the hulls of boats, customarily seeking forage.

Normally, the boat is stopped when tuna foray on the chum-line, often ignoring the jigs: chumming continues,

Like Michigan's coho fishermen, Southern California's anglers are filled with enthusiasm during the albacore season.

The southland's anglers reap thousands of tuna during the brief albacore season.

When albacore invade Southern California's waters, it's like a gold rush.

Left, Below: Floating live-bait receivers are anchored inside the many harbors, maintaing an adequate supply of lively anchovies during the albacore season.

Action reigns when a cooperative school of albacore is located.

When gaffed, albacore explode the surface.

Albacore are a streamlined, dynamic fish.

drawing the school close to the boat. Should the tuna be observed afar astern, the boat is returned to circle the area or to drift while chumming. Should the albacore fail to strike, the search continues.

A distant "jumper" (grayhounding albacore) is a welcome sight to a seasoned yachtsman. Immediately, he shoves the throttles ahead for flank speed, veering sharply to port or starboard, steadying on the target, hastening the blood through the anglers' veins, silencing the engines upon arrival, again chumming. Often this maneuver is trailed by an exploding wake as albacore charge as a brigade up the chum-line, ultimately striking the terrorized anchovies which are impaled on the weightless lines of tensed anglers. Then the proverbial mass hits the fan! Suddenly, the long trip is worthwhile! Soon the albacore are gaffed and swung aboard as gleeful shouts rally through the salty air. When the school departs, there is a tremen-

dous let-down.

Although the pelagic saury provide a prime forage, albacore will often streak like lightning towards a few anchovies which have been chummed amid countless sauries, pretty much as a hobo passing up a cold hamburger for a sizzling steak! The elongated saury attain lengths of approximately ten inches, displaying a dark back and grayish sides, shaped like a tiny wahoo. The anchovies are much smaller, usually less than seven inches long, displaying a black back and silvery sides.

"Follow the birds!" is a familiar expression among salt-water fishing circles; likewise, it's good advice for tuna fishermen. Occasionally, an albatross will follow a craft for miles, demanding admiration as it gracefully glides at great speed with fixed wings, like a glider, swaying, gaining and losing altitude, passing the boat, returning astern, veering suddenly, circling above tuna, signalling

The day's pack pot is decided by a hand-balancing scale.

an alert yachtsman. Likewise, seagulls circling wildly over an area, diving intermittently like arrows, often herald the presence of tuna. By the same token, seagulls occasionally nestle on the surface where tuna have sounded, patiently waiting for the tuna to surface again, foraying to their delight. The sea's birds, including the small, dark, sparrow-like "albacore" birds which follow the schools, have guided skippers to tuna countless times, denying an otherwise un-rewarding day. Areas void of sea birds and marine activity are often unproductive.

It is interesting to note that whales are also good signs. Occasionally, forage will trail whales, thereby attracting tuna. Like yellowfin tuna, albacore will also follow dolphin (porpoise), possibly attracted by their playful cavorting. The bizarre-shaped mola mola, whales, sharks, striped marlin, swordfish, tuna and forage often traverse the same currents. Although sharks are scorned, they normally do not lag too far behind the abounding schools of albacore, playing havoc with the angler's hooked fish.

While trolling for albacore, light tackle may be used. However, seasoned anglers and skippers prefer medium or heavy trolling tackle with 50- or 80-pound-class Da-cron line. Admittedly, this is *not* sporting tackle for the comparatively small tuna. However, when albacore strike trolled jigs, they are often trailed by tons of tuna which are prone to follow leaders. Should the jig-striking tuna be allowed to run excessively as the boat is stopped, which is often the rule with light tackle, the school will normally follow the hooked tuna, dispersing and fleeing *away* from the chum-line. Conversely, jig-striking alba-core, which are retrieved quickly, will draw the trailing

Excitement reigns when albacore churn the surface to a froth.

school up the chum-line to the stern, but fast! *This* is the ideal way to attract tuna to the boat. Therefore, many skippers prefer stout boat lines to trolling tackle.

When the boat is stopped, lively anchovies are chummed sparingly over the leeward corner of the stern. Normally, the tuna churn the "spot" continually, provid-ing a prime target for anchovies cast on weightless lines, often struck successively at jet speed. Should the albacore be chummed excessively, the overly-fed albacore, which have a very small stomach (necessitating frequent forays), will streak away, occasionally followed by the school. Two lively anchovies chummed at intervals of five seconds are normally sufficient. Should the tuna remain distant, the chumming is temporarily increased, drawing the tuna close to the boat, like feeding chickens or domestic pigeons.

The standard trolling tackle includes a stout, six-foot-six-inch, tubular fiberglass trolling rod with a heavy action,

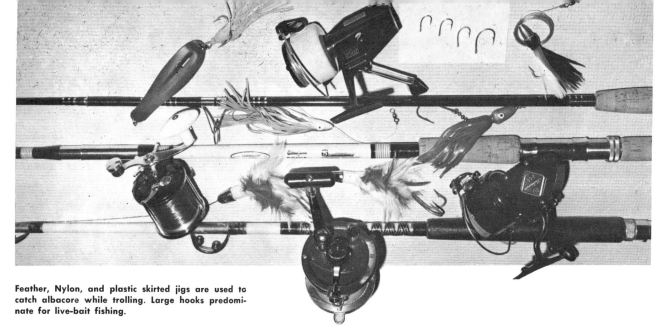

Feather, Nylon, and plastic skirted jigs are used to catch albacore while trolling. Large hooks predominate for live-bait fishing.

adorned with roller guides and tip top, plus a sturdy reel seat which supports a 4/0 trolling reel filled with approximately 250 yards of 50-pound-class Dacron line, or a 6/0 trolling reel, filled with equal yardage of 80-pound-class Dacron line, withstanding the occasional strikes of striped marlin. The popular trolling reels include the True Temper and Penn No. 4/0 and 6/0; Shakespeare 30 and 2153; Pflueger 1788 and Garcia 624, all with metal spools. Albacore play havoc with plastic spools, even when they are cushioned.

One end of a Sampo 100-pound-test ball bearing swivel is attached to the end of the Dacron line to prevent the line from twisting. To the opposite end is attached a three-foot length of 80-pound-test monofilament. Its end is threaded lengthwise through the lightweight heads of two tandem feather, Nylon, or plastic skirted jigs, about five or six inches long with a bullet-shaped head of a pearl or a chrome finish. The end of the monofilament is adorned with a Mustad 8/0 extra-strong trolling hook, or a single Mustad Nikkel, or Pflueger O'Shaughnessy hook of comparable size. The improved clinch knot is used for all connections.

The standard colors of albacore jigs are red-and-white and green-and-yellow. Other effective colors include purple-and-black, blue-and-white, black, purple-and-brown, red-and-black, green-and-white and pure white. Like other gamesters, there are occasions when albacore prefer certain colors, such as purple-and-brown, while denying all other combos. Consequently a colorful rigged array should be included within every angler's tackle box.

At times, the albacore will remain deep. Therefore both weighted and unweighted lines should be trolled simultaneously with variously colored jigs, including red-and-white and green-and-yellow. A multitude of jigs are used, including the Raja, Weber Hoochy, and No-Alibi. Luhr Jensen's Twin-Fin, which is an adjustable depth regulator, is an excellent device for towing the jigs at varying depths.

The standard balanced tackle for live-bait fishing includes one- and two-piece tubular fiberglass rods, varying from eight to ten feet lengthwise, with a quick taper and a light or medium action. Large graduated spinning guides are preferred, affording use with either a spinning or conventional (revolving metal spool) reel, filled with approximately 200 yards or more of 20-pound-test monofilament line. Two, additional balanced tackle outfits with 15 and 40-pound-test monofilament lines provide ideal alternates

Lively anchovies are impaled with large hooks for albacore.

when the tuna are indifferent, or while angling aboard a crowded boat. The large array of suitable live-bait reels include the Shakespeare 2091 and 2151; Pflueger 600 and 2777; True Temper 905M; Zebco 870; Garcia 600A; and Penn 500.

Ordinarily albacore are not hook-shy. Consequently a large 1/0 Mustad tuna hook (color immaterial) is fastened to the end of the weightless line with the improved clinch knot. The lively anchovies are impaled by passing the point crosswise through the nostrils or by passing the point upward just inside the collarbone, which is located on the top, right side of the head alongside the gill plate, continuing penetration until the point and barb emerge atop the head. When the albacore are wary, a 4/0 tuna hook is used with a 12- or 20-pound-test monofilament line. Should the albacore remain deep, a sinker with a rubber core is attached to the line approximately three feet above the hook, varying from a half-ounce, dependent upon the depth, and the speed of drift or current involved.

Striped bass fishing is great sport anytime. But to double your catch – or more – bide your time until the sun goes down.

Here's Al Anderson with a speedy outboard runabout he uses while fishing for stripers in Rhode Island. Al does almost all of his striper fishing at night, for he's found that's when the big ones most often feed.

FISH AT NIGHT AND CATCH STRIPERS GALORE!

BY MILT ROSKO

Here's Wilfred Fontaine holding a nice 28 pound striper just landed by Jim Patterson. Jim was fishing with a live eel at night on the rocky submerged ledges located off the Rhode Island coast. Daytime anglers seldom take fish of this size during the summer months. Only a handful of seasoned regulars ply the dark waters at night, but they make many fine catches.

Here's a bull striper landed by the author from the surf while using conventional casting tackle. Pictured are some of the lures he often uses, including Hopkins lure, Creek Chub Popper, rigged eel, Atom swimmer and block tin squid with feathered hook.

It was the most wicked kind of night. A raw wind whistled in from the northeast and brought along intermittent showers. The seas were running heavily and just trying to keep solid footing on the moss and mussel covered rocks was not easy. Now and then a huge, cold comber would crash down on the jetty, showering us with water.

By daybreak I was beaten. The dampness had penetrated through my foul weather gear, my eyes burned from the salt spray and I had "dishpan" hands which were constantly wet. My fishing companion Johnny Celaya was even in worse shape because the salt had burned into several cuts on his hand which he had received in the excitement of unhooking big striped bass.

When we arrived at a coffee shop located on the banks of Shark River and within sight of the inlet which empties into the ocean, we looked as though we needed a good night's sleep (which indeed we did) and as though we'd been through the wringer (which we had been)! Our first thought was to eat a hearty breakfast. But being preoccupied with gulping down gallons (it seemed) of hot coffee, we failed to mention to the fishermen gathered there what we'd caught.

Thus began a story.

That morning a large group of anglers congregated and were discussing (naturally) how frustrating striped bass fishing was and can be. It seemed that several of the lads had fished for years and never really drawn striper blood. In fact, two of the brethren claimed they'd never even seen a striper caught and wondered if such a fish existed!

My friend Johnny just couldn't sit idly by. He retired to the trunk of the car and dramatically revealed to the disbelievers the result of one night on the rocks—fighting

Heading for the rocky ledges offshore, Al Anderson and Howard Beyer plow through rough seas on the way to the striper grounds. Most bass men who run up good annual scores, catch most of their bass after sundown, when there is minimal boat traffic.

His hand firmly under the striper's gill, Bob Stankus drags a striper up onto the sand, as the breakers crash behind him. This heavyweight grabbed a rigged eel cast into the breakers with a medium weight spinning outfit.

It took a drifted sandworm to fool this striper being unhooked by Howard Beyer. It's amazing, but anglers can often fish some areas for days on end without hooking bass, but once the sun goes down the very same areas produce fantastic striper sport.

the elements. We had six stripers from 12 to 39 pounds apiece. And as many more had been lost in the heavy seas.

Suffice to say we made several believers that morning, for as we finished our breakfast a group of the really interested anglers sat down at our table and asked some very pointed questions. Specifically they couldn't understand why they weren't enjoying at least fair results. During our discussion it was revealed that they were using basically the same equipment and lures that Johnny and I used. In fact, one man had fished the day before on the same Deal and Elberon, N.J., jetties where we'd made our good catch and never had as much as a strike.

Therein was the answer. He'd fished during the day while we did our striper fishing at night.

While stripers are active and feed whenever the mood strikes their fancy, they do feed most extensively at night. In fact in many areas they feed only infrequently during daylight hours, preferring the period between sunset and sunrise to satisfy their hunger.

As a result of the nocturnal feeding habits of striped bass, you will find that most successful regulars along the seacoast do their fishing after dark. This applies to all bass men, whether they seek *Roccus saxatilis* from the surf or jetties or when fishing bay, river or ocean waters from a boat.

As oversimplified as it may sound, for more than a score of years I've recommended to many anglers that the easiest way for them to start catching stripers is to stop fishing daytimes and start fishing nights. This alone has resulted in many anglers becoming consistent bass catchers.

There is, however, quite a difference between fishing for bass when the sun is up and fishing when the waters are shrouded in blackness. Any angler who develops the cat-like sense necessary to function efficiently at night will naturally catch many more bass than the sportsman who aimlessly wanders about in the darkness.

To be successful at night you must thoroughly acquaint yourself with the area you plan to fish. During the day this isn't quite so important because you can observe visually where rips and eddies are located, or where there is a bar formation along the surf, or exactly where the deepest water is located around a jetty. At night you have to depend on your memory, otherwise you might be fishing in spots that are completely devoid of bass.

Most of the better bass men I know make it a point to frequently survey the spots they like to fish at night during the height of day and especially at low tide. When the sun is high, visibility is good and when the tide is low you can see many things that might otherwise be covered on the flood.

In the case of boatmen it is necessary to know the exact location of sand bars and particularly of submerged rocks, jetties, old pilings and other obstructions that could damage your boat as you cruised along in the darkness.

Humorous as it may sound, there are many anglers who try night fishing and fish for hours on end with their bait resting on a sandbar with only a foot or so of water on it! So you see the importance of knowing just where to fish. This holds true of jetty anglers too, who must know where submerged rocks are located so they can keep a fish clear of them once they are hooked up.

Some of the finest surfing grounds on the Atlantic coast are located along New Jersey, Long Island and Cape Cod beaches that are frequented by bathers, skin divers, surfboarders and water skiers during the daytime. Some believe that this great amount of activity during the day causes stripers to keep their distance. But once the sun goes down these very same areas come to another kind of life as old linesides moves into the wash to hunt for a meal.

Frequently schools of bait will lay offshore during the day. Toward dusk the bass start harassing the schools and they move into the surf in hopes of eluding the marauding stripers. At such times the bait will often move into the wash, frequently being washed right onto the sand as a wave breaks. Then you can often see them nervously fluttering on the surface. When a bass cuts through the bait you'll see the small fish leaping into the air. While this may sound like a difficult thing to spot at night, you'll be surprised at how adept you can become if you concentrate and watch for it.

When there is an abundance of bait along the surf and around the rocks of jetties, bass will often move extremely close to feed on it. Often they will chase the bait within ten feet of the rocks and sand. Hence it becomes important to concentrate night time casting effort in close, especially when the concentrations of bait are evident.

This takes a bit of skill on your part because anglers frequently have a tendency to reel too quickly as their lure approaches the sand or rocks in order to make another cast. As the lure approaches where I'm standing, I've learned to concentrate even harder, slowly retrieving until the lure literally slides onto the sand or over a rock. Over the years I've experienced a greater proportion of strikes within two rod lengths of where I was standing than way out at the end of a cast.

Some anglers speculate that fish follow the lure in and maybe they do. But more often I believe they're waiting right in close all the time, particularly when baitfish such as herring, mullet, menhaden, sand launce, spearing and mackerel are also sticking in close to shore.

When stripers are chasing bait at night there are many lures that the caster may employ. But rather than burden myself with a sack full of lures that I wouldn't even have time to use, I limit myself to just a few which have produced well over the years and I find they usually score.

It has been my observation that on calm nights with little water movement, surface lures produce the best. With conditions such as this swimming plugs such as the Dasher or Scudder are perfect. The minnow-type surface swimmers which have a sloshing, side-to-side movement when retrieved slowly also get lots of strikes, as do the larger-size surface swimmers. The former produce best when mullet, baby menhaden and mackerel are plentiful, while the latter 5″ to 8″ plugs bring the most strikes when big herring, mackerel or menhaden are being sought by the bass.

It never ceases to amaze me how many anglers fall into the bad habit simply casting these lures out and unceremoniously reeling them in. That's the easy way to do it. But too often we've observed that bass men who aren't scoring well are retrieving much too fast. They use just one speed and that happens to be the wrong speed, if they receive few strikes. I do not mean to imply that a fast retrieve will not catch bass; it's only that a slow retrieve will get many more.

Torpedo-shaped surface plugs with propellers fore and aft are very good on calm nights, as are surface darters. Both make the kind of surface disturbance which attracts bass.

When there is plenty of white water rolling—a wild sea—you'll find that sub-surface lures bring more strikes after sundown. The finest after-dark lure we've ever employed in this event is a rigged eel. In reality it is not a lure at all, but rather a natural bait rigged on a block tin squid to give it action. It is cast and retrieved much the

Striper fishing from jetties at night is tough work. Here's Milt Rosko cautiously leading a bull striper to his waiting gaff while fishing from a moss and mussel covered rockpile.

same as an artificial lure. In recent years several manufacturers have brought out plastic eels designed expressly for striped bass and they seem to be accounting for catches just as good as those made on the real McCoy. But bear in mind that common eels or sand launces are basically lazy, slow swimming fish. So when retrieving rigged eels take it very slowly and easily. The eel should "swim" through the water in a lazy, lifelike manner. When it does you will get your share of strikes.

Sub-surface plugs such as the swimmers, darters and mirror-types are good when the water is discolored. Stick with plugs the size of the local natural bait and you will find yourself enjoying more strikes. Quite naturally the stripers are more apt to strike a lure similar in size to the bait on which they have been feeding.

Always keep alternating the speed and method of your retrieve. With the deep plugs, especially the mirror-type plug, an irregular retrieve causing the plug to dart ahead and falter, brings far more strikes than a steady retrieve.

Bucktail jigs can also be depended upon to bring strikes at night. Both lima-bean shaped jigs and bug-eyed jigs are great lures, especially when used in rivers and inlets where there is a swift current. In situations such as this, the stripers frequently take up station in the depths, waiting for bait to be swept down the current. With the lures discussed earlier it is very difficult to get them down deep enough in fast water. But with a heavy bucktail jig it's a snap. All you have to do is cast *up* into the current, strip off some line, and permit the jig to settle deep. As the current carries it along you will suddenly feel it bouncing on the bottom, at which time you can start a slow retrieve, alternately lifting your rod tip to give an added bit of

Here's Milt Rosko putting the gaff to a Sandy Hook striper. The husky linesider walloped a big subsurface swimming plug in the wee hours of the morning, when there was no boat traffic at this famous bassing ground.

The author's mighty pleased with this striper. He landed it from a jetty located adjacent to a bathing beach—a spot where stripers are never caught during the daytime, only well after dark, when they come into the wash to feed.

action to the jig. Dressing the jig with a pork strip will enhance its action. In fact, many anglers of my acquaintance never use a jig unless there's a bass-size piece of pork rind attached to it.

Bass which hang around in inlets are seldom cooperative during daylight hours, especially during the summer. For one thing there is a constant parade of pleasure boats using the cuts, or openings, to the ocean. This probably keeps the fish on edge and "off their feed." After dark, when all is quiet, it's quite another story.

Boatmen employ many of the lures just discussed as they hunt for stripers during hours of darkness. Usually they troll, for in this way they can cover a great deal of area and as a result catch more bass. But quite a few boatmen we know prefer to drift and cast, believing that this offers more of a challenge than trolling.

So they seek out spots where bass are known to feed and ply their trade with casting tackle. There are many spots along the seacoast where surfmen and jetty jockies cannot fish. Nor can trollers. I'm speaking of the fringe of submerged rocky ledges far from shore, or jetty fronts which have been tumbled into the sea by constant pounding of the ocean. Spots such as these are a natural for the caster because bass often are schooled up and feeding here. And seldom are they exposed to the constant parade of lures they are elsewhere.

While lures take a great toll of stripers during hours of darkness, there are many fine catches registered by anglers who use live baits. Of course, fishing with live bait presents a few problems, for often you have to catch your own and keep it alive until the bass grounds are reached.

Common eels are a rather easy bait to obtain and one of the best all-around live baits to use for stripers. I've seen them used everywhere along the Atlantic coast and each season they account for a great many big stripers, especially when fished after sundown. Eels have nocturnal habits too, which make them a natural for stripers when fished on night tides. The fact that eels are a sturdy bait which stay alive a long time makes them especially popular.

Terminal rigging for fishing a live eel consists of a 6/0 or 7/0 Eagle Claw style hook which is tied to a three-foot-long piece of 30 or 40 pound nylon leader material. This in turn is tied to the line with a tiny barrel swivel in between. The eel is placed on the hook by running the point of the hook into the eel's lower jaw and out its upper jaw. You can use either spinning or conventional tackle with equal effectiveness.

The bait is then cast out and slowly retrieved along the bottom in areas where there is little current, or simply cast out and drifted along the bottom where there is sufficient tidal flow or current to carry your boat over a productive rocky ledge or through a swirling tide rip.

This basic live bait technique may be employed effectively at night with live mackerel, menhaden, herring or mullet. Sea worms such as sandworms and bloodworms also make excellent striper baits. Shedder and soft-shelled crabs annually account for many stripers as they drift along with the tide, a hook carefully concealed within them.

As with most types of fishing, the striper angler belongs to one of two schools: those who stay in one spot and wait for the fish to come to them, and those who constantly keep on the move, searching for feeding bass. I found that in some areas, such as in tide rips and around rockpiles that are inaccessible at high tide, you have no alternative but to wait for the fish. But, on the whole it pays to move around quite a bit, rather than to stay put. Over a period of many years I've found that immediately upon arriving at a very good spot I would have action. However it was seldom worth the effort to stay if fish weren't hooked within the first half hour. This rule applies to fishing from a boat, beach or jetty.

One thing you're certain to notice once you commence night fishing for stripers is the rather limited amount of fishing activity once the sun goes down. Often where there were dozens of boats trolling during the day there may only be a handful at night. The same applies on jetties and along the beach. Frankly it often gets really lonesome.

This has caused me to wonder why more anglers do not fish at night and has resulted in my making a careful analysis of my personal logbooks to determine just what kind of an edge night fishing gave me. When comparing the results of any given month of the season, on an equal time basis of hours expended during the daytime as opposed to night, I've caught almost four times as many bass after sundown, as at any other time, including dusk and daybreak!

With odds like this you would think that everybody would be fishing at night. While I don't really think anglers are afraid of the dark, I do feel there is a bit of hesitancy to get started with this madness of probing around in the inky blackness with a boat, or stumbling around coastal rockpiles too.

One thing that causes many newcomers some concern (and I've found this to be true of fresh water bass men and trout fishermen as well) is that it's so dark that you can't enjoy fishing, because you can't possibly be functioning as efficiently as during daylight. This isn't the case. Once you become accustomed to night fishing it's sheer pleasure. The easiest way to get used to seeing in the dark is to keep all lights out, except when you absolutely need them. This is a trick that infantry soldiers are taught. By working in the dark your eyes become accustomed to the inky blackness and it's remarkable how well you soon can see. Indeed, after a while you become adept at changing lures, baiting hooks and moving about without the aid of any lights.

For those occasions when a light is required, I've found a miner's type headlamp with 4 D size dry cell batteries to be ideal. I wear mine around my neck, when fishing from boat or beach, for in this way it's always ready for instant use.

Throughout my travels along the striper coast I've met many successful bass men who studied stripers and their habits, and who developed patterns of fishing at certain stages of the tide, the moon, or when the wind was from a preferred quarter. Some even used solunar tables in planning their striper sorties. While I am among the first to respect a successful bass man's techniques and theories, I've found that in almost every instance if I used a native's manner of fishing at an optimum period, but did so after the sun went down, I came away enjoying unbelievable striper fishing!

As simple as it may sound, the most surefire way of increasing your striper catch is to fish at night. By doing so you'll join that select fraternity along the striper coast who catch more and bigger stripers than all daytime anglers combined.

Unhappy with your present work?
Here is a guide to new careers
in fisheries and fish management.

SO YOU WANT TO WORK WITH FISH!

A FISHERMEN'S DIGEST *SPECIAL SERVICE FEATURE*

Today there are a surprising number of opportunities for young men and women to do fisheries work in the outdoors. And the field grows broader every day. There are jobs that require every conceivable type of skill and a few that require little skill at all. Some are routine and either research or library oriented; others would have to rank with the most thrilling, even the most dangerous jobs on earth.

For instance, there is a team of biologists now probing the bed of the ocean with electronic equipment and underwater cameras. And another team of game technicians on loan to an African government is studying tigerfish and the giant Nile perch.

Today there is a need for experience in law enforcement and in freshwater fish culture, for farmers and X-ray technicians, for all kinds of fisheries men, clerks, chemists, engineers, real estate appraisers, naturalists, and lecturers, for full-time employees as well as for part-time summer workers. Since more and more people are getting outdoors more often, there is also a naturally growing need for outdoor recreation specialists. According to Joe Linduska, Associate Director of the U.S. Bureau of Sport Fisheries and Wildlife, "Recreation is becoming of extremely great concern to *all* conservation agencies. We have even given thought to how recreation might fit into our National Wildlife Refuge system, without detracting from the basic principles for such areas—which is to furnish sanctuary for wildlife, often for rare wildlife."

The best estimates show that about 55,000 are employed full time in the outdoors. More than half of these have at least something to do with fish. Many more are engaged part time, and the number of both is expected to double before another decade passes. The three main employers are the Federal government, the various state conservation bureaus, and private industry.

Employment with the Federal government is not limited to the Bureau of Sport Fisheries and Wildlife, although that may be our main consideration here. Jobs are also available with the Bureau of Commercial Fisheries, the National Park Service, the Bureau of Indian Affairs, the Bureau of Land Management, the U. S. Forest Service and U. S. Soil Conservation Service. Appointment to nearly all posts with these agencies requires passing a competitive Civil Service examination. Information on these examinations can be obtained from the U. S. Civil Service Commission offices in the nearest of the following cities: Washington, D. C., Boston, New York, Philadelphia, Atlanta, Chicago, Dallas, St. Louis, Denver, Seattle, San Francisco, Honolulu, Anchorage. Or ask for copies of two pamphlets called "Working for the U. S. A." and "Futures in Federal Government."

All fifty states (as well as the Canadian provinces) employ officers to enforce fishing laws (they are variously called game wardens, game protectors, wildlife officers, fish wardens and so forth), and specialists in fish propagation, conservation, wildlife study, and management of fish. Most of these positions also are awarded after Civil Service tests. But in too many states today, particularly in the South, conservation jobs are awarded on the political spoils system. It is more a matter of who you know than what you know. Here new jobs go on the basis of political affiliation and little money is left for a few worthwhile management programs. Job applicants are always wise to check this situation locally.

The names of various state employing agencies differ, but a letter simply addressed to any state fish and game department will get results. All of these are located in the state capitals except for Pratt, Kansas; New Orleans, Louisiana; and Portland, Oregon.

Perhaps the most rapidly expanding field for outdoor careerists is in private industry. Commercial wildlife preserves and fishing clubs are hiring qualified wildlifers. Men are needed to run private hatcheries, to transport fish and to act as guides. One tackle company, Arbogast in Akron, employs a full-time wildlife biologist to investigate the behavior of fishes and to discover why they strike. Others may eventually follow suit. Even the U. S. Corps of Engineers and the strip-mining industry, both in the category of despoilers and pillagers, suddenly feel it is wise, politically, to hire a few wildlifers and fisheries experts.

Also in this private-enterprise category would have to be the communicators—the outdoor writers, columnists, radio and TV broadcasters. Some of these work for magazines or newspapers; others are freelance or self-employed. Add also the personnel who work for such national organizations as the Wilderness Society, Trout Unlimited, National Wildlife Federation, National Audubon Society (which employs many field personnel), Wildlife Society, Wildlife Management Institute.

It is very important to mention a few basic points here about all outdoor careers, government or private enterprise. First, the more education you have, the better opportunity there is for a challenging job. College educations are necessary just to make application for certain posts. For many positions, good physical condition and stamina also are important. All these facts cannot be emphasized enough for the young man who is looking ahead to a life outdoors.

Also these are not jobs in which to get rich. The reward is largely in the enjoyment, the dedication, and the freedom of being in the open at least part of the time. Compared to a newly graduated chemist or engineer, for example, fish biologists begin their careers with a state agency at a modest salary. Scales vary, but the average starting pay is around $6,000 per year with the chance to advance to $9,000 or so. Some fish biology posts may reach $15,000 or beyond, but these are uncommon. Unless you relish the work, that is not a great reward for the time spent studying and for the frequently hard, frustrating work afield.

Conservation worker getting lake trout ready for transfer from a Wisconsin hatchery to a fishing lake.

Each year the U. S. Bureau of Sport Fisheries adds new men to its roster. Some are hired right out of college, on graduation; others leave state jobs for the greater scope and security of Federal employment. Both state politics and the desire for advancement precipitate such change-overs. According to the director of the Bureau, love of the outdoors, hunting, and fishing is helpful in working for that organization. But far more valuable is a thorough knowledge of fish and their management.

Most career appointments with the Bureau fall into the following classifications: fishery biologist, wildlife biologist, fish hatchery manager, U. S. game management agent (federal game warden), U. S. fish management agent, and engineer. There are also clerical, administrative, and stenographic jobs to fill. Inquiries about any of these (and the titles are practically self-explanatory) should be addressed to the nearest office of the Bureau of Sport Fisheries and Wildlife, U. S. Dept. of Interior, in the following cities: Portland, Oregon 97208; Albuquerque, New Mexico 87103; Minneapolis, Minnesota 55408; Atlanta, Georgia 30323; Boston, Massachusetts 02111; Washington, D. C. 20240.

There are a few satisfying fisheries jobs in the National Park Service. Most of them offer opportunities to live and work amid scenes of the most exquisite natural beauty in the world. Job titles cover everything from park ranger to naturalist, icthyologist, and curator. Besides the regular, full-time Parks assignments, many summertime rangers are employed during the middle of the peak vacation season. Inquiries on all Parks employment should go to the Personnel Director, National Park Service, U. S. Dept. of Interior, Washington, D. C. 20240.

In many National Parks, nongovernment summertime jobs are available to college students and application for them should be made to the various concessionaires—such as the Yellowstone Park Co., Helena, Montana, for Yellowstone Park. They have such jobs available as fishing guide and boat operator. More than one college student has started with one of these somewhat menial jobs and used it as a springboard to a summer ranger's or fish management post.

The basic government work week is an 8-hour day, 40-hour week, but in the field it always adds up to more. Quarters are furnished at isolated posts, with some small deduction made for rental. New appointees are expected to pay their own transportation to the first job; after that the Government pays transportation costs for the whole family and household goods when an employee is transferred. Vacation leave is thirteen to twenty-six days a year, depending on length of service, plus thirteen days of sick leave may be accumulated each year. A good retirement plan, group life insurance, health benefits, and an incentive-award program all work in a Federal employee's favor.

It is only natural that there should be many applicants for the state game warden positions which become available every year. The life of a warden is generally a good one; he is necessarily a healthy, active, intelligent, enthusiastic man. In many states a county or area game warden is a jack-of-all-trades, although his main responsibility is law enforcement and education. The pay for this in some states is as low as $4,500 and elsewhere as high as $8,000 per year. Some states require a college education for all new wardens, followed by several months of on-the-job training.

Many applicants see the game warden's job as a chance to go fishing all the time. But it never works out that way—at least not for very long. Too many nights will be

Fish management aides operating weed cutter which opens up weed-choked channels to fishermen.

spent watching lonely country roads for fish poachers, attending sportsmen's club meetings, teaching gun safety to groups of boys, checking anglers, and appearing in court. The best game wardens do not work 8-hour days; they are on call at all times.

This can also be a dangerous job. Although most wildlife law enforcement involves misdemeanors rather than felonies, a game warden contacts more armed persons (hunters) in any year's time than any other law enforcement officer. In almost every state, game wardens have been killed in the line of duty.

Few people get more satisfaction from life than a game warden who really loves his work, even though the job is seldom easy. Such a man makes his own job. He practically lives in and works out of his car which is a miniature quartermaster depot. More often than not it's crammed with writing pads, a sleeping bag, maps, binoculars, license blanks, hip boots, outboard motor, firearms, two-way radio, thermos of hot coffee, and maybe an old beagle that rides along for company. This man is in the public eye; lots of people know him so he must be a good example to other sportsmen. But his assigned territory, usually one county, is his own domain and no boss breathes down his neck all day long.

How can you prepare for a job (or for an examination) as game warden? First read all you can find on conservation and natural history. Know your own state's conservation problems. Improve your physical fitness. Two books now available may be of some help: "Manual for the Conservation Officer," by Irving Isaacson, Legal Publications, Lewiston, Me.; and "Wildlife Law Enforcement," by William F. Sigler, Wm. C. Brown Co., Dubuque, Iowa. Some of the correspondence school courses can also be helpful to the high school graduate.

Fingerlings like these were foundation for Ohio's successful musky program. (See "Ohio's Musky Explosion" elsewhere in this issue.)

Fish hatchery worker checks water temperature to insure survival of fish eggs.

Game warden checks fisherman's license and makes creel census on Ohio stream.

It's a rugged, but important job to remove such trash fish as carp and suckers from Lake St. Marys, Ohio.

Perhaps the most rapidly expanding area of the outdoor job field is communications. This field takes in writers, artists, photographers, and lecturers, both in and out of government employment. Every state employs conservation communicators; many newspapers and a few magazines and companies do; and some individuals are able to make a living in this field on their own, doing freelance work. For these interested in this growing field a valuable handbook was published recently. The Outdoor Writers Instruction Manual is available for $3.00 from the Outdoor Writers Association of America, Outdoors Building, Columbia, Missouri.

There is great opportunity in the so-called I & E (Information and Education) sections of fish and game departments for people who can write well or take pictures. And there is a great demand for them *if* they also have a solid background in some phase of scientific wildlife conservation. Specialists in this field might start at $5,000 and in a short time double that figure. But the person must have ability, energy, and originality—and he must

produce. No other segment of the outdoor career field is more filled with individuals who only want to write, or think they want to write, but never really get around to it.

This is another area where education is very important. But at the same time all the journalism and photography courses ever offered by the best schools will not make an outdoor writer or photographer. Great desire is necessary. So is the compulsion to sit down and keep writing—or filming.

The greatest potential for outdoor writers exists in American newspapers. Even though most of the stadium sports continue to decline in popularity as compared to the mushrooming interest in the outdoors, baseball and basketball produce enough exciting writers to make the coverage of these sports all out of proportion to reader interest. A good, original outdoor journalist will have no trouble selling his product as a regular column to a newspaper.

FISHERMEN'S DIGEST, FIELD & STREAM, SPORTS AFIELD, OUTDOOR LIFE, WESTERN OUT-

Important job in every state is test-netting waters to study fish population.

With snowbanks on the ground and the weather cold, the biologists seine native cutthroat trout from the icy brook.

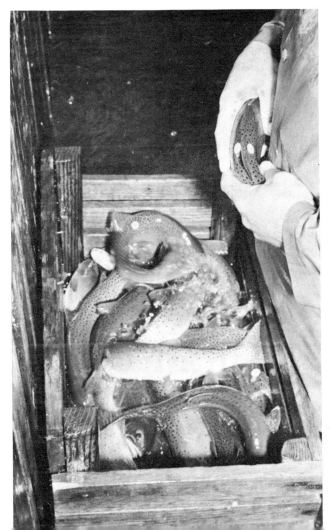

DOORS, and several other magazines buy outdoor material from writers and photographers, although the total annual amount is only a fraction of the copy that newspapers and conservation agencies use. But it is the very best material. Some of it is produced by fulltime freelancers (who have usually reached this status by gaining proficiency with other media) or by individuals also employed by newspapers or company public relations departments. A very few magazine staff positions are also available.

So far most of the emphasis in this article has been on fisheries jobs that require training, considerable skill, or experience. However there are also many positions available for the man who has only his own enthusiasm and strength. These might be called the conservation "aide" jobs, some of which are quite challenging. Aides

National Park fish biologists tag spawning cutthroat trout at fishtrap in Yellowstone's Pelican Creek.

Above: A Montana fisheries crew flies into remote Goose Lake in the Beartooth Mountains. Their mission is to capture spawning trout in Goose Creek and to transplant them to other fishless lakes.

Left: The successful air-drop is made. Survival of trout is good and a new fishing lake is created. This is typical of modern fisheries work today.

Fisheries workers trap-net a musky, which will be tagged and released again.

Biologist scrapes scale off cutthroat so that age and growth of the trout can be determined later in the laboratory.

Pilot for the Montana Fish & Game Dept. readies his plane and special equipment for air-dropping trout caught at Goose Lake to another Montana lake.

perform such important tasks as tagging fish, excavating ponds, treating lakes with chemicals, building fishing access sites on public areas, seining or trapping rough fish, working at hatcheries, counting salmon, repairing boats or nets, and operating anything from airboats and aquatic weed cutters to bulldozers and electronic fish finders. Requests for information on these jobs should be addressed to the same state and Federal agencies mentioned earlier. Some of the aide jobs are salaried, others are hourly.

All right, suppose you have decided to make some phase of fisheries or conservation work your lifetime goal. What is the best college or university to attend? What should you study?

In the first place you should have been getting the best possible grades in high school. That means you can pick your college rather than be forced to take what is left. But let's examine details.

Approximately seventy-five universities and colleges offer courses in ichthyology or fishery biology, although not all offer a major in the field. Potential outdoor workers should get a thorough foundation in undergraduate school in the following courses: zoology, botany, geology, agronomy, mathematics, physics, chemistry, social studies and the humanities. The Sport Fishing Institute recommends that prospective fishery scientists postpone specialization in fishing science subjects to the graduate level of training and concentrate in undergraduate years on fundamental courses in the sciences, mathematics, social studies, and the humanities.

Graduate schools offer advanced courses, seminars, and research problems under experienced instructors. Cooperative units have been set up in several universities and colleges with the Bureau of Sport Fisheries and Wildlife and state conservation departments cooperating. Scholarships and research fellowships are available at several schools. For a list of institutions and professors offering fishery biology and related courses in United States colleges and universities, write Sport Fishing Institute, 413 Bond Building, Washington, D. C. 20005.

For the fisheries or conservation writer, a few universities offer special curricula designed for technical journalists, that is, journalists whose main work will be the translation of technical knowledge into attractive and easily understood material. A university may list this as "technical journalism." Schools giving majors in this curriculum include: Iowa State University, Oklahoma State University, Kansas State University, Colorado State University.

Some schools famous for offering wildlife conservation studies and extensive training in journalism and English are Cornell and the Universities of Michigan, Missouri, California, Minnesota, and Wisconsin.

From all the careers in fishing we have mentioned will come tomorrow's conservation leaders. And we surely need a bumper crop of good, capable ones. But even when a man reaches the top with a comfortable salary, his troubles do not disappear. There are the same old politics and politicians to cope with, the same criticisms from people who do not understand the importance of conservation. But there also are rich rewards for a vital job well done.

For anyone who genuinely loves the outdoors there is no more satisfying career than one spent in behalf of conservation.

MINI-TACKLE

For The Mini-Fish . . . or

how to make the most of panfishing

By Charles Waterman

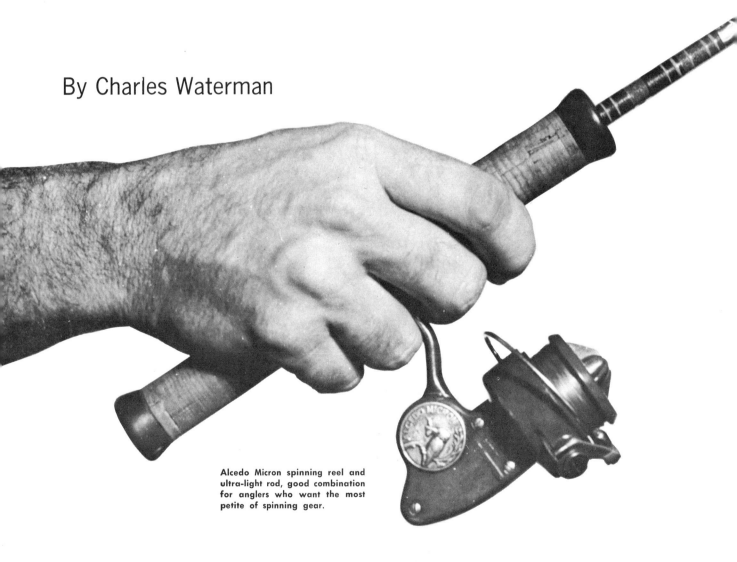

Alcedo Micron spinning reel and ultra-light rod, good combination for anglers who want the most petite of spinning gear.

A black crappie, favorite of the bottom bouncers, with some of the little lures that work best on panfish.

When casting champion Bob Budd arrives home from an international tournament in Europe, he steps off the airliner and — believe it or not — heads straight for his favorite bluegill hole. If an angler who has collected a string of national casting championships prefers to use miniature spinning and fly tackle on panfish, while a world of bigger fish is waiting, it must be top-notch sport.

Certainly catching a mess of bluegills is no way to become famous but plenty of expert fishermen figure panfishing with ultralight tackle is distinctly superior to trolling for sailfish or chasing steelheads. Of course it's just a matter of using tackle matched to the fish. But the miniature gear often catches more fish than heavier equipment, and it's always more fun and less work to handle.

Budd's own ultralight spinning outfit is one of the most versatile I've seen. With slight modification it will cast plugs as heavy as 5/8 ounce but it was designed for and performs best with pee-wee lures. After testing countless rods, Bob decided on a delicate five-foot stick, and he completed the outfit with four-pound-test monofilament line and a light closed-face reel designed to mount below the rod. In normal casting the line is controlled with a finger as it slides over the rod grip, but Budd found he could cast more accurately with a special nylon trigger-like device he designed. The line passes through this gadget and can be pressured so delicately with the forefinger that he won a bunch of accuracy casting events with it.

Budd was so proud of the fingering device that he tried to market it, but evidently fishermen didn't want a white, nylon whatzit taped to their rod handles even if it did help their casting. Anyhow Bob still had quite a few fingering devices left the last time I saw him and he wasn't even trying to sell them.

Budd also makes his own tiny spinning lures. He figures the occasional six-ounce sunfish that grabs a six-inch bass plug is an unlucky extrovert. A more appropriate spinning lure for panfish may weigh as little as 1/24 ounce. Even a bait *that* small will cast fairly well with 4-pound-test line and a rod light enough to bend with it.

Lure manufacturers are notably reticent about indicating lure weights on the sales card or box, but 1/4 ounce is the average weight of freshwater spinning baits. With a lot of effort you can make almost any spinning outfit throw 1/24 of an ounce — but not very far. Casting a miniature bait easily all day long takes a pretty soft rod. The little 5-footer is handy and extremely accurate, and even a light fly rod or combination rod fitted with a spinning reel can serve in a pinch.

Any angler using ultralight equipment for panfish will probably want a small, light spinning reel to match the

Lightweight Orvis flyrod (6½ feet long) favored by the author for panfishing. Tiny reel is a nameless antique but complements the rod in size.

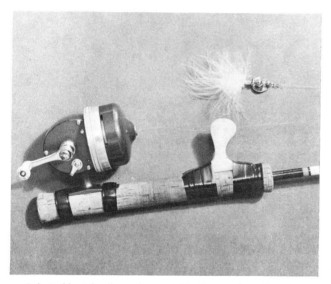

Bob Budd's "doodle outfit" and his favorite lure, featuring marabou streamer and beaded spinner.

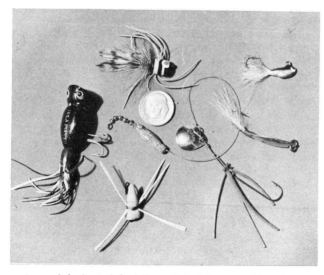

Some of the best of the little panfish stuff poses with a dime. Rubber spider at bottom is about the most productive of all surface lures. Lure made from rubber band is at lower right.

rod, although the reel isn't too important in casting dynamics. It's the rod and line that are critical, and if you use monofilament heavier than four-pound-test, you'll have trouble getting casting distance and proper lure action. Incidentally, don't count on your 4-pound line testing that much after it's been tied to a lure and frayed on weeds and snags underwater. It may test only two pounds.

Not only will a rod that's too stiff fail to throw midget lures far enough, but it will also break a light line easily when you strike a fish too hard. If you tend to be heavy-handed or over-enthusiastic, a lighter rod — or a slightly longer one — might save plenty of line, lures and fish you would lose with a stiffer rod.

One day when fishing for crappies from Bob Budd's boat and catching about one to his ten, I happened to stick a hook into a trophy-sized Florida bass. I was using one of his miniature outfits and managed to break the fish off in roughly four seconds. I told Bob my drag was too tight.

"Don't use the doggone drag!" he told me. "Play your fish with your finger! Drags are no good for light outfits like this!"

As soon as he hooks a fish he backs his reel handle to release the line and lets the fish run with no drag at all other than the pressure he carefully applies with his forefinger. Of course if you use a conventional open-faced reel it's difficult to release the line from the bail. In that case you'll have to use the drag, but keep it light. Anyway you don't need much drag pressure to set such tiny hooks in a fish.

Budd occasionally ties into really big fish on ultralight tackle. Recently he caught a 4-pound line record black bass that weighed nearly 13 pounds. He also whipped a 7-pounder on 2-pound line, and I suspect that might be a record too. Of course many anglers will find 2-pound threadline a bit too delicate, especially for fishing in snags.

All types of ultralight baits are available — plugs, underwater spinners, spoons and jigs. All of them should be fished slowly, and that's one of the main reasons they must be light. A heavy quarter-ounce lure generally must be reeled fairly fast to keep it off the bottom and fast lures seldom appeal to panfish. That's why spinners must be light and tuned to turn at a breath, even when installed on a surface plug.

When fishing for bluegills with a top-water bait, work it very, very slowly. If your lure has a slow-turning spinner that tosses little drops of water into the air the bream will get all a-twitter. The same bait will appeal to rock bass, green sunfish and most of the other sunfishes for that matter.

The hooks on your baits should be very small and kept needle sharp with a hone. For positive hooking most experts like trebles, despite their tendency to hang up on snags. Most of the sunfishes will often nibble and bump a surface lure, and a fish sometimes will take several tastes of a bait before getting hooked. Chugging a surface bait briskly a couple of times will often bring a curious fish into the area. When I suspect a fish is watching my lure, I rest it on the surface for a few moments and then twitch it slightly to provoke a strike.

Underwater spinners are most effective when worked slowly and are especially deadly with tails that squirm at the slightest movement. Little marabou streamers tied on the treble hooks especially in white, yellow and yellow-and-red combinations can just about double the attractiveness of a spinner. But be sure the feathers don't trail too far behind the hook or you'll get a lot of tail-end nibbles you can't snag. As a boy in Kansas I fished for bluegills and green perch with a tandem spinner and figured the tail of the bait wasn't too important. Now I'd like to fish

Paint Creek again with a marabou tail to replace the stiff guinea feathers I used then.

Tiny plastic worms on single hooks are also effective fastened behind small spinners, and pieces of narrow rubber band tied to a small hook have put plenty of fish in my skillet too. In fact I've often found the rubber bands more productive than more sophisticated baits. Like the marabou, the worms and rubber bands keep wiggling even when the lure travels very slowly. Squirrel hair and bucktail have long been popular for spinner tails too. And some fishermen simply fasten on a rubber spider, giving the bait an untidy appearance but producing plenty of strikes.

The panfish spinner gets its casting weight either from metal beads fastened to the wire shank of the lure or a small lead body. To cast extremely light spinners I usually

Panfish taken on miniature lures and with ultra-light spinning tackle.

Bob Budd plays a good fish with his miniature rig. With light line he doesn't use the reel's drag, depending on an educated forefinger for resistance.

A mess of bream (bluegills) that took a tiny, rubber-legged popping bug for Jack Gowdy in Florida

fasten a small sinker ahead on the line. The sinker makes casting a little sloppy but gives the spinner plenty of weight.

Ordinarily panfish don't seem to care whether the spinner blade is brass, nickel or gold, but there are days when one finish will work better than the others. What's really most important is that the blade spins easily.

Thumbnail-sized spoons are deadly for panfish too but must be fished very slowly. They'll even get strikes when simply sinking erratically. For this fishing I use a fly rod because most spoons heavy enough to cast with spinning tackle will hit the bottom while the fish is still looking for what fell in. When used with a small porkrind, tiny spoons are even effective on pickerel.

Bottom-bumping jigs in small sizes are often deadly on deep-lying crappies, which will hit on the surface occasionally but prefer the depths. One of the best crappie fishermen I know makes short casts and lets the jig sink to the bottom before beginning the retrieve. Then he gently lifts the lure and reels slowly before bumping bottom again. If the lure doesn't hit bottom solidly when it drops back, he sets the hook. A soft-tipped rod can be a great help in detecting a light crappie hit. And remember that almost anything that swims the bottom will take a tiny jig occasionally, so be prepared.

Perhaps it has occurred to you that many of these ultralight baits can be fished with a cane pole. In fact many anglers who own the finest of equipment will resort to a pole when after panfish. But a fly rod is more versatile and can even throw natural baits — but not with orthodox fly casting technique. Use the rod like a cane pole. A long, soft spinning rod also will cast worms, grubs and small minnows fairly well, but shorter rods intended for snap casts will tear them off.

Of course the first ultralight panfish lures were fished with flyrods years before spinning came to America. But most solid lures are abominations for the fly caster. Even the tiniest spoon or wooden plug can become a lethal missile in a high wind, and many panfishermen of pre-spinning days carried neck and ear scars to prove it. What's more, a flyrod and line heavy enough to throw a small spoon would also be suitable for 100-pound tarpon and will cornfield a bream if you set the hook too hard.

Although I often use sinking fly lines I think it's on and near the surface that the flyrod really comes into its own for panfish. The sinking fly line will definitely take a streamer to the bottom, but it's tough to pick off the water for a new cast and generally requires a lot of false casting to get distance again. So the fly angler has a difficult time competing with spin fishermen in deep water, especially for crappies.

But for top-water angling for most of the smaller sunfishes and big shallow water crappies, the ultra-light flyrod is an invaluable tool. Your flyrod should be the lightest you can find in either bamboo or glass, and six or seven feet long is about right. Or you can go all out with a short four- or five-foot stick — or even use just the tip section of a long rod — but unless you're a very good caster you will surely run into difficulties. For one thing the very short rod won't lift your line easily over the rim of weeds that frequently lines fishy water. It's tough, too, when you're trying to keep your line above lily pads and especially when you're fishing from the bank.

For several years I've used a light 6½-foot bamboo trout rod for many species of small gamefish. It takes a #4 weight forward or double taper line, but a level line will work nearly as well for most panfishing. The rod weighs slightly more than two ounces, but a glass rod of the same length might be somewhat lighter.

Although many fly fishermen would almost rather be caught with live bait than with an automatic reel, automatics are quite handy for the short casts and short runs of panfishing. But automatics are heavy, and you might prefer a small, light single action to fit your light rod. Incidentally, it's a good idea to spool a little backing under your fly line since all kinds of fish sometimes take flies intended for rock bass and bluegills.

While it isn't a very aesthetic number and many trout fishing purists would be nauseated at the thought, the sponge rubber spider with little plastic legs is probably the deadliest surface fly known for bluegills and other sunfish. You don't need great skill to manipulate a rubber spider. Just cast it on the water and let it float motionless, twitching it occasionally to make the stretchy legs wiggle. The spider doesn't have to float high in the water, and often panfish will hit it even if it soaks and sinks a few inches.

Keep your leader light with a tippet no heavier than six-pound test so the spider will have a natural appearance. Set the hook gently when a fish bumps the bait. Don't be in a hurry to strike — often a fish can't decide whether he wants the spider even after swimming several feet toward it. When there's no fish in the area big enough to take the whole bug, the three-inchers will wrestle with the individual legs to keep you amused.

Unfortunately, rubber spiders seem short on appeal for bass and other large fish, which frequently are bonuses for panfishermen. But if you want to catch both big bass and panfish, a fairly small popping bug with rubber legs is a good compromise. A big pumpkinseed or bluegill will hit it, and it's just the right size for rock bass and yet not too small to tempt an occasional bass. On Ozark streams my favorite bugs are actually a little small for bass and slightly large for panfish but reasonably effective for both. Keep in mind that if a bug is too big your light rod just won't cast it smoothly.

With all bugs a very slow retrieve is most productive for panfish. Often saucer-sized bluegills will tentatively sample a rubber leg before deciding to shoot the works and slurp the whole bug. I know successful bluegill and bass fishermen who just cast a bug to a likely spot and never even move it. But I get more strikes if I twitch the lure gently every few moments.

Although feeding panfish are usually suckers for almost any tiny bug or midget lure, they can be finicky at times. Often — especially during the heat of the day — bluegills and their kin will absolutely refuse surface baits. At such times you have to use a small plug, spoon or spinner and fish it deep. When the fish move into the shallows in the evening, on the other hand, they may ignore everything but top-water lures. One fisherman I know uses his spinning rod all day and then takes up his flyrod when the surface feeding starts at dusk.

Once on California's Tuolumne River I spotted several bluegills in such a shallow pocket they stirred up surface wakes wherever they swam. My size 12 black gnat would snake out a fish on every cast as long as it floated but couldn't get a tumble when it sank. After several wasted casts with a slimy, sinking fly I'd apply a dab of floatant dressing, and the fish would climb on again. The difference between "dry" and "wet" was no more than six inches of water but the bluegills were as selective as any brown trout.

But no matter whether you fish the surface or the depths, give miniature tackle a try. You just might hang up your heavy equipment for good.

Bottom-bounced jigs accounted for this hefty string of crappies.

*There is always something new and exciting
in saltwater fishing. Now, at last . . .*

THE PLASTIC WORM GOES TO SEA

BY RUSSELL TINSLEY

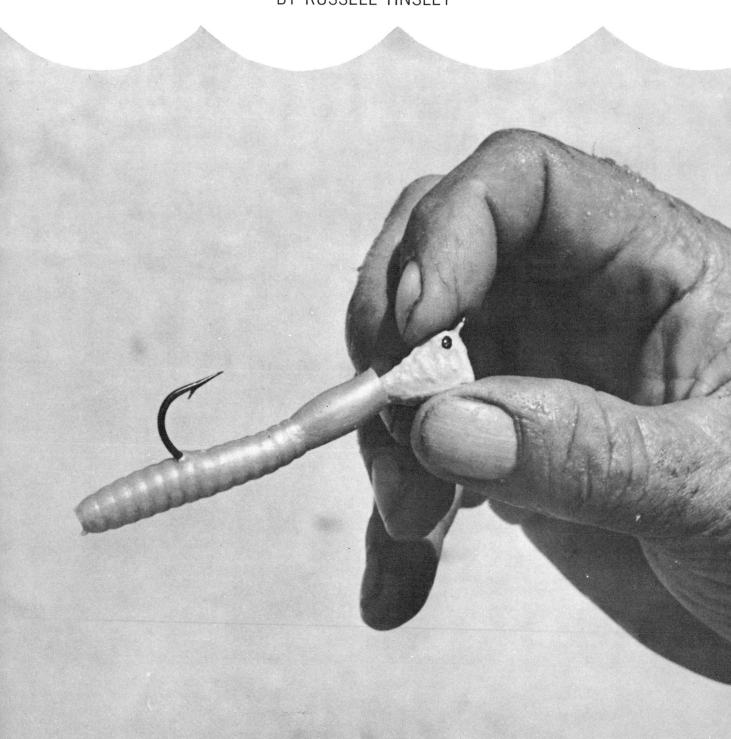

It has often been said that success talks. For Eddie Hudson it literally screams — someone else's success, that is.

Hudson, owner of a window-cleaning business in my hometown of Austin in central Texas, is an avid fisherman. Nothing rankles him more than when someone is catching fish and he is not. He has a lot of pride and determination.

This sunny summer afternoon was particularly painful to Hudson. He was standing on a pier jutting into the Gulf of Mexico at Port Aransas on the Texas coast and casting various artificial baits, but getting only exercise for his efforts. Now it would have been easy for Hudson to dismiss the fishless session as "just one of those things." As any fisherman knows, there are days when nothing will work and the human may as well accept these dry spells philosophically, for there is nothing he can do about it.

Perhaps Hudson could have blamed it on the lack of cooperation by the fish if it hadn't been for another angler nearby. This man didn't seem to be doing anything that Hudson wasn't doing, except for catching fish. Hudson said he was dragging in a large sea trout on practically every cast.

"I kept trying everything in my tackle box, figuring that *something* had to work," Hudson remembered. "While I caught a fish occasionally, this smart aleck down the pier kept hauling 'em in."

Every man has a breaking point. With Hudson, it came when the fisherman strung about his 20th big fish.

"When he pulled those trout up, a stringer full, I couldn't stand it any longer," Hudson went on. "I swallowed my pride and walked over and said, 'Doggone it, mister, what kind of bait is it you're using anyway?'."

Imagine Hudson's surprise and almost disbelief when the angler held up "a bait I'd been using in fresh water for years, a bait I've got a tackle box full of."

It was a common plastic worm—the kind commonly used to catch largemouth black bass.

Hudson didn't become a convert overnight. He had too many tried-and-proven lures in his tackle box. Like most new baits, Hudson went to it only when all his pet standbys wouldn't produce, which isn't giving the lure much of a chance. But lo and behold, he caught fish on the plastic worm and he started using it more and more. Today his tackle box carries an assortment of homemade leadhead jigs in various weights, hundreds of highly colored worms and practically nothing else.

When the plastic worm first appeared on the Gulf of Mexico coast, no one took it seriously. But then as it produced fish, by word-of-mouth its popularity spread. More and more fishermen tried the worm. By odds, since many fishermen were exposing the bait to many fish, it enjoyed phenomenal success. More manufacturers commenced bringing out their versions and styles of the salt-water worm and now the sight of it on shelves of sporting goods stores is commonplace.

In its basic form, the salt-water worm is nothing more than a six-inch, bass-size plastic nightcrawler cut in half, and the three-inch chunk of worm threaded on a leadhead jig.

Where this idea of a plastic worm in salt water originated, no one knows for sure. T-Sgt. Phillip J. Scudder III of Orlando, Fla., claims he was the pioneer. Unless some rebuttal is forthcoming, we'll take his word for it.

"In October of 1956 I was wading the flats of East Bay near Panama City, Fla., when I noticed several dead marine worms floating in the water," he recalled. "These worms were as long and large as a pencil and were of a very flimsy texture.

"Gathering the few I could find, I used them under a float and fished them as you would any bait. Having good luck with these few and unable to locate more, I substituted a plastic worm. The nearest imitation to the worm I could find was a yellow plastic worm with tiny black dots.

"I tried it under the cork a spell without results," he went on. "Then I removed the cork and simply cast the worm and retrieved it. Casting the light worm was difficult; so I pinched on a small sinker for weight.

"Right away I began to get strikes, yet I caught only a few trout since they were merely grabbing the end of the worm and not getting hooked. Remedying this was simple; I pinched off the worm about two inches beyond the hook. The birth of the salt-water plastic worm as we know it today occurred at that moment."

If so, it was a historic moment worth recording for posterity. While the plastic worm never will supersede time-proven baits like the spoon, plug and bucktail and nylon jig, nonetheless it already has left its mark and undoubtedly it will be with us, a standard item in the salt-water fisherman's tackle box, from now on.

What's the secret of this revolutionary new bait? What makes it tick?

Like most salt-water artificial lures, it has negligible action of its own. The way it is manipulated by the fisherman gives it any lifelike qualities. In the water it is not unlike the common leadhead bucktail jig. It is fished in exactly the same way.

Yet for some inexplicable reason it sometimes will produce when a bucktail jig will not. I remember, for example, the first time I tried the plastic worm in salt water. Bob Hill and I were prospecting along the rock jetties which protect the ship channel at Port O'Connor, Texas. Bob had pinpointed a school of cooperative trout near the rocks and we were casting to them. He'd tied a yellow worm on the business end of his line while I elected to use a yellow bucktail jig. The color of the two baits was almost identical. Yet Bob was putting five or more fish in the boat for every one I caught. I've got a stubborn streak and I've caught too many fish on the bucktail jig not to have confidence in it. But it didn't take Bob long to make a convert of me. Success has a way of doing that.

Almost every fish that swims in the brine has a mouth bristling with sharp teeth. When action is hot and furious, a plug or a jig can take a beating. While catching kingfish (king mackerel), I've actually had all the hair stripped from a jig after catching only two or three fish. My only choice, when that happened, was to take time to tie another jig on my line. It meant carrying quite a supply in various colors.

A plastic worm is even more fragile than a bucktail. But once the plastic becomes mangled, it is a simple and quick procedure to slip on a new worm, using the same jig. That the painted head gets scarred, makes no difference. Eddie Hudson doesn't bother to paint his jigs, using only the worm for color, and he's about as successful a salt-water angler as I know.

So the plastic worm is more economical than the bucktail jig. Many anglers I know mold their own jigs and buy bass-fishing worms and cut them in halves. Even with a commercial worm rig, the jig part can be used time and again, merely substituting a new worm when the original goes to pot. Instead of lugging about a huge tackle box filled with lead, the angler can get by with maybe ten to a dozen jigs and a pocketful of worms. Bought in bulk, plastic worms cost just a few cents apiece.

Nowadays the plastic worm is available in practically every color imaginable. This is another reason for its success. Some of the hottest plugs along the Gulf of Mexico coast have traditionally been in outlandish hues like glowing pink, iridescent red, fluorescent orange and the like. What appeal such unlikely colors have to fish, no one can explain. Fishermen just know they produce, which is all they care about anyway. But the drawback of the plug is that often the fish are on or near the bottom and the bait simply doesn't dig deep enough. The bucktail jig would get down to the right territory, all right, but the color selection always has been limited. Available dyes for coloring the hair have limited the choice.

So in a way the worm rig incorporates the best features of the bucktail jig and plug. The worm jig can be worked deep and slowly, and because of its single upturned hook it isn't prone to grab every underwater obstruction; and it is available in the many colors which hitherto could be had only in plugs.

Any type of jig can be used for fishing the worm. For all-around use, the ⅜-ounce jig is best. One of this weight will hug the bottom on retrieve, and it will sink even when a brisk tidal current is flowing. Many fishermen who mold their own jigs use ½-ounce jobs.

Primarily the worm jig has been used for taking bay and estuary species. The plastic worm really hasn't moved into the surf or offshore yet, but it should work equally

Bob Hill hauls a small trout that went for worm into the boat.

Hill unhooks a redfish that was taken on worm jig bumped along bottom.

A gafftopsail catfish got in the act and hit a bright yellow worm.

Bob Armstrong with a large trout he caught while casting off a rock jetty.

The worm has proved most effective on speckled trout (weakfish).

A catch of trout made along Port O'Connor, Texas, jetties on plastic worms.

well here, or anyplace the bucktail jig produces.

Dennis Baurle was telling me of a recent trip he took on the Texas coast. It was a calm day and the Gulf was flat with just a mild surf. In his outboard runabout, he ran parallel to the coast, at the fringe of the surf, where the initial rollers were forming. Every time his fathometer would indicate a depression in the Gulf floor, he'd stop and prospect it with a plastic worm. Practically every gut held fish, and he had a couple of bull redfish (channel bass) of 20-pounds-plus to show for his ingenuity.

But the plastic worm has had its most faithful following among those who pursue the spotted weakfish, or speckled trout, as it is more commonly known. The weakfish has long shown a weakness for the bucktail jig and bright-colored plugs. It prefers a lure worked slow and easy. The trout is a school fish and where you catch one, you'll likely take several. Some fishermen even use two quarter-ounce jigs simultaneously, and when the trout are in a cooperative mood, it isn't uncommon to catch them two at a time. Two dropper lines are tied on a three-way swivel, one slightly longer than the other, and the two jigs are fished just the way you'd manipulate one.

The plastic worm also is quite effective at times when fished under a popping cork. Live shrimp has been the old standby of the cork fisherman, but often a worm will do just as well with considerable less fuss and bother. The elongated cork has a scooped-out head. The worm jig, quarter-ounce size, is tied about 18 inches to two feet below the cork. The bobber rides upright when at rest, but when pulled, it leans over and the head scoops into the water to create a burping sound, like the sound made when trout are feeding on the surface. The pulling also causes the jig to dance up and down and appear alive.

The popping cork is particularly effective when fished in grassy bays. The grass holds tidbits like shrimp which trout eat, but it is impossible to fish a plug or bucktail jig in the thin strata of water covering the grass at the slow speed desired. But with a cork, the dropper is just long enough to dangle the worm above the grass, where any trout lurking below can spot it.

Eddie Hudson prefers just a simple round bobber when fishing over grass. He casts and pulls the cork steadily and slowly over the grassbed, and the worm jig riding below sort of humps along like a swimming shrimp.

Just as it revolutionized the taking of black bass in fresh water, the plastic worm has revolutionized saltwater fishing. While the worm is most predominate along the vast Gulf of Mexico coast, from Florida to Texas, it slowly is beginning to appear along the Pacific and Atlantic coasts. Whether it will catch on at these two far-flung places remains to be seen. But I'm not betting against the worm. It has made a believer of me.

A Texas redfish and the worm jig it was taken on.

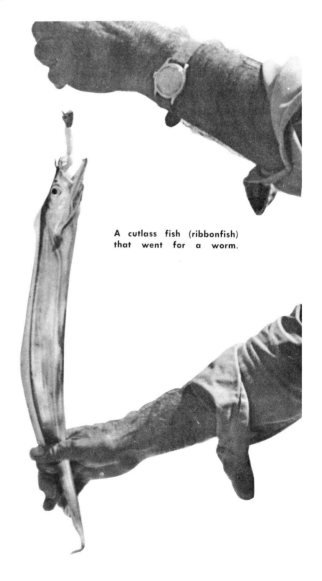

A cutlass fish (ribbonfish) that went for a worm.

Even this flounder hit a slowly fished plastic worm.

TACTICS FOR TROPHY FISH

It's been said that all men are equal before fish—that you have the same chance as the guy in the next boat.

Of course that's true but there are anglers who somehow stack the odds in their own favor. These experts don't work unusually hard at fishing, but they do pay attention to the details of tackle, casting, retrieving and playing fish.

In this country and in others I've seen many outstanding anglers in action, and I'll try here to describe some tricks that will score whether you're after big bass, trout, muskies or other fish. These aren't complicated strategies—just minor but effective tactics that any angler can apply. A fisherman determined to catch *trophy* fish *must* apply them.

By Dick Kotis

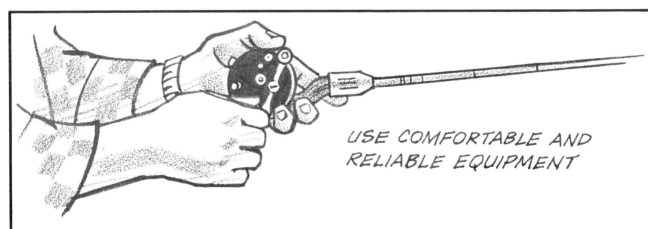

USE COMFORTABLE AND RELIABLE EQUIPMENT

First—and I'll admit this is elementary—you should use reliable and comfortable equipment. Too often anglers come to the water's edge with a dime-store rod and grinding reel, stuff that would be right at home in the county dump. Then they're surprised at losing big fish. Often these are the same fellows who use only the most expensive golf clubs.

A good rod, once you're used to it, should feel almost like an extension of your casting arm. The reel should operate smoothly, with a non-sticking drag. Compared to golf clubs, rifles, shotguns, camping equipment, boats, motors and other outdoor gear, high quality fishing tackle is inexpensive and durable.

Among your tackle there should be lures which swim at various depths—surface baits, shallow runners and deep diving or sinking lures. In each category you also should have different baits designed for slow and rapid retrieving, to suit the mood of the fish.

Most anglers know fish move through various depths but few know exactly which level to fish at what time. Usually fish distribution and activity depend on water temperature, although oxygen content, food supply and other factors also contribute. The best the angler can do is figure where the water is most comfortable for the species of fish. He knows that bass like warm water, trout like cold water, and so on, and he looks for those conditions.

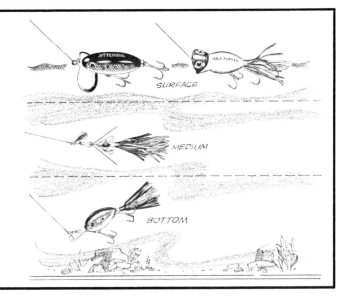

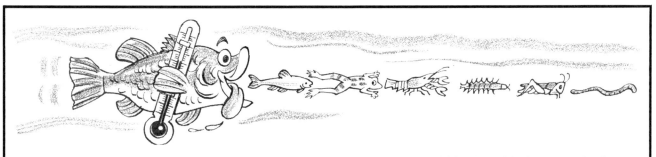

In winter the most suitable water is usually deep. In spring the fish move into the shallows as the sun warms them. In summer the surface becomes too hot for nearly all game species, and the angler fishes deep. Of course he may find feeding fish shallow in early morning, late evening and at night when the water cools somewhat. Then in autumn when the shallows cool again most fish return briefly to the surface. Wherever the fish are, deep or shallow, they'll be near some type of cover—brush piles, boulders or weeds.

One way to pinpoint the most productive fishing depth is to use a water thermometer. A simple mercury thermometer tied to a string with a bulb or cup to trap the water will work, but one of the electronic thermometers now available makes it possible to take a series of deep readings more quickly and efficiently. With these you simply use a chart showing the preferred temperature range of any fish —say, 60 to 70°F. for smallmouth bass or 40 to 50° for lake trout. You locate the proper depth and select a lure to reach it.

Whatever depth you determine, fish near the bottom. That's where most species like to rest. If the best temperature is 30 feet deep, for instance, find a place where the bottom is 30 feet down. If you also have an electronic depth finder and can locate a dropoff or underwater obstruction, so much the better. Of course it isn't necessary to own any of these instruments to catch fish. Just use common sense about water temperature and time-of-day.

To reach the bottom with different lures you must adjust your retrieving speed. With a bait that floats at rest but dives when reeled, for example, you must reel rapidly. The faster you crank, the deeper it dives. Most of these baits— the Arbogaster, for instance—have diving lips which help bounce the hooks over the snags.

To reach extreme depths you must use sinking lures and reel them slowly. With a fast retrieve they just climb through the water. Spoons and weighted spinners fall into this category, and should be allowed to sink after the cast.

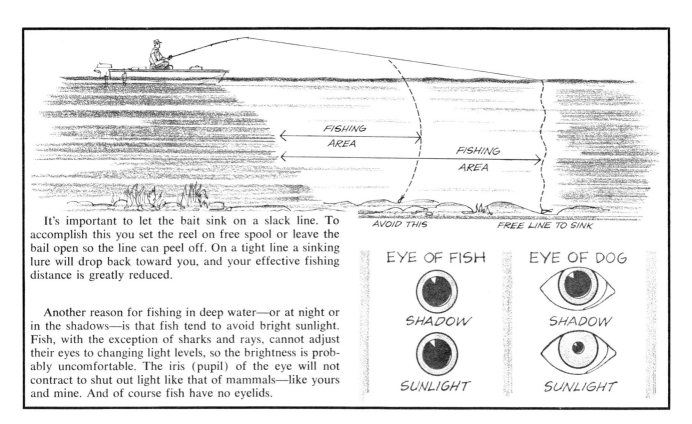

FISHING AREA

FISHING AREA

AVOID THIS

FREE LINE TO SINK

EYE OF FISH

SHADOW

SUNLIGHT

EYE OF DOG

SHADOW

SUNLIGHT

It's important to let the bait sink on a slack line. To accomplish this you set the reel on free spool or leave the bail open so the line can peel off. On a tight line a sinking lure will drop back toward you, and your effective fishing distance is greatly reduced.

Another reason for fishing in deep water—or at night or in the shadows—is that fish tend to avoid bright sunlight. Fish, with the exception of sharks and rays, cannot adjust their eyes to changing light levels, so the brightness is probably uncomfortable. The iris (pupil) of the eye will not contract to shut out light like that of mammals—like yours and mine. And of course fish have no eyelids.

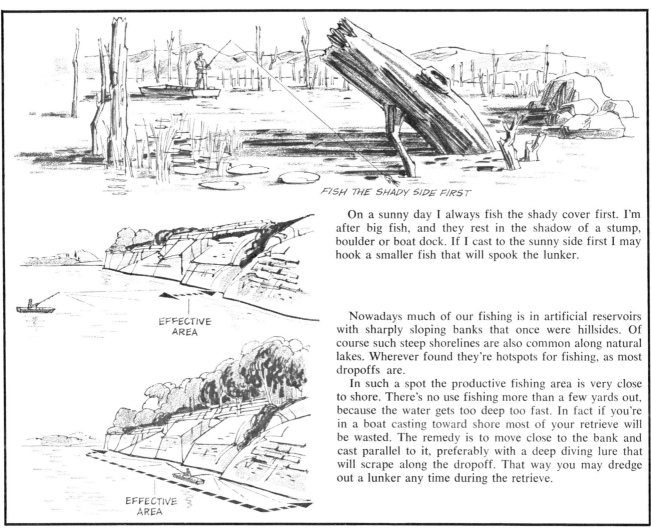

FISH THE SHADY SIDE FIRST

EFFECTIVE AREA

EFFECTIVE AREA

On a sunny day I always fish the shady cover first. I'm after big fish, and they rest in the shadow of a stump, boulder or boat dock. If I cast to the sunny side first I may hook a smaller fish that will spook the lunker.

Nowadays much of our fishing is in artificial reservoirs with sharply sloping banks that once were hillsides. Of course such steep shorelines are also common along natural lakes. Wherever found they're hotspots for fishing, as most dropoffs are.

In such a spot the productive fishing area is very close to shore. There's no use fishing more than a few yards out, because the water gets too deep too fast. In fact if you're in a boat casting toward shore most of your retrieve will be wasted. The remedy is to move close to the bank and cast parallel to it, preferably with a deep diving lure that will scrape along the dropoff. That way you may dredge out a lunker any time during the retrieve.

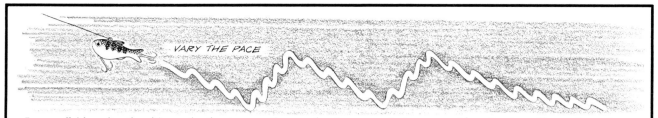

In any fishing situation it's productive to vary the speed and action of the retrieve. I'm sure most anglers know this, but few consistently practice it. We all (I'm guilty sometimes too) tend to reel at a steady, monotonous pace. You've got to concentrate on working the lure like a live minnow, frog or other critter. Alternate rapid reeling with slow, and experiment with rod-tip action until you find a pattern which gets strikes.

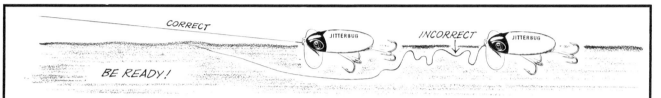

Stop-go retrieves are particularly effective with surface lures. Usually it's best to fish these baits slowly and with long pauses. What's most important is to keep the line nearly taut when the lure is at rest. The bait usually drifts toward you, and if slack develops—even a little slack—you won't be able to hook a striking fish. This simple detail explains why anglers miss so many surface hits. By the time the fisherman jerks up the slack the fish has already spit the bait out.

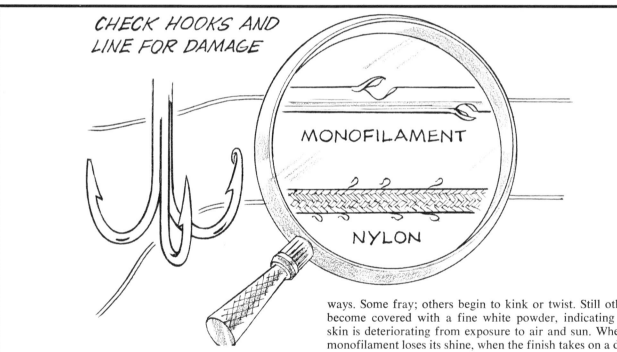

CHECK HOOKS AND LINE FOR DAMAGE

Perhaps the most common error anglers make is to use old, weak line. "Old" is a relative term. The line you used just yesterday may already be badly worn, particularly if your rod guides are scored and rough, if you've been casting among weeds or rocks that abrade the line, or if you've stretched the line repeatedly while fighting fish or loosening snags.

Monofilament spinning lines, which are used increasingly in bait casting, wear very rapidly. By far the strongest part of the monofilament is the thin outer skin, and when this layer is nicked or frayed only a fraction of the original strength remains. Of course it's worn away partly by the action of repeated casting and reeling and by scraping through the line guides.

Monofilaments wear at different rates and in different ways. Some fray; others begin to kink or twist. Still others become covered with a fine white powder, indicating the skin is deteriorating from exposure to air and sun. When a monofilament loses its shine, when the finish takes on a dull, scored appearance, it is usually time to change. A good rule of thumb is to wind on new monofilament after two days of fishing. Using old lines is false economy. Too often anglers empty their wallets on lodging, travel, and guide service only to see the trip ruined by rotten lines.

Braided nylon lines of the type usually used in bait casting don't wear as rapidly. Still they should be checked frequently while you're fishing. Watch for tiny frayed fibers and cut back the first few feet of line frequently.

While you're checking line look very closely at the point, barb and bend of your hooks. A snag, a fish, or repeated scraping along the bottom can bend or break the point. Carry an inexpensive hone in your tackle box and touch up your hooks frequently. It's also a good idea to check a new lure before using it.

FLIES
FOR KELP BASS
By Al Pearce

Author casts in the kelp outside Mission Bay.

Possibly I'd never have fished flies for kelp bass if not for an incident—an accident, actually—several years ago in Baja California.

My brother Dale and I were fishing from the rocks near Punto Santo Tomas. We'd been unable to charter a boat that day, so we were using our energy throwing cut bait at kelp bass.

The shoreline was perfect for this type of fishing. Rocks were conveniently spaced for us to jump from place to place until we were fishing in the middle of a kelp bed. Kelp, is case you don't know, is a rooted, leafy plant which reaches to the ocean surface and sprawls into a canopy. It forms a sort of underwater forest.

With spinning tackle we'd caught and released a few bass when suddenly I hooked something that was unwilling to play our game. It objected to the hook and had the muscle to lend emphasis to its objections.

I started moving for a better spot on the rocks, and that's when the accident happened. It was mid-tide and the rocks were as slippery as a frozen pond in mid-winter. I jumped to a rock that looked like a good fighting platform, and my right leg went east, my left west, and I was upended like a circus clown.

A quick check revealed I wasn't hurt, but the last I'd seen of my rod was the handle slowly disappearing beneath a cluster of kelp. After Dale was sure my scattered pieces were back together, he evidently thought the whole event was funny.

"That's not the way you're supposed to do it," he kept saying.

"Suppose you show me how," I suggested.

"Well, to begin with, you're supposed to bring the fish to you . . ."

"Forget it," I said.

Dale and I had brought only one rod each when we left camp. Now that I'd lost mine — and it was a good one, too — I either had to quit fishing or hike back after another one. It was a good half-mile to camp, but walking was better than listening to Dale.

Sometime later, I was rummaging through the camper for another rod and stumbled across a fly outfit I'd used several weeks earlier in Oregon for salmon and steelhead. At first I laid it aside, but then had second thoughts.

"Why not?" I asked myself. I quickly put the rod together, grabbed a fly box and returned to the rocks. I felt about ten feet high, as I always do with a fly rod in my hand. I really didn't expect to catch much, so I was totally unprepared for the action that followed.

The stick was equipped with a fast-sinking, shooting taper. Since I had no tapered leaders I stripped a section of 10-pound monofilament from a spool and tied on a Silver Abbey fly I'd used effectively on the Oregon salmon.

"Are you sure you didn't land on your head?" Dale asked.

I couldn't think of a single reason why kelp bass wouldn't take a fly. I'd fished for them many times with freshwater bass plugs and had tremendous success. So why not flies? I carefully cast to a spot where two long shoots of kelp opened slightly to form a little channel. It looked like just the place.

It wasn't.

After many more tries, I tied on a Squirrel Doctor . . . then a Ross Special . . . then a Silver Gray . . .

"Would you like me to keep a couple of extra fish for your lunch?" Dale asked.

"I'll eat cheese," I said.

"You mean crow, don't you?"

Finally I tied on a large streamer fly with a three-inch tail and long wing of bucktail. It was one of the Brooks' Blonde patterns that a friend had given me on a recent yellowtail junket. Like many flies used by saltwater fly-rodders, it resembled no natural critter in particular. I tossed it out into the kelp, took a deep breath waiting for it to sink and then started the retrieve.

It was hit instantly, but I reacted too slowly to set the hook. And I was so shaken by the strike that I also missed the next one.

The third time I connected. The kelp bass were fighting among themselves for the fly. And an hour later, Dale was trudging back to camp for his own fly rod.

Since that day three years ago, I've become an avid ocean bass fisherman. Before then, I generally chased them as a substitute for other species that weren't biting, but now I plan ocean-bass trips as carefully as any other expedition.

One such jaunt was near Oceanside in southern California. There was a large kelp bed not far from the harbor entrance which was virtually destroyed during the late 1940's and early 50's by kelp farmers. Eventually the cutting of kelp was brought under regulatory control, and wholesale destruction was stopped.

With the disappearance of the kelp, the fish that lived there also disappeared. But the kelp appears to be coming back now, and so are the bass.

At the time, I was planning to fish with Dutch Greenlund, a retired Air Force officer. I'd told him that kelp bass were suckers for flies and he wanted to fish right then, that very minute. He was like a race horse at the starting gate. "What size rod do I use?" he wanted to know. "What else do I need?"

I explained that in my experience any rod suitable for freshwater bass-bugging was good enough for kelp bass fishing. I generally use a stick that will throw a number

seven line or number eight line. I usually carry at least two rods and several extra line spools.

Ocean bass are found at various depths, and the fly rodder must fish wherever the fish happen to be. For this reason, I always have both fast- and slow-sinking lines as well as a floater. The floating line, which should be a weight-forward taper, must be heavy enough to throw large, wind-resistant flies or bugs. Ocean bass often feed near the top, and these surface or near-surface lures can be effective.

Dutch and I arrived at the kelp beds shortly after sunrise the following morning. In kelp bass fishing you don't have to be on the spot before the cock crows. You can wait until the rooster has worn his larynx to a frazzle if you want.

When fishing near kelp beds, you have a few things more to consider than when fishing in the lettuce of a freshwater lake. There are the problems of currents, of constantly moving kelp and of greater water depths, to mention just a few.

I've found over the years that the best way to tackle a kelp bed is to drift along its edge in a boat. Generally this requires a lot of starting and moving; but occasionally a current will carry you parallel to the kelp. At all times, you should fish on the side of the kelp where the current is working. The current often carries food into the vegetation and the larger fish will be there waiting. When Dutch and I tackled the kelp beds off Oceanside, it was a day when the current permitted us to drift lazily along and cast into the openings always present in kelp.

You might expect the long tentacles of kelp to wind around each other and form tight patterns, but they don't. Kelp beds are full of holes where you can cast. And I've never found it difficult to get a boat out of kelp if I stayed along its edge. A whirling propeller seems to push kelp away if it's not too thick.

Dutch and I tied on the long bucktail streamers I described and started casting. I was using a slow-sinking line

Sometimes bass can be taken from the rocks, particularly if there are kelp beds nearby.

Author boats average-sized kelp outside Mission Bay.

Mexican skiffs carry anglers to
nearby kelp beds for a small fee.

Oversize bucktail streamers
are most productive flies. Color
of lure doesn't seem to matter.

and Dutch started with a floating taper. But he changed lines quickly when I hit pay dirt 15 feet down. I used the cast-and-count method. That is, when the fly hits the water, I let the fly sink while I count. On the first cast, I count five, on the second, ten, until I reach a depth where I get strikes.

"I got one," Dutch roared a few minutes later. "And it hooked itself."

"You haven't got it yet," I warned. "You have to lead it through that kelp."

That maneuver is probably the most difficult aspect of fishing the kelp. It's easy for a fish to loop around the nearest stalk and bind himself to the bottom. Sometimes— and only sometimes—the fish will untangle itself if you relax and keep the line taut. If not, hand-hold the line and pull. Don't attempt to work it loose with the rod; a rod shouldn't take that kind of punishment.

"Holy mackerel." Dutch was shouting, "I must have a real whopper."

He didn't, of course. I've yet to see a fisherman who didn't think he had a whale by the tail the first time he hooked a kelp bass—*any* kelp bass—with a fly rod. He worked the fish expertly, giving as little line as possible, to keep the critter from tangling in the kelp. I couldn't have given him better instructions. The line would barely start moving in one direction before he pulled in the opposite direction. The action was a pleasure to watch.

"There's the fish, Al," he shouted after a couple of minutes. "I can see it." And after a short pause he added, "Aw, it's just a small one."

Actually, it was 15 inches long, about average size. I might say at this point that a fast retrieve is very important, the faster the better. A kelp bass, I believe, will grab its food by the tail and shake it violently before attempting to swallow it. The fly must be moving fast enough to make the bass lunge for it, grabbing enough to take in the hook. I've lost many hits because the three-inch streamer was not in the mouth far enough.

That day at Oceanside was no exception. I lost several strikes, but not all. In fact Dutch and I were catching at least two bass for every one taken by anglers in nearby boats. It's usually that way. Most of the time the fly-rodder can outfish the bait angler two to one. That's especially true if the bass are close to the surface.

I was fishing with James McCormick of San Diego recently and we ran into an exceptional feeding spree. We were fishing the kelp beds off Mission Bay, near perhaps 50 other boats. As usual, I started with a sinking line, but I didn't connect. It was an hour later when I finally decided to try a floating taper. Actually I turned to it just for something to do. Nobody was catching anything anyway.

I tied on a fresh-water bass bug and heaved it into a large opening. I can't be sure, but I think it was actually hit before I started retrieving. A lunker came shooting from somewhere and grabbed the bug and was on its way back down in less time than it takes to snap your fingers.

"Try the top," I shouted to James.

He quickly changed line and tried for some surface action. His first cast was whammied, just as mine had been.

I won't discuss further what great sport an ocean bass is on a fly rod. There's really nothing quite like tangling with ocean bass on the surface, with any tackle. When you get surface action, it's often hot and heavy. It's not unusual to connect on every cast. As in fishing with sunken flies, the retrieve must be fast. At times I've seen a bug hit the instant it strikes the water, but a motionless lure or one retrieved slowly just doesn't do the job. The fish may come up and mouth the tail, but that's about all.

James and I had released at least a dozen fish each before the action abruptly ended. For reasons known only to themselves the bass had left.

I looked at my tattered bug and remembered that morning long ago off the coast of Baja California. I had traded a lost rod for hundreds of torn-up flies and beat-up bugs.

It was a fair exchange, I thought.

Charter boats and small craft alike gather whenever kelp bass are eager to strike.

Above—Catalpa worms which are larvae of the catalpa sphinx moth, may be best blue-gill baits of all. Right—Native (upper fish) and hatchery golden shiners vary slightly in color, shape and, some say, in bass catching.

TRY THESE "Collectors' Items"
By Will Graham

Many anglers seem to think that a live bait is a live bait. In other words a worm is about as good as, say, a minnow, and it's embarrassing to be caught using either of them. Usually these same guys know—and use—a chestful of different artificial lures by their catalogue numbers.

If there's such a thing as a live bait specialist, I suppose I'm one of them. I've fished naturals for more years than I like to admit, and I've found certain ones unusually effective. Among these "collector's items" are some common baits—certain minnows for instance—any many oddities—gar eggs and bonnet worms. I've also learned that fish can be highly selective, so it pays to try several different live baits.

Here's a listing of my favorites, along with tips on how to collect and use them:

MINNOWS

Not all small fish are minnows. Only the shiners, daces, chubs, goldfish, carp and others of the family *Cyprinidae* are true minnows. Of course anglers often use other fishes for bait, including suckers, darters, perch and small catfish. What few anglers realize is that certain of these bait fishes are far more effective than others.

Perhaps the deadliest minnows of all are the delicate, silvery shiners of the genus *Notropis*. These include the emerald shiner (known as "lake shiner" in the Great Lakes region), common shiner, spotfin shiner, spottail shiner, rosefin shiner, redfin shiner, rosyface shiner and several others. They're particularly effective baits for smallmouth bass and walleyes, but it takes very careful handling to keep

Dwarf sirens are legless salamanders. They're unusually tough bass baits.

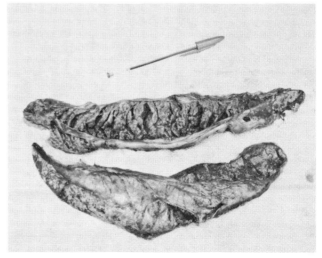

Gar egg mass, though repulsive in appearance, may yield up to 60,000 panfish baits.

"Horse" golden shiners attract only the biggest bass and are nearly as much fun to catch as to fish with.

Dry cloth or sand on hands makes holding the siren easier.

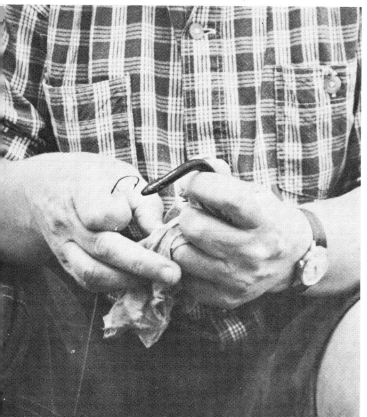

them alive. The fisherman who makes the extra effort to use them usually makes a heavier catch.

The emerald and common shiners are occasionally available in bait shops, but in most places you'll have to catch your own from local waters. Before starting, check with your state conservation department for regulations on seines, traps and waters where bait may be gathered. Working by yourself you can handle a short seine in a small stream or weedy cove. With a larger seine, two men can wade in shallow water, starting a few feet deep and hauling toward shore. It's also possible to anchor one end of a long seine on shore and swing the other around until it reaches the bank.

After the drag, form the seine into a bag just under the water and carefully select the minnows you want with a dip net. Don't empty the seine on shore or you'll destroy much valuable aquatic life—tiny minnows, immature game fish, crustaceans, and insect nymphs.

Another way to catch minnows is to use the old glass or wire trap with funnel openings. These devices are considerably less efficient than seines, but also require less effort to use. Scrape out a depression in the streambed for the trap, place the entrance facing downstream and bait with bread, cracker crumbs, or balls of oatmeal.

The exact collection technique you use may depend on the habits and habitat of the particular minnow species. For illustration let me describe how I catch some favorite minnows where I live in Florida.

For most of the year, the red minnow, *Notropis maculatus*, swims about in silvery-tan anonymity. But come spawning time, it shucks its drab coloration and dons a cloak of bright red. When "the red minnows are in," fish and fisherman are never far behind.

Generally distributed from Mississippi through Florida, the red minnow is found in large lakes and rivers. An incomplete lateral line and a black dot at the base of its tail—along with the bright red seasonal coloring—are identification give-aways.

Spawning is somewhat spasmodic, starting as early as March (in Florida) and frequently extending well into the summer. There is no way to predict exactly when and where the minnows will be, but once discovered, word of mouth spreads the news from fisherman to fisherman. Camp operators are a big help, too.

There's another restriction. Like other *Notropis* species, red minnows don't store worth a darn. They're tender in captivity and even if you get them over this hump, they quickly "bleach out" to the pale coloration. This means you must catch them in the act of spawning, which actually isn't too difficult. You need to know generally where they are, of course, but other clustered boats will reveal this. Occasionally you can spot them, but normally they swim too deep for visual sighting. Quivering pads or weeds indicate their presence, while sharper disturbances nearby indicate bigger game is also in the area.

Though a rigid, commercial umbrella net will work, a smaller home-made model of flexible wire screening (no framing—just lines tied to all four corners) can be poked down into the pads with an oar handle if necessary. After a few moments' settling-down time, a quick retrieve may yield a quart of these carmine-colored fish attractors.

Cane poles are the standard rig for red-minnow fishing with no special techniques involved except perhaps to put two or three minnows on the hook when the action slows down. My catches with red minnows have been very good, and I've heard reliable reports of fish-hogs taking bass in numbers too shameful to report here.

Another minnow—one that's often as effective as the red but can withstand rougher handling—is the golden shiner, *Notemigonus crysoleucas*. In Florida it's the bait most old-timers prefer for really big bass, but it actually ranges throughout the eastern and central United States. It's brassy-colored with a slightly upturned mouth and forked tail, and reaches a length of 12 inches or more.

Hatchery golden shiners have largely replaced natural shiners for bait, with anglers considering the convenience factor. Many swear, too, that the hatchery shiner is hardier on the hook. For me, it's a consideration of time. I can always pick up a dozen shiners from the local bait dealer. But when time isn't involved, catching your own can add to the sport.

For collecting wild golden shiners, a few hardy individuals use a cast net, but more often they're caught with a lightweight cane pole, using a long-shanked size 14 hook. Bait can be bread, flour balls, oatmeal, or a tiny worm fragment, but for me, oatmeal works best. In a likely area around weeds or lily pads, I throw a handful of oatmeal as chum,

Small caledonia, big fish. Bass both love and hate these baits, so you can't miss.

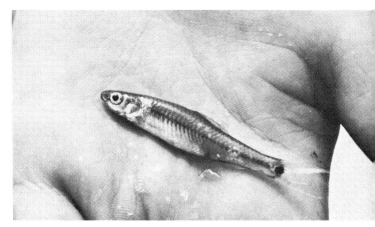

During spawning, red minnow lives up to its name, but reverts to straw color for rest of year.

Salamanders are popular and highly effective bass baits in some regions.

then lash at it with a cane pole to attract the shiner's attention. Then I take another handful of oatmeal and moisten it just enough so fragments can be rolled into tiny balls for the hook. Shiners are typically "nibblers," but can be entertaining to catch. In some instances you can fish for shiners on one side of the boat, and use them to catch bass on the other.

Wild shiners have the annoying habit of zooming out of your bait bucket or live-well whenever they get the chance. Hatchery shiners seem a little more agreeable in this respect.

Shiners can be fished on the bottom with a slip sinker or held near the surface with a float. With a spinning outfit, my favorite method is to let the shiner swim freely, hindered only by a hook in the mouth or back.

In Florida, huge native shiners a foot long are used to entice the lunkers from hotspots like the St. Johns River. Cranking in a shiner that big is a thrill in itself, let alone a 12-pound bass wrapped around it!

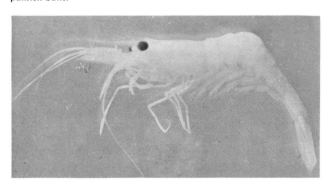

Freshwater shrimp, smaller than saltwater species, are outstanding panfish baits.

Another excellent bass minnow is the caledonia, which, unfortunately, lives only in peninsular Florida. It's pearlish-grey, cigar-shaped, nearly transparent, and has scales with black-dotted edges. Also called "bullhead" or "stoneroller" (from its habit of kicking up puffs of sand where it feeds or spawns), this up-to-eight-inch fish is technically known as *Fundulus seminolis,* or caledonian, usually shortened to "caledonia." Although there was once a commercial supplier of this bait on Lake George and there are still isolated fish camps where it can be purchased, the caledonia is usually another "collector's item."

Caledonias can be seined along the shallow sandy stretches of the larger Florida lakes (they don't occur in all lakes). Or, there's a unique method of night collecting which can be productive—provided you don't forget the mosquito repellent. You use a piece of stove pipe or two five-quart cans soldered together with their ends cut out, a lantern with enough light to "freeze" the caledonia to the bottom, and your minnow bucket. As you wade along shallow, sandy lake edges, the light immobilizes the caledonia, you clap the pipe over it and merely reach down to grab it.

Another popular method of caledonia collecting is to fish for them with a cane pole, light monofilament, a fragment of cork, a tiny BB shot, and a size 14 to 16 hook. Thread a quarter-inch of worm over the hook and barb, and fish in shallow water along the weeds. Often it pays to jiggle the bait along. But keep the hook point covered or you'll wind up with nothing in the bait bucket.

I figured why bass go for calendonias so passionately. On the one hand, they love them for their taste appeal and ideal eating size. On the other hand, bass may attack them because calendonias raid bass nests for eggs and fry.

Lively on the hook, caledonias can be "held down" by standard sinkered terminal tackle, but with a spinning rig and a bass hook, thread both lips or pierce lightly behind the dorsal fin for an ideal free-roving, bass-attracting rig. If you want your bait (and this works with shiners, too) to

Spearing, where legal, is an exciting way of collecting gar eggs for bait.

Golden shiners are deadly baits for winter bass fishing.

Caledonias may be caught on hook-and-line, as here, or netted or "stove-piped."

swim downward, hook it in the lips; in shallow water, hook it in the back. Frequently a caledonia will jump from the water with an open-mouthed bass close behind. That's bad for your heart, so hook your bait accordingly. Let the bass run with the bait until it has the opportunity to turn it around head-first in its mouth, tighten the line, set the hook, and hang on.

By the way, contrary to their ruggedness on the hook, caledonias are delicate, nervous fish in confinement, which explains why they are not readily available from bait dealers. In cool, dark water, however, they can be kept with some degree of success. I've been told the addition of a couple of aspirin tablets to the water helps settle them down.

SALAMANDERS

Perhaps the deadliest bass baits of all are salamanders and newts. They're effective for both largemouths and smallmouths, and in some areas—the mountains of North Carolina and eastern Tennessee, where they're incorrectly called "lizards"—they're sold in bait stores. Elsewhere you must find your own under rocks, logs and undercut banks near streams or other moist places.

From southern Georgia through Florida, a few anglers fish with "eels" which actually are narrow-striped dwarf sirens, cousins of the salamander. The siren has tiny three-toed forelegs and external gills, is as big around as a lead pencil, and as tough as a steel cable. It commonly grows to six inches, occasionally to ten, and if I were limited to a single bass bait, it's what I'd choose.

Collecting sirens can be a rough proposition. They live in floating hyacinths, entwining among the roots, dining on grass shrimp and other tiny organisms. The bait-hunter must wade in belly-deep water, year around (all our weather isn't exactly the chamber of commerce type!), working a floating screen box under the hyacinths. He then sorts out the hyacinths contained in the box, shaking them over the screen, leaving an assortment of insects, grass shrimp, an occasional snake—and hopefully some eels.

Shrimp are often common along weedy shorelines,
where they're easily collected with dip nets.

Several years ago I followed a group around in the misty dawn's light, wading among ghostly dead cypress trees, pushing solid rafts of hyacinths aside at each step, concerned mostly for my camera on the mucky, slippery, logered real estate beneath my tennis shoes. Cattle breakfasting on the succulent green plants eyed us curiously.

With four people working, we uncovered only 11 dozen eels in a half-day's work. And I understand things are rougher now with so much spraying, drainage, and land-manipulating going on. Ideal eel habitat, never abundant, is becoming scarcer.

Instead of wading, I've collected from a boat, shaking hyacinths over a wood-framed screen. Frequently, too, this bass bait supreme can be spaded up under hyacinths left on dry land after a sudden drop in water level.

If not too crowded, sirens will keep indefinitely in a bucket with water and a clump or two of hyacinths. Of course the water will need changing occasionally.

Sirens are as slippery as the proverbial eel so a rag or a can of dry sand to help hold them is essential for baiting-up. Hook the critter in the back above the spinal column or through the lips. Use a thin wire hook and be prepared for a disconcerting and pathetic little squawk when the barb penetrates.

The baits are unusually tough; I've caught eight bass on one. They don't stop kicking—and even if they do, you can use them like you would a plastic imitation. The only difference is that the siren, even dead, will attract more bass.

FRESHWATER SHRIMP

Frequently the best baits are right under a fisherman's boat, in abundance, and free for the taking, baits that game fish have grown up with and eaten most of their lives. Yet these baits are overlooked by most fishermen.

The fresh-water shrimp (or grass shrimp) is an example. Common in Lake Erie, the Illinois River, the Carolinas and Florida, this diminutive tidbit is high on the list of food found in most game fish stomachs. *Palaemonetes paludus* deserves more recognition than it gets.

In Florida, however, this transparent morsel seems to be increasing in stature as a fish bait. My favorite tackle dealer informs me that more and more anglers come in to ask for a "net to catch grass shrimp." Fresh-water shrimp live in the vegetation of most Florida lakes and rivers. Hyacinth roots, maidencane, and eelgrass seem to be favored hangouts.

Except for a more hump-backed appearance and small one-inch size, they're similar to the edible salt-water species and very likely they perform the same function as a staple food item. Only isolated dealers or camps offer them for sale. While they are easy to catch, they're somewhat difficult to hold in large numbers. One fish camp near my central Florida home town of Eustis has some success keeping them in a wire cage and selling them by the handful—about 100 to 150—for a dollar.

You can fashion a dipnet from wire screen, but for a few dollars you can buy an ideal net known as a "bait net." This net, used by dealers to scoop minnows from tanks, has a straight and wide leading edge, a deep fine-meshed nylon bag, and a four- or five-foot handle. The deep bag is essential because the shrimp will ricochet out of anything shallow. Drag the net through some underwater vegetation and you may come up with anywhere from 0 to 100 of these zippy little speedsters. A short minnow seine makes an efficient gathering tool, too, if you don't mind wading.

Bonnet worm is deadly bait for bluegills, other sunfishes.

A few Florida old-timers use cast net for golden shiners.

Author uses wire screen to catch minnows in weedy Florida lakes.

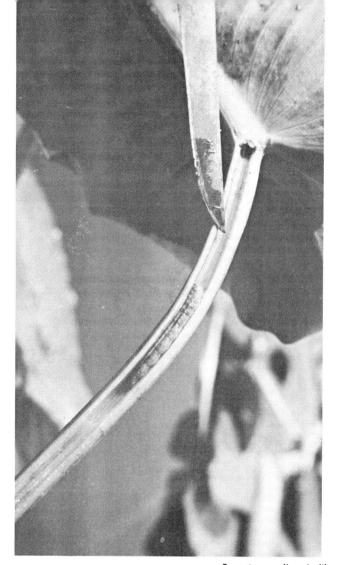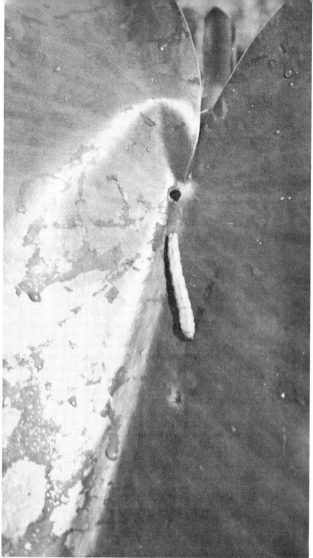

Bonnet worm lives in lily-pad stem and becomes
a dull-colored moth — if not eaten first by fish.

Most fish chew on this tasty crustacean with gusto, but it's particularly attractive to crappies, redeared sunfish, and all the catfishes. Commercial catfishermen use shrimp on their lines, coming up with some surprising catches for such a tiny offering. For crappies and redeared sunfish, cane poles rigged with a hook no larger than a No. 8 are ideal. Hook the shrimp through the tail and watch that float!

While dead shrimp will turn soft and be worthless, if you have any extras or fresh dead ones, put them in the sun on an absorbent paper towel. They turn firm and crunchy, and they work. In fact, what they gain in odor might be even more appealing to the fish.

CATERPILLARS

At least twenty kinds of caterpillars are commonly used as bait, and they're highly effective, particularly for panfish. Among the best are waxworms, catalpa worms, corn borers, corn earworms, cutworms, armyworms and bagworms.

One of the lesser known but readily available spring and early summer baits that I frequently turn to for a stringer of panfish is a moth caterpillar which lives in the stems of lily pads. At times, this creeping critter, usually called a "bonnet worm," will hold more appeal than any other offering.

What you'll be looking for is a drab, whitish caterpillar with a reddish-brown head. The length is about 1½ inches, the diameter less than that of a lead pencil. Ultimately it turns into a nondescript moth with a wing span of a little over two inches. It's a tough bait, sometimes accounting for a half-dozen or so bluegills before it is too tattered for further use.

A give-away to the bonnet worm's presence in a lily pad is a neat round hole bored in the leaf where it is attached to the stem. The general appearance of the pads where they are working will be unhealthy, with brown, curled edges. If the pad looks sad, chances are the bonnet worm has already wriggled to a fresher home. Don't waste time there; watch instead for a healthy pad with a new hole. Frequently there will be a mound of chewings at the entrance which indicates the pad is inhabited.

If you like exercise, you can pull the pad until the stem breaks. It's easier to cut the stem with a knife about a foot below the surface. Split this stem carefully, and you'll probably see your quarry humping hurriedly along, concerned at the great upheaval.

Bonnet worms can be stored for a few days in a bait bucket; throw in some stem sections to keep them happy. By the way, use a metal or hard plastic container, because they can chew through the Styrofoam type. I know from first-hand experience. Head- or tail-hook these worms, using a cane pole or light spinning outfit.

I've been asked if a bonnet-worm gatherer can't ruin a section of lily pads by his cuttings. But the answer is simple: any pad with a bonnet worm in it dies anyway.

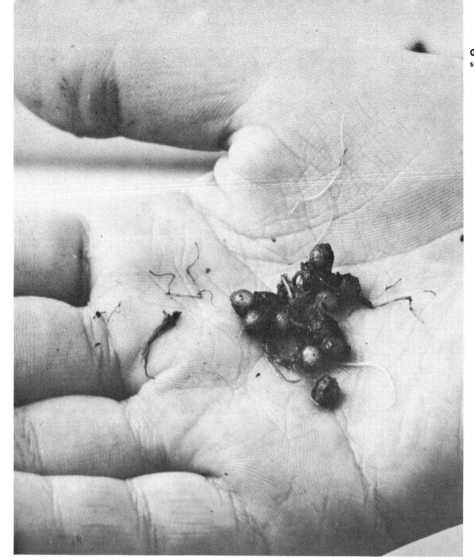

Gar eggs are dirty-white in color and somewhat sticky.

GAR EGGS

Gar eggs are as sporty to collect as they are productive to use. BB-sized, dead white in color, and somewhat sticky, they're a favored bite-sized bluegill tidbit. The bluegills follow the spawning gars, inhaling the eggs as they are expelled.

Occasionally you'll find a dealer who sells frozen gar eggs, particularly in an area where there has been a gar spearing contest or commercial seining. But usually you'll have to gather your own—which can be fun.

In the warm spring months, particularly in morning and evening, gars undertake their spawning chores in the shallower water around floating or rooted vegetation. During their frenzied activity, I've even seen them flip a few of their eggs out onto the tops of lily pads (the grackles love them). It's possible to collect enough eggs for a fishing foray with a small strainer or your hand, if you know what you're looking for.

The best method is to spear the bigger gars, which are usually females. Make sure spearing is legal in your state, however. The ovaries of a big female gar may yield 60,000 eggs.

To fish the eggs, use a stout cane pole, monofilament line, split shot, and a small thin-wire hook, spearing one or two eggs through the barb. Sink the bait where there has been gar-spawning activity. Normally, the bluegills don't recognize the deception until it is too late.

When action is slow, one enterprising gar-egg specialist beats the water with his cane pole to simulate spawning gars, then fishes with previously collected gar eggs to haul in the betrayed bluegills. With an abundant supply, you can afford to resort to further trickery by combining chumming and pole-lashing to create your own "instant" bluegill fishing.

WORMS AND CRICKETS

Though worms are a popular bait, they are no longer a popular bait to collect. The worm-raising industry has made it convenient to part with a few pieces of silver for a neat container of healthy worms. Somehow this is more appealing than digging your own under a hot sun.

In Florida a few folks gather them from compost piles or along the shores of lakes where the critters live in damp or soaking-wet sands.

There is a style of worm collecting in the swampy panhandle section of the state which bears mention, some families earning a pretty good seasonal living at it. They pound a stake into the ground, saw another piece of wood across the top of it to set it screeching and vibrating. The worms pop to the surface where they are easily gathered. I confess I've never tried this trick myself.

Crickets, too, are raised in such quantity nowadays that overturning rocks or running around in a field with an insect net is a thing of the past.

Worms, gar eggs, bonnet worms and the rest—give all these collector's items a try where you fish.

Basic Ice Fishing

by Ed Hutchins

A discussion of frostbite fishing fundamentals, plus advice on ice fishing baits and how to raise them at home

In most of the northern states fishing is a seasonal sport identified with such symbols of warm weather comfort as shaded river banks, outboard motors and rolled up shirtsleeves. However there are exceptions to every rule and those whose fishing fever cannot go unsatisfied during the winter months must either journey to a warm climate or take up the sport of ice fishing.

Notwithstanding its demand on personal comfort, ice fishing is an increasingly popular form of winter recreation. In fact one recent study showed that ice fishing popularity in many sections of northern United States where the ice is thick enough to support the fishermen may nearly equal that of the summer anglers. And it even exceeds summer fishing in certain localized areas.

Ice fishing has long been recognized as one of the most productive forms of sport fishing. On a fish-per-hour basis, ice fishing is in a class by itself, especially where bluegills and yellow perch are abundant. However, good catches of walleyes, crappies, bass, catfish, northern pike, lake trout, carp and several other species are made in certain waters. In general, any body of water that provides good fishing in other seasons will most likely be productive for ice fishing. Farm ponds and other small lakes are an especially good bet because of their large populations of bluegills.

Ice fishing should not be attempted until the ice is at least two inches thick. Even then the fisherman must exercise extreme caution in areas where spring water or some other warming influence might have reduced the safety margin. Since ice fishing ordinarily takes place under conditions of low temperature often accompanied by bitter winds, it is almost impossible to dress too warmly. An outfit that has become virtually the ice fisherman's "uniform" consists of a heavy parka with hood, a good pair of gloves (perhaps two pairs) and insulated boots. The heated, portable shanties used in some areas are probably the ultimate in ice fishing comfort, but are seldom practical for the man who fishes only a few hours at a time and would have to transport the shanty to and from the lake. Many fishermen use portable windbreaks which can be carried over a shoulder or hauled on a small sled.

Although there are several devices on the market intended to simplify cutting holes in the ice, the most practical tool for the average fisherman is the "spud bar," a heavy iron bar with a broad chisel-like end.

However, where the ice is unusually thick and many holes are to be made, power saws prove to be very practical. Ideally, ice fishing holes should be eight or ten inches in diameter, with 12 inches sometimes the largest that can be made legally, obviously for safety reasons. After the fisherman spuds a hole in the ice, he cleans out the slush with a small strainer or sieve.

Some fishermen cut holes at each of the various locations where they suspect fishing might be good, or perhaps where they have made good catches previously. It is a good idea to fish each hole for a few minutes and in this way determine which holes produce the best results. Fishermen tend to concentrate at points where a few good strings of fish have been taken, and this does not necessarily detract from the area. In fact, some veteran ice fishermen believe that added light and air made available from the greater number of holes actually serve to attract fish to the area. As a general rule, the deeper the water, the better the chance of good ice fishing. An especially choice spot is where there is a source of spring water several feet under the ice.

During the past few years many ice fishermen have been using electronic devices, such as the Lo-k-tor to find schools of fish. This effects a great savings in valuable fishing time.

There are several combinations of equipment popular with ice fishermen. These range from the simplest hook and line outfits to some fairly elaborate "tip-up" devices which can be left unattended and will signal when a fish takes the bait. Local regulations should be checked for the maximum number of hook and line and/or tip-ups permitted each fisherman. Rods for ice fishing need not be expensive—in fact, very few of them are.

An old flyrod tip or simply a short stick or piece of heavy, stiff wire is usually all that is needed. Most fishermen prefer to sit close to the hole and use the typical, short, ice fishing rods. However, a few ice fishing addicts insist they have better success with a slightly longer rod which allows them to sit back a few feet from the hole, thereby reducing the chance of fish seeing them or their shadow.

Of course, it is a subject of debate whether fish can see the fisherman through several feet of water plus a covering of ice and snow, but the relative wariness of fishes no doubt varies with local conditions with the relative clarity of the water perhaps being the major factor. In general, winter usually brings about an extreme slow-down of fish metabolism with a proportionate decrease in all activities and sensibilities.

The line preferred for most ice fishing is monofilament of approximately four-pound test, with a short leader section of lighter material used when the fish are not biting readily. The most popular hook size for panfish is about No. 12, with gold-plated hooks or ice flies often preferred because of their shiny appearance which is probably attractive to fish. Many experienced ice fishermen use two hooks or flies on each line. One is tied to the end of the main leader, and a "dropper" is on another length of leader tied to the main line a foot or so from the bottom. This allows the use of two different kinds of lures or baits at same time and at different depths.

Opinions vary as to whether a float or bobber should be used. When using a float, it should be set to position the bottom hook six inches or less from the bottom. An easy way to determine the depth of the water is to temporarily attach a sinker to the hook and allow it to go to the bottom—then to set the float accordingly, and remove the sinker. In certain waters where there is a current, a sinker must be used when actually fishing or else the line will be swept out under the ice and never reach the bottom. When

After spudding out a hole, the ice fisherman uses a sieve to strain out ice and slush. Next he dunks his bait. The angler is Lowell Woodrich, editor of the Outdoor Beacon.

a small amount of weight on the end of the line is desirable, the little metallic ice fishing flies might be used in preference to a sinker.

Ice fishing without a float requires extra skill on the part of the fisherman as he must be alert for the almost imperceptible tugs on the line indicative of a nibbling fish. A trick used by some of the experts who fish without a float is to put a kink in the monofilament line just above the surface of the water. When the kink straightens out, it is very likely a fish has taken the bait. At certain times, a gentle up and down motion of the rod tip serves to impart a waving action to the flies which makes them appear more lifelike and usually adds to their effectiveness.

In the wintertime, fish are not apt to feed as readily or as heavily as in the warm seasons, and they ordinarily show a definite preference for live baits, usually in the smaller sizes. A good trick is to use ice flies baited with small grubs until the fish are located or until they begin feeding actively. Then, a little experimentation quickly indicates whether the grubs or the ice flies can be eliminated.

The most popular baits for ice fishing are waxworms, which are larvae of wax moths; mousies, or rat-tailed maggots, larvae of syrphus flies; and "spikies," or blow maggots, larvae of blow flies and flesh flies. Some fishermen find mealworms as effective in winter as in the summer. Mealworms are larvae of darkling beetles. Minnows, of course, are always popular and a good bet to have along on an ice fishing trip.

Some fishermen have discovered there is an excellent source of live bait awaiting the man who will hunt weed fields and woods edges for goldenrod plants that show the characteristic swelling or gall of the goldenrod moth larva. However, most of the gall worms reach the adult stage and emerge from the gall by fall, so the fisherman often must cut into several dozen galls before finding one larva, or worm suitable for fishing.

Most of the popular live baits are readily available in bait stores, but some of the more avid ice fishermen like to rear their own live baits with a preference shown for mealworms and waxworms. There are two kinds of mealworms, namely yellow mealworms and dark mealworms. They are very similar except for color.

Mealworms derive their name from the fact they feed on grain. In fact, they are a serious pest when they get into stored meal, bran, grains, coarse cereals, oatmeal, and similar products. They also occur in meat scraps, among dead insects, or in mixtures of feathers, refuse, grain and other litter in chicken houses. Mealworms are the larval form of the darkling beetle. The mealworm is sometimes called the false wireworm, but it can be distinguished from the true wireworm by the presence of an upper lip in front

Angler Lowell Wodrich, editor of the Outdoor Beacon (Oak Harbor, Ohio) makes a perch double on Lake Erie. The bait: emerald shiners.

Lantern furnishes light for night fishing and also helps keep angler Dick Kotis warm at Mogadore Reservoir near Akron, O.

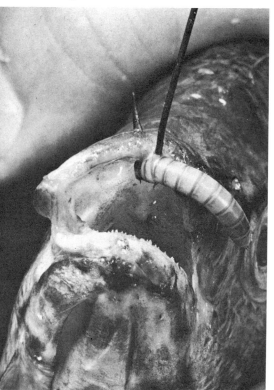

Close-up of mealworm used to hook a large bluegill thru the ice.

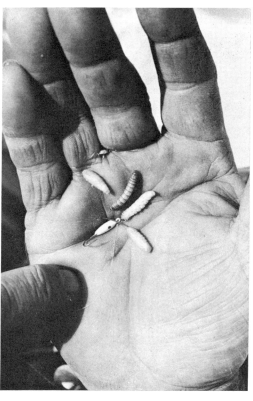

Popular ice fishing baits clockwise: ice fly, spikie, mealworm, waxworm, mousie.

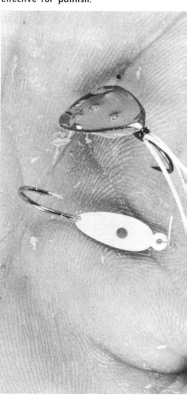

Typical ice "flies" which anglers now fir effective for panfish.

of the mouthparts. Most mealworms also possess a tail-end which is smooth and usually without prominent, paired, sharp appendages.

Dr. Alvah Peterson, Professor Emeritus of Entomology at Ohio State University, in his book "Fishing with Natural Insects," gives a good account of how to rear mealworms at home. He says he used wheat bran mixed with a small amount of brewer's yeast placed in a large covered glass jar, earthenware pot or other container to a depth of three to six inches. Some breeders use a mixture of graham flour and meat scrap. Dr. Peterson says that brewers' yeast usually increases the size of the larvae.

The adult darkling beetle lives an average of 84 days and the female lays an average of about 460 eggs. Mealworms pass through nine to 20 moults and are at least one inch in length when fully grown. For satisfactory growth of the larvae, a constant supply of moisture must be maintained, but one should avoid excessive moisture which may result in molds that are toxic to the larvae. Carrots, cut potatoes, lettuce or pieces of cabbage placed near the top of the bran provide ample moisture.

Before the larvae are fully grown, pupation material should be provided. This may be pieces of rough burlap, strips of one inch wide corrugated paper, crumpled pieces of paper toweling, or cellucotton. Full-grown larvae crawl into these products and change to naked pupae without

forming a pupal cocoon or cell. For best results they should not be disturbed in this stage. When the black beetles emerge from the pupae they should be removed from the cultures for maximum protection. It is apparent that many adults in a culture probably eat the eggs and otherwise disturb the pupae. The development of nearly grown larvae can be retarded if they are kept in a cool place (refrigerator) at 40 to 50 degrees F. To get your start with mealworms, they can be obtained from a breeder or dealer, and adult darkling beetles are fairly easy to collect where they occur under stones, logs, rubbish, beneath loose bark, and even attracted to lights at night.

Probably the favorite bait for ice fishing, and one of the most easily reared at home, is the waxworm. Although they are available on a year-round basis, many bait stores stock them only in the winter because of the demand by ice fishermen. The waxworm is the larval stage of the greater wax moth. It has a head, three pairs of jointed legs and five pairs of fleshy feet. It is about one inch long when fully grown and is grayish-white in color.

Waxworms occur infrequently in properly managed honeybee colonies, particularly in the northern states where low winter temperatures kill the larvae. However, wax moth eggs are usually present on old, stored bee combs which can be obtained from a beekeeper. The best combs for this purpose are old brood combs containing

anglers have a ready supply of baits (the gall th larva, here) from goldenrod stems standing in the fields.

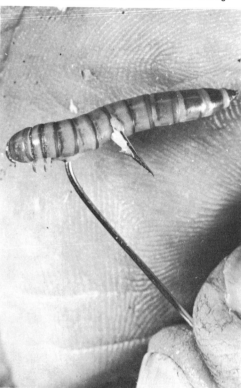
Close-up of how mealworm, larva of darkling beetle, is impaled on a hook for ice fishing.

Waxworms, larvae of the greater wax moth, make excellent ice fishing baits.

pollen and honey as well as many years' accumulations of larval skins. The old brood combs that have been exposed to wax moths can be placed in a widemouth fruit jar, covered with fine mesh wire screen (40 to 60 mesh) and held at average room temperature (70 to 75 degrees F.). The period of time required for development of waxworms varies somewhat, but the larval period averages close to a month. The larvae feed at first on the comb itself and are first detected by their gradual assemblage in a mass of webbing from which tunnels of web material extend through the remainder of the comb. As the tunnels are built, wax is consumed and the comb finally weakened and destroyed.

Fishermen who know the waxworm prefer full grown larvae, just ready to spin cocoons, and larvae within cocoons. The period of time that waxworms are full grown within cocoons may be five days or less. Development of the waxworm after it is in the cocoon may be delayed for a week or longer if the cocoons are placed in a refrigerator at 40 degrees F. When waxworm production is completed, the old bee comb should be carefully destroyed by burning to rule out any possibility of spreading diseases that affect honeybees.

Great quantities of waxworms are sometimes produced quite by accident. A few years ago an OSU graduate student of my acquaintance, who was also a beekeeper, stored his annual crop of honey, still in the combs, in the basement of the house where he roomed. Unfortunately, heat from the nearby furnace provided optimum conditions for development of waxworms and the basement soon became infested with all stages of the greater wax moth. For some reason, the landlady took a negative attitude toward wax moths in her basement and the student was given only a few days to remove the honey, the wax moths and himself from the premises.

Ice fishing is a marvelous winter sport regardless of how seriously one takes it up. When the fish are hitting, almost everyone makes good catches, expert and novice alike. Another interesting thing is that the success rate of most ice fishermen improves as the season progresses and is ordinarily far better during late winter than in the early part. It has been conjectured that fat stored during the fall may be reduced by the latter part of winter so that the fish become more interested in taking food. Fish that are taken through the ice are almost always in prime condition for table purposes. Furthermore, the removal of large numbers of bluegills from ponds and lakes is highly desirable from the management standpoint since it helps maintain a proper equilibrium between bass and bluegills. But probably the best thing of all about ice fishing is that it helps abate the winter form of a human affliction known as fishing fever.

ONE OF SPORT FISHING'S ALL-TIME GREAT PERFORMERS
REVEALS HIS SECRETS IN

HOW I CATCH
GIANT FISH

ON LIGHT TACKLE

BY STU APTE

The action began when our mate, Lucho, saw a sailfish jump at least a quarter mile off our starboard beam. Immediately Capt. Jaime Archibald turned the 31 foot Bertram sharply, increasing his rpm at the same time, in order to lead the direction of the fish and make an intercept. As we approached the area in which we saw the fish, Archie reduced the throttle setting to a fast trolling speed. My wife Bernice and the mate put a pair of artificial squid teasers over the side.

Suddenly a bill appeared behind each teaser. Bernice and the mate slowly reeled the squid teasers away from the fish. They moved them just fast enough to keep them away from the slashing bills of the excited sailfish. I slipped a cut bait with a hook into the water. The fish lunged at my bait and the furious battle began. When it ended I had landed another record fish.

And catching record fish has been both my vocation and avocation for much of my life.

But catching this fish really began long before Bud and Joan Williams had invited me to try some of the fabulous fishing at their Tropic Star Lodge in Pinas Bay, Panamà. A few months before Fred Wintzer, Ed Keller and I (all of us involved in DuPont's Stren Division) were discussing the possibility of catching a giant Pacific sailfish on very light tackle spinning gear. We knew it would be difficult, but then all things are possible and when Bud's invitation came, I leaped at the chance to try. But first we had to agree upon what constituted catching of giant fish on light tackle.

Should the fish weigh 500 pounds or over to qualify? Certainly not! Of the different fish I have caught on light tackle, an 82 pound sailfish is one of my proudest achievements. Why then, when the all-tackle record for this species stands at 220 pounds, am I as proud as can be of this 82 pounder? Because the catch was made on 5 pound test monofilament line! This fish weighed over 16 times the breaking test of my line.

Depending upon the tackle you are using, the fish (in my opinion) should weigh 10 times the breaking test of the line or leader to qualify as a giant fish on light tackle. Because of the specialized nature of catching giant fish on light tackle, attention to details and technique that may not be critical in every day angling suddenly assume the utmost importance.

Whether your choice is fly, plug, spinning or conventional tackle with bait, the first thing to do is to pick your adversary. Learn all that you possibly can of the species' feeding habits, fighting characteristics, where and how to find him, the time of year he is in greatest abundance. For, you see, the catching of big fish on light tackle usually requires more than just one chance. The more opportunities you have at catching your giant fish, the better are the odds in your favor.

I think one of the most exciting aspects of fishing is not knowing just how big the next fish will be. While working as a guide I had the pleasure of fishing Russ Ball of Bryn Mawr, Penna. It was March 10, 1963, and I was poling Russ over some prime tarpon flats while he stood ready to cast on the stern of the boat, with the bail of his spinning reel open. Suddenly, without warning, a school of about 20 fish appeared off our starboard quarter.

Russ quickly cast to try to intercept our quarry. The water boiled as the fish attacked the lure. Russ struck hard, again and again. Then 170½ pounds of furious tarpon made the first of its magnificent leaps for freedom. But in only 43 minutes Russ had set a new I.G.F.A.

record for 12 pound line class, topping even the existing 20 pound record.

Russ's spinning reel was fully loaded with brand new 8 pound test monofilament line. Attached to this with a small swivel was 2 or 3 feet of 80 pound monofilament leader. On the business end of the leader was a Bill Smith lure. This lure works like a breathing-type fly. It has just enough of a cork body to make it castable, it weighs about ⅜ oz. and has orange feathers behind. We used a simple clinch knot to attach the lure to the leader. This is about the only time I use a simple clinch knot, as it is only about 70% perfect. Always be extremely careful when pulling up a knot. I wrap a handkerchief around my hand to hold the mono and a pair of pliers to hold the hook. Pull slowly, but hard and especially pull it up *smoothly* until the knot is tight.

Russ Ball's accomplishment was by no means a one-shot situation. Russ had been fishing the Keys several times a year for nearly ten years. He spends the majority of his time in the pursuit of tarpon and always uses spinning tackle. He has also learned about his adversary the tarpon, its feeding and fighting habits. However, none of us in the boat that day — Russ, his friend Andy Duggar, or myself — will deny that our "lucky charms" must have been working when the giant 170½ lb. silver muscle succumbed to spinning tackle.

Once you have chosen your adversary, check your tackle. Start with your rod. Make certain that every guide on the rod is firmly wrapped and that none of the windings are frayed. Inspect the reel seat for damaged hoods and don't forget to inspect the guides for rough spots or nicks that could fray or cut your line. Neglect of the guides is one of the most common causes of lost fish. Remember that the odds are in the favor of the fish. So why put yourself out of the fight before it even starts by using a guide that will wear down the line before *you* wear down the fish?

Your reel should be well oiled and *clean, in perfect working order*. Special attention should always be given to the drag. A high spot or roughness in the drag could add the proverbial straw that in this case would break your line at the most inopportune moment.

Do not take chances with false economies. Use only NEW line that has not been long exposed to harsh light

Apte strives to land fish that weighs ten times the breaking strength of his line.

or sunshine.

Your leaders should not only conform to the class regulations of the tackle you are using, but should also be of the highest quality. Make your connections with utmost care. Because a chain is only as strong as its weakest link, your connections or knots are of paramount importance. You cannot afford to lose over-all line strength because of weak knots. Using your tackle to its utmost, to the best possible advantage, is the secret of success. As you will be placing maximum pressure on your equipment, the *knots MUST be stronger than the breaking strength of the lightest line used.*

One of the most important knots involved in light tackle trolling is the Bimini Twist, (sometimes called the 20 times-around knot). If I am fishing with dacron line, I find it best to splice a loop in the 15 feet of double line allowed.

Remember that I.G.F.A. allows 15 feet of double line *and* 15 feet of leader, a total of 30 feet; while International Spin Fishing Association regulations allow only a total of 15 feet.

The Bimini Twist or double line knot is a 100% knot. That is to say the knot is as strong as the line. When properly tied, the break should never be in the knot. The double improved clinch knot is in the 90% bracket and very often 100%. Therefore the line, not the knot, should be the weakest point of your tackle.

I often use the Bimini Twist when plug casting or spin fishing as it is easily cast through the guides and can even be wound all the way up to the reel. This gives added strength when the fish is ready to be boated and also gives additional protection against abrasion.

I always use a hone or file to sharpen each and every hook before the day's fishing begins. This includes the hooks on *all* my flies, lures and plugs. The best results are obtained by triangulating the point of the hook. To do this, flatten the hook behind the barb with a file and taper the barb to form the third point of the triangle. All of these things and more are important in catching giant fish on light tackle.

Using the right landing gear can make the difference between success or failure. Many anglers underestimate the importance of selecting the proper gaff. It should be sharp, the points triangulated in the same manner as the points on your hooks. In choosing the right gaff, many factors must be considered. There are different gaffs that are made for landing different fish. Once the basic type is decided upon, you must take into consideration such factors as the size of the fish, the strength of your line, the type of leader, the weather and height of the boat.

For example, when fishing for black or blue marlin, you certainly would *not* try to use a little hand gaff or a release gaff. This type is used to lip gaff tarpon so that they can be released unharmed. But you most certainly would want a big flying gaff. This is a gaff hook that detaches from the pole after the fish is gaffed. A cable is attached from the gaff hook to a cleat on the boat.

For the record there are four types of gaffs: the lip or release gaff, various hand gaffs that can be used with one hand, large two-handed hand gaffs which are generally 8 feet long, and flying gaffs.

In every phase of light tackle angling for giant fish, everything from choosing the right tackle to the proper boat is of critical importance. But granting that you have the best of everything, your chances are still not the slightest without a really good amount of angling competence. Just as with the man who can run the four minute mile, practice and training are the basic vehicles to success. Just as most men will never run the four minute mile, you (even with the proper tackle) will probably never catch a 10-to-1 fish unless you (like the successful athlete) condition yourself for it.

Go out and practice! Do it on the front lawn, while out fishing, but not over the giant fish that are the prize you seek. The giant fish doesn't come into casting range every five minutes, but when he does, you must make the most of the opportunity.

Tail-walking Pacific sail tries to throw Apte's bait and hook.

Fly-hooked sailfish tires near side of boat.

Author with fly rod world record tarpon of 150½ pounds.

Can you turn the handle of your reel several thousand times in a few minutes? Or will your hand freeze up? Don't wait until the wrong time to find out, *train for it*. Actually I do not recall ever having caught a giant fish on light tackle when I did not hurt physically both during and after the fight.

Let me tell you more about the catch I described briefly in the beginning of this story. I was using conventional trolling tackle at Pinas Bay, Panama, except that I *was not* trolling with the 5 pound test line. Such light line could be weakened by trolling the ballyhoo bait. So instead we used heavier tackle to troll a pair of decoys without hooks. If a sailfish attacked one of these baits, the mate would reel it in while I substituted another in its place rigged with a hook on the 5 lb. test mono. That way my light line would be in *new* condition at the beginning of the fight.

The first day we ran into fish early in the morning. The midnight-blue Pacific waters were calm. It was precisely the kind of day I had hoped for. When the first bright-lined sailfish was sighted speeding toward a decoy bait, I dropped my bait over the side and dropped it back to where the teaser had been. The sail took it furiously. I held my breath for an instant and then it struck.

I hardly felt the hook set, but still the line popped with a sickening sound. The drag on my Penn Master Mariner was too tight, so I backed off half a turn, re-rigged and soon had a second chance.

Almost exactly the same thing happened. I broke the fish off at the moment of the strike. A feeling of frustration and helplessness overcame me, but I re-rigged again and this time set the drag as lightly as I dared. If it was too light, I'd never hook the fish and if it was too tight . . . well, I already knew what would happen.

It did not take long for the third hungry fish to show. The moment my bait was within range, this sail rushed it with an open mouth. After an agonizing length of time I set the hook three or four times. With such a light drag it was hard for me to believe I had hooked anything, except for the line running out. Then a 100-pound sailfish made his first jump.

This was only the beginning of a show that still lives in my memory. I couldn't put too much pressure on him, not on 5 pound test mono. For 45 minutes I played him, coaxed him. When he jumped, I'd bow. I pushed the rod far out in front of me, allowing for slack line the moment he was in the air, moments when he weighed his full weight, when the buoyancy of the water was not a factor in my favor, and the slightest extra tension would have me out of the battle.

Finally the leader showed. The mate got his hands on the leader and was about to grab the fish's bill, when suddenly the blue powerhouse began to surge. The leader slipped through the mate's hands and the instant the 5 pound line touch his hand, it popped.

It took a long while to wind 400 yards of new line on the spool, but twenty minutes later I was glad I had. It was a beautiful day, the weather and fish were doing their best for us and soon I was solidly hooked to the fourth sailfish of the day. It took an hour of hard work and everything went well. I was extra careful but I did not underplay the fish. I put all the strain that I dared on the tackle until, finally, I boated the handsome 82 lb. Pacific sailfish.

Now let's talk about spinning tackle for giant fish. One of the single most important parts on a spinning reel is a rolled on the bail, which truly rolls. The friction at this spot is tremendous, as the line has to make a 90 degree turn-out at this point. I take my rollers to a jeweler and have them polished to eliminate as much porousness (or roughness) in the metal as possible. Then I keep an eye on it to see that it rolls freely. I watch it the way a politician watches his rival for office.

Erwin Bauer, noted author, photographer and adventurer, was fishing at Pinas Bay when I caught a very big sailfish on plug casting tackle. I was using an Ambassadeur 6000 reel and a six-foot tubular glass rod similar to those used for largemouth bass fishing in sweet water. I had 275 yards of 10 lb. test Stren fluorescent monofilament on the reel and was using an Arbogast Scudder plug, then in the experimental stage. A sail suddenly chased down one of the ballyhoo teasers, the captain quickly put the engines in neutral, and I cast the large plug to the hungry predator. The fish charged and I set the hooks hard. Once, twice, three times in order to deeply inbed the sharp hooks into its boney mouth. This exciting battle culminated in the boating of a 110 lb Pacific sailfish.

In order to qualify as a saltwater fly rod record, a catch must be made within strict rules and regulations. The most important regulation is the one which governs the test of the leader. There are four categories for records as kept by the SWFRA: 6, 10, 12 and 15. To meet fly rodding regulations the leader tippet must be monofilament and at least 12 inches long. The over-all leader has to be at least 6 feet long. I normally use between 9 and 13 feet, depending upon the type of fish and the conditions that I am fishing under.

I always recall a day in April 1967 when the fishing was slow on the Florida Keys. Guy Valdene who had just caught his first large tarpon on fly, offered me a chance to fish while he poled the skiff. He was too tired to try another duel. It did not take long before we spotted a school of about 40 tarpon cruising just out of casting range. It was calm and I knew that they would probably be spooky, so I crouched down to cut the size of my silhouette against the sky until I was within casting range.

I cast and a large fish took my yellow and orange saddle hackle streamer fly.

Next I set the hook instinctively and braced for the explosion that I knew was coming.

The fish reacted mildly at first, but then began a frantic head-shaking and a series of mighty leaps that ended in gill-rattling fury. What drama on the flats! This fish behaved erratically, darting back and forth in figure eights. One rub of the leader on that scaly monstrous back or against a fin and the fight would have been over. I coaxed him into a short run which produced several more magnificent jumps. Finally the tarpon tired. It was only about 18 minutes since I had hooked him. But what an exciting 18 minutes!

We weighed the tarpon at the Sea Center, Big Pine Key, which is an official Metropolitan Miami Fishing Tournament weighing station. For a moment I could not believe my eyes. The scale read 151 pounds. I had a new fly rod world record by 2½ pounds.

How did I do it? I had used excellent tackle in perfect working order and was in training for the occasion. With the addition of Lady Luck, the formula was complete.

Is my record on light tackle going to last for a long time? I doubt it. There are too many skilful anglers capable of beating it and someday *soon* a well prepared fisherman is going to land another giant tarpon on light tackle. I lay the odds at about 10 to 1.

Stu Apte displays 82 pound sailfish taken at Pinas Bay, Panama, on 5-pound-test line.

Furiously leaping sailfish can easily break extremely light lines Apte uses. Apte says the angler must train himself, study his adversary carefully, and rig his tackle carefully.

The author with the 136 pound sailfish he caught on a fly rod, Pinas Bay.

STU APTE IMPROVED BLOOD KNOT

For tying a heavy "Stren" monofilament shock leader to a lighter "Stren" monofilament line or tippet. (Two greatly unequal diameters of monofilament)

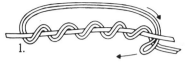

1. Double a sufficient length of the smaller diameter line so that it can be wrapped around the standing part of the larger diameter line with at least five turns. Place the doubled end down between the strands.

2. Hold the looped line between the thumb and the forefinger at the point marked "X" to keep from unwinding.

3. Now, wind the larger diameter line around the standing part of the doubled line three times, but in the opposite direction. Insert the end upwards through the loop at the same point marked "X".

4. Pull the knot up slowly and tightly to keep it from slipping. Use the fingernails to push the loops together, if necessary.

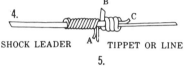

5. Now, cut off the ends of the doubled loop (A) and the end of the heavy line (B), both about a quarter-inch from the knot. Cut off the loose end of the doubled line (C) about a quarter-inch from the knot.

NAIL KNOT

The Nail Knot is used to tie the butt end of your leader to the forward end of your fly line. It is also used to tie backing to a fly line. This knot gives a smooth, streamlined connection and the flat-lying knot will move freely through the guides of your rod, and if tied properly this knot cannot slip, cut, or pull out.

This knot is tied using either a tapered nail or piece of small tubing. Here's how to tie it.

Hold the line, leader and tapered nail or tubing alongside each other as shown in Fig. 1. Allow ample overlap. Then wind leader downward around nail or tubing, line and itself six times and run end of leader back along nail or through tubing up under loops, Fig. 2. Pull both ends of leader tight. Slip knot down nail or tubing, tightening by pulling both ends of leader as it goes. Slip nail or tubing out and retighten by again pulling leader ends, Fig. 3. Finally, pull line and leader tight and clip end of line and leader close to knot, Fig. 4.

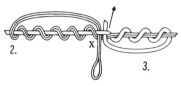

Looking for an exciting change of pace? Try bowhunting for this outlaw fish.

Target: Carp

BY KEN BOURBON

The carp were in. Even at 1,500 feet we could see the telltale brown discoloration from Manila Bay blend with the gray-green water of open Lake Erie. Frank cut the throttle, cranked the stabilizer of his Cessna 195 and began a sharp banking spiral to lose altitude and to get a better look. At about 700 feet he leveled off and made another pass over North Bass Island.

The carp were there indeed. Moving along at slightly faster than a stall, we could see the spawners churning and splashing along the margin of the bay, a small swamp indentation on the island. The shadows of others were visible, lying in echelons around the shallow entrance to the bay from the open lake. And still others cruised along in great schools just off shore.

It was late spring in the Great Lakes country — a restless time for all the carp now so numerous in those waters. Moving into any shallow water they can find to spawn, the fish concentrate in some of the more suitable areas and then the event becomes an amazing, turbulent spectacle. North Bass Island, just inside the U.S. international boundary, is one of these concentrating points; I know of no place where so many big carp collect at one time. I'd seen them come and go several times. For a long time I had plotted and planned ways to catch them, but it was little use. Spawning carp aren't feeding carp and all the dough baits ever concocted have no value here.

Then liberalized fishing laws in Ohio came to the rescue. Following a new philosophy of as few restrictions on fishermen as possible, no-holds-barred angling for all rough fish was made legal. Sportsmen could take them any way they wanted except, of course, with poison or explosives. At the first opportunity then, I was back with a pair of companions, Frank Sayers and Al Staffan. But instead of regular fishing tackle, we were armed with something far more deadly — bows and arrows.

Frank circled a narrow, cleared landing strip sandwiched between a woods and the vineyards that comprised about half of the island. He had to cut his approach pretty fine for the strip was neither too long nor too well mowed. A heavy clump of sumac crowded the runway at one precarious point. But Frank touched down easily in the high grass and then rolled to a stop over a rough, corduroy surface, scattering pheasants in all directions. We stepped outside to look the place over.

We were a bare half hour from home in Columbus, Ohio, and less than that from Cleveland, Toledo or Detroit, but except for the vineyards and the crude landing strip we might have been a thousand miles from civilization. Actually, North Bass Island is a bleak and lonely place. Perhaps 18 people, all grape growers, share the two-square-mile island with a pheasant population as heavy per acre as that on neighboring and better-known

Pelee Island just to the northeast in Canada. For a few days when the ringneck season opens, islanders are hosts to a small invasion of hunters. Otherwise the place is as remote and forgotten as it looks.

We unloaded our gear and prepared for the cross-country hike to Manila Bay when a vintage Ford lurched up the rutted and dusty road along the airstrip. The car was almost old enough to be in style again and the driver was a pleasant, plump lady who offered to taxi us anywhere we wanted to go. She said she was Mrs. Wires, the post-mistress, the grade-school teacher (four pupils), book-keeper for the island's largest vineyard and mayor without portfolio. She met all the planes, she assured us, which wasn't very much trouble outside of the hunting season because nobody landed there. Gratefully we piled into her jalopy. It might have been easier to walk.

Among other things, Mrs. Wires was a splended navi-gator. When the road ran out, she just shifted into creeper and hacked a path through dense woods as high as the car, flushing pheasants like hens in a barnyard and finally emerging on the gravel beach of the island's east shore.

"This is as close to the swamp as we can get," she said. "But I'll be watching for you to get back. I'll take you to the plane." With that she backed off into the brush and disappeared.

Walking the gravel beach wasn't as simple as it sounds.

Heavy northeast winds during the winter had gouged into the shore and toppled large willows and elms into the water. But walking around them, sometimes chest deep on the water side, was better than fighting the inland vege-tation Mrs. Wires had managed in her Ford. All along the beach we flushed carp that were lying close or cruising in an almost unbroken line. It was a temptation for Frank to try to stalk them, but we pushed on to the Bay. Al and I had watched with longing the jumbos that collected there last spring. The brief glimpse from the air indicated they were back again — so we kept Frank moving.

It was exactly like the year before. Maybe more so. In small schools all around the bay, carp noisily wallowed and thrashed about in the shallows — sometimes in water so shallow the critters were half exposed for seconds at a time. It was a sight for an archer's sore eyes. It was enough to make stringing my bow a more nervous job than usual — hampered by ten thumbs.

Frank made the grade first. He bent a laminated-glass-and-maple recurved bow over his knee and slipped the loop of the bowstring into place. Next he taped his "reel" — nothing more than a tapered block of wood with round-ed edges — to the bow, just beneath the grip. He pulled several feet of line off the end, as from a spinning reel, and then tied the loose end to a metal-harpoon type of arrowhead.

Frank Sayers in action at Manila Bay, North Bass Island. All these carp are big female spawners. Notice the wood block "reel" taped to the bow in picture at right. The carp in picture on left weighs 28 pounds.

He sharpened the point quickly with a small hone, inserted an aluminum-tube arrow into the harpoon tip and slipped easily into the water. Al and I followed close behind.

A scant 20 feet from where Frank entered the water a gang of carp rolled gently on the surface, disappeared, and then came wallowing back to the top. Frank took a couple of steps nearer — the line tied to the arrow greatly limits range and accuracy — and drew an arrow. He held the draw for a second on the biggest carp in the group, followed it and let fly at an exposed, scaly back.

That carp took off as if pricked with a red-hot pitchfork. Hit too far back toward the tail to bother him much, the fish cavorted over the best part of half an acre of water. Frank just held on to the line and had a strip of hide scraped off the palm of one hand for all his trouble.

The arrow had gone completely through the fish and the whole shaft was acting like a barb which couldn't be escaped. Even climbing halfway out onto the bank wouldn't do it — so Frank horsed in the writhing fury, hand over hand. It was an 8-pounder.

With the line rewound nearly on Frank's reel again, we waded out side by side. Al moved off in another direction to stalk fish spawning noisily beneath a fallen elm. None of them had long to wait. I heard Al's bow zing behind me at precisely the moment more carp schooled just ahead.

"Let's take 'em together," Frank said.

We moved up easily, waited for them to show again and then drove a couple of harpoons hard into them. With an eruption you could hear across the bay, the school spooked — that is, all but one of them.

My partner had tagged a 5-pounder right behind the head and had stiffened the fish on contact. I retrieved nothing but a pair of scales the size of new quarters that were still sticking to the barb.

From there we started harvesting carp in earnest. We made some good hits, had plenty of misses and few dull moments — for shooting carp with bow and arrow is one of the fastest actions a man can currently find in the fishing field. Most states have given it their blessing in recent years. The fish are plentiful enough to be a nuisance and they're unwary enough in springtime to make good riddance possible on a grand scale. Find the beasts spawning and you've found a frantic and exciting way to do a little conservation work on your own. You'll get wet often and cold, sometimes, but you'll never get bored from the game.

I waded to shore for a break, soaked and slightly bruised. My shins had suffered from stumbling over underwater snags I couldn't see in the water roiled by carp. And I'd become so absorbed in the action that I didn't notice it when the wrist guard on my bow arm slipped out of place. Repeated twanging on bare skin by the bowstring had raised a muitlcolored welt. That's a good lesson for prospective archers: wear a wrist guard for continuous shooting. It's good to wear a glove or at least a partial glove on the drawing hand to prevent wear and tear on those fingers when the bowstring is released. A pair of Polaroid glasses is helpful, too, particularly of the type Florida bonefishermen wear. They make spotting the target a lot easier, especially on extremely bright days.

Actually, very little equipment is necessary for taking carp Indian style. The essential pieces are neither expensive nor complicated. Any adult with normal coordination can learn to shoot quickly and well enough to be successful. And an entire outfit that will last for years can be purchased for less than $25.

No special bow has been designed for carp shooting; any hunting or target model will shoot hard enough and straight enough for the job. There are almost as many kinds of reels and harpoon heads as there are archers — and nearly all of them are good. Probably the wooden block reel that Frank Sayers prefers is by far the simplest and best.

But there are circular models, some the size and shape of wooden cheese boxes, that double effectively as sighting apparatus. The gadget is mounted so that the grip is in the center of the box and the archer looks through the reel to aim and shoot. Line pulls easily off the end.

Aluminum-tube arrows are best because they float and can be retrieved. Wooden arrows break and splinter too easily for this kind of rough use. Glass arrows will stand the gaff, but they sink and often too much time is wasted in retrieving them.

Harpoon heads should be kept sharp and the line knot should be inspected frequently since it will wear badly at that point. The barbs should be built for the roughest handling. Soft line that stays coiled and testing no less than 25 pounds is the best.

Where boats are available or practical (punt boats are best; canoes next best) it's often possible to get nearer to carp, especially the bigger ones which exhibit wariness even when occupied with the absorbing matter of spawning. But there can be no banging of oars and oarlocks against the gunwales or heavy thumping on the bottom. The quarry won't tolerate it.

Waders may be comfortable on cool days, but generally they're just a hindrance to the best maneuverability. The new light plastic waders are some improvement. But tennis shoes or sneakers are enough for me — just something to protect my feet on sharp and jagged bottoms.

It's well to learn the fundamentals of archery and to practice on targets with field arrows before going after carp. Shooting is simple and easy to learn, and it is most helpful to have a certain familiarity with the proper handling of the equipment.

I made a swing around to the entrance of the bay which was actually just a shallow sand and gravel bar over which the surf broke and then washed gently for some distance before dissipating into the muddy water inside. In that narrow strip between the break and the dirty water, carp were finning side by side, almost as close as sardines in a can. They seemed to be waiting for their turns in the bay — every few moments one would give a curious wiggle and then disappear. Immediately another would move into the vacancy. The whole operation was easy to see for in that one spot the water was clear and no more than 18 inches deep.

Moving around from behind, generally a good direction from which to approach carp, I tried to maneuver close enough for a shot. But I must have moved one step too far for all the fish within range suddenly scattered. I stood motionless then, and soon they began to filter back into place. One came poking along uncertainly right toward me. Twenty feet away it paused for a moment, then 15 and finally at about 10 feet, it turned broadside. I drew hastily and fired.

You never have time to wonder whether you scored or not in this game. If you miss, usually nothing happens. The carp flush out of range. If the arrow connects, the spot fairly explodes. I caught this one just a few inches forward of the tail fin, the arrow going completely through and coming free from the harpoon on the other side. I was literally tied to an 8-pound carp. I just hung on — there wasn't anything else to do when that fish turned on the power.

Even though it burned across the fingers on my hand, I

had to give line rapidly—but I got a break when the carp made a circle and tried to cross that part of the bar where the surf was breaking — and the water most shallow. The fish floundered there, unsuccessfully tried to turn back, and then beat a wild tattoo on the gravel. I sloshed toward the fish and grabbed it before it could reach deeper water.

After that first carp was dispatched, I eased back to the others waiting in the bay's entrance, this time keeping a safe distance and relying on longer shots. The first two efforts fell way off the targets, which spooked out of the picture. But finally I learned the knack of correcting for light refraction in the murky water and then recorrecting for the "pull-down" of a heavy line on the arrow. The third shot and also the fourth connected with solid thuds. The result was like pitching a hand grenade in the water.

I was soaking wet before I could get my hands on the fish. That was enough action for awhile so I waded over to shore and sat down to watch platoons of gulls and terns that began wheeling and diving over a spot out on the lake. Probably a school of white bass was feeding on emerald shiners.

Frank joined me on the shore. He said that if I'd anywhere near held up my end, he figured we'd bagged about 40 carp altogether. But none were big. We'd seen some old sockers, but getting a decent shot was something else. Once, just after we'd started, I had a snap draw and release on one carp the size of a brood sow. But the miss only produced a deep wake into the bay.

There's nothing particularly restful or contemplative about this shooting carp with bow and arrow. It's a vigorous business no matter where you find the brutes, and that's

almost everywhere. It was a sad day a couple of generations ago when they were imported from Europe, but now they're here to stay. The best efforts of biologists and trained fisheries men have failed to get rid of them — there's no choice but to try to make the best of the aliens, and the best way, perhaps, is by bow and arrow. The breed is far too clever to ever give much sport on hook and line. The wariest of old brown trout have nothing on carp in the mental department.

No matter where you find them, carp behave exactly like their Lake Erie cousins when springtime rolls around. They make for shallow water. From rivers they move into the backwaters, bayous and oxbows, or they even collect on the soft mud bars in midstream. At a fairly low stage for that season of the year, I've seen them spawn in the middle of the Great Miami River which is diagonally op-

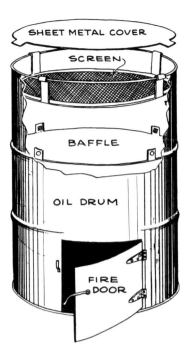

Sketch showing how a backyard carp smoker can be easily made from a discarded 50 gallon oil drum.

Frank Sayers demonstrates excitement of bowhunting carp, this time in a Lake Erie marsh near Port Clinton.

posite Ohio from the Erie islands. And I've seen them surge into the marshes and swampy places that border most of the lakes in between. If your waters have carp, you'll see them in spring. And if you want to harvest some of them try a bow and arrow, providing the law allows it there.

When prospecting for carp, never neglect the extremely shallow places lush with vegetation — places that may be bone dry later in the season. Watch for movements along the fringes of cattails and for unusual bulges beneath patches of pond weeds and lilies. Closer inspection of these telltale signs often turns up an assembly of carp — amorous and vulnerable.

While Frank and I talked strategy on the bank, Al shinnied up into a giant elm that drooped far out over the water. He almost fell out of it, seeing in the bay below huge carp moving leisurely around — like submarines with scales. Even though we'd been out among them, they evidently had just moved out of our paths. And we weren't in the best spot to see them when we were so close to the surface.

With an aerial spotter on the job, Frank went to work again. Al picked out a pair of big ones and following his directions, Frank began the stalk, as slowly and cautiously as he could. "More toward one o'clock," Al called.

An old hand at stalking everything from honkers to whitetails, Frank ran into trouble with these carp. Spawning season or not, they gave him the slip simply by easing away into the most convenient clouds of roily water. But Frank doesn't give up easily.

Al picked out another and gave directions for getting close, but it was the same story. He scanned the bay carefully for other targets. Then suddenly:

"Stand still, Frank," he cautioned. "There's a dandy working toward you from your left. From ten o'clock."

Frank didn't move an eyelash, let alone a muscle.

"Coming closer," Al called. "Don't move!" Then Frank

picked out an indistinct form approaching him. A tail — or maybe a dorsal fin — broke the surface almost imperceptibly.

Turning slightly, he drew an arrow. But the carp stopped. Painfully Frank held on to his 65-pound draw — afraid to make a sudden move. The minute the carp moved again, he let the arrow go in the direction he figured was correct — with splendid calculation, for the harpoon hit with a solid, satisfying "whump." The first thing that carp did after lunging into the air was to barge right between Frank's legs, cracking him across the knee with the aluminum shaft and breaking it. Faster than he could follow the action, the carp was wound around both his legs and in and out of the air again twice before Frank could grab the heavy line which had pulled completely from the reel.

Carp never jump? Put an arrow through a big one sometime and see!

The contest ended quickly. Wet and still enmeshed in the line, but grinning, Frank dragged the fish to land. Hit fairly hard amidships, the carp acted a little like a tarpon and a lot like a wild bulldog. Before Frank eventually cleaned and quartered him for the smokehouse back in Columbus, the bruiser weighed in at 28 pounds.

Then the action started all over again. Al called the shots like an artillery observer and we took as many of them as we could. Al swears he was watching 40- and 50-pounders swim around below him and from his tree perch, he couldn't resist several shots at long range with hunting arrows mounted with razoredged broadheads. It's no small trick to draw an arrow while wrapped around a long limb, but it was a futile effort for there's no way to recover the misses which disappear into the muck below. Al made one hit but lost that arrow, too. We saw the last of it swishing through the water like a periscope — Canada seemed to be the destination.

I did get an arrow solidly and dead center into a 20-pounder. That one didn't move very far but for several moments I doubted if my heavy line would hold. The big carp surged away blindly, rolled, and then turned back and barreled head on into my ankle. It rolled once more and turned on its side — all this with a metal shaft lodged completely through just behind the gill cover.

Frank stopped a 24-pounder coming head on. It came out of the water just once before it was pitched on our growing pile and then made a series of wild flurries. Frank was showered every time the old carp flipped its broad tail to try a new direction; he just turned his head and held on. Meanwhile more excited all the time, Al kept

scouting big fish from his precarious perch. Suddenly the inevitable happened — we lost our observer. There was a loud splintering of wood followed by a heavy splash. Al had become too enthusiastic and had edged his way too far out and become our unwrung hero of the day.

But I was ready to quit anyway. A carp had just snagged my line, taking my last arrow and harpoon tip along, and my arms and shoulders were complaining after the sustained shooting binge. There was a substantial pile of carp to lug back and we had definite plans for those fish, too. Actually there's never much reason to leave carp for the crows and gulls after a big shoot. No finer, more hearty fare exists than carp properly brined, then smoked over apple and hickory-wood flames; Lake Erie folks pay up to 80c a pound for it while smoked whitefish and smoked salmon go begging around the commercial fish houses.

Smoking is a simple operation at home. It can be done in an old 50-gallon drum with top removed to insert a couple of shelves and with a fire door cut in the bottom. Or simpler still is an old-type icebox in which an electric hot plate is installed on the lowest level. The smoke is provided by piling hickory and apple chips or shavings on the hot plate.

Before smoking, carp should be scaled and "hog-dressed." The larger the fish, the better for smoking. Cut the fish into sections of about a pound each and keep them in a brine solution heavy enough to float an egg for at least 24 hours. Then give them the smoke treatment for from three to five hours depending on your smoker and the intensity of the heat. Generally it will require the least smoking in an icebox that is fairly well insulated and will hold the heat better.

Mrs. Wires was a welcome sight waiting for us there on the beach as she promised.

It's a mystery how she guessed we were coming at that time. We'd hung all the carp we could handle on a willow pole and, taking turns, carried them back down the beach, over the deadfalls and around the trees. They must have been a strange spectacle, still hanging on the pole which we lashed to her spare tire outside the car. The rest of us slumped inside.

Our hostess was a big help at the airstrip too, for she voluntarily made a couple of fast passes back and forth in her old Ford to scatter the pheasants. A couple of big cocks in the propeller could have made a messy business out of our take-off.

The gracious gal was still waving when Frank circled around for another look at Manila Bay and then dipped his wings, heading south, in farewell.

Great white heron filmed while on bonefish trip to Florida Keys.

Cedar waxwing is a handsome bird familiar to springtime fishermen when it migrates northward.

Serious fishermen know the sight of circling sooty terns means schools of game fish feeding in the waters below.

Double the pleasure of every fishing trip by —

Watching the birds

By Karl Maslowski

It's hard to decide just what made my first fishing trip of the season last March so memorable. Was it the seven-pound bass I caught — trophy size for an Ohio farm pond — or was it the sight of a flock of over eighty cedar waxwings as they fed fearlessly, almost within a flyrod length, in a multiflora rose hedge?

Or, come to think of it, was it really the big 28-pound dolphin (my first ever), or was it the sight of a sooty tern (also my first ever) that excited me most on a May afternoon in the Dry Tortugas Islands of Florida? And I suspect it was a toss up as to just what started my adrenalin flowing one summer day on an un-named lake in Canada's Northwest Territories. For at just about the same moment I hooked my first Arctic char an old-squaw hen and her downy brood of ducklings became an irresistible attraction as they paddled out of a nearby cove.

Now it's not that I am an indifferent angler. When I was still in my early teens some of my closest friends accurately predicted that I had already wasted too much of my youth fishing to ever hope to become President. Actually, fishing has always been a passion with me, but at just about the time I discovered things like Meek reels, Arbogasters and Hawaiian Wigglers, I also discovered birds.

It is a fact of existence that all animals need water for survival, and birds are no more an exception to this rule than are the fishes. So it is almost axiomatic that where you find fish you will find birds, or vice-versa. Because of this, I have had, as the chewing gum ad says, "double my pleasure" almost since the very first time I dangled a hook in the water. While I have fished I have watched birds, and I have indulged in this double hobby from the Arctic to Capetown, South Africa, with countless stops along the way.

Worldwide there are about 8600 different kinds of birds, and more than 1700 species live on the North American continent. Knowingly or unknowingly, I am sure that every one of the North American species has been seen at some time or another by anglers. If you would like to get twice the fun from angling too, don't feel there is a lack of opportunity for birding along the fisherman's waterways.

Birds like grebes, ducks, geese, herons, sandpipers, gulls, terns, puffins, and murres are among the most likely to be noted. However, some of my most memorable experiences have been with land birds, including finches, warblers, and thrushes. My one trip up famous Hazel Creek in the Great Smokies did not produce a single trout — later I found I was using the wrong fly, only the female Adams being acceptable that day; but I have never heard such a chorus of black-throated blue warblers. There must have been a singing male every 50 yards along the stream for miles on end.

On my very first try for trout in Glacier Park in 1939 I had even better luck. Not only did I catch lots of trout, but also I made the acquaintance of the dipper, or water ouzel, that slate-gray bird that looks like a sturdy aquatic catbird. At first sight the dipper is enough to make even the most experienced angler lay aside his flyrod and watch. This is a land bird, but it swims and walks *under water!*

Bird watching may sometimes lead to a fishing bonanza. My good friend Milton Trautman, the keenest ornithologist-ichthyologist of my acquaintance, taught me this years ago in the Put-in-Bay area of Lake Erie. Along in June and July he would simply watch for milling flocks of common terns and gulls on the horizon to locate big schools of feeding white bass. When such a flock was located he would crank up the outboard and rush us to that spot where we would begin casting with small spinners or flies. It was the rule rather than the exception to catch a boatload of white bass along with a few husky smallmouths.

The terns and gulls were attracted by myriads of minnow which were driven to the surface by huge schools of feeding bass. This method of watching the birds to locate schools of feeding fish still works, not only on Lake Erie but on many other waters, too.

Actually, the presence of an abundance of fish-eating birds is generally indicative of waters rich in fish life. When I find a waterway abounding in kingfishers, herons, cormorants, and the like, I KNOW I'm going to catch lots of fish.

Perhaps the best place to bird watch and fish at the same time in the U.S. is off the Florida Keys. I have seen my good friend Dick Kotis of the Fred Arbogast Company even lay aside his tackle to watch — enviously, I might add — the angling tactics of brown pelicans, great white herons, snowy egrets, ospreys, and bald eagles near Big Pine Key. Normally, Dick is so single-minded about angling that the first manned moon shot could be going off on one side and the Miss America pageant on the other and he would not take his eyes or mind off the tackle he held in his hand at that moment.

Indeed, the variety of avian action an angler can observe is almost endless. I once spent a very pleasant hour watching a ruby-throated hummingbird tend her young in a walnut-sized nest on a maple bough that arched over one of my favorite smallmouth bass pools of the Eastfork River in Clermont County, Ohio. On another occasion, while doing a bit of very early spring jig-fishing on Lake Cumberland in southern Kentucky, I put my nearly frozen hands in my pockets to warm them for a half hour while I watched with amusement as a phoebe tried fly-catching flakes of snow. Then there was the Goliath heron Erwin Bauer and I watched as we fished at St. Lucia in South Africa. It spent at least ten minutes grooming its head feathers with the comb-like margin on the middle toe of its right foot.

A fellow can do a lot of naked-eye bird watching while fishing, but a pair of lightweight 7 x 35 central focusing binoculars are a worthwhile light burden to carry along. There are a number of guide books to help with problems of identification. Perhaps the best of the lot are *A Field Guide to the Birds* (East, West, and Texas editions) by Roger Tory Peterson, and *A Guide to Field Identification, Birds of North America,* a Golden Press publication.

The time between strikes will seem a lot shorter if you look and listen for the color, action, and songs of the birds that share the waterways with you.

Anglers on northern fishing trips might spot an old squaw duck, like this one, with a brood of ducklings.

Author Maslowski thrilled to the sight of nesting hummingbirds while fishing for smallmouth bass on a stream near his home in Cincinnati.

This fellow fisherman, the bald eagle, isn't too plentiful along our waterways anymore. "Progress", pollution and insecticides have taken a great toll of a great bird.

The beautiful wood duck, or summer duck, adds color to any bass fisherman's day almost anywhere in America.

Balanced tackle is necessary to deliver a dry fly (here a Royal Wulff) accurately to a target.

Assembling an outfit which casts easily and accurately is no longer a deep mystery.

How to match fly rod equipment

BY LEON MARTUCH

Tackle manufacturers keep repeating that fly *fishing* is easy, yet the beginning fly fisherman often finds that fly *casting* is too difficult for him. The explanation is simple. Too often the fly fisherman starts out with mis-matched or poorly matched equipment — equipment that even an expert fly caster would find difficult or impossible to use.

Although there are a number of balances that must be drawn in fly fishing, as there are in spinning or bait casting, the balance between the fly rod and the fly line is the one that gives most fishermen the most trouble.

In spinning, the fisherman should match the weight of the lure and the size of his line to the action of his rod, and, to a much lesser degree, his reel. The fly fisherman should also balance his tackle to his type of fishing. He should balance his leader to the fly and the fly line, but his biggest problem is matching a rod and fly line.

What is a balanced fly rod outfit? *It's a combination of rod and line that works together to make casting easy and effortless.* The proper combination of rod and line makes the tackle work for you and requires the least work on your part. It makes fly fishing easier and more fun. A poorly balanced combination makes casting difficult, if not impossible.

All casting is based on weight. In bait casting or spinning, the lure provides the weight; in fly casting, the line provides the weight. The fly rod fisherman is really a fly line caster, not a fly caster. He casts the line; the fly just goes along for the ride. The fact that the fly line must provide the weight to bring out the action in the rod explains why the fly line is larger in diameter than a spinning or bait casting line.

Jumbo brown trout such as these are extremely shy. Sloppy casting with unbalanced tackle will spook them out of casting range.

How do you go about finding a combination of rod and line that results in a balanced outfit? Today, it's simple.

The American Fishing Tackle Manufacturers Association (AFTMA) has set up a numbering system. Under it, each fly line has a number that indicates its weight. This number designation is determined on the basis of the weight of the front 30 feet of line, since this is the amount of line that is most commonly cast. The numbers range from #1 to #12. The lightest is #1; the heaviest, #12. Line weights most commonly used for fishing range from #5 through #10. Although the AFTMA weight standards allow a manufacturing tolerance, all lines that have the same number will have the correct weight to balance satisfactorily with the same rod. Once you know the number representing the weight of line that balances best with your rod, you can easily buy a line that will match that weight. For example, if your rod balances with a #7 line, any line that is a #7 weight line will balance with your rod.

The fact that all lines of the same number will balance with a rod is true, regardless of the taper of the line and regardless of whether the line is a floating or sinking one. The explanation is that a #7 sinking line has the same weight as the #7 floating line. The sinking line has a smaller diameter and that's the reason it sinks.

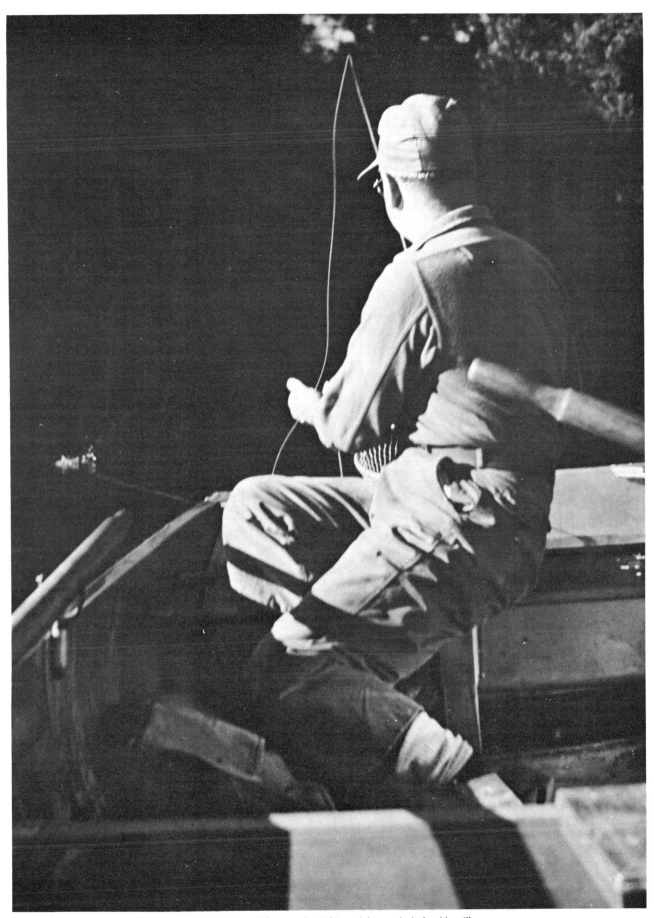

This angler is using a very light fly casting outfit to fish a small Michigan lake at dusk for bluegills.

Balanced tackle makes fishing these Montana streams a pure pleasure.

To put the system into use, let's suppose that you have a rod and that you need a new fly line. How do you go about buying a line that will have the correct amount of weight to match the action of your rod?

There are a number of ways. Most rods of recent vintage have a marking indicating the correct weight line. For example, your rod may say "balanced for a #6 line." If your rod doesn't have such markings and if you're quite sure that your old fly line is of the correct weight, you can duplicate the weight of your old line. Before you do this, however, you might want to check to be sure that the line weight you've been using is correct. In our work in fly fishing clinics, we've found that at least three-quarters of the fishermen have a line that is not the correct weight for their rods. In many cases, the weight they have been using is

satisfactory, but not the best weight for the most effortless casting. As a result, these fishermen are doing more work and their rods and lines are doing less work on each cast.

If you're pretty sure about your old line, you can cut off the front 30 feet and ask your druggist to weigh it for you. The table at the end of this article gives the allowable weight range for each line weight number. Refer to it to find the line weight number that matches your old line, then simply ask your local sporting goods dealer for a line of that number.

But if you're not sure about your line, you might borrow lines from your fishing pals, assuming that they know the weight numbers of their lines. A final choice might be of more help to you. Starting in 1964, Scientific Anglers has cast with and determined the best weight of line for almost

Classic trout water in Montana.

all models of rods produced by major rod manufacturers in the United States. Your local sporting goods dealer likely has a series of these charts that he could refer to, if you know the length, model number and manufacturer of your rod. If he doesn't, send a self-addressed, stamped envelope to Scientific Anglers, Inc., P.O. Box C-95, Midland, Michigan 48640. Be sure to include the name of the manufacturer, the model number and the length of your rod. Also include any other markings found on the rod. Chances are that we will know the correct weight line.

Suppose you have the other problem: you have a perfectly good line and you know the line weight. So you need a new rod. How do you find one that will balance with your line?

Here, too, a little caution is in order. We've had any number of fishermen ask us to recommend a model number of a rod for their type of fishing. When we question them, we invariably are told that they have an old rod but it isn't any good and they need a new one. Most often, we find that when we put the right weight line on that old rod, it suddenly changes into a very good rod. There was never anything wrong with the rod; it was just not matched with the correct line weight.

But if you really do need a new rod and you know the

Even bass popping bugs which weigh as much as 1/16 ounce can be cast with accuracy on balanced tackle.

line weight, it's quite simple to purchase a new rod that will balance with your line. Again, refer to the rod markings to see what line weight is recommended for a particular rod. Some manufacturers do not mark the recommendation on the rod but do list it in their catalogs. Your dealer can help you here. And if that fails, ask your dealer to see his Scientific Anglers' line recommendations chart, LR-5, listing the correct weight lines for some 508 different 1968 or 1969 fly rods. If you'd like your own copy of the chart, send a self-addressed, stamped envelope to Scientific Anglers, Inc. Ask for the free line recommendation bulletin, LR-5.

If you're really starting from scratch, how do you find a balanced outfit? Today, many manufacturers are selling combinations or kits of rods, reels and lines. You can be sure that the kit will be a balanced outfit, and although they are generally inexpensive, they give good value for the money. If you prefer to select your own rod and line, however, you can again refer to the markings on the rod, to the manufacturer's recommendation in the catalog, or to Scientific Anglers' bulletin LR-5.

With a balanced fly fishing outfit, you'll find that fly casting is easy and that fly fishing is not only more fun but a most productive way to take fish!

AFTMA FLY LINE WEIGHT STANDARDS

AFTMA Number	Weight (grains/30′)	Tolerance		
1	60	Plus or minus	6 grains	
2	80	″	″	6 ″
3	100	″	″	6 ″
4	120	″	″	6 ″
5	140	″	″	6 ″
6	160	″	″	8 ″
7	185	″	″	8 ″
8	210	″	″	8 ″
9	240	″	″	10 ″
10	280	″	″	10 ″
11	330	″	″	12 ″
12	380	″	″	12 ″

Miss Print buries her nose in a sea. She can take rough going.

Having dunked thousands of lures and chunks of bait from the decks of hundreds of boats, I finally fell victim to every coastal fisherman's common malady and began dreaming up designs for the "perfect" coastal fishing boat. But, unlike most anglers, I actually got my dream boat built. I've owned her almost four years now, and she still stops traffic when I pull into a dock.

Meet *Miss Print*, 23 feet of pure fishing machine, able and tough, a go-anywhere boat. She has fighting chairs, walk-around decks, and loads of stowage space.

But there's more to *Miss Print* than meets the eye. The special problems of salt water fishing were the first consideration in her design.

I wanted, first of all, a boat that would face offshore seas, and make light work of the slop sometimes encountered in an inlet. For rough going, I wanted a self-bailing boat, and one that would provide a reasonably soft ride.

But at the same time I wanted a craft that could negotiate the shoals — get up on the bonefish flats and work the shallow edges of bars on an ebbing tide. In short, I planned a boat that could take her skipper and crew after any kind of fish — from blue marlin to bonefish.

The answer to this problem wasn't as difficult as it might seem. *Miss Print* is an outboard, for only the reliable kicker allows you to easily cruise shallow waters. It tilts up in seconds when you run up on the flats. She is also a conventional, hard-chined design, with flat buttocks, no deadrise. She draws only four inches of water, with the outboard tilted up. This and outboard power, give shoal water capability.

This go-anywhere
coastal craft is
nearly ideal ... it's

One man's dream boat

by Jim Martenhoff

How about going offshore? The answer to that one was fairly simple, too. She's 23 feet long—a big, husky hull. Conventional hard-chine designs appear old-fashioned in these days of deep vees and cathedral hulls designed for rough water. But sheer size makes a huge difference. Her 23 feet of length allow her to bull her way through seas and rough chop with reasonable ease.

And one other design factor helped to lighten the slapping and slamming: Borrowing from ocean powerboat racing, I designed the stand-up steering station aft of amidships. Vertical motion is reduced when you move aft, and when you stand at the wheel your knees bend to take out most of the bumps. I've had *Miss Print* offshore in 30-knot winds when even large charter boats were forced to wallow out to the reef line, plunging and plowing into the seas. Yet my boat could run on plane — slowly, to be sure, at a little under 20 knots, but planing just the same. It was a wet and wild trip, but she made it.

The fighting chairs on the boat are mounted forward on the bow deck. This arrangement is ideal for the small boat, especially for an outboard. Every coastal angler knows you use the boat when you battle a big fish. Husky charter boats can successfully back down on a fish, but the offshore outboard cannot.

So on *Miss Print* I can troll conventionally, anglers facing aft. But when a fish is hooked, I spin both angler and boat around to fight the fish bows on! Facing the action means I can chase that fish all over the ocean if I want to. I have maneuverability, and the seas stay out of the boat. Back down into them and they flood in over the transom.

The fighting chair arrangement seems unusual to anyone accustomed to seeing them installed aft in a boat. But it has worked out extremely well, and when you think about it the logic is almost overwhelming. The chairs *belong* forward in the small boat!

Miss Print's wide, walk-around decks allow casting artificials on light tackle on inshore waters and provide plenty of room to fight stubborn gamesters that like to circle the boat. Even if the convertible top is raised, I can still trot around on deck. The top covers only the steering station and does not extend out to the covering boards or gunwales.

As for other features, they're rather obvious needs for most anglers. There is an extraordinary amount of storage space in large compartments beneath the bow deck and at the steering station and in four small compartments at the cockpit sole level. There's also a built-in, insulated fish box-ice box and a battery compartment that accommodates tools and small spare parts.

Most unusual factor of all is the hull construction. *Miss Print* is a sandwich. She has two plywood hulls. The space between them is filled with foam, which takes the place of the customary skeletal structure — ribs, keelson, and so forth. The boat is all skin and no skeleton, for she doesn't even have a stempiece! The inner hull was nested in the outer one, and the space between filled with the expanding resin foam. When it hardened, it made a light-weight hull that was very strong and durable. The sandwich was then fiberglassed, after which the interior structures — decks, steering station — were added.

The boat was built at Allied Marine in Miami. I had raced offshore as navigator in the crew of Allied president

Ruth Martenhoff (author's wife) fights fish from Miss Print.

Jack Manson. Jack became interested in my novel hull form idea, for the foam sandwich boat is not only light and tough, it is virtually unsinkable. Break it up into three parts, and each of the three pieces will still stay afloat.

Manson's carpenters built *Miss Print* as an experiment. She turned out so well he tried producing a smaller version as the "Allied Angler" but one problem arose no one had foreseen: the sandwich construction is costly. So the boat was discontinued.

But *Miss Print* went into service. She is kept in a dry marina on Jewfish Creek, where the Florida Keys, an angler's genuine gold-plated paradise, begin. From the docks it is but a 20-minute run to the offshore reefs of Florida's Pennekamp Coral Reef State Park. On the way outside I pass one of the best bonefish flats in the Keys, in Largo Sound. Twenty minutes in the other direction takes me to redfish and trout country, and — in season — tarpon fishing.

The boys at the marina finally had to store *Miss Print* on the highest rack in the building. It was sheer self defense. Fishermen who spotted her in the building had to examine every detail. She has been a howling success, and has influenced the design of other boats.

But that doesn't mean she's perfect. I made mistakes, none of them serious, some I'll correct soon.

To begin with, her center of gravity is too far forward. She was designed this way originally, because I wanted to race her at least once in an offshore powerboat contest. I needed weight forward for two reasons: To keep the bow down when running into rough seas and — should the boat jump off a sea completely clear of the water — to bring her down nearly level. With the weight too far aft, ocean racers come down on their transoms. For this reason most offshore racers have built-in ballast tanks forward, into which seawater can be pumped for more weight at the bow.

It made her fast in rough water when she had big twin outboards on the transom. But a fairly lengthy convalescence from illness prevented me from racing, and I took one of the outboards off. I had no need for the speed when she was just to be used for fishing.

That put her center of gravity too far forward. Rain water can now accumulate in the bow compartment — until I step aboard and stand aft for a few minutes. The weight of one man is enough to restore her balance, and the water drains out aft. I plan on removing the two 33-gallon fuel tanks now located forward. (Gas tanks forward is contrary to general practice, but ocean racing is different. With racing out of the picture, however, I'll move the fuel supply aft where it belongs.)

Another mistake was the flush hatch on the bow compartment. I didn't want anything to project that might catch a fly line. But the flush hatch is not watertight. Again, this is contrary to recommended engineering and design practice, but I was thinking of fishing first. If I had it to do over, she'd have a hatch with a coaming or recessed gutters.

I also think I would redesign some of her stowage compartments, especially to provide rack space for an extraordinary number of rods and reels! *Miss Print* once left the dock with 17 rods aboard and only two anglers. We were on our way to a tournament where two men may fish with four or five rigged rods ready to hand at all times.

But virtually everything else has stood the test of time. Some people have asked why I didn't design into her a tiny cuddy, with a couple of bunks. The answer to that one is easy. She's a fishing boat, not an overnighter. And

Author with a husky African Pompano taken plug casting on reefs from Miss Print.

Miss Print at dusk . . . Note fighting chairs forward.

Depth sounder is one of many angling accessories . . .

Hatch opens on giant bow storage area.

Bill Ward, friend of writer, and wife Ruth Martenhoff prepare to leave on fishing trip. (Author behind camera, but there!)

Convertible top, when raised, covers only steering station. Miss Print still has walk around decks—and room to walk around!

Vinyl cover—with glassine inserts—prot dash from weather, allows use of fol chart also.

because she's so light, she's reasonably fast even with one 100-hp outboard. She'll do 30 miles per hour and hit 40 with the twin engines.

Why stay out overnight when you are only 45 minutes away from the nearest dock? A reasonably fast boat is the answer for an angler. Build her for fishing. Run back to a waterside motel if you want to stay overnight and sleep in comfort. You can be back on the fishing grounds at any morning hour you choose.

The space we saved by keeping her wide open for angling is what makes her a unique fishing machine. She even poles well on the bonefish flats, and I once poled her a quarter mile upwind just to prove she would handle satisfactorily. I prefer, of course, to pole across the wind and tack downwind on the flats. That way I cover more territory with less work.

In four years I have received hundreds of letters from all over the world. A handful come from Australia where correspondents told me her design appeared ideal for Down Under coastal waters. I had to prepare a mimeographed stock letter to handle the flood of mail at one point.

But *Miss Print* is not a stock boat and no plans for her exist. Plenty of small boat builders who still work in plywood could produce a facsimile of conventional lines, with her storage and walk-around deck features built in. Some commercially produced craft come close to her, although none possess her range and capacity.

Besides the 66 gallons of fuel in the two fixed tanks forward, there are four portable tanks beneath her steering console bringing the total capacity to 100 gallons. This gas supply was intended primarily for racing, but allows

fishing trips beyond the range of most boats.

There are two radios in the steering console compartment: A standard ship-to-shore, and a Citizens Band. I often take a "shoulder-talkie," or one-watt CB, when cruise-fishing with another boat lacking radio. It gives us communications.

Although the boat has a load of storage space, emergency gear is located where it is instantly accessible. The first aid kit is held by shock cord on the inside of the console compartment door. Fire extinguisher and a water-activated emergency light, meant to be tossed overside should a fisherman accidentally fall overboard at night, are near the wheel. Life vests are held by that always useful shock cord on the underside of the bow hatch — fully protected from weather, yet available in seconds.

The compass is unique — and again was borrowed from the ocean racing world. It's a surplus military aircraft compass, electrically operated. The magnetic sensor is located in an area away from ferrous metal objects, so there is no deviation error. The read-out dial is on the dash by the wheel and has a grid which I set on the course I wish to steer. Keep the compass needle in the grid, and I'm on course.

A vinyl cover protects the instruments, but a glassine insert allows me to see them. A similar insert to port of the wheel allows a folded chart to be read at a glance.

Every design feature, and all equipment, was intended to simplify boating chores and enhance *Miss Print's* "fish-a-bility." She's a go-anywhere boat, able to carry a hardy angling crew anywhere the spirit moves them — chasing anything from blue marlin to bonefish.

And she can do it in almost any weather!

Truck has plenty of clearance, to get you to the spots away from other campers and fishermen.

SAVE MORE VALUABLE TIME FOR FISHING WITH A SUMMER COTTAGE ON WHEELS

Camp Coaches for Anglers

BY BYRON W. DALRYMPLE

Last summer I took my family on a camping trip into Colorado and New Mexico. My two boys and I are ardent fishermen and needless to say the moment we get to a fishing spot we like to wet our boots, not spend endless hours setting up a comfortable camp. And we like to keep the fishing going right to the bitter end, not have to quit a half day early to tear down and pack up camp.

Happily, we discovered several seasons ago how anglers can lick the time-consuming labor of camping. We'd tried about every camping outfit. But finally we switched to a pickup coach and found it's by all odds the best outfit any angler can utilize. Let me illustrate from a random day of that Colorado-New Mexico family trip I mentioned.

That day I had driven about 300 miles, heading for a stretch of flies-only water on the Rio Grande way up between South Fork and Creede in Colorado. It was late in the afternoon when we arrived. As we pulled off the highway and down beside the rollicking river, I noted that although this was state property and camping was permitted, there were no facilities. But that made no

difference. Our water tank was full, we had a self-contained full bathroom, lights, heat, and of course cooking facilities. We needed nothing more except a place to park.

Here's how we set up camp. I pulled in beneath a big cottonwood, looked at my leveling device attached to the cab to check for tilt sideways and fore-and-aft. I was off a little on the left. I laid down a short piece of 2 x 6 carried for this purpose and backed the left rear wheel onto it.

The boys had been riding in back, in the coach. It's perfectly legal and extremely comfortable. Riding in a travel trailer is not legal in many states, nor very comfortable. They had been getting tackle ready as we drove. We'd conversed about it on our intercom between pickup cab and coach the last few miles before homing in. By the time I had the rig leveled — about five minutes — they were ready to go.

We hauled out waders and were into the stream less than fifteen minutes from the time we left the highway. Meanwhile the boys' mother had waited for them to get out of the way, then had gone inside, taken a couple of chickens from the refrigerator, readied them and some potatoes for baking, and popped all this into the oven of our butane stove. Then she lounged on the dinette divan, watching the river out the big side window as we worked for trout until dusk. When we came back to the camper shivery and hungry with a half dozen rainbows for morning breakfast, she had a warming toddy for me already stirred up in the galley. We sat snug and cozy, relaxing and watching darkness enfold the valley until it was time to take dinner out of the oven.

Granted such comfort and convenience can be duplicated with certain other types of camping outfits, such as the small trailer. But there are distinct advantages that only the coach has. I was struck by one of them next morning, for during the night it rained hard and the temperature dropped below freezing. We awoke to see some tenting neighbors drying out, hunched around a weak fire, and some tent-camper neighbors on the other side sitting in their car with the motor running.

Nor was that all. A man farther down the river had

A truck can get into spots where passenger cars may fear to go—and here is boat & camp all there, easily maneuvered.

pulled in the previous evening with a late model car towing a fair-sized travel trailer. He got started out but on the very steep grade leading up to the highway he was stopped cold. I went over to see what I might do to help.

"If you'll block your trailer wheels and get unhooked," I said, "I think maybe I can help you."

The pickup carrying my camper was a 1967 GMC V6 with the large motor, a three-quarter ton with automatic transmission, big 10 x 16½ tires, and a limited-slip rear end. Under slick or muddy conditions, particularly on grades, the weight of a camper on a pickup is a distinct asset, not a liability. The weight allows the truck to perform with plenty of traction.

But the real magic was that I had a heavy step-type rear bumper with a stout trailer hitch tab and ball welded to it. The reason I have this — like hundreds of other coachers — is that a pickup coach is the only fully-equipped recreational vehicle capable of towing a boat. In addition, I often tow a horse trailer, taking our own horses or rented horses to locations where we camp in the coach and ride back to more remote fishing areas. All we did now was to hook the gentleman's trailer to my coach. I pulled it up the hill to the highway shoulder with no problems. You can bet this man was coach-minded

by the time he drove away!

The pickup coach is a fairly recent innovation in camps for sportsmen. But it has gained fantastic popularity and there have to be logical reasons for this to happen. Ten years ago I could locate less than a half dozen firms in the coach business seriously enough to be identified. Today there are some 250,000 pickup coaches on U.S. highways, scores of firms producing them, and the projection for 1970 is at least three times the present number of coaches in action. Surveys show that these coaches are used for a variety of purposes. But they also indicate that the greatest percentage of owners are *fishermen*. Anglers use their coaches part of the time with one or two friends who are fishermen, part of the time for family travel wherein fishing plays a great part.

As I've said, there have to be reasons why coaches are outselling all other recreational vehicles, and especially reasons why fishermen are so sold on them. Travel Industries of Oswego, Kansas, who make the well-known Dreamer Coach, which I have used in various models for many years, have gathered by surveys some interesting

In New Mexico, in open area without shade, I bring a string of walleyes in for lunch. Coach is cool and comfortable, and we can park near boat, so it is safe.

A self-contained coach on an unfished saltwater channel with no camping facilities is a real home. This one also brought a boat here, large enough to use in outside waters on calm day.

answers to "why." Here are a few of them.

1. A coach allows one to have the most comfort with the least work — no hooking up, unfolding, etc.

2. Pickups, or four-wheel-drive vehicles with special coaches, can go to back-in waters where other outfits can't.

3. Coaches are allowed on many big roads, especially in the east, where even small trailers are prohibited.

4. Parking in tight spots is easier than with tow rig or large motor homes.

5. Stopping in towns is easy, for shopping, etc., but with a trailer it can be difficult.

6. One can tow large boats suitable even for bluewater fishing along the coasts. Particularly for the numerous large freshwater impounds fished by the majority nowadays, a substantial boat larger than "cartop" is needed, and the coach-and-pickup can tow it.

7. With modern built-in jacks, the coach can be removed and replaced. Thus a fisherman can set up a headquarters for family comfort and use the vehicle to scout other locales.

8. In many camp areas where trailers are still not allowed or no facilities are available for them, coaches are no problem.

9. Using a coach is economical. Today's streamlined, full-comfort pickups are catching on as second cars in many families. They are sturdy, the best buy in the automotive field and have high resale. A coach can be added cheaper than any other camping unit with comparable comforts.

10. Safety of travel both on highways and back country due to ruggedness of vehicle.

11. The coach can be set up as a "summer cottage" at a lake lot near home, while the pickup is used to go back and forth and to haul the "cottage" home in the fall.

12. Coach can double as a houseboat and cabin fishing boat, set on a special pontoon-and-deck, driven by outboard.

13. Better fishing can often be reached because of pickup ability to travel mountain roads, wood trails, lakeside undeveloped areas away from other campers and fishermen.

14. A group, family or otherwise, can ride in full com-

Photo illustrates ease with which coach rig handles boat, to get it into the water almost anywhere.

We drive up along many a salt water canal or inlet & stop to fish. Those who don't fish can relax inside in full comfort. It's a great way to keep everybody happy.

For those who really want to rough it, Dreamer builds small coaches specially designed for short-wheelbase 4-wheel-drive vehicles, as here.

For the angler who doesn't want to take a horse along, a special bracket on back of coach will carry a trail bike to get one to back-in fishing spots.

257

fort, even sleeping, making lunches, etc., en route.

15. Greatest ice-fishing shanty known to man. Set tip-ups and watch out window from position of solid comfort.

16. Ditto for surf fishing. Sit inside out of boiling sun, for example, or bad weather, and watch surf rod held by sand spike right outside the door.

17. Best way to prevail upon a wife who doesn't like discomfort to go into the wilderness places that have passable roads, where a husband wants to fish.

18. Saves a great deal of fishing time that would otherwise be wasted doing camp chores in off-trail or off-road spots when other type outfit is utilized.

19. Perfect full comfort and safety for family when children are small while still allowing the male angler of the family to get to his favorite backwoods lake or stream.

20. Economy of fishing-trip travel for group of anglers who want the comforts plus ability to take a good-sized boat along.

The list might go further. However, included in all of the above are some convincing arguments for the camper and pickup combo. Obviously the first question most prospective owners will want answered concerns cost. Look first at the pickup. If you buy a year-end model new, almost any of the makes will run around $1900 to $2400, depending on what extra equipment you want. Earlier in the model year prices will be a bit higher. Regardless of make, you should buy a ¾ ton, even for a coach of modest size. A four-speed transmission is good. So is an automatic, if you get one with multiple-shift. The two-speed automatic is useless for coach toting.

Small six-cylinder motors leave much to be desired. The powerful GMC V6 is fine. So are the various eights of all makes. Don't fret too much about gas mileage since performance is far more important. If you want to climb mountain grades to get to good waters, you need plenty of horsepower.

I've used both power brakes and power steering in the units I've owned. Both increase safety and comfort for the coaching angler. And I'm sold on the newfangled large tires — the ten-inchers. They're a great base to hold a coach on the road and are excellent for sand or mud, for beach or back-in. I'm sure most readers will know that air conditioning is also available nowadays in pickups for hot-weather travel. I wouldn't be without it for my southwestern bass and saltwater trips. Even in mild weather, traveling with the windows closed tires you less. Also, by

all means I'd get a custom cab with full foam cushions, arm rests, twin visors, etc. A pickup with all these extras will run around $3000 to $3500, still less than a comparable passenger car. And it will last longer, if anything be *more* comfortable, far tougher and double beautifully as a second car around suburbia. It will sell secondhand far more readily and for more money than a comparable passenger auto.

The cost of coaches varies greatly due to the different styles and lengths available and the numerous items of optional equipment. The old saying, "you get what you pay for," goes all the way, too. A low price on a new coach means either mediocre construction or few comforts. Here are some general price ranges for coaches of different sizes and styles, variously equipped.

Begin with the standard 8-foot coach, with over-cab bunk. In general such coaches will sleep four persons comfortably, have as basic equipment a water tank and pump, stove with oven and broiler, ice box, and lights running from the car battery. The dinette makes up into a double "downstairs" bed. Generally a space heater, a hot water heater, and a toilet, or toilet and shower, will be extras. With standard equipment the 8-footer — which can be mounted on a pickup with either short or long wheelbase — will cost around $1100 to $1400.

Next step up is the standard 10-foot or 10½-foot slide-in model. Both this one and the above 8-footer slide into the pickup bed and are secured there. Base prices on the larger coach will run from $1350 to $1600. The 10 or 10½ will more easily accommodate a bathroom and other optionals. A full bath costs in the neighborhood of $250 to $350. Heaters, good ones fully and properly vented, run from $60 to $100. A butane refrigerator as a rule will be $200 or more. And so on. If you want all of the optionals, you're better off buying one of the fancier models in any standard line. Most of these will cost, depending on equipment, from $1800 to $2000.

Next step up are the on-frame models, which I like a great deal. I have used over thousands of miles such models as the Dreamer Explorer in 10½- and 12-foot lengths. The single disadvantage is that the frame-mounted model cannot be easily removed from the truck chassis. And if it is removed, then a pickup bed or box must be mounted to use the truck. The long coaches — in 12- and 14-foot models — are mounted permanently on stretch-frame trucks, which makes it impossible to remove and replace

A unique use to which we put coach: we tow horse trailer, take our own or rented horses to high country, then ride in to roadless waters, using coach for base camp. Here son Mike exercises a horse before loading for a trip.

with a truck bed, unless a special one were made.

In other words, the on-framer is strictly a recreational vehicle. With full bath (my 12-foot Dreamer had a full bath and dressing room across the rear that could be completely closed off with an accordian-type door) such a coach will cost around $2000 in 10 or 10½ feet to $2500 or $2800 for fully-equipped 12 or 14 footers. You can have all sorts of conveniences if you wish, such as power-pumped water. Just turn a tap and an electric motor pumps the water. The great advantages of the on-framers are: a great deal more room inside; additional room because there are no fender wells to get in the way as in a pickup bed; and a much lower center of gravity, which makes these large coaches handle beautifully on the highway even if they look mighty huge.

Quite obviously the cost and the use you intend for the unit will dictate what you will buy. Even if you have plenty to spend, you must realize that although a compact 8-footer may be less plush inside, it can go places a big on-frame 12-footer can't. I have taken both 10½'s and 12's into some astonishing off-trail locations at fairly remote lakes and streams. Nonetheless, they do have their limits. But I have run an 8-footer practically anywhere I wanted to go. The only real limitation is overhead clearance. You have to watch for low limbs, etc. And of course a trail too snug at the sides is hard on wide mirrors and edges of a coach. But few anglers will need to get into situations where a small coach can't make it.

There is still another coach for fishermen who really want to go rough. These are special coaches built for the various 4-wheel-drive trucks. I ran a long and rather severe test not long ago on one of these trucks outfitted with Dreamer's small coach designed for it. It must be understood these coaches are not meant for sprawl-out

comforts for a whole family. The interior length of the downstairs portion is only about five to six feet at best. When a lower bed is made up from the dinette, it takes up just about all the floor space. However, with an over-cab bunk such coaches can sleep four. Most are outfitted only with the basics — sink and water pump and tank, butane stove, ice box, wardrobe and storage space.

When buying such a coach I would strongly advise getting a vehicle with a big motor, if there is a choice. For example, one test unit I ran for several months in some exceedingly rugged fishing country was a 4-wheel drive with a small 6 motor. With the coach overhang at the rear, this unit was a little bit light in the front end. On some of the hair-on-end grades where I put it, I could have wished for more up-front weight. The large motor offers this. I'd say that if you own a short-wheelbase vehicle such as Bronco, Scout, Toyota, Jeep, Datsun, etc., one of these small coaches for weekending or back-in jaunts is fine. Or, for trips into Mexico or the Canadian bush, excellent. But I doubt that buying a coach and 4-wheel-drive outfit for general family use is necessary.

Of course a fat book could be written about coaches and their uses and advantages for anglers. We can only skim the important factors here. Enlarging on that list from the survey, I'd say that economy of travel for a group, once the initial investment is made, is exceedingly important. Add to this the solid comforts that in themselves save many hours of time and labor that can be spent instead in fishing, and the investment begins to shape up as sound indeed. I know one group of four anglers who bought a camper together. One of them already owned a pickup. This is a unique idea, and might be well worth investigating. After all, tens of thousands of people nowadays are already pickup owners, and the pickup truck becomes ever more popular as a

We use the new type big tires—10x16½—on my GMC Camper Cruiser, and move right down to the surf line on almost any beach.

suburban runabout.

The coach cost these men $1850 and had virtually all the latest conveniences. Each man put in $462.50, and they agreed that the fellow who owned the pickup would be left out of gasoline and truck expenses on trips. All four split food and incidental costs. Granted such arrangements work well only among close friends. But this group has used the coach on two-week fishing vacations for five years now. That makes roughly $92 per year for each, invested in the coach. Gas, food, etc., would cost about the same no matter how these anglers traveled, if they did their own cooking.

So they've spent about $7 per day per man in the coach for those two-week vacations. But they have also used the rig many weekends which we might consider free. And they still have the coach, which retains a substantial resale value of perhaps fifty percent. This cuts their lodging fee down still more, to maybe $3.50 per day on the long trips and for-free on the weekends. The truly important aspect is that they've been able to actually go places where none could go without the coach. That is, to off-trail locations ordinarily available only to tent campers.

For that matter, economy is not everything. Nowadays I think most sportsmen know well they can't get their fishing for nothing. They don't expect to. What they want is the enjoyment, the thrills, and they are not unwilling to pay for it. Viewed from this angle, and considering the fact that boats for fishermen are so popular nowadays, I am convinced one of the most important coaching bonuses is the ability of the pickup coach to tow a boat. Few anglers consider just how drastically fishing has changed over the past two decades. As a younger fellow I fished constantly with a light cartop boat. One of the most-used boats I ever owned weighed only forty-eight pounds.

But as the years flew by, more and more impoundments were built coast to coast, border to border. Over the past twenty years fishermen have moved *en masse* from small waters to the hundreds of large reservoirs. These larger waters and the ever-growing popularity of saltwater fishing have made bigger boats a necessity. The cartop boat is almost literally a thing of the past. I remember when in the Great Lakes states every second or third car passing on main highways during vacation season had a boat on top. Now each has a boat towed behind it.

The motorist who tows a tent camper or travel trailer must stick with a cartop boat or none. But the coachman-angler can tow any boat he selects. With a powerful pickup he can tow the boat and piggyback his coach — camp into all sorts of tough areas. He can also park his camper close to a large boat that is not easy to put in and out, and at times this has tremendous advantages. Much as we hate to talk about it, there are still vandalism and theft in the land. A boat left tied up in an end-of-road location is safer if the owner is nearby.

While we touch the business of boat towing, let's look more closely at the pontoon-&-coach idea. This unusual use of coaches has not been explored to any great extent so far. But it is my prediction that within the next few

This is how coach on special pontoons & deck looks, and operates.

One of the great advantages of the pickup coach is its ability to tow a good sized boat. Here an on-frame 10½ footer makes fine camp for lakeside use.

From coach-houseboat, one can fish from deck, as here—and note those big bass on deck and in water.

years it will see increasing interest. As far as I know, Bud Coons of Dreamer was the first to experiment purposefully with the pontoon-coach idea. He and I were riding around on and in one of these unique outfits ten years ago. It is a tremendous idea worthy of much more attention by anglers.

The idea is to mount a slide-in coach on your pickup and tow a set of pontoon-and-deck on a transport trailer specially built for the purpose. The deck sides fold down so the rig won't be too wide to be legally towed. There is a raise-&-lower motor bracket at back. At the lake where you intend to camp and fish, you raise the coach from the pickup bed on coach jacks. Then you ease forward, pulling the pontoon and deck under the coach. From here on you let the coach down in precise place, secure it with the turnbuckles installed for the purpose, and pack up the jacks. Then the deck sides and motor bracket are raised. The motor is attached — we've used outboards of 15 and 25 to 40 horsepower with satisfaction — and the rig backed down the ramp. Set her afloat and you have a full-fledged houseboat.

Don't misunderstand me. Nobody claims this is a flick-of-the-wrist operation. It takes some time and work. Too much nonsense is written nowadays about products that can be whipped together in 20 seconds by a two-month-old baby. The point is that this conversion is not very difficult, nor very strenuous. But it probably takes about two hours to do properly. Obviously for an afternoon or a single day it is not worthwhile. But for a week or more, or a whole summer of back-and-forth runs from home to lake, it's a tremendous idea. You have a coach that doubles whenever you wish as a real houseboat. It is safe and sea worthy and has all the comforts, even to a shady seat at the wheel, placed under the overhang of the overcab bunk.

Granted also this is not a cheapie. But it's not prohibitively expensive. The pontoons and deck cost from $800 to $1000, the towtrailer to carry them runs about the same. Truck, coach (figure an 8-footer for low cost), pontoons and trailer will total at least $5000 and probably more. But the uses for this multiple outfit and the enjoyment it can offer an angler or family of anglers are tremendous.

I happen to consider the coach without question the most perfect beach rig. After all, the myriad contrived and contrapted "beach buggies" one sees can hardly compare with coach comforts. And the big coaching tires available nowadays are ideal for sand travel. In addition, for trips to camp areas with limited or no facilities, such as back-in National Forest sites where the fishing is best, the comforts of a coach — if you are taking your wife and family on a vacation — keep everyone happy. Many an avid city-dwelling angler settles for a nearby stream where he's in danger of losing an ear to a pack of competitors, just because his mate hates tenting or is afraid of it.

Perhaps she shouldn't be blamed. Times change. We are no longer a nation of pioneers. We are an urban population. A full-comforts coach in effect moves suburbia to the out-back. Admit it, Mr. Fisherman, you too are softer than your forebears. But happily the pickup coach has evolved to solve your problem. And it's the best camp yet for traveling anglers. ⋖══⋗

Here's how it looks, the coach turned houseboat, as it is launched.

Coach, with special pontoon deck and trailer, can double as excellent house boat. Here jacks are being put under the coach, to get set to place it on pontoon.

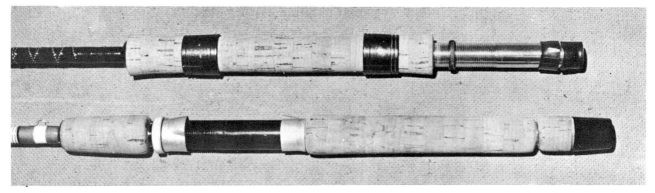

Combo rods come with various handles. The Fenwick has the conventional rings and attached fly reel seat, while the Shakespeare handle disassembles to move the seat from its spinning position back to the fly reel position.

Keep a tiger in your trunk

by Bill Resman

All about pack rods—and how any angler can make the most of them.

A tucked-away pack rod is a blessing on portages. There's enough loose gear as it is!

In all but the fly fishing field, rods are getting longer and longer. Not too long ago, a 4½ to 5 foot rod was standard for baitcasters, but with the introduction of spinning and spincasting the rod grew like Pinocchio's nose. Like that nose, the rods became more vulnerable. Car doors, screen doors, and the interior of compact cars became virtual smash traps.

The person using public transportation had even more of a problem. Even broken down into two pieces and cased, a rod was still a cumbersome object to carry. If you submit it to the sardine-packed maws of a luggage or freight compartment you don't know how it will come out. (At one time I shipped my rods ahead and they arrived on site labeled "mop handles." You can imagine how gently they were handled!) Carried personally with you in the passenger compartment they're as clumsy as a pair of crutches.

Back in the bush, the problem becomes even more apparent. Neither rods nor rod cases fit well in bush planes, tie well to mules, or portage easily.

There were solutions to the problems years ago, but they weren't good ones. Telescoping beryllium copper and hollow steel rods were plenty compact, but they had all the action of a loosely fitted car antenna. The rods were fine for emergencies or for trolling, but fairly creaked at the joints when you used them for casting.

Anglers were ripe for a good, moderately priced compact rod, and with the advent of fiberglass, they got it.

The first really successful rod of this type was introduced by Wright and McGill in their "Trailmaster" series. For several years they seemed to have the market pretty much to themselves, but then two newer modifications began to emerge.

The first of these was the "luggage." Falling between the average two and three piecers and the bona fide pack rod, this rod was not aimed at the boot-clad portage-pounder, but at the businessman or executive who could tuck one of these into a train case. As might be expected, many of these latter rods are top of the line, beautifully adorned and fitted with plush cases.

The next rod to emerge was the rebirth of the tackle box rod in fiberglass. Pretty much pioneered by Old Pal and South Bend, these rods break down into five or six pieces and fit easily into any moderately sized box.

While these lines of rods were being developed, another offshoot developed with them — again for the sake of compactness. These were the combo rods which could be used for more than one purpose. Most commonly they are combinations of spinning and fly rods, but an occasional maverick gets into the pack which combines even more uses.

All of the foregoing rods, however, are met with a common skepticism that runs something along these lines: A one-piece rod has the best action, a two-piece rod a less perfect action, and a three-piece rod worse yet. So how can a four- to six-piece rod come up with even a DECENT action?

This skepticism gets a further push from many fishing columnists who have never used the short rods. Ever notice the typical answer to a question about pack rods? It usually goes something like this:

QUESTION: I am contemplating a canoe trip and am wondering whether a pack rod would be a good choice for me?

Almost invariably this comes back:

ANSWER: A pack rod would be convenient to carry, but you certainly can't expect it to have as good an action as a two piece.

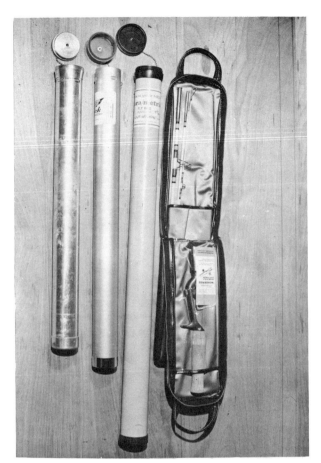

Variance in cases is shown here. At left are Fenwick and Wright & McGill aluminum cases. Then follow Berkley's plastic case and Shakespeare's soft luggage case. The padded cases are good for luggage travel, but the tubes are preferable for rough going.

Rod caps can be either screw-on or slip-on. The aluminum case at left is the most substantial, with no exposed threads on the case.

The luggage rod allows the businessman to take his fishing where it comes. This bass was taken just a five minute drive from the office.

It can't, huh? That's not what my findings show! In an attempt to find out just how good these compacts are, I obtained a sampling of rods from various tackle companies.

These were first "back yard" tested, with the author switching alternately from the multi-piece rod to a similar two-piece one.

There is a variation among rod makes, of course, but I'd be willing to bet that the average angler, blindfolded, could not tell the difference in action between a four-piece rod and a two-piece! This ought to straighten out a few who have stayed away from pack rods because of their "lousy" action. Those four-piecers with glass ferrules felt a little better than those with metal, but if a person was trying to decide between the convenience of a pack rod and the "smoothness" of a two-piecer, I'd take the pack rod every time.

When you get into the five- and six-piece rods, you can definitely tell the difference from a two-piece, but the difference is that the rod merely seems stiffer.

This was true of all the pack rods, for that matter, but note that the difference is STIFFNESS, not SMOOTHNESS! A person looking for a soft parabolic action spinning rod would not be pleased by pack rod actions, but he could probably get close to what he wanted by going to a lighter action. In short, a four-piece light action rod feels and casts somewhat like a two-piece medium action.

There are certain characteristics that one should seek in a pack rod.

The first of these is proper-sized guides. In some cases, guides have been used which are too small. This is apparently an attempt to fit the rod into a more compact case, but it cuts down casting distance. There is no real reason for the guides to be smaller on a compact spinning rod than in a conventional two-piece rod. Watch too, for guide materials. Stainless steel guides are almost universal, but it's desirable to have at least a tip guide of carboloy, carbide or agate.

Better yet is having both the gathering guide and the tip guide made of carboloy, particularly if the rod is to be used steadily. Logically, a full set of carboloys would be best, but this gets to be a toss up choice because these guides are heavy and could dampen the action of a light rod.

Ferrules, too, take on greater importance than in a conventional rod, if for no other reason than that there are more of them. These run a full gamut from nickel silver, to sizematics with neoprene "o" rings, to no real ferrule at all in the glass ferruled rods. As shown in the photo, the latter permits a smoother flow of action since there are fewer dead spots that do not flex. Regardless of the type, the ferrules MUST fit tightly or the rod will feel like a handful of dry chili beans.

Type of action is an important consideration in the combo rods. There are spinning rod actions with tacked-on fly reel seats, and fly rod actions with reel rings and spin guides. This can't be determined by just looking at the rod, for all two-use combos look like modified spin rods. The action of the rod can best be determined by referring to the company's catalog. It's a rare store clerk indeed who could tell the difference!

The combo action should then be picked to match its primary use regardless of whether it's for spinning or fly use. The rod may LOOK like a spinning rod, but it might be a better fly rod.

Cases for the compact rods vary a lot and they should be picked to fit the need. The flat plush padded case looks luxurious and works well confined within the hard shell

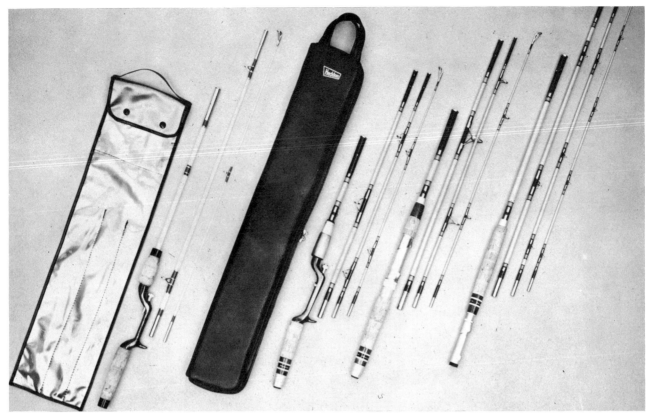

HEDDON PACK RODS: Two series of fishing rods packed in their own cases and ready to travel. These are the Starcast at left and the Mark V pack rods at right. The Starcast is a 3-piece rod which fits into a 25" carrying case. It is available in a choice of 6' spin cast or spinning rod. The Heddon Mark V, right, is a 4-piece, deluxe Mark V rod in a 27", cushioned Naughahyde case. It is available in 6' casting or spin casting, 7' spinning, and an 8' fly rod.

of a suitcase, but it offers little protection against crushing type blows which might be sustained in a pack or in the trunk of a car. The round hard case is dandy for taking abuse, but is comparatively heavy and the very dickens to pack clothes around in a suitcase. Any rod carried in these hard cases should also come in a cloth bag to prevent eventual damage by friction. I've found that one must occasionally buy a separate bag because the one furnished is so flimsy it lasts for only about one season.

A review of the rods actually tested will help to get some idea of what the angler can expect in given price ranges.

The first rod tested was a four-piece Trailmaster by Wright and McGill. This veteran rod has been around for many years and deservedly so, since it's still one of the best under-thirty-dollar rods available. The rod has a near parabolic action with nickel silver ferrules and butt cap. I'd like to see that butt cap touched off with some non-skid material though, because the rod slides almost every time you stand it up on a hard surface. It may be an Eagle Claw hallmark, but it sure is slippery. Guides are stainless steel, with the gathering guide somewhat on the smallish side

Finish and workmanship are excellent, and it's the only pack rod I know which comes with an unconditional guarantee against breakage.

This includes car doors, screen doors and even clumsy foot damage! The case is the most indestructible thing I've seen for holding rods. Made of heavy aluminum, it has a reinforced lower end, and a screw type lid machined from a block of aluminum.

The same company's Heavy-Duty 7½' pack rod comes in a different case. Made of leatherette and an aluminum tube, the 26" case contains the mightiest mittful I've seen

in a compact package. This spin rod is easily capable of punching out lures well over one ounce in weight, and its 19½" handle makes this a good two-hand rod. Since it's somewhat clumsy for use with one hand, it could hardly be called an all-around freshwater rod but it could sure serve the ticket for the now-vaunted Coho or for the northern pike or muskie fisherman who dislikes baitcasting.

Finish and workmanship are similar to those on the lighter rod, but the ⅝" gathering guide is small for a rod with this heft and length. This rod would probably be used with reels in the light saltwater class. Since these have comparatively large spools, the small guide could create quite a bit of drag. No one, however, could knock the strength of the guides — they're the beefiest I've seen on any pack rod.

Garcia has a 5½' fast taper spinning rod that's a good one. They call it a luggage rod, but it's available with both hard or soft cases, and its eighteen-inch aluminum case turns it into one of the most compact pack rods available.

This five-piece rod could be tucked away almost anywhere including the very common 18" tackle box. Normally I'm rather touchy about fast taper rods, but this seems to be one of the good ones. The fairly steep taper can handle lures from one-eighth to one-half ounce, and is even all the way down so that there's no floppy tip.

One unusual feature is the comparatively short handle. From winding check to rubber butt cap, the handle spans only 10½" as compared to the average 13 to 16 inches. The short handle feels strange at first, but when you think about it, what use IS a long handle? In days gone by you could theoretically adjust your handle rings to adapt the rod for different lures and this was some justification at least for a long handle. Sliding rings are now

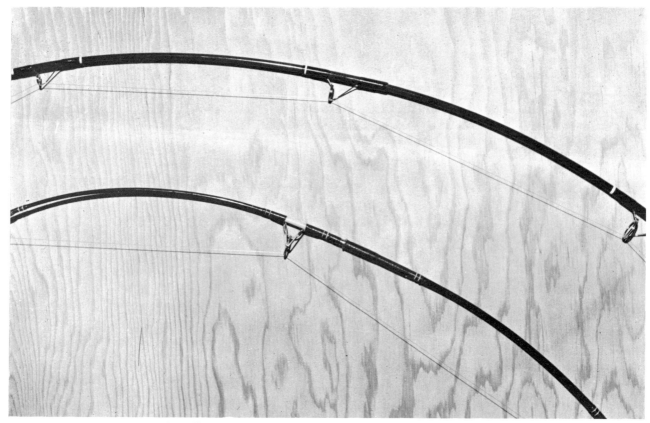

The difference between glass and metal ferrules is shown here. Note the smooth uninterrupted flow on the upper (Fenwick) ferrule.

getting to be passe except on ultra-lights or combo rods, so why should one need a long handle with a fixed seat? Sure you can stick those long corks into your tummy when fighting a big fish, but this is also a dandy way of breaking a light rod!

Guides are stainless steel and of good size. Finish and appointments are very good on the B545, as on any Garcia rod in this $25 price bracket. Case is aluminum with plastic cap.

South Bend makes a whole series of six-piece rods. The one tested was their fly rod, which without the case, will easily fit into an 18″ tackle box.

Even though the rod is made up of six pieces, the action is good, although somewhat stiff and fast. A beginner would have to watch his timing carefully with this one.

The rod comes in a slip-in case with reinforcement rod, and while the rod is short enough for a pack rod, the case offers no protection against crushing action. Finish and workmanship are good, although not quite up to what one would expect in this just-under-thirty-dollar rod.

Zebco has come out with two compact outfits: the 2495 and 2795. Both of these are spincasting rod and reel combinations, but are designed for different purposes.

The 2495 is an "ultralight" outfit, equipped with hollow glass shaft and combined reel and handle. Although at first glance it looks like a kid's toy, it is nicely engineered, with good workmanship. Use proves it definitely is not a toy, for the four-piece rod is equipped with a carboloy tip and has a very good light action. I used this outfit on panfish and had myself a ball — certainly more fun than with a standard stiffish rod and ordinary spin casting reel. The outfit comes in a padded slip-in case and sells for under twenty-five dollars.

The 2795 is also a compact rod and reel combo, but for medium size fish. The reel is Zebco's 606 and detach-

able. The rod is a four-piece solid glass item with good action. Unfortunately, like many solid glass rods, it makes the outfit tip heavy in feel. Workmanship is good and the whole works sells for under thirty dollars. A non-padded slip-in case is included.

Moving into the more expensive rods, we encounter the Berkeley Para/metric fly rod at just under fifty dollars. This 7½′ stick comes in a heavy plastic tube with screw-on cap. Not quite as substantial as aluminum, but a far cry better than those "sturdy fiber" tubes that some manufacturers insist on using for even their best rods.

This four-piece rod, like all other Para/metrics, was computer designed, which in part, I suppose accounts for the high tab. I must admit, however, that the computer must have been thinking for the action is excellent and quite similar to a regular "dry fly" action. The rod feels stiff, as do the other Para/metrics, but it's very versatile for a fly rod. It will easily handle a 6-weight line, a 7-weight line, or even a comparatively short length of 8 line, which makes rod-to-line matching much easier.

The rod has flexible ferrules which are part of the rod itself. The male portion of the ferrule is a short shaft inserted into the center of the lower section. The female portion of the ferrule is the hollow shaft of the next section. Although I was disappointed with the fittings I saw on the earlier Para/metrics (considering the price), I have to revamp my opinion. This fly rod is very well finished, with excellent workmanship and even THE final touch of a walnut reel seat. This, by the way, is an excellent rod for sinking lines. Many rods can delicately deliver a number 7 line, but when it comes to lifting a sinker out of the water they fold up like a goldenrod tipped with a soggy blackbird. The Para/metric keeps it up and moving for a good backcast.

The Mark V "pack" spinning rod by Heddon is really

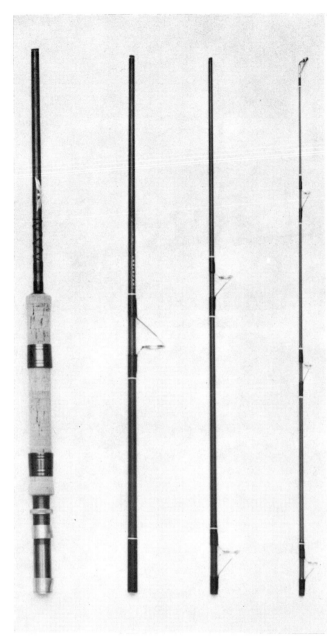

Combination fly-spin rod by Fenwick features glass ferrules for smooth action, light weight.

a four-section luggage rod with what Heddon calls Controlled Flex Action. This action has an almost parabolic flow from the tip to about two-thirds of the way down the shaft with the last third quite stiff. Preference for various acions is a personal choice of course, but I'd rate this with the best actions available. It keeps away from the sloppy tip, and yet that stiff one-third adds leverage that really pushes out a cast.

The rod is stiffer than the conventional two-piece rod in this action, and more closely approximates the heavier Heddon action called Power Flex. It's therefore most suitable for lures in the ⅜th- to ⅝th-ounce range. The rod has carboloy tip and gathering guide. Finish and workmanship are top drawer including such deluxe appointments as stainless steel guide windings and walnut insert. This sixty-dollar rod comes in a padded case with leather-grained vinyl outside and lining of blue vinyl.

A conventional combo fly/spin rod becomes unusual when it's made by Fenwick. Called the Feralite, the SF 74-4 has ferrules that are merely the lower shaft inserted into the hollow of the next shaft piece. I say merely because it looks simple, but I sure can't figure how they do it without showing a bump or any variance in the taper of the rod. Once the rod is assembled, you'd be hard pressed to find even one ferrule. When I first got the rod for testing, I almost ruined it by trying to take it apart at a guide wrap where there wasn't any ferrule. How is that for invisibility!

Action of the rod is excellent. I don't think I could distinguish it from even a one-piece rod, since its four pieces don't even have a tendency to feel stiffer than a conventional rod. Because of the lack of metal, the rod is also very light for its power. Even with the extra fittings of spinning guides and reel rings, the fly rod action rod weighs less than some conventional fly rods with similar "strength."

As a spinning rod, the stick performs best with lures in the ⅛th- to ⅜th- ounce range. As a fly rod, it performs very well with a number six or seven line. Finish and workmanship are excellent on this forty-dollar rod, and the shaft has a gleam I've never seen excelled on any rod. Guides are flexible stainless steel with a carboloy tip top.

The most versatile multi-purpose rod I've seen is the SP999 Jet Set by Shakespeare. This is an executive-type luggage rod packed in black leather grained, padded vinyl case. The rod makes into a 7-foot spinning or fly rod, or 6½-foot spincasting rod.

Although one might wonder how well such a wide variety of methods might be served by one shaft, the outfit does surprisingly well. It performs best as a spinning or spincast rod, but works well enough as a baitcasting or fly rod to satisfy all but the pickiest purist.

The finish and workmanship on this fifty-dollar rod are very good and equal what might be expected of a rod in this price range. The only disappointments are the lack of even a tip guide of something harder than stainless steel and the fact that some spinning reels will not fit the reel seat when it is set up for spinning.

There are, of course, many other compact rods than those represented here, but those tested prove that the "pack" rod is much more than just the second rod you throw in the trunk just in case your first love breaks. Eventually you'll probably carry the pack rod with you in the car all the time. Then when you visit your wife's third cousin, and he suddenly decides to take you fishing (and offers you his son's one-ninety-eight Super Shaft) you'll feel that you *have* got "a tiger in your trunk"!

Pitch a comfortable fishing camp

A guide for all anglers on
basic camping techniques.

By Erwin A. Bauer

This camp on Buckhorn Lake, Ontario has everything: access to fishing water, seclusion, shade during heat of the day.

This summer the largest army of anglers in history will go fishing and for many it will be a camping-fishing trip. They will pitch tents or unfold camper trailers wherever there is water and spend happy summer holidays under canvas. Just *how* happy the holiday will usually depend as much on whether the camp is comfortable or not as on the fishing success.

But nowadays there is no reason for camping to be anything *but* comfortable as well as uncomplicated. Modern gear is so skilfully designed and easy to use that any fisherman can be an expert on his first camping trip. But planning ahead is very important. So is being fully acquainted with your equipment. Add also a knowledge of basic camping techniques.

Let us assume you already have the camping essentials: Tent, stove, lantern, cooler, utensils, enough bedding for all in the family. The next step is to pack it so that it will be out of the way when traveling, yet handy and easy to reach when you arrive at a campsite.

If the party is large, or if you do not own a station wagon, this may call for renting a simple two-wheel luggage trailer or a cartop carrier. Rentals for both are very inexpensive. And today there are excellent cartop luggage racks on the market which are easy to install and which will not injure a car's finish. Remember that anything carried on top of the car must be covered sufficiently to protect it from rain and road dirt. Double check also to be certain that the cargo is lashed securely to the carrier.

Storing the larger items — tent, sleeping bags — isn't difficult. In a station wagon, it is often a good idea to unroll all bags and pile them in the back to make a comfort-able "traveling pad" for any children. Or one fisherman can sleep during long trips while the other drives. But storing smaller items — pots, pans, foodstuffs, lantern, as well as tackle — is a little more difficult. Without proper storage, they can be broken, scattered, lost or misplaced when you need them the most. At the very least, they should be packed neatly in boxes. Pack cushioning material around glass.

But the wise camper will carry a portable pantry. This is an upright cupboard which easily fits into the back of a station wagon and by trip's end can be worth its weight in gold. It contains drawers or shelves of sizes specifically to fit, say, the two-burner stove, one or two gas lanterns, a tray of utensils, nesting pots and pans, cans of food. When the cupboard doors open outward, they furnish a flat working space for the cook, either right on the tailgate of the car, on a picnic table in camp, or on collapsible (folding) legs.

These portable pantries are available ready-made by several manufacturers. But most campers prefer to build them in home workshops (of plywood or aluminum sheeting) to suit their particular needs. Either way they are the greatest time and space savers on any camping trip.

It is excellent advice to carry camp tools in a separate sturdy container which is easy of access because some of these will be used immediately on reaching camp. A list of essential tools would include an axe, rope, folding hand saw, pliers, small funnel (for refueling gasoline appliances), shovel, extra stakes, folding grill.

The first step on arriving in a campground is to erect the tent or camping trailer. That way you have shelter in

Idyllic situation for a fisherman's camp at Gates of the Mountains on the Missouri River, Montana. Tent is right near water edge.

case of rain. No modern tents are difficult or slow to erect; still you should have practiced this several times on your lawn or garage apron before making a trip. Any tent should be ready for occupancy in less than ten minutes.

If you have a choice of sites on arriving in a typical campground, keep the following points in mind: ask the campground ranger for permission to drive around the area before choosing a site. Select high ground rather than low ground, for better ventilation and for a dryer camp. Lakeshore sites are handy because you can be close to your fishing water and boat at all times, but be certain the spot you pick is not boggy. It is well to be near the water supply and toilets, but avoid locating on main paths to these facilities used by other campers. If you prefer peace and quiet, keep a good distance from concessions or organized playgrounds. Pick a site which offers at least partial shade.

Of course during very busy periods in popular fishing and camping areas, you may not have a great selection of sites. In such cases, campground custodians simply assign a spot and that is that. Then you just make the best of it. And the first thing to do is to police it. Pick up any bits of litter which previous campers may have left. Keep the place clean at all times.

Locate your tent on the smoothest, highest portion of your camp site, wherever it is. In some campgrounds the tent site will already be leveled and marked. If not, you can do some minor grading with a shovel. If you have a tent trailer, level it carefully. Face it so that the door opens out onto your main "living area" rather than away from it. You might want to consider the prevailing breeze, and thereby let nature air-condition your quarters.

Perhaps in a few years, pitching a tent will only require pushing a button and stepping back while it pitches itself. But 1969 campers will find it is still a minor, though not unpleasant chore, once they have translated the written instructions into plain English. No two of today's models erect in the same manner, but there are a few rules for getting the job done quickly and correctly. First spread the tent (floor down) out on the ground exactly as you want to place it. Stake down the four corners. Next erect the center pole or assemble the framework and raise the canvas into position. Add any other stakes necessary and complete any rigging. Finally dig a shallow ditch completely around the tent to carry away water in case of a rainstorm. Incidentally, a small amount of ditching elsewhere around low spots of a campsite can make things

This fishing family uses a fold-out camper trailer for their lakeshore camp. Late arrivals might miss out on choice sites such as this one.

Fishermen here will have shade and seclusion when their camp is pitched.

Good selection of camp stoves like these are available to make cooking in camp easier and more pleasant.

more pleasant.

It may sound strange, but often what makes a more cozy and comfortable camp is a good supply of rope. Stretched between trees, this will serve as a clothesline and a place to hang sleeping bags for airing in the sun. Short lengths of light rope temporarily tied as necklaces around tree trunks will make good hangers for everything from shaving mirrors and lanterns to soup ladles and fishing rods. Do not drive nails or use wire for this purpose; you will only destroy the trees and other campers will recognize you as inexperienced or inconsiderate.

If open campfires are permitted (they aren't everywhere) or fireplaces are provided, do not chop down trees or cut firewood in the immediate camp area. The normal erosion caused by camping is serious enough without further thinning the vegetation. On the other hand, check with the campground ranger about fuel. Nearly everywhere firewood is available free or for sale at nominal cost.

Some sportsmen keep so busy fishing that a simple, dry place to eat and sleep is accommodation enough for them. But if you plan to spend considerable time just relaxing in camp, you might as well add a few conveniences. For example, erect a canvas fly leaf over the dining and/or cooking area. It is an especially easy thing to do, especially if there are enough trees onto which to lash the four corners. A single center pole will prop up the middle. The result is both shade and shelter from occasional summer showers.

Unless you are very short of space during travel, extra plastic water cans are very handy. With them you can keep an abundant supply of water on hand right at the campsite. In some more primitive areas, you may even be able to prop a can of water in the fork of a tree and use it as a portable shower.

1969 fishermen hopefully will find more and better places to camp than they did in recent years since there has been a great push to build new facilities almost everywhere. Still it is very, very important to plan ahead — to pick out camping areas far in advance of starting a fishing trip. In other words you might build your trip around places to camp.

Avoid reaching the most popular camping areas (Yellowstone, Cape Cod, Hatteras, Florida Keys, and many others) during the peak vacation periods of summer or especially on busy weekends. And once underway, actually traveling, get an early start in the morning and stop early in the evening before the best sites in any campground are already filled. That last is a tip already well known to experienced campers who always wind up with the best overnight spots. A camp pitched early also allows a chance to go fishing during prime evening time.

Altogether about 15,000 campgrounds will be open in 1969 in the United States and Canada. A good many of these are on or near fishing water. Most are public and are located in state parks, National Parks and Forests, plus a number in county and municipal parks. All of these are on a first-come-first-serve basis and advance reservations will not be accepted. The average fee is seldom more than $2.00 per night for a family. But the fisherman planning to camp very often in federal government areas anywhere should purchase a Golden Eagle Passport (at many Park entrances, from local AAA offices, from the U.S. Dept. of Interior, Washington, D.C.) for $7.00. It permits camping for an entire family all year long in federally-operated campsites. It's quite a bargain.

Nowadays most public campgrounds are located by name, symbol or both on all new road maps issued by the major oil companies. A postcard to any Department of State Parks in the State Capital will produce a list of that state's camping facilities. For information on camping in National Forests, write to the Regional Forester, U.S. Forest Service in the nearest of the following cities: Missoula (Mont.), Denver, Albuquerque, Ogden (Utah), San Francisco, Portland, Upper Darby (Pa.), Atlanta, Milwaukee, Juneau. The Director of the National Park Service, Washington, D.C. 20025, will send information on Parks campgrounds.

More and more privately operated campgrounds are opening for business and with most of them it is possible to make reservations. One new chain (Kampgrounds of America, Box 1791, Billings, Montana 59103) operates 350 camping areas in 35 states. Most of the camping guides (Rand McNally, Trail-R-Club of America, Mobile, Atlas, Camping Maps U.S.A., Camper's Bible) now available on newsstands contain complete, up-to-date lists of all campgrounds, public and private.

This much is certain: setting up a comfortable camp was never before easier than in Summer, 1969.

Fisherman gets ready to cook fish, fresh caught, in camp.

Author running one of the many Caddo bayous.

Bragging fish are plentiful down in bragging country, so

HIT THE HOT NEW LAKES OF TEXAS

By Al Eason

Catch of August bass from Lone Star Lake. Note spotted bass in string.

Twenty years ago even Texans cussed the poor fishing in eastern Texas. The truth was that water was scarce in the area, and waters suitable for game fish were virtually nonexistent. Consider that Texas oil once sold for ten cents per barrel, while water went for a dollar per gallon in some early oil-boom towns, and it's easy to see why there wasn't much fishing.

But that's no longer the case. Now anglers from all over the country come to sample the superb fishing for black bass, white and yellow bass, crappies, bluegills and several other species. New lakes covering over a half million acres have sparked a full-scale fishing revolution in eastern Texas. In a rush to preserve precious water, state and federal agencies have built reservoirs—and are still building them—at a fantastic rate. Even as I write, three new lakes are filling, and a score or more are in the planning stage.

As each lake is completed, its fishing productivity follows a predictable pattern. For a few short years there's a fishing boom, when almost everyone takes home a full stringer. But then, as some of the lake's natural fertility becomes depleted and silt accumulates on the bottom, the fishing inevitably begins to drop off.

Since all the lakes are located within a 75-mile radius,

Author's fishing rig on launching ramp at Sam Rayburn Lake.

as well as the best season for chain pickerel. Pint-sized cousins of the northern pike, the pickerel strike hard and execute fancy acrobatics. A large one from Caddo will weigh 3½ pounds, and it's not unusual to boat thirty or forty in a single day during the prime winter months.

The fastest bream fishing—and the best popping-bug bass angling—starts in early May and continues through most of the summer. Bluegills and redears commonly reach one-pound size, and it's possible to catch a whole stringerful in one spot after the fish are bedded.

The favorite baits for bream are worms and crickets. But fly fishermen can have wonderful sport with these little battlers on a light trout rod and dry flies. May flies hatch on Caddo, and a fisherman floating a tiny gray hackle can catch a grab-bag of different fish. One of my favorite tricks is to move along a row of cypress trees and knock the flies to the water with a boat paddle. After doing this I can see where the largest fish are taking the fallen flies and fish in those spots.

Caddo has many fishing camps where launching ramps and fishing supplies are available. Several camps are located at the village of Uncertain, about fifteen miles from Marshall on Highway 43. There are a number of experienced guides who have spent their lives on the

local fishermen move from lake to lake as each reaches its peak. This practice has spawned a new breed of fishermen spoiled by easy angling success. As a result, many older lakes still affording excellent fishing by any standards go begging for anglers.

Caddo Lake, the only natural lake in Eastern Texas, is a prime example. This ancient body, said to have been discovered by Hernando De Soto's band of adventurers in 1536, contains more species of fish than any other Texas lake.

Caddo is a lake of meandering bayous, cypress-covered islands, and countless hidden coves, offering the fisherman some of the most beautiful fishing water this side of Florida. And while the man-made lakes boom and bust, Caddo fishing is good year after year.

Like all lakes in the area, Caddo produces fish year-round. But the best crappie angling occurs during the spring spawning run, sometime between mid-February and April. During this period both black and white crappies are taken by the hundreds around the big cypress trees and in the shallower water of the cypress brakes. Most local fishermen use live minnows, but anglers using tiny feathered jigs and spinner combinations have had good success too.

At the same time bass move into shallow water where good catches are made on plastic worms and safety-pin type lures. Caddo bass are small compared to those of other lakes in eastern Texas, but, perhaps due to a chemical change in the lake during the last few years, the fish are growing larger each year. A five-pounder is considered a good bass on Caddo, but the average is from one to two pounds.

As soon as spawning is completed, bass move back to open water, where they school up and raid schools of shad on the surface. Tearing and slashing into the bait fish like salt-water bluefish, the schooling bass will hit almost any bait in your tackle box. While many of the surfacing fish are small, anglers have learned to take lunkers by casting plastic worms and allowing them to sink to the bottom of the school.

Winter is the best time to take the larger bass on Caddo,

A scene on Caddo Lake, showing the Florida-like scenery.

John Ellis, Lake O' the Pines guide, and client admire fish.

First-year catch of bass from Sam Rayburn Res.

Author shows string of Caddo bass taken with plastic worm.

lakes and will take you after either crappies or bass. Guide fees average about 15 dollars per day. Roy Butler of Jefferson has 20-foot john-boats and guides for float trips down the bayous leading into Caddo. An all-day trip for two including boat, motor, guide, lunch and beverages, costs 35 dollars.

Lake of the Pines, a man-made reservoir, is only 15 miles from Caddo. An open lake of 18,000 acres with clean shorelines and many camping areas, LOP is considered one of the best bass fishing holes in Texas. But fishing methods contrast sharply with those used at Caddo.

Although bass school in Lake of the Pines also, the bragging-size fish are taken from deep holes scattered around the lake. Plastic worms are the favorite summertime baits, while jig-and-eel combinations work best during the winter months.

Fishing the shallow water in the upper ends of coves produces bass during the spring spawning season. Most of the coves are tangled with logs and brush where timber left standing when the lake filled has fallen into the water. This natural cover is a favorite bass hangout during the spring months. A Rapala-type lure worked slowly around the snags or a large-bladed spinner skittered across the surface will usually produce a good catch.

Author lands chain pickerel on Caddo Lake.

For crappies, night fishing under lanterns is the deadliest method. Small motor-driven barges are popular on Lake of the Pines, and many families take lunches and spend the night fishing for crappies.

Deluxe quarters and excellent guides are available at Tejas Village on LOP. John Ellis, who works out of Island View Landing, is one of the best guides in the area. The fee for guide, boat and motor is about 25 dollars.

Northeast of LOP, at 20,000-acre Lake Texarkana, crappies up to three pounds are not unusual, and bass fishing is excellent when water is at the proper level. Since the lake is used for flood-control, water level fluctuates, causing fishing success to blow hot and cold. And when Texarkana is hot, fishing is fantastic, but at other times, it can be disappointing. Shortly after construction of the lake, a Texarkana fisherman took over a thousand bass weighing over five pounds each. This remarkable feat was accomplished in a single year.

The race below the dam on the Sulphur River is a favorite spot of white bass anglers. When large amounts of water are released, fish run upstream and become trapped in the water below the dam. This is a signal for hundreds of anglers to gather for the phenomenal fishing in the concentration of fish.

A number of fishing camps on the lake offer facilities for the fisherman, and numerous public ramps are available for launching boats. Deluxe accommodations are available at the Kickapoo Lodge, north of Atlanta.

Four small Wood County lakes, located north of U. S. 80 between Hawkins and Mineola, offer excellent fishing. These lakes—Hawkins, Winnsboro, Holcomb, and Quitman—each covering 400 to 600 acres, have produced bass up to nine pounds. Most of them are spring fed, and as a result the water is extremely clear. Anglers, suiting methods to prevailing conditions, have found night fishing for bass most productive on Lake Quitman. A black Jitterbug is the favorite lure of the nocturnal anglers.

While all four lakes are adaptable to fly fishing, Winnsboro is best suited for this method. The lake contains abundant moss beds and submerged timber, making it a fly fisherman's dream. There's at least one fully equipped camp on each lake, and launching ramps and camping facilities are open to the public.

Tawakoni, a black jack country lake, is well past its prime for crappie fishing, but consistently produces good catches of bass. Tawakoni is a large lake, containing 36,700 acres of water. Because of the wide reaches of open water, boatmen should use extreme caution when crossing the open lake. Professional bass guides use 16 foot boats and 40 h.p. motors, and anything less could be quite dangerous when the wind blows over 15 miles per hour.

Tawakoni is one of the most productive bass lakes in Texas, but the unitiated would be wise to hire a guide. Bob Uhler and Mike Carmichael, both working out of White Deer Landing, are two of the best on the lake. Dave Hawk and his wife Elaine are also top guides. Elaine, while of the so-called weaker sex, consistently produces fish for her clients. Inquiry at the lake will reveal where the Hawks are currently working. Launching ramps and fully-equipped marinas are available at several spots on the lake.

Cedar Creek Reservoir, another black jack country lake, is in the second year of a fish population explosion. Two miles north of Malakoff off Highway 31, this lake last year produced some of the most fantastic fishing ever seen in eastern Texas. Catches of 100 to 150 crappies were common, with day and night fishermen enjoying equal

Two hour's catch from Striker Lake, "hot-hole."

success. In fact, due to the amazing abundance of crappies, there is no limit on them at Cedar Creek.

Since crappie fishing has been so hot, few fishermen try for bass. But those who do fish for them make consistently bigger catches as the lake grows older, taking bass up to 6½ pounds. Three-pound crappies have been caught, and a good stringer will contain many fish in the two-pound class.

As in most man-made lakes in the area, the plastic worm (with weedless hook) is a great favorite at Cedar Creek. The numerous brush-filled coves and submerged timber in the open lake are the favorite spots for both bass and crappie. Floating baits and spinners skated on the surface both take heavy strings of bass from the cove. Anglers using the weedless worm can fish the thickest brush tops and snake many good bass from the maze of underwater limbs.

At present only two marinas are in full operation at Cedar Creek. Don's Port Marina on the west side of the lake near the village of Tool and Big Chief Marina at the east end of Highway 85 bridge both have launching ramps and full facilities for fishermen. Only two or three professional guides are working the lake now. Local inquiry will help to locate their base of operations.

Sam Rayburn Reservoir, the largest lake in Texas and one of the best bass lakes in the South, sprawls over 144,-000 acres in the heart of the piney woods country. The bass angling is red hot—Rayburn is now and will be at the very peak of a bass population explosion. Fish from the original stocking have reached 5½ pounds, and even nine-pounders have been taken. The bass strike a wide

Proud anglers display catch from Lone Star Lake. Best bass fishing at Lone Star is during the usually unproductive months of August and September.

Top: Dallas anglers and one-day catch of crappie from Cedar Creek Res.

Right: Bob Uhler, Lake Tawakoni guide, with string of fish taken drift-fishing plastic worms.

variety of lures, and are boated by almost every method known to sport fishing.

Government agencies maintain scores of beautiful campsites and launching ramps around the lake, and commercial marinas are opening.

Sam Rayburn is a MUST for any fisherman visiting eastern Texas, since many veteran anglers consider it the hottest lake for medium-sized bass in the nation.

Lake Murvaul, though small, with only 3890 acres, is the BIG bass lake of eastern Texas. Although catches have dropped off since the incredible run of tackle busters three winters ago, this is still the best hole in the area for a "hang-'im-on-the-wall" bass. Trophies of nearly eleven pounds have been taken from Murvaul, and seven- and eight-pounders are common. It's the only lake I've ever fished in over 40 years of bass angling where a five-pounder could actually be considered a small bass.

Although most of the larger fish are caught by anglers

trolling with deep-running baits, worm and jig-and-eel fishermen still boat plenty of lunker bass. The prime time for big bass is December, January and the early February, but anglers make occasional catches of large fish throughout the year. Murvaul also produces crappie and bream, especially during the summer months, and good camping facilities and well-equipped marinas make it ideal for camping fishermen.

Lone Star Lake, about the same size as Murvaul, is northwest of Lake of the Pines on Highway 259. In contrast to Murvaul, Lone Star has shown the best bass runs during the usually unproductive months of August and September. Almost any fishing methods will produce in this lake, but trolling and casting to the surface schools seem most deadly. A day's catch from Lone Star will include both native largemouths and Kentucky spotted bass.

Only one fishing camp—Scenic View, near the town of Lone Star—is in operation on the lake. The owner, an

Top left: Morning catch of bass from Cedar Creek Res.

Roy Butler and guide on bayou float trip.

Big black puts up brawling battle on Lake O' the Pines.

Well-known bass fisherman Dick Kotis with a pair of bragging-size largemouths from Lake Murvaul. This lake has been a great producer of bass in recent years.

Angler Carl Lowrance finds plenty of action at Lake of the Pines. It's a bass caster's dream come true.

Fishing the timber on Lake O' the Pines.

inveterate bass fisherman himself, will direct the newcomer to the current bass hotspots. Lodging, launching ramp, and fishing supplies are available at the camp.

There's unique winter fishing for both black and white bass at Lake Striker, 17 miles south of Henderson. A steam-turbine generating plant on this lake discharges heated water creating a "hot spot" attractive to fish. Bass tend to congregate along a timberline where the warm water creates a current. Catches of bass up to nine pounds from this spot are not uncommon. Plastic worms are favorites for summer fishing at Striker, while winter anglers boat the most bass by casting Hellbenders. Fish are easily located because of the unique conditions, and anglers casting from anchored boats often catch six to ten bass weighing over four pounds each in an hour.

White bass school at Striker in both winter and summer. While the surfacing fish are often small, many fish run well over two pounds. Fishing is usually fastest in early morning and evening. Anglers frequently make catches of thirty to forty white bass in the late afternoon. Irwin Cross, who operates a marina on the lake, fishes every day and knows where the fish are located. He's always helpful to anglers fishing Striker for the first time.

In addition to the lakes I've mentioned, eastern Texas has numerous municipal lakes, many of which offer good fishing, although some have special fees and regulations. All the lakes I've discussed lie between Dallas, Texas, and Shreveport, Louisiana, within a seventy-five mile radius of the Texas town of Kilgore.

Eastern Texas is truly a fisherman's Shangri-La, and with more lakes built each year, local anglers find it tough to pick a favorite. The frenzied activities of the lake builders prompted a local wag to remark: "If them fellers keep building lakes so fast, it's soon gonna be to where a fellow will have to use a pirogue to go to the privy." Could be, but think of the wonderful fishing!

Author casts big bass water on Caddo Lake.

Lady angler displays fish from deck of barge at Lake of the Pines.

TENNESSEE:

BONANZA FOR TROPHY FISHERMEN

by Lea Lawrence

Speaking of bragging size fish, the Volunteer State has a few claims to fame

The former North American brown trout record holder, a 26-pound, 10-ounce fish, was taken below Dale Hollow Dam.

A friend from Florida, visiting me in Tennessee a couple of years ago, was browsing around in my den and he came across a stack of fishing rods and reels in a dusty corner.

In the assortment were several heavy-duty outfits, one a good-size star drag reel on a hefty boat rod and the other a spinning rig suitable for use in the ocean surf. A gleam came into his eyes immediately. He's a salt water fishing addict, and he had previously given me his general opinion of fresh water fishing: light gear, little fish.

"Too bad we're not where we could use these," he said. "Just think of tying into a dolphin, or a cobia, or a . . ."

I interrupted and stopped him short.

"We *are* where we can use it." I said, "I don't use that tackle for saltwater. There's plenty of opportunity right here in Tennessee to give it a good workout!"

I'll never forget the look on his face. We had been friends for a long time, and I could tell he thought I was lying. Or maybe that I was somewhat balmy. So I pro-

Big muskies, such as this one taken by Willie Speck from Dale Hollow Lake, provide a really fine challenge.

ceeded into an explanation as rapidly as possible.

"You're just not that familiar with inland waters, particularly Tennessee, and I'm sure you're not aware of what kind of big fish action is available here."

He still wasn't convinced.

"OK" I continued, "how about a big musky, say 25 pounds? Or maybe a 17-pound brown trout? Or a 25-pound walleye? Or a blue catfish of 78 pounds? Call those fish big enough to get your attention?

He appeared incredulous, and I kept talking.

"You wouldn't be interested in smallmouth bass of, say, 10 pounds? Or how about a largemouth of 12 pounds. Certainly something like rockfish wouldn't whet your appetite. So as you have already indicated, this kind of fishing isn't much to offer a jaded old salt water fisherman like you!"

His look by this time had changed to that of a cat stalking a mouse. His eyes narrowed and his nostrils dilated. I tossed in the Sunday punch.

"I forgot to mention alligator gar, but they're only seven or eight feet long. Nothing like that ocean stuff."

He was down for the count, but it didn't stop him from talking. And sometime in the wee hours of the morning when we finally turned in, he had planned enough fishing trips in Tennessee to keep us both busy for the rest of the year.

Actually my friend had learned something in a short time that isn't common knowledge among fishermen in the eastern United States, especially those who want really big fish for a challenge. The truth is that there are countless opportunities to tangle with big fish in fresh water, and Tennessee has an especially broad offering.

Part of this is because the state has a tremendous variety of fishing waters, ranging from the cold mountain streams of the Appalachians to the warmer waters of the Mississippi River. In between lies a complex of rivers and man-made impoundments created by the Tennessee Valley Authority, the U. S. Army Corps of Engineers and the Game and Fish Commission. These impoundments range in size from a few hundred acres to the huge 155,000 surface-acre Kentucky Lake, and the tailwaters of many of these lakes are terrific fishing spots.

Another important factor is the fisheries program of the Game and Fish Commission, which has resulted in the importation of several species and the improvement of many waters in which native big fish species are found.

Notable among these projects has been a highly effective musky hatching and rearing operation; a rockfish program, utilizing both the hatching and importation of fry; the development (in conjunction with South Carolina) of a rockfish-white bass hybrid; a lake and tailwater trout program which is second to none in the nation; and a supplementary walleye stocking plan which has shown excellent results.

In total, it all adds up to great fishing opportunity and especially for some tackle-busting species. To provide a more detailed look, here follows a complete rundown.

MUSKY—Tennessee always had a small number of native muskies, although they were confined for the most part to a small area on the Cumberland Plateau in Daddy's Creek and the Obed River.

Several years ago the Game and Fish Commission began purchasing eggs from a northern source, hatching and rearing the fish, then stocking them in selected waters. Now by supplementing the egg supply with eggs from the brood stock, the program has been greatly accelerated.

Presently muskies are in Fort Patrick Henry Lake, Woods Reservoir, Dale Hollow Lake, Norris Lake and Laurel Hill Lake, and the state record musky (just over 28 pounds) was taken from Dale Hollow in 1967. Norris has produced plenty of 15-20 pound fish, and Laurel Hill, a state lake, has shown phenomenal success.

King-size spoons and Arbogaster plugs are the best bets for muskies, along with big minnows, and they are taken the year around. Some of the biggest fish taken in Norris Lake showed up in December.

Muskies from impounded waters must be 30 inches in length to be legal with a daily limit of three.

WALLEYES—Top fishing for big walleyes occurs in the cold, early spring months when the fish are on spawning runs. The Cumberland River above Old Hickory Reservoir (where the world record walleye, 25 pounds, was taken) produces more walleyes at this time than any other place in the state. Leadhead jigs, Hustlers and minnows are the best baits used separately or in combination. It is very cold fishing, but well worth it if the payoff comes!

Spring, summer and fall fishing in the lakes for walleye shouldn't be overlooked, either, with Dale Hollow, Watauga, Center Hill, Norris, Old Hickory lakes and Woods Reservoir being the hottest spots. During these seasons, a nightcrawler with a spinner ahead trolled slowly is a deadly bait. Lead-head jigs with pork rind, spoons and big minnows are also good. Another method commonly used is drift-fishing—bumping a nightcrawler along the bottom or using a minnow just off the bottom. This is a fine night fishing trick, too.

There is no size limit on walleyes, and the daily limit is five.

TROUT—An angler looking for big trout in Tennessee has a broad selection of waters, but the top areas are the larger lakes and their tailwaters below the dams. Ten of these tailwater trout locations exist, with the best being Watauga, Wilbur, Norris, Chilhowee and Dale Hollow Lakes. Others are South Holston, Appalachia, Fort Patrick Henry, Daniel Boone and Center Hill reservoirs.

The former North American brown trout record was held by a 26-pound, 10-ounce brown from below Dale Hollow dam. But the finest stretch of big trout water in the state is the 33-mile stretch of the Little Tennessee River below Chilhowee Dam. At least two 17-pound browns have been taken there, and 10-pound browns and rainbows aren't uncommon. Float trip fishing is the best method, with small spoons, spinner-fly combinations and balsa-bodied lures the favorites.

Lake fishing for trout is best in Watauga where the state record rainbow (12-pounds, 14-ounces) was grown, and in South Holston and Dale Hollow, which has received over two million trout over the past two years and which will get another million soon due to the presence of the new Dale Hollow National Fish Hatchery just below the dam. Cilhowee is presently an experimental area for cold water fisheries for the Game and Fish Commission.

Most lake rainbow trout are taken with plugs or spoons trolled deep with lead-core or steel lines. Fishing worms and minnows deep at night is also productive. In early

The famed "boils" below Pickwick Dam, one of the best areas in the nation for big catfish.

A 54 pound blue catfish taken from the tailrace of Pickwick Dam. Every season produces many giant cats like this one.

The rockfish-white bass hybrid have created quite a stir on Cherokee Lake. The second and fourth fish from the left are examples.

Bass fishermen will find Tennessee a paradise. How about a string of smallmouths like these?

spring months when the water is still cold, plenty are taken on lead-head jigs with pork rind, and on live salamanders.

Trout season in the impoundments and tailwaters is open the year around with no size limit. A daily creel limit of seven applies.

CATFISH—The famed Pickwick Dam area still remains the best spot for really big catfish, and to fish the "boils" below the dam is an experience to be long remembered. Pickwick is the site of the annual Catfish Derby, and blue cats from this location have consistently been tops in the nation.

While lots of fishermen try to tackle the cats from the bank, the boat fishermen, using the unusual "reverse trolling" method score best. This is accomplished by heading the boat into the swift current just below the dam at a speed only slightly less than that of the current. The bait (cut bait or shad guts) along with as much as four to eight ounces of lead, trails behind the boat downstream while the fisherman constantly raises and lowers the rod tip to keep the bait bumping on the bottom as he slowly backs down the river. Heavy gear with lines of 100-pound test or more is used, since catfish of 50 to 60 pounds aren't uncommon. The top rod and reel catch on blue catfish is 78 pounds, with a 136-pound blue cat having been taken on commercial gear. The big cats, plus the effect of the current, make for a battle royal every time! Often the fish aren't boated within sight of the dam, although they are hooked below it.

Other impoundments and tailwaters in the state, particularly in the Tennessee River system, produce some big catfish and not only blues, but also of other varieties. Kentucky Lake, Douglas Lake and Fort Loudoun Lake are good spots, as are their tailwaters.

Bait is the best offering, although some cats are taken by trolling lures. No size limit exists and there is no creel limit, except in Game and Fish Commission state lakes where a daily creel limit of seven is imposed.

ROCKFISH—This exciting exotic stocked in Tennessee water only a few years ago is showing great promise. When fishermen learn how to go after them, excitement should really explode across the state.

Kentucky Lake, Barkley Lake, Cherokee Lake, Fort Loudoun Lake. Hales Bar Lake and Watts Bar Lake have rockfish, and recent findings have proved that the fish have migrated all up and down the Tennessee River system and even up into the Cumberland River.

Rockfish grow fast and provide plenty of action as well as being excellent table fare. To date the largest rod and reel catch on rockfish has been fifteen pounds, but biologists are certain much larger rockfish already exist in some of the impoundments. And there have been indications of natural reproduction which certainly brightens the outlook for future rockfishing.

The rocks like big jigs and feathered spoons, and probably part of the reason more aren't taken is that few fishermen use big enough gear. Once some of the techniques used by fishermen in the North and South Carolina lakes which hold rockfish drift into the Volunteer State, the bonanza could begin!

The rockfish-white bass hybrid is certainly worth mentioning here because this could prove to be one of the most interesting species in the nation. This hybrid resulted from a cross between a female rockfish and male white bass in a joint project of the Tennessee Game and Fish Commission and the South Carolina Game and Fish Commission conducted at Monck's Corner, S. C.

Some 80,000 fry were hatched, with each state taking half. The South Carolina portion of the fry did not sur-

Big walleyes like this show up in the spring spawning runs.

Team of anglers battle a huge alligator gar in a Tennessee tributary of the Mississippi. These gars may exceed ten feet in length.

vive, but those brought back to Tennessee did, and after being released into Cherokee Lake, the fish showed a terrific growth rate, passing the five pound level in less than two years. And they're still growing! If natural reproduction occurs between these hybrids, a great new fresh water species may emerge.

The hybrids are readily taken in the spring spawning run in the Holston River above Cherokee Lake in the early spring months on lead-head jigs and spoons. Once back in the lake, they feed with the white bass schools, tearing into schools of shad minnows, at which time spoons and lures both are effective.

A daily creel limit of two applies to both the rockfish and the hybrids, with no size limit.

GAR—While this is a somewhat restricted fishery, especially for the huge alligator gar, these fish can provide all the challenge and action of other big game fish species, since they attain lengths of up to sixteen feet, with seven-footers taken frequently.

The Mississippi River and some of its tributary streams

hold most of these monsters, and taking them requires very stout tackle. The best method is the use of a length of steel wire or line attached to a plastic jug. The bait is a fish, usually of from one to two pounds, with a hook the size of a small gaff. Several of these rigs are tossed into the river and allowed to float slowly downstream. Fishermen in the boat follow. When a jug stops and then begins moving back upstream, the boat moves along behind, giving the gar plenty of time to swallow the bait. Then they get set for action by detaching the steel line, re-attaching it to a heavy rod and reel outfit and, finally, setting the hook.

What happens after that is best compared to hooking a tarpon because the gar is a spectacular jumper! He's also a furious fighter, strong and hard to tire. Battles with gar can last for an hour or more.

Once the fish is worn down and brought alongside the boat, a pistol or rifle shot, or shots, finishes off the job because a big gar still alive can wreck a boat and injure its occupants.

The spotted, long-nose and short-nose gars are found in impoundments across the state, but few fishermen seek them since they do not reach the size of the alligator gar. There's no limit on any of them.

BASS—Tennessee has some of the most consistent largemouth and smallmouth bass fishing in the nation and bass can be found almost anywhere in the state, from fabulous Reelfoot Lake in the west to mountain stream-fed Watauga in the east.

The fastest bass fishing occurs in the winter and early spring months, both times when many fishermen find it too chilly to be appealing. However the biggest strings of bass to show up during the year are taken then, mostly with lead-head jigs and pork rind, deep-running plugs, weighted spinner-fly rigs and plastic worms. Center Hill and Dale Hollow Lakes are topnotch winter bass locations, as are Watauga and South Holston Lakes. Actually, most all of the larger impoundments, fished properly, are good winter bass areas.

Best times of the year other than the cold months are mid-spring and fall, and at these times all of the lakes across the states are in good shape. Crappies, bluegills, white bass and other game fish also are active then.

There is no size limit on bass, and the daily creel limit is ten, combined. Remember that the world record smallmouth came from Dale Hollow Lake.

So Tennessee, with year around fishing available, trophy fish of several species, and all the elbow room any fisherman could ever want, is a fresh water bonanza. Try it and see!

Non-resident fishermen can obtain a three-day permit for $1.50, a ten-day permit for $2.00, an annual license for a minimum of $5.00, or the fee is the same as the cost of a similar license in the visitor's state of residence. Those non-residents fishing for trout must have a $2.00 trout stamp, the same price paid by residents.

Additional information on Tennessee fishing, as well as maps of the region, can be obtained by writing: Tennessee Game and Fish Commission, 706 Church Street, Nashville, Tennessee 37203.

Here's a pair of big blue cats from below Pickwick Dam—some real tackle-busters!

Trout reach trophy size in many Tennessee reservoirs and tailwaters. Ten-pound browns aren't uncommon in some areas.

BACKPACK
TO BETTER FISHING

by Bob Bauer

Hiker packs out catch from back-country lake: cutthroat trout, plus large brookie (center).

It was September — a Yellowstone September, with frost on the morning meadow but hot dust on the midday trail — when I made my first backpacking trip. Jon Parsons and I had just left a fishing lodge on Great Slave Lake in the Northwest Territories, where we'd been summer fishing guides. Though not tired of fishing, we were perhaps a bit weary of lodge life, of the occasional disagreeable guest, of the noisy outboard motors, and of the race to produce more and bigger fish than the other guides. I suppose we wanted the simplicity of backpacking — the chance to be in wild country on our own.

We flew from the lodge to Winnipeg, Manitoba, and then drove to Mammoth Hot Springs in Wyoming. The road west from Mammoth (which is in Yellowstone Park) crosses the ravine of Blacktail Deer Creek. There we started on foot downstream. Our packs were light, loaded only with sleeping bags, a fishing outfit apiece, hip boots and food enough for five days, assuming we'd catch some trout.

The warm afternoon sunlight tilted into the canyon, and a cool breeze skated along the rock walls as we descended to the Yellowstone River junction. As we neared it, we heard the hollow roar of water, and the clumps of sagebrush gave way to stands of pine and spruce.

At the river, before we even thought of fishing, Jon and I grounded our loads and dove into the cool water. We found a high cliff to dive from with a deep green pool below. From there we floated a narrow deep run to another pool farther down. The water was colder than we'd realized, and after perhaps 45 minutes Jon looked like — and I suppose I did too — an albino prune.

We broke out the fishing gear, Jon's spinning outfit and my flyrod. And before the afternoon ended, we'd each whipped a half-dozen cutthroat trout, more than enough for dinner, and perhaps twice that many whitefish, which we released. The catch that afternoon — and those on the days that followed — wasn't spectacular, certainly nothing to match the 20-pound lake trout we'd caught that summer, but just being able to fish for five days without seeing another person was pleasure enough.

Hiking boots with lugged soles are most suitable for mountains.

Angler here has pitched mountain tent,
hooked good trout along Montana stream.

Here's sample of lightweight dehydrated
or freeze-dried foods for the hiker-angler.

We fished our way downstream, perhaps two miles each day, and pitched camp wherever we found ourselves. One night it rained, but we kept dry sleeping under a rock overhang. To make our food last longer, we ate trout nearly every meal, which, of course, was no hardship at all. On the sixth day we hiked into Gardiner, Montana, about ten miles downstream from our swimming hole of the first afternoon. It had been the kind of holiday any angler could enjoy almost any time, without elaborate preparations, reservations, travel agents or bankruptcies.

The basic equipment for the backpacker is some sort of frame, bag or basket to carry his load. Among the most popular are packsacks with integral metal frames, usually of lightweight aluminum. Generally there's a wide band of nylon webbing or other material across the base of the frame which transfers part of the weight to the wearer's hips. Most metal frames are constructed to leave an airspace for ventilation of the hiker's back.

Packsacks are made of either canvas or nylon, preferably the latter which is slightly lighter in weight. Some models

Wildnerness fisherman prepares
meal on tiny camp stove.

Angler here is on trail to trophy
trout in Montana's Missouri River.

The going is sometimes tough in mountains but may pay off in fast fishing.

Trout anglers find cave in Appalachians for overnight shelter.

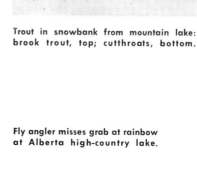

Trout in snowbank from mountain lake:
brook trout, top; cutthroats, bottom.

Fly angler misses grab at rainbow
at Alberta high-country lake.

have separate compartments on the front and sides for convenient storage of smaller items — raincoat, camera, or other items which should be kept handy.

It's imperative that the pack have comfortable shoulder straps at least two inches wide. The strap material should also be thick, to minimize curling and cutting into your shoulders. It's not difficult to make excellent straps yourself from wide strips of sheepskin.

Other types of backpacks are available for special purposes. Small rucksacks, for instance, are designed to carry only a few items and are suitable for one-day hikes. There's also the large Duluth pack, which has a tumpline instead of a packframe. The tumpline straps across the forehead and transfers much of the shoulder weight to the neck muscles. It's practical for carrying heavy weights short distances — on portages during canoe trips, for example. Another old favorite is the Maine packbasket constructed of hardwood splints and often used by trappers. The packbasket will hold traps, axes and other rough items without jabbing the wearer. But its additional weight makes it impractical for most fishing jaunts.

I have seen extremely good rucksack buys at prices as low as $25 and there are others made for professional mountaineers (but great for neophytes as well) with price tags of $125 and more.

Before buying a carrier, it is a good idea to consult with an experienced backpacker and to try "wearing" as many as possible before making a final selection. If buying in a sporting goods shop, try to find one which specializes in such trail gear, rather than in general outdoor merchandise. It is also good advice to write for the catalogs of the several companies which manufacture backpacks. All of these also offer free booklets on how to select a pack and on successful backpacking in general. This is very valuable material, except that actual advice on how a pack should fit — how the load should be carried — is sometimes conflicting. That's why I recommend trying different models to get one which best suits your own physique.

The amount of weight that can be carried comfortably varies with the hiker. If you're inexperienced it's wise to start with 30 pounds. For a man in good physical condition who intends to take a long hike, 40 pounds is about the maximum. Of course it's possible for some individuals to lug more, and the only way you'll find out is to try. But remember that any pack, by the end of the day, may feel like a load of anvils.

Many wilderness fishing waters such as this in Colorado are accessible only to backpackers.

Evening meal comes shore on Alberta la

Hiker takes time out along remote stream in Northwest Territories.

Typical backpacker's equipment includes: sleeping bag, rain jacket, sweater, dried foods, trail rod, camera, mess kit, insect repellent, matches.

Many of best fishing waters in eastern mountains are accessible only to backpackers.

Here are two types of packing gear: lightweight packsack with aluminum frame (left) and military-style frame onto which equipment is lashed.

Of course you must haul no unnecessary gear. Plan your food needs carefully, and throw in some emergency rations. Also carry your mess kit, knife, extra clothing, matches, a light sleeping bag, several pairs of socks, first aid kit, rain jacket and some sort of shelter. The matches should be kept in waterproof containers and stored in several different places. That way, if you lose some of your matches, you'll still have others. The extra socks are very important; changing them every day will help avoid blistered feet.

A ten-by-ten-foot sheet of polyethylene can be used as a tarp for a light and waterproof shelter. The mountain tent made of nylon with aluminum poles is both light and valuable for mosquito protection at night. Its only drawback is its lack of room, especially for two persons. A heavier tent such as the canvas pup tent can be used but is more practical when there are two hikers to alternate carrying it. Occasionally a tent may not be necessary. During dry seasons in dry country (such as parts of the Southwest) or where there are natural shelters (caves or overhangs) a light waterproof cloth will do.

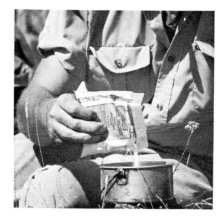

With packaged dried foods angler can easily carry week's rations.

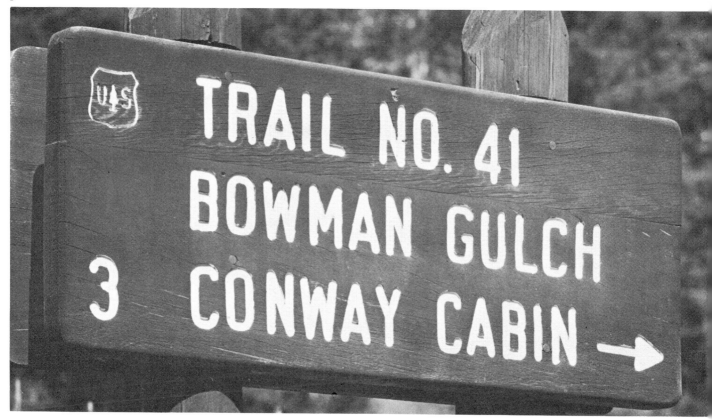

U.S. Forest Service marks many wilderness trails for hikers.

You'll also want camera and film, canteen, compass, halazone tablets to purify water, insect repellents, topographic maps, soap, foot powder, sunglasses, binoculars and perhaps field guides. If you're going to high country where wood is scarce you can carry along a small gas stove.

Go as light as possible on fishing tackle, but don't skimp on lures or extra spools of line. Rods should be placed in a sturdy aluminum or plastic tube which can double as a walking staff. Short pack rods of four or more sections can be tied to the packsack. If you're going on an extended backcountry trip, it may be wise to take two rods.

Soft leather, lightweight boots from 8 inches to 10 inches high and which fit the foot snugly are the ideal footgear. These should give good arch support and have lugged rubber or composition soles to grip a variety of surfaces. But most of all the boots should be well broken in long before attempting any long trip. In addition, changes of clean dry socks are necessary for pleasant traveling afoot.

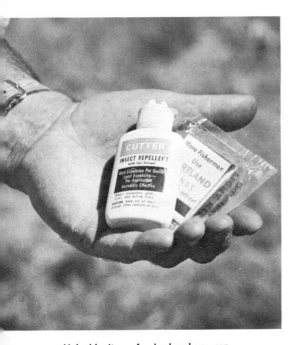

Valuable items for backpackers: concentrated insect repellent, matches sealed in waterproof wrapping.

Hikers compare map with trail sign in Banff National Park, Alberta.

If any phase of backpacking has changed radically — and for the better — since John Muir and Bob Marshall wandered across our western ridges, it's in the matter of food. Nowadays it is as easy to carry a week's supply of concentrated or freeze-dried foods as it was formerly to carry a day or two of regular rations. A number of companies prepare and package food, even entire meals especially for trail use. These reduce both weight and bulk of foods to as little as a fourth or a fifth. They also reduce to a minimum the amount of aluminum cookware which is necessary to prepare a meal. There are aluminum military-type messkits which can be used both for cooking and for eating. The wise backpacker prepares a menu for the entire trip in advance and thereby can save additional space and weight.

The main thing when planning a trip is to select foods which pack as much nutrition as possible into the smallest and lightest packages. Do not carry canned juices and soups, for example, but rather take dried soup mixes and powders. Besides the concentrated foods already mentioned, some high energy foods popular with skilled backpackers are chocolate, raisins, jerky, peanut butter and honey thickened to eliminate bulk.

But no matter how carefully a hiker has selected his equipment and planned his trip, the venture can end in unhappy failure unless the hiker gets into proper shape physically before starting out. The less active life a person leads, and the older he is, the more important this becomes.

Getting in shape isn't difficult and can actually be very pleasant if done correctly. In most cases correctly means slowly — gradually — over a long period of time.

Jogging is an excellent tuneup. So is swimming every day. Bicycling is even better and when doing this I add athlete's training weights to my shoes and wear a light pack on my back to start getting the "feel" of it. I also wear the training weights when doing normal gardening chores and when jogging.

It isn't wise to try a long or hard trip right off the bat, at least not without having experienced backpackers in the party. Instead try short weekend expeditions to test both your equipment and yourself. An excellent way to get started on the right track — and very inexpensively, too — is to join one of the numerous backpacking expeditions organized each summer by conservation groups as the Sierra Club (1050 Mills Tower, San Francisco, Calif. 94104), the Wilderness Society (729 15th St. NW, Washington, D.C. 20005) and Trail Riders of the Canadian Rockies (Box 448, Banff, Alberta). All of these treks are led by experts and some include interpretive services. The hikes are of various durations and may cost as little as $5 per person daily.

Sheepshead grow big. Ten- and 20-pounders are sometimes taken, though two-pound fish are average. Anglers usually fish deep with live baits or weighted artificials.

a different drum

By Horst Redding

I guess Stan Washington didn't have much use for sheepshead. When one would steal his expensive crawfish he'd storm from stern to stem, calling it a "rubber carp" or other names that can't be printed here. One time I suggested that sheepshead were fair eating, and he fell to a horrible gasping and gagging. "Them . . . them *things*," he finally said, "ain't even good for garden fertilizer."

But Stan was a smallmouth bass fisherman or, depending on the season, a walleye, perch, catfish or white bass fisherman. Lake Erie was loaded with game species and he could afford to do a little selective gagging. In time his tune may change, because Erie game fishing is no longer booming.

Which reminds me of an old-timer I met along the Ohio River. This fellow was dozing in the shade of a floppy old Stetson, down among the rocks below the Greenup Roller Dam. He'd wake long enough to haul in something—I couldn't tell what from a distance—and release it. "Oil," he told me later. "Pollution. Damn fish taste like oil, can't eat 'em. Used to catch everything here. We liked sheepshead—you might call 'em croakers—best. Always wished there was more of 'em."

The sheepshead dispute really isn't new. Over a hundred years ago the pioneering naturalist Jared P. Kirtland voiced the general opinion of the time that sheepshead from Lake Erie were "hardly edible" while those from the Ohio River were always "fat, tender and delicious." Probably the difference was that superior food fish including the whitefish and lake sturgeon were available in the lake but absent from the Ohio drainage. Still in 1858 Kirtland advised that drum from the Ohio be introduced into Lake Erie in the hope that

"the rich and delicate White Perch or Sheepshead" of the Ohio might supplant the "worthless" Erie fish.

In almost any lake or river there are better fish than sheepshead to eat. Almost no one denies that. But when cleaned properly they're good eating, better than most anglers like to admit, whether deep fried, stuffed and baked or prepared into chowder. The secret is to peel away the thin outer layer of dark meat when the fish is skinned.

The sheepshead is also known as the freshwater drum. As the name suggests it's the only member of the drum family in inland waters, and they're considered "different," and not really a game species. But like the various saltwater species sheepshead are tough battlers. They don't make spectacular jumps or long fast runs. Instead they bore stubbornly for the bottom, and the fisherman might think he's somehow hooked onto an anvil.

The species grows big too. Though no one bothers to keep official records on sheepshead, they are occasionally reported to reach 50 pounds. Fish that big are rare, but 10- to 20-pounders are taken fairly often. Sheepshead bones found in excavated Indian villages indicate possible sizes of 200 pounds. But in most waters, including Lake Erie where sheepshead are most abundant, two-pound fish are average.

Erie charter captains, like guides elsewhere, are frequently saddled with beginning anglers. When the so-called game species aren't hitting, the neophyte (who doesn't know the prejudices) is turned loose on sheepshead. When he hangs one he usually thinks it's a trophy bass, and if told different he doesn't know whether to be elated or disappointed. But it's a sure bet he'll want to catch more of them.

Early in the season—say, early June in the northern latitudes—the fish form tight schools above the shoals and you can spot their fins clustered and circling together. The formation is similar to that of baitfish "balled" by feeding sailfish. You can wrestle these schoolers until your arms and wrists feel like worn-out rubber bands, and there's really no quicker way to forget about bass fishing.

Drum are scattered throughout eastern North America. Their natural range is the entire Missouri and Mississippi River system and the cleaner large rivers from southern Manitoba to the Yucatan Peninsula of Mexico. Pollution has squeezed them out of many waters, but in others, where pollution is severe enough only to eliminate competitive fishes, they're now more abundant. Their preferred foods are mollusks and snails, which also are reduced by pollution, siltation and dams. In many waters today their diet consists of small fishes, insects and crayfish.

Drum are most abundant in the lower Great Lakes, particularly the Bass Islands of western Lake Erie, and in the lowland streams of Louisiana and Texas. Remnant populations exist in the Ohio and Mississippi Rivers, and in some localities they are caught commercially. Almost everywhere drum populations fluctuate; they decline repeatedly and unexplainably after periods of great abundance.

The drum's name derives from its ability to make a drumming sound in the water. And it often surprises unsuspecting anglers by drumming when out of the water. How the fish makes this peculiar noise is debatable. Perhaps it's by grinding the throat (pharyngeal) teeth or by expelling air from one part of the swim bladder to another.

Whatever the noise, it's responsible for the names croaker, grunter, grinder, thumper and thunderpumper. And the fish has still other labels including gaspergou (in Louisiana) gray bass and silver bass, not to mention the ones Stan Washington used. It's often misidentified as white perch, a name which properly belongs to another species found in salt and brackish waters along the Atlantic Coast. At Lake Erie the few anglers who appreciate sheepshead—I could count them on one hand—call them "reef bass." Probably only mothers-in-law are called more names.

Since sheepshead are primarily bottom-feeders, your best bet to catch them is a live bait fished on or very near the bottom. Crawfish are probably the most effective, as Washington's empty bait box and emptier wallet often prove, but you'll also score on minnows, nightcrawlers and hellgrammites.

There is no use buying soft craws or spending long hours seining them. No matter how hard the craw shell, drum have teeth enough to crack it. And it doesn't matter whether the craws are dead or alive or what size they are, or if they're whole, or anything.

The most exciting way to catch drum is with artificials. They'll usually hit lures as readily as live baits, particularly in the spring and summer. Probably the most effective artificials are weighted spinners of one-quarter to one-half ounce that will sink deep in the water. Small deep-diving plugs and jigs bumped slowly along the bottom also take their share of fish. Sheepshead don't really strike a lure they just—"glomb," one angler described it—glomb onto a lure. The initial hit, however, doesn't reflect the powerful struggle to follow.

I think this slow, deliberate strike was what irritated Washington most. He was a painstaking fisherman who would count carefully as his lure sank, then be cranking away, concentrating, working the lure with his rod tip when gradually he would realize he was playing a fish—a sheepshead—and his mouth would start to work and the angry flush would spread across his face the way it happens to characters in movie cartoons. "No strike, there wasn't any strike," he'd mutter, tight-lipped. And then as the fish swung aboard the words quit coming. One time I think he threw a rod overboard in disgust, but he claimed it slipped because of the sheepshead slime.

You can fill your stringer fastest—Washington would howl at the thought—by drifting over a submerged rocky reef, gravel bar or other obstruction. When you catch a fish, throw out an anchor to pinpoint the spot. There are probably more sheepshead nearby, perhaps with concentrations of other game fishes.

Don't run your motor over the area where you catch fish. Instead wait until the wind carries you past the spot, then crank up and run around for another drift. If the wind is strong and the fish are concentrated in a small area, it's best to anchor in position over the hotspot.

Drum aren't attracted to a fast retrieve. Allow your lure to sink deep, then work it just above the bottom, reeling no faster than necessary to keep the spinner blade turning. It was on such a retrieve, slow and patient, that an Erie guide once hooked an exceptionally heavy drum. He'd borrowed my spinning outfit, a light one with 6-pound monofilament, and he knew what he'd hooked. While the fish emptied the spool about all he could do was hang on and hope. After several minutes he'd regained no line, couldn't even budge the fish, then said he'd better "pour the coal to it." The line snapped at the rod tip and sprung several feet onto the water's surface, where it coiled benignly like a shrunken snake skin.

Anglers work sheepshead near boat on Lake Erie.

He started the engine, nudging the boat to port, retrieved the line and barrel-knotted it together. Probably he was less intrigued with the sheepshead than with the thought of setting some new record. In either case he set to hauling the fish, and with me working the rudder he finally boated it. It was a 15-pounder, the damnedest drum he'd ever seen, and in the net it looked like a side of beef. Suddenly I wished that Washington were along to see it.

If you ever walk along a beach or streambank where sheepshead are abundant, you may find a small disc-shaped stone, or perhaps a pair of them. A closer look will reveal the letter "L" etched into their faces. These are sheepshead ear bones or otoliths, better known among anglers as "lucky stones." Some fishermen collect them in various sizes from sheepshead they catch and use them to make bracelets or other jewelry. I cannot remember any exceptional luck from them, except that any angler—anyone but Washington—who catches a stringer of sheepshead can surely count himself lucky.

Mike Laycock fishing with Campbell on an early Orange
Lake outing, when Campbell took this 10 pounder.

*A strange lake
where islands float
and fish lurk
underneath them*

ORANGE LAKE and BLACK BASS

by George Laycock

On my first visit to Orange Lake south of Gainesville, Florida, I met the rugged looking angler credited with taking the biggest bass ever recorded from that lake. The man was the late R. W. Campbell. His bass weighed 17¼ pounds. And it may have been the largest ever taken on a topwater lure. No wonder it created a great stir, even around that bass-conscious country where a nine-pounder, they say, may or may not be a keeper depending on the mood you're in.

Campbell was casting one evening in mid-March along the edge of one of the floating islands for which Orange Lake is famous. His line tangled in a giant size backlash and his topwater plug fell short of its mark. Campbell, grumbling about losing fishing time, kept picking away at the snarled line. "That plug must have been there five minutes without moving at all," he said.

With the line finally straightened out he took up the slack. He gave the plug a twitch.

The bass sucked the bait in, almost gently, and Campbell, with no idea of what he had in store, set the hook. The lake surface frothed and rolled. There was a frightening weight against his rod. It bent crazily and the line pulled tight enough for a banjo string. "I thought," says Campbell, "that I had hooked an otter."

He soon saw that it was a bass and a big one. He wanted to keep the fish from muscling its way back among the roots that hung from the bottom of the island. He wondered what he would do about getting the fish into the boat. He could never remember feeling as weak in the knees as he was at this moment.

The big bass did most of his fighting beneath the surface. "I was lucky when he headed for the open water," Campbell says, "out there I could handle him."

Eventually the fish was in alongside the boat. Campbell, expecting momentarily to lose the biggest fish he had ever hooked, finally managed to wallow the bass into the boat. "He was too big to go into the live well," says Campbell, "and I was afraid to let loose of him." The only thing he could think of to do was head for the dock across the lake holding the big bass in his lap. He went all the way back tending the motor with one hand and clutching his giant bass in the other.

People from all around came to see the big fish and take pictures of it. One of his visitors wanted it so badly to take back north with him that Campbell gave the fish away. "Maybe," he said, thinking back on it, "I should have had that one mounted myself."

Orange Lake is one of the strangest swampland lakes in the South. Some six miles long and three miles wide, it covers about 22,000 acres. Orange Lake is rimmed with great royal palms. Its water is the color of weak coffee. The lake bottom is ooze, half liquid, half solid, with an endless accumulation of black organic sediment. In the waters of Orange Lake cavort some of the biggest of all America's largemouth bass, a point R. W. Campbell has helped to prove.

Campbell was an ex-deputy sheriff from Mississippi. For nine years he wore the badge. "Then my man," he

Campbell and Mike heading out for fishing spots on Orange Lake.

explains with the conclusive fatalism of the southern political worker, "got voted out."

Campbell headed south for Orange Lake where he had fished often. For a few years he lived by guiding other fishermen. Then he began operating his own fishing camp.

Throughout Florida, Orange Lake is famous for its floating islands. Some of them cover 40 acres. On them grow sweet gum and oak trees 20 to 30 feet high. Marsh rabbits live there where it's too boggy for man to pursue them and dogs almost never venture. Water turkeys, shore birds, herons, egrets and an occasional alligator keep the rabbits company around the floating islands.

"A stranger on this lake can really get turned around when the islands start shifting," said Campbell. "It may look entirely different in the evening than it did when you started fishing that morning."

When a good wind comes up the islands begin to move, gently at first, then with increasing speed until they're going for the far shore. Perch fishermen have found that the perch bite well right along the edge of the floating islands. So they just tie their boats to their favorite island and move on across the lake with it.

The islands sometimes move into narrow necks of water and seal off bays. Fishing camp operators sometimes push the islands back out into the lake by getting behind them with a couple of outboards. One visitor from the north, after watching an island being pushed, is said to have given up his daily toddy.

The islands are chunks of bog that break away. Sometimes when the water goes down in a dry summer an island settles until the roots of the trees and bushes touch the mucky lake bottom. If the water stays down long enough the roots get a grip on the lake bottom. The longer they grow the more firm their grip. Then the rains come and the lake level rises and the island tries to rise and stay above the surface. But it can't. It is anchored and gradually the coffee colored waters of Orange Lake cover the island. "Those sunken islands," said R. W., "make mighty good places for bass."

My own first visit to Orange Lake was one damnably hot day in early September. I was told before I got there that no one was catching bass. Some fishermen may accept such talk as a challenge. I don't. I like to go where they are catching them. But now this far from home, and having heard about Orange Lake's big bass, I tried it anyhow. I should have stood in my sleeping bag. We didn't catch enough to make a small size pot pie. But Campbell showed me pictures of his 17¼ pounder and told me at some length of other big ones he had taken. I was coming back.

Another time that I fished Orange Lake was with Dick Kotis and Earl Pease, and later with big jolly Ben Curry, an ex-Kentuckian who came to Florida a non-fisherman and became one of the most serious and successful bass fishermen around Orange Lake. "I'm going out this evening," Ben said, "come go 'long." That was all the invitation I needed.

Ben figures any bass under five pounds is "little." A few evenings previous Ben took a 10 pounder. "That was in my favorite place," he said, "across the lake. We'll go there at just the right time, about 5:30 and fish it 'till dark. I'll even take you over there without blindfoldin' you, since you're not from 'round here."

Ben took a death grip on the throttle, put the bow of his boat high in the water and headed for the nearest bay. Finally he looked at his watch. "Let's go," he said, and we headed out for the far side of the lake. Still a couple of hundred yards from the chosen spot he cut the motor back and moved in ever so gently. "They can hear you coming," he said. We eased up within long casting distance of a tangle of branches sticking through the lake surface. "Never been skunked here yet. Old sunken island," explained Ben. He made a long skillful cast right into the middle of the sunken jungle and began bringing his top water bait back with short whipping jerks of his rod tip.

We had cast two or three times each when Ben tangled with the first of several, a three-pounder, and unceremoniously brought him through the limbs out into the open water and over the gunwales.

Then in winter, along with my son, Mike, who delights in trying to outfish me and sometimes accomplishes it, I drove into Campbell's Holiday Fish Camp early one morning in midweek.

Campbell, busy with chores around his launching area pointed to a 16-foot fiberglass boat and said it was ready to go. "You can fish around back of the camp here anywhere in this bay," he said, "while this fog is heavy. Come in after a while and I'll go back out with you. We can use the houseboat for a base."

Mike and I fished around the quiet bay, shrouded in early morning fog. We were casting artificials with spinning outfits. In the times I've fished Orange Lake, I've never used anything but artificials. Mike was using a medium-sized silver spoon and I was trying a top-water plug. A few casts brought Mike a scrapping pound-and-a-half

At roadside baitshop this 14 pounder whetted our appetites.

Mike and Campbell compare their bass.

On another Orange L. trip Kotis took this
husky four pounder from the lily pads.

bass. He boated the fish smoothly, released it gently back
to the water and went right back to casting.

Meanwhile I was forcing myself to let the top-water plug
rest for long periods between movements. Nothing I made
that plug do seemed to bring a fish up to consume it. Then
I dropped it far back toward a point of the boggy shore
and right in the middle of a patch of brownish grass protruding above the surface of the lake. The plug rested
there. The ripples moved further and further away and
the water became plate-glass smooth again around the
patch of grass. I waited another 30 seconds. A gentle
twitch of the rod tip moved the plug ever so slightly.
As it moved I saw the water pushed up in a short, steep-
walled V.

The bass moved in and clamped down on the plug and
began immediately to cut a windrow of hay through his
patch of grass. I applied pressure to bring him out of the
grass, and he left it only to head for a spot of deep water
a dozen feet distant where a couple of small limbs, protruding slightly above the lake, should have been ample
warning of trouble on the way.

This bass was headed for the deep woods. Nothing I
tried changed his mind. And there was precious little time.
Down now among the submerged brush he took a half
hitch with my monofilament on the handiest snag. I'll
never know how he made out afterwards. As for me, I
lost the fish, the plug and the most exciting fight of the
morning.

The fog lifted slowly and hung like a blue-gray back-
drop behind the royal palm forest. The lake looked as it
must have a thousand years ago. I had Mike put me off
on a point with my cameras while he continued to cast
around. Before he returned to pick me up he had taken
another medium-sized bass, perhaps a three-pounder.

When we went back to camp in mid-morning Campbell
was all primed to take his 32-foot aluminum houseboat
out. He bought the houseboat a few years ago and operated it first on the Suwannee River before moving down
to Orange Lake. He cut across the end of the lake for a

big palm-rimmed bay. There was no need now to go back
to camp for the rest of the day. The houseboat provided
solid comfort and gave me a vantage point from which
to make pictures.

Action had been slow for a half hour. I was making pictures of an anhinga through the back of the houseboat and
the bass was well worn down fighting against the spinning
rod before I realized Campbell had one on the way. He
had hooked him on a noisy surface plug and kept the drag
set for every ounce the line would stand. Campbell, who
had big bass go right through landing nets, now carried
a husky, long-handled gaff hook in his boat. "Get the gaff,"
I heard him say to Mike. The big fish was in close to the
edge of the boat now. Mike reached for him and missed
as the fish rolled and pulled out a dozen feet of line.

Campbell carefully worked him back. This time Mike
snagged the fish, and he and Campbell brought the old bass
aboard and stood over it puffing and grinning. "He's a
black old cuss," Campbell said when they came in alongside the houseboat. "Lot of fish in this lake are dark like
the color of the water. Some are a little greener. The color
even varies with the section of the lake they come from."

"Would you say eight pounds?" Mike asked.

"Eight anyway," Campbell answered as if he caught
them every day.

It's well-known that largemouths grow bigger in the
Sunshine State than anywhere else in North America. In
his first year of life a Florida bass can become a husky 12-
or 14-ounce fish that measures 10 to 12 inches long, and,
as Ben Curry says, "gets fat as his skin will hold him."
Bass of two or three pounds are probably two-year-olds.

The non-resident fishermen on Florida's fresh waters
pay $3.25 for a 14 day license and $2.25 for a five day
trip license. You're allowed 10 bass a day with a possession
limit of 20 after the first day, and there's no limit on size
and no closed season. A limit of Florida bass, if you hit
it right, can total 50 or 60 pounds or more and be heavy
enough to make you walk lopsided.

And I can't think of a finer way to get lopsided.

More leisure, better transportation, the search
for adventure . . . so of course

ANGLERS ARE GOING

FARTHER NORTH

By Turner Smith

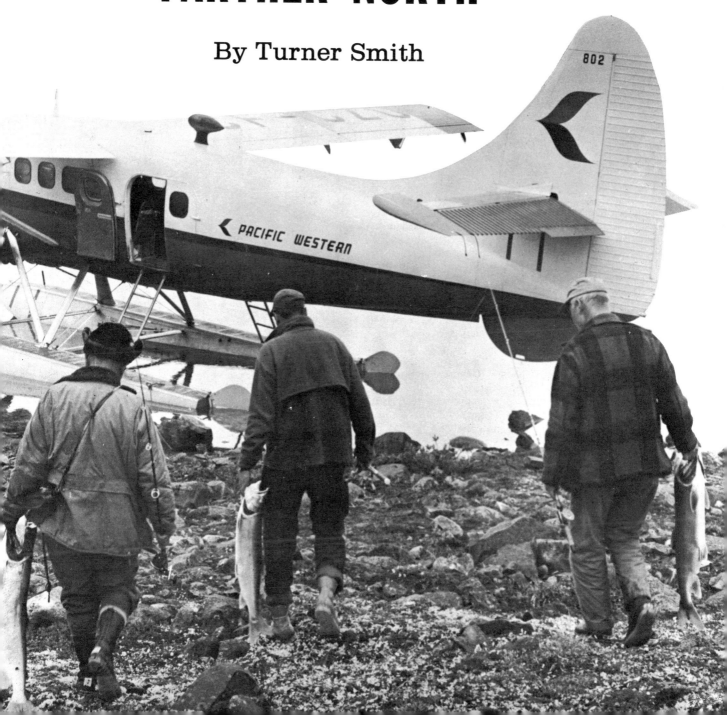

Pioneering anglers these days have turned their eyes to the far north toward the last great fishing frontier on the North American Continent. Canadian officials are inviting fishermen to come to the vast Northwest Territories, and fishermen are going — more of them every year. In that cold, bleak land they are finding fishing they will always remember.

Some years ago, on my first trip into the Arctic to fish, I was amazed by the endless procession of lakes that marched across the tundra beneath us. Half the area seemed covered with irregularly shaped bodies of water of all sizes. And almost nowhere was there a fisherman or for that matter anyone else. Today, several years and several trips later, the Arctic landscape looks the same.

Except for the Yukon, the Northwest Territories occupies all of Canada north of the provinces. A single island in the territories — Baffin Island, cold, bleak and barren, is bigger than all the province of Manitoba.

But across this region of land, lakes, and bays at the top of North America, live only 23,000 people. Of these 8,900 are Eskimos, and 4,500 are Indians — the original fishermen of the Canadian North.

In the last half-dozen years these native people have seen more and more flying fishermen from the south. Last summer, during a stop at Rankin Inlet on the west shore of Hudson Bay, we saw a class of young Eskimo outdoorsmen assembled from around the north for the first of a new summer school for guides. At the end of summer they returned, fully trained, to their home communities. Fishermen visiting their settlements in remote northern areas in years to come will find trained and skilled guides waiting to serve them. This is indicative of the part the government expects sport fishing to play in the economy of the north country.

There are three fish which account for the growing interest in this cold land. Foremost is the lake trout. They are found in many waters across the north and especially in the big deep lakes. It is not unusual for a fisherman on his first trip to the Arctic to catch a lake trout weighing 35 pounds or more. During the week's fishing he may catch several of 20 pounds, and as many 12 and 15 pounders as he cares to bring to the boat. I have seen fish of 45 pounds from these lakes on several occasions and others up to 55 have been taken by anglers.

Best known of the lake trout waters in the Far North is Great Bear Lake. Half a dozen years ago Great Bear opened up to sportsmen with the building of the first lodges there. Now there are four lodges on the lake, the limit permitted by the Canadian Government in the interest of maintaining high quality fishing.

The fishing season on Great Bear covers scarcely two months of the summer. Ice doesn't go out until summer is well along in southern areas, and the first flurries of fall snow come early. July and August are the times to plan a far north fishing trip. Even then you will want to dress in woolens and thermal clothing, more as you would for a late autumn deer hunting trip than for a summer fishing adventure. Some days, temperatures may soar to 70, but most of the time it hovers considerably below that mark. Rain gear is especially important.

The other fish anglers want — and one even more attractive than the lake trout to most fishermen from the south — is the Arctic char. It is difficult to make generalities about this magnificent fish. They are found in both salt and fresh water at various stages in their life history, and they come in a wide range of colors ranging from a silvery color to brilliant reds and oranges.

The most colorful Arctic char I ever saw were taken from the Tree River on my first trip to the Arctic several years ago. At that time, the Tree was the hottest char fishing stream in the far north. We arrived the last week in August as the fishing season was already drawing to its close for the year. At this time the char were moving into the streams for spawning.

Our flight began at a fishing lodge on Great Bear Lake where we had experienced several days of amazingly successful lake trout fishing. We flew almost due north to the Eskimo village of Coppermine which is a collection of low, colorful, wooden buildings on the edge of the Arctic Ocean's Coronation Gulf. Coppermine was slightly out of our way but we wanted to see an Eskimo village as well as to refuel our plane.

Most Eskimos have moved from the country to live in the more civilized settlements. Only rarely any more do

The author holds a 20 pound lake trout beside the Kujjaac River near Minto Inlet on Victoria Island—on the top of Canada.

you find a fishing or hunting camp of native people far removed from the settlements. In Coppermine they can go to the Hudson Bay Store for their provisions and are able to purchase everything they need or want including tape recorders and cameras. But they still travel by dog sled in winter, and their lines of half-starved sled dogs are staked out everywhere. One must take care not to pass too close to these beasts when wandering about an Eskimo village.

At the little government craft shop in Coppermine we bought a few soapstone carvings then were soon back in the plane and headed due east some 80 miles to the mouth of the Tree River. That stream rolled and tumbled down from the tundra-covered hills past banks of clay that gave it a strange grayish white appearance.

After landing on the river we caught Arctic char up to 20 pounds. The biggest ones were among the world's most brilliantly hued fish. Flashing brilliant red on the sides grading to a darker color on the back, they had blood red ventral fins edged in half-inch borders of pure white. They carried the under-slung jaw typical of the salmon to which the char is, in fact, related.

Near the end of the day we brought our shore lunch box from the plane. We started a fire of willow twigs and butchered a 10-pound char. In large cities to the south it would cost $2 a pound. We cut one-inch steaks in cross-sections, and after they had cooked in the sizzling butter in our iron skillet, we experienced an unforgettable treat. Here, plainly, was one reason for going north for Arctic char. Many consider this the world's finest fish for eating.

Word of the Tree River's treasure spread and fishermen flocked to the banks of that stream. The fishing fell off quickly until today it no longer offers the spectacular fishing it did half a dozen years ago. Meanwhile flying fishermen have located other char caches. But they are still searching for streams that have big red male Artic char as brilliantly colored as those we found in the Tree.

On Victoria Island there are now known to be some excellent char lakes. On one of these spots there is a com-

Average size lake trout found all across sub-Arctic Canada.

This huge lake trout weighs 43 pounds, but is not a record at Great Bear Lake, N.W.T.

fortable tent camp in the middle of the barrenlands. It accommodates 12 sportsmen at a time, in perhaps the most northern sport fishing camp in the world. Opened for the first time in the summer of 1966, it is known as Arctic Outpost Camps. Its operators live in Cambridge Bay, NWT, which is as much address as anyone needs. Although the fishing season didn't get underway there until July 23rd last summer, visitors could make the most of their time because of the 24-hour daylight. In the Arctic summer, you can fish the clock around if you care to. To Arctic visitors, the problem is sometimes knowing when to go to bed.

The third fish that attracts visiting anglers to this northern country is the grayling. The record grayling of five pounds was taken in 1966 from Great Bear Lake. Grayling are not so flashy as the char, but they are excellent fish for the fly rod man. They can be taken on a wide variety of wet or dry flies as well as many kinds of small spinners. They are found in cold, clear, fast-flowing streams along the shores of larger lakes, especially where the shores are lined with headsize boulders.

Perhaps the finest grayling fishing I ever found was at the head of the Bear River which carries water from Great Bear Lake down to the MacKenzie River. At this fishing spot near the Indian village of Ft. Franklin, you can, if you hit it right, catch as many grayling as you want. And you can see them swimming down there in the crystal clear water. You watch them until the moment they sight your lure and begin their purposeful rise toward it. Most fishermen consider grayling inferior to char as a food fish. The grayling tends to be more oily.

As fishermen have become increasingly interested in Arctic trips, the government has received a number of applications from people who want to open far north

Mosquitoes collect on Lou Klewer of Toledo Blade as he admires string of pan-size lakers at Blue Lake on the Arctic mainland.

fishing lodges. With the short growing season and limited food supply, however, northern fish grow at amazingly slow rates. There is concern about catching all the trophy fish out of some waters, as they apparently were from the Tree River. Consequently, the number of fishing camps is limited, and those permitted are well dispersed.

Most fishing trips into the north are for periods of one week. Lodges on Great Bear as well as some other waters offer package deals from either Edmonton or Winnipeg. A week's fishing on Great Bear Lake, including this round-trip transportation, may cost between $700 and $900. Some fishermen fly their own small, float-equipped planes into the north on fishing outings. But this is tricky business and visiting pilots often lack the caution and respect the bush pilots — at least the living ones — have for the unpredictable Arctic weather. Some charter flying services haul fishermen, along with all their supplies and camping gear, into choice fishing spots, then come back a week later and pick them up. This is the most economical plan for fishing the far north.

Those fishermen interested in traveling northward toward the top of the continent should collect as much information as they can on the subject. The best place to start is by writing to Bud Styles, Senior Tourist Development Officer, Northwest Territories, Department of Indian Affairs and Northern Development. The address is 400 Lourier Avenue, Ottawa.

Since that first Arctic trip I have gone back as often as I could arrange it. I am already thinking ahead to the next one. As I have on earlier ones, I expect to find new seldom fished waters — perhaps places no white man ever fished before. I know what the country will look like. It will be barren, uncompromising, harsh, — and to an adventuresome fisherman — beautiful.

Author lands lake trout on Kent Peninsula near Arctic Ocean. Best lures here are spoons.

Great blue heron is common wading bird — and
fellow fisherman — in marshes and along streams.

my fellow fishermen

BY KARL H. MASLOWSKI

Left—Green heron followed author along stream, begging for small sunfish and minnows. Below—Mink eats rockbass on bank of Ohio stream.

Because all wildlife must have water for survival, our waterways are always a focal point for animal activity. At least that's true of waters that are not coated with oil, saturated with silt, polluted with acid, or doused with nonbiodegradable detergents.

A healthy waterway, besides providing sport and recreation for human fishermen, may also provide sustenance and solitude for a wide variety of furred and feathered anglers. These "fellow fishermen" are responsible for some of my most memorable stream and lakeside experiences.

Back in the early 1960's I built a 60-foot-high tower within 50 feet of a bald eagle eyrie in the marshes just off Sandusky Bay in Lake Erie. I'm a professional wildlife photographer and I wanted to film and observe the home life of our living national emblem. There were days when the light was too poor for filming, so I would take a canoe

and go fishing in the waters that surrounded my tower and blind. With satisfying regularity largemouth bass and bluegills walloped the various-sized hula poppers I used. But I missed all too many strikes because my eyes generally were searching the skies for the parent eagles. Often they would soar effortlessly overhead as though checking to see how I was doing. Then they would disappear from sight, but soon I would see them laboring back to the nest with a fish of some kind clutched in the talons, as though to indicate that to catch fish you had to remain alert. That's a good lesson for *any* fisherman.

When the sun shone I was generally concealed in the box blind atop the tower, and from there I could easily see just what kind of fish they fed their single young. I soon learned they weren't competing with me, because the only species I saw them deliver to the young during two nesting seasons of observation were coarse fish such as gizzardshad, carp, and suckers. Not once did I record a game fish delivered to the nest.

A pair of eagles still maintain territory in that area, but they have hatched no young the past three years. Perhaps the toxic pollutants in Lake Erie are to blame for these failures.

Wading birds, including green, great blue, and black-crowned night herons, are among the favorite fellow fishermen I meet regularly on streams throughout the midwest.

Like all successful anglers, the 14-inch-long green heron is usually a bird of infinite patience. It may stand rock still — except for an occasional twitch of the tail — for five to ten minutes, waiting for a small fish to venture within capture range. But last summer while fishing the East fork of the Little Miami River not far from Bantam, Ohio, I encountered a youngster which exhibited typical childish impatience. The bird was very naive and permitted me to wade within fifteen feet. While I cast it moved constantly back and forth along the rocky shoreline peering intently into the shallows. I caught several husky green

Above—Author photographed this adult bald eagle at nest from specially-built tower in Lake Erie marsh. Left—Young bald eagle eats fish at nest.

sunfish and everytime one splashed about on the surface prior to landing, the youngster would crane its neck and hop around crazily.

As I was about to release a four-inch-long sunfish I looked shoreward, and if a bird can ever wear a begging expression that green heron did. I flipped the little sunfish onto the rocks just behind the bird, and it was instantly seized. The heron probably hadn't learned to catch fish yet, but it surely knew how to eat them! In the next 15 minutes it gulped two more small sunfish I tossed to it. When I offered a fourth fish the little heron, evidently stuffed, just stood there hunched up and ignored it. But I returned to the same pool the next evening and again caught the heron's supper.

Incidentally, you may have read that herons "spear" fish with their beaks. Not long ago I had the opportunity to

take high-speed pictures of a green heron capturing minnows. Exposures at 1/3500 of a second invariably showed the bird seizing the fish, using its mandibles like a pair of forceps or needle-nosed pliers.

On another midwestern limestone creek I was fishing at dusk when I heard a mewing and splashing at one end of a favorite pool. The disturbance was caused by a baby raccoon that couldn't have weighed much more than two pounds. When I approached, the youngster galloped toward me through the water and started to climb my wet trouser leg. It reached my shoulder, probed in my ears, and thoroughly tousled my hair. I called to my companion, Jeff Kraemer, who was fishing below me, to turn over a few rocks and catch a crayfish. That done, we offered it to the youngster which grasped it with a growl, and for the next half-hour we were kept busy catching small minnows and crayfish to

Above—Young raccoon once trailed author along fishing stream, climbed onto his shoulder when fed crayfish and minnows. Below—Tracks along muddy streambank reveal presence of fellow fisherman —a raccoon.

satisfy the baby's voracious appetite. Obviously it had been orphaned somehow and was on the point of starvation.

We tried to leave him on the stream, but he would have none of that. Every time we put him down and started to walk away he would scamper after us, climb onto one of our shoulders and purr contentedly. We finally brought the youngster home and raised him for three months, giving him ample opportunity to practice catching crayfish in the creek behind my photo studio. Finally we released him on the stream where we found him. Needless to say, we didn't catch any fish the night we found the raccoon, but even if we had, we doubtless would have forgotten them and remembered only the baby raccoon we'd met that evening.

Then there was the mink I watched dragging a rock bass along the streamside. Mink seem to reflect two extremes of temperament — they're either the shyest or the boldest fellow fisherman you'll meet along the waterways. This animal was one of the boldest. I was standing in about six inches of water when I heard a bumping sound behind me. Turning I looked squarely into a mink's face not five feet away. Dripping from its jaws was a struggling rock bass. We stared at one another for some moments and then, to my everlasting surprise, the mink began to eat the head of its fish while I stood by. Once the head was downed, the animal bounded along the bank for another 30 feet and vanished from sight amidst the roots of a sycamore tree.

The list of furred and feathered anglers you may meet while fishing is almost endless. Included would be kingfishers, cormorants, pelicans, ospreys (in ever diminishing numbers, sad to say), otters, and bears. You also will meet some that wear scales and shells, including alligators, snapping turtles, and banded watersnakes. Research has shown me that none of them offer the sport or commercial fisherman any real competition. So enjoy their company and treat them as fellow sportsmen. Chances are you'll have some fascinating stories to tell — ones that won't bore your listeners with details of how the big one did or did not get away.

Author Hutchins with his Ohio record largemouth bass—9 lbs., 8 oz.—from a farm pond.

Pressed for time?
Unable to plan a
long vacation to
the wilderness?
Then —

Why not fish the farm ponds?

by Ed Hutchins

For the angler who wants to escape the crowds on public waters, but cannot travel to a remote lake or stream, farm ponds are made to order. In many areas of the country, farm ponds are virtually unfished. Many are capable of providing faster action and more fish harvested per hour than almost any other fishing waters.

In the not-too-distant future, farm ponds may become the last close-to-home refuges for anglers who want to forget they're part of society — at least while they're fishing. If the U.S. population soars from the present 200 million to the predicted 350 million persons 30 years from now, the number of fishermen will probably double and the over-all demand for outdoor recreation will more than triple. That is indeed a frightening prospect.

Public lakes, reservoirs and streams, especially those near highly-populated cities, must somehow endure most of this vastly increased fishing pressure. Even if biologists can maintain adequate fish populations in these waters, the crowds of people and myriad boats resulting from multiple-use philosophy could create situations that will be something less than quality recreation for many fishermen.

Fortunately, the construction of new farm ponds is keeping pace with population growth, with more than 50,000 ponds built every year. It's estimated that there are now over three million ponds on farms and ranches in the U.S. That's about 60,000 per state or approximately 1,000 per county. Of course they're not so evenly distributed nor can all of them properly be called fishing ponds.

Probably most ponds are build with some fishing in mind, at least as a fringe benefit, but fewer than one-fourth of them provide really worthwhile fishing. Sometimes agricultural use of a pond prevents establishment of a good fish population. Most ponds heavily used as watering places for cattle or sheep are in this category, as well as ponds built to provide irrigation water which are reduced to little more than mud holes in dry seasons.

Farm pond anglers should learn to recognize productive ponds before trying to get permission to fish them. There is little value in asking to fish a pond that is too small, too shallow, or otherwise unlikely to produce fish. With a little experience, an observant fisherman can learn to "read" farm ponds just as a grouse hunter learns to spot grouse cover or an experienced wildfowler knows just where to set his decoys.

Although most farm ponds are privately owned and may seem generally unavailable to you, it's often surprisingly easy to gain access to them simply for the asking. But remember that the landowner should be respected for his right to refuse as well as to grant permission to fish. It's usually wise to seek his permission well before the time you want to fish and under no circumstances should you walk up to his door with rod and a stringer in hand. The U.S. Bureau of Sport Fisheries and Wildlife reports that approximately 32 percent of all farm ponds are open to public fishing and even more can be fished if you courteously ask permission.

Pond owners and anglers quickly learn that merely impounding water and stocking it with fish does not always produce good fishing. The farm ponds that provide the best angling are usually those built and managed primarily for fishing. In general, the larger the pond the better the chances it will support a desirable fish population for a long time. However farm ponds across the nation average little more than one acre in size, and only the rare pond is three or four acres or larger.

While size is important, several other features of location and construction also have a lot to do with good fishing. Ordinarily the best fishing ponds have relatively little shallow water (three feet deep or less). In deeper water less sunlight reaches the bottom, which helps cut overproduction of fish and discourages excessive growth of aquatic vegetation. As a general rule, a pond should be at least eight feet deep if the fish are to survive under stress conditions.

In most parts of the country largemouth bass, bluegills, and sometimes redear sunfish and channel catfish are recommended for stocking farm ponds. But everything from trout to goldfish are occasionally used. Crappies and carp are seldom recommended since they compete heavily with small bass for food, and carp frequently stir up mud, causing extreme turbidity in the water. Furthermore, pond carp are not easy to catch.

Ordinarily trout cannot survive in farm ponds, except in relatively cold climates or in ponds fed by spring water. Trout thrive best in water of 55 to 68 degrees F. If the pond water becomes warmer than 70 degrees F. six inches below the surface of the deep water, it probably won't support trout during the summer months. Besides needing cool water, trout have a relatively high oxygen requirement that prevents their survival in most ponds.

In most areas expert advice on pond construction, stocking and management, tempered for local conditions, is available from state, county and federal extension personnel. They should be consulted early in the planning stages, and often the U.S. Soil Conservation Service will even share the cost of construction.

Fish should be stocked in the species and numbers recommended by the consulting biologists of the agencies giving assistance. An Illinois study pointed out that there is nothing to be gained by excessive stocking of a pond since there is a definite limit to the poundage of fish any pond can support. If two identical ponds were stocked, one with 1,000 fish and the other with 10,000 fish, both would contain about the same poundage of fish one year later. But fish from the pond stocked with only 1,000 would be much larger than those from the other pond.

There are probably as many opinions on farm pond management as there are ponds. But most experts agree that a pond constructed according to the recommendations of the consulting agencies and carefully managed in its early years can nearly self-regulate an equilibrium (or balance) between the different species of fishes stocked. Most ponds, though, are not in this category. Instead they follow a predictable pattern characterized by high productivity in the early years, followed by fairly rapid deterioration until the pond is over-populated by stunted fish.

Good pond management dictates that fishermen keep only bluegills the first two years and return any bass that are caught. Bass do not reproduce until they're two years old or about nine or ten inches in length. Assuming the pond was stocked with fingerlings, bass should not be harvested before the spawning period of the second or perhaps the third year is completed.

Underfishing the bluegill population is probably the biggest reason many ponds get out of balance. Research in Illinois revealed that the average farm pond will support about four times as many pounds of bluegills as bass. For every pound of bass harvested, three to seven pounds of bluegills should be taken. That means about 20 times more effort should be directed toward catching bluegills than bass.

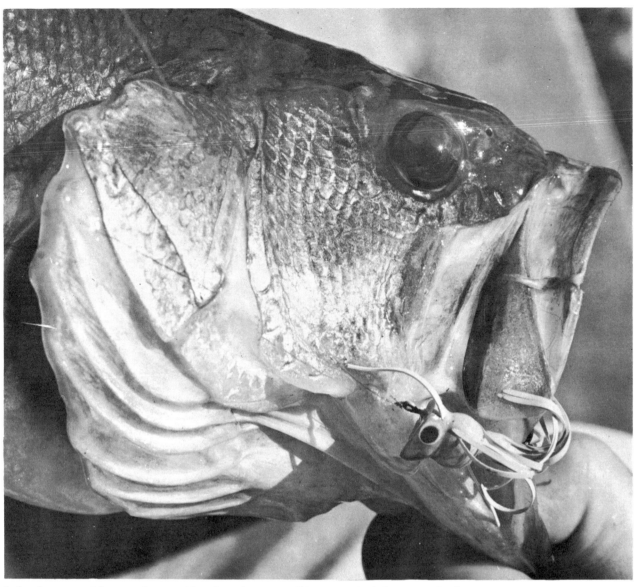

Surface lures account for many farm pond bass in early summer. This one was hooked on a popping bug.

A largemouth bass has just managed to elude the grasp of a fisherman in Indiana.

In lakes where bluegills are underfished, they should be systematically trapped or seined out of the pond to prevent over-population In many ponds it has proven beneficial to destroy most of the bluegill nests. If a pond owner does not plan to fish for bluegills or otherwise control them, he should not even stock them. Instead he can plant golden shiners or fathead minnows in the pond as food for the bass.

Some owners of very small ponds have considerable success allowing no one to keep bass for the first three years, and none under 12 inches in length thereafter. In other small ponds, good-sized patches of cattails prevent overfishing of the bass by making about half of the lake virtually unfishable from the shore. (However, the cattails create other management problems.) If such measures restricting bass fishing seem unreasonable, consider that some experts say a skilled fisherman who keeps all his bass can actually throw a small pond out of balance in one day when the bass are hitting. Incidentally, it's always wise to use artificial lures (vs live bait) for bass fishing so most of the fish released will live.

As in all fishing waters, the angler's success in ponds depends chiefly on his skill in appraising the fishing conditions and choosing the proper lures or baits for the occasion. The farm pond season lasts the entire year, with some of the best catches being made by ice fishermen. Tackle for farm ponds ranges from cane poles to the most sophisticated fly fishing, spinning and bait-casting outfits.

Bluegill specialists ordinarily use a lightweight fly rod with small flies, popping bugs or rubber spiders. Hook sizes for bluegills range from 8 to 12. When bluegills are feeding on the surface, tiny popping bugs are an extremely good bet, while the most popular live baits for bluegills are mealworms, small earthworms, crickets, roaches, catalpas and various kinds of caterpillars. Bluegills provide the bulk of pond fishing and a heavy harvest of them should always be encouraged. I never return an undersized bluegill to a pond, since it can only contribute to the usual damaging over-population.

Largemouth bass angling in farm ponds is more specialized than bluegill fishing, due at least in part to the smaller number of bass. Artificial lures are generally more productive than live baits for pond bass, probably because there is a great deal of action built into most artificial lures and fishing them demands less skill than the proper presentation of live baits.

Too many anglers think that live bait fishing is simply a matter of soaking a worm or soft craw, but a highly-skilled live bait fisherman is the man who will catch a bass or two when fishing is the poorest. But minnows ordinarily should not be used because of the possibility of introducing unwanted species into the pond. Farm ponds typically have a super-abundance of bluegill minnows with which the fisherman can seldom compete anyway.

Bass fishing in farm ponds is at its best in spring and early summer, especially for anglers who fish at the right time of day. Bass seem to have more or less definite feeding periods, evidently related to natural conditions such as food availability and light intensity. Early morning and late evening are the times when largemouths ordinarily move into shallow water and to the edges of weed beds and deep-water shorelines to feed. Their feeding periods may last for an hour or more or sometimes only a minute or two. Often it seems that the entire bass population is feeding at once, while at other times only one or two fish seem be feeding.

Spinners, deep-running plugs, flies and most rubber eels and worms will take bass in ponds. But many experts

Jumbo farm pond bluegills taken on popping bugs with rubber tails.

Gal angler flycasts for bass on southern farm pond. Notice the handy stringer.

This fisherman has just plugged a good bass from a pond in Illinois.

think there's far more sport in surface bait fishing. Ordinarily bass feed on the surface only when the water temperature is 68 degrees F. or above, and fishing is definitely fastest in the early morning or late evening, although it's occasionally productive in midday.

Any plug or popper that floats well can be used for bass on the surface, but some baits are obviously better than others. A few surface-plug fishermen still prefer the old wooden plugs to plastic. This is particularly true with the darter-type plug in which the wooden models seem to pop to the surface faster after being pulled under than those of plastic.

Some surface plugs such as the Jitterbug have enough built-in action that the fisherman needs only to cast and retrieve them for fairly good results. Other models require considerable twitching of the rod tip. The Hula Popper is a good example of this. In almost all situations, it is good practice *not* to begin the retrieve until the disturbance caused by the plug striking the surface has completely quieted. Then the bait should be retrieved with frequent stops and starts, and sometimes be allowed to rest motionless for long periods of time.

One ingenious fisherman I know constructs his own rubber-band-powered bass bugs that are probably the last word in gimmicks to take smart bass which have defied all previous angling efforts. He makes the lure from a hook, a matchstick, paper, glue, and a rubber band. The bait is used only once, but there's an excellent chance of retrieving it with a big bass attached.

The bug is assembled with the rubber band twisted in model airplane fashion and attached to miniature wings. When the device is fished, it is cast to the precise spot where the fish ordinarily feeds. Minutes pass before the water soaks loose the glue, finally allowing the wings to flutter in a highly realistic manner. Hopefully the bass is convinced it's a real insect.

Even farm ponds that have fish populations out of balance and seem to be fished-out will hold a few good-sized fish. But they are tough to catch. One trick that often works is to check very carefully the times when the pond is fished. Some ponds receive heavy fishing pressure in the afternoons and evenings but are never fished in the hours between dawn and noon. I have made some remarkable catches simply by fishing a pond at times no one else does. There is a distinct possibility that the feeding habits of fish assume certain patterns of time and place regulated by more than just the natural conditions obvious to fishermen. Thus fish accustomed to feeding at times of low fishing pressure would seldom be exposed to hook and line and could grow to be old and large. But the imaginative fisherman who will vary from the routine of hours and methods always has a good chance of catching such fish.

It's estimated that within 30 years the number of fishermen in the United States will reach about 63 million, or approximately double the number today. And as I've mentioned, the total population of the country is expected to reach 350 million in the same period. It's very possible the over-all resource demands of such a huge population will shift the emphasis on farm pond use from recreation to food production.

Dr. Milton B. Trautman, widely known fisheries expert and author of "The Fishes of Ohio," points out that while Americans do not consume great quantities of fish now, history shows that most over-populated countries depend upon fish and rice for food, both products being grown under water! Trautman hopes that increased use of fish for food will not detract from sport fishing. He states that in the event we can not maintain sufficient quantities of fishes that combine food and sport value, we can always fall back on carp and goldfish for food fish. That is surely a bleak prospect.

A U.S. population of 350 million persons would bring such great demands for multiple use on public lakes and streams that we would probably see a further decline in their value as fishing waters. If that happens, farm ponds may become the only places where a fisherman can forget society and be alone with a fish. Sad, but true.

FISHING TACKLE MANUFACTURERS DIRECTORY *

Tony Accetta & Son
932 Avenue E., Riviera Beach, Fla. 33404
Lures & Baits, Fishing Accessories

Acme Tackle Company
69 Bucklin St., Providence, R.I. 02907
Lures & Baits, Fishing Accessories

Aero Precision Engineering Co.
6728 Point Douglas Dr., S. St. Paul, Minn.
55071
Fishing Accessories

Airlite Plastics Company
P.O. Box 649, Omaha, Neb. 68101
Fishing Accessories

Aitken-Warner Company
427 Beech St., Green Camp, Ohio 43322
Lures & Baits, Fishing Accessories

Al's Goldfish Lure Company
516 Main St., Indian Orchard, Mass. 01051
Lures & Baits, Fishing Accessories

Alladin Laboratories, Inc.
620 S. 8th St., Minneapolis, Minn. 55404
Rods & Reels Fishing Accessories

Allan Manufacturing Company
325 Duffy Ave., Hicksville, L.I., N.Y. 11801
Fishing Accessories

Alliance Manufacturing Company
3121 N. Milwaukee Ave., Chicago, Ill. 60618
Fishing Accessories

American Sportsman Bait Company
21744 Dequindre Ave., Warren, Mich. 48091
Lures & Baits

Angler Products, Inc.
868 Mercer Rd., Butler, Pa. 16001
Lures & Baits

Angler Rod Company
1426 Oakland Ave., St. Clair, Mich. 48079
Rods & Reels

Anglers' Manufacturing Corp.
7729 N. Eastlake Terr., Chicago, Ill. 60626
Fishing Accessories

Fred Arbogast Company, Inc.
313 West North St., Akron, Ohio 44303
Lures & Baits, Fishing Accessories

Ashaway Line & Twine Manufacturing Co.
Laurel St., Ashaway, R.I. 02804
Fishing Lines, Fishing Accessories

Axelson Fishing Tackle Manufacturing Co.
1559 Placentia, Newport Beach, Calif. 92660
Fishing Accessories

B & B Tackle Company
P.O. Box 220, Lufkin, Texas 75901
Lures & Baits, Fishing Accessories

---

*Members of the American Fishing
Tackle Manufacturers Association

B & M Company
P.O. Box 231, West Point, Miss. 39773
Rods & Reels, Lures & Baits, Fishing Acces.

Jim Bagley Bait Company
P.O. Box 110, Winter Haven, Fla. 33880
Lures & Baits

Bass-Buster Lures
P.O. Box 66, Amsterdam, Mo. 64723
Lures & Baits

Bay de Noc Lure Company
Box 71, Gladstone, Mich. 49837
Rods & Reels, Lures & Baits, Fishing Acces.

Bead Chain Manufacturing Company
110 Mountain Grove St.,
Bridgeport, Conn. 06605
Lures & Baits, Fishing Accessories

Bear Paw Tackle Company
P.O. Box 177 Farmington, Mich. 48024
Lures & Baits, Fishing Accessories

Berkley & Company, Inc.
1617 Hill Ave., Spirit Lake, Iowa 51360
Rods & Reels, Fishing Lines, Fishing Acces.

Best Tackle Manufacturing Co.
P.O. Box 123, Unionville, Mich. 48767
Lures & Baits, Fishing Accessories

Bevin Wilcox Line Co., Div. Brownell & Co., Inc.
95 Skinner St., E. Hampton, Conn. 06424
Fishing Lines

Bluegill Tackle Manufacturing Co.
P.O. Box 57, Fuquay Varina, N.C. 27526
Lures & Baits, Fishing Accessories

Bluegrass Tackle Company
205 Robin Rd., Russell, Ky. 41169
Lures & Baits

Boone Bait Company, Inc.
P.O. Box 571, Winter Pk., Fla. 32789
Lures & Baits

Browning Arms Company
Route 1, Morgan, Utah 84050
Rods & Reels

Brunswick Corp., Sports Div.
69 W. Washington St., Chicago, Ill. 60602
Rods & Reels, Lures & Baits, Fishing Acces.

Burke Flexo-Products Company
1969 S. Airport Rd., Traverse City, Mich. 49684
Lures & Baits

California Tackle Company, Inc.
4060 E. Gage Ave., Bell, Calif. 90201
Rods & Reels

Carry-Lite, Inc.
3000 West Clarke St., Milwaukee, Wis. 53245
Fishing Accessories

Challanger Manufacturing Corp.
94-28 Merrick Blvd., Jamaica, N.Y. 11433
Fishing Accessories

H. C. Cook Company
28 Beaver St., Ansonia, Conn. 06401
Fishing Accessories

Cordell Tackle, Inc.
P.O. Box 2020, Hot Springs, Ark. 71901
Lures & Baits, Fishing Accessories

Cortland Line Company
67 E. Court St., Cortland, N.Y. 13045
Fishing Lines

Creek Chub Bait Company
Garrett, Indiana 46738
Lures & Baits

Creme Lure Company
P.O. Box 87, Tyler, Tex. 75701
Lures & Baits

Cuba Specialty Manufacturing Co.
P.O. Box 38, Houghton, N.Y. 14744
Fishing Accessories

Ed Cumings, Inc.
2305 Branch Rd., Flint, Mich. 48508
Fishing Accessories

Daisy/Heddon, Div. Victor Compt. Corp.
414 West St., Dowagiac, Mich. 49047
Rods & Reels, Lures & Baits

Daisy/Heddon
P.O. Box 220, Rogers, Ark. 72756

Daiwa Corporation
1526 W. 166th St., Gardena, Calif. 90247
Rods & Reels

Les Davis Fishing Tackle Company
1565 Center St., Tacoma, Wash. 98409
Fishing Lines, Lures & Baits, Fishing Acces.

Davis Mills, Inc.
Blue Mountain Rd., Blue Mountain, Ala. 36201
Fishing Accessories

Dayton Marine Products, Inc.
7565 E. McNichols Rd., Detroit, Mich. 48234
Fishing Accessories

DeLong Lures, Inc.
80 Compark Rd., Centerville, Ohio 45459
Lures & Baits

Depew Manufacturing Company
359 Duffy Ave., Hicksville, L.I., N.Y. 11802
Rods & Reels, Fishing Accessories

DeWitt Plastics
26 Aurelius Ave., Auburn, N.Y. 13021
Rods & Reels, Lures & Baits, Fishing Acces.

Dor-Mar, Inc.
1812 N. Cliff, Sioux Falls, S.D. 57101
Fishing Accessories

Dragon Fly Company
P.O. Drawer 1349, Sumter, S.C. 29151
Lures & Baits, Fishing Accessories

E. I. du Pont de Nemours & Co., Inc.
1007 Market St., Wilmington, Del. 19898
Fishing Lines

Dynaflex Manufacturing Corporation
1075 W. 21st Place, Hialeah, Fla. 33010
Rods & Reels

Lou J. Eppinger Manufacturing Co.
6340 Schaefer Hwy., Dearborn, Mich. 48126
Lures & Baits

Glen L. Evans, Inc.: See Gladding Corp.

F. B. Spinning Reels, Div. Feurer Bros.
77 Lafayette Ave., N. White Plains, N.Y. 10603
Rods & Reels

Falls Bait Company
1440 Kennedy Rd., Chippewa Falls, Wis. 54729
Lures & Baits, Fishing Accessories

Famous Keystone Corporation
1344 W. 37th St., Chicago, Ill. 60609
Rods & Reels, Lures & Baits, Fishing Acces.

Felmlee Enterprises
409 Woodland Ave., Lewistown, Pa. 17044
Lures & Baits

Flambeau Plastics Corp.
801 Lynn St., Baraboo, Wis. 53913
Fishing Accessories

Fly Fish Kit Company, Inc.
612 N. Mantau St., Kent, Ohio 44240
Lures & Baits, Fishing Accessories

Fo-Mac, Inc.
2621 N. Iroquois, Tulsa, Okla. 74106
Lures & Baits, Fishing Accessories

John J. Fox Championship Baits
Route 4 - Box 43, San Augustine, Tex. 75972
Lures & Baits

Frabill Manufacturing Company
2018 S. First St., Milwaukee, Wis. 53207
Fishing Accessories

Isaac Franklin Company, Inc.
630 N. Pulaski St., Baltimore, Md. 21217
Fishing Accessories

The Gaines Company
Gaines, Penna. 16921
Lures & Baits

Gapen Fly Company
2335 Main St., Anoka, Minn. 55303
Lures & Baits, Fishing Accessories

The Garcia Company
329 Alfred Ave., Teaneck, N.J. 07666
Rods & Reels, Fishing Lines, Lures & Baits,
Fishing Accessories.

Gladding Corporation
South Otselic, N.Y. 13155
Rods & Reels, Fishing Lines, Lures & Baits,
Fishing Accessories

Gladding Corporation
P.O. Box 260, Syracuse, N.Y. 13201

**Gladding Corp. — South Bend Tackle Co., Inc.
Div. Gladding Corporation**
4275 NW 77th Ave., Miami, Fla. 33148
Rods & Reels, Fishing Lines, Lures & Baits,
Fishing Accessories

The Gliebe Company
1154 Myrtle Ave., Brooklyn, N.Y. 11221
Rods & Reels, Fishing Accessories

Great Lakes Products, Inc.
312 Huron Blvd., Marysville, Mich. 48040
Rods & Reels

Gudebrod Bros. Silk Co., Inc.
12 South 12th St., Phila., Pa. 19107
Fishing Lines, Lures & Baits, Fishing Acces.

John S. Haddock, Inc.
P.O. Box 7768, Tulsa, Okla. 74105
Fishing Accessories

Hall Line Corporation
Park Ave., Highland Mills, N.Y. 10930
Fishing Lines

Harrison-Hoge Industries, Inc.
104 Arlington Ave., St. James, N.Y. 11780
Rods & Reels, Fishing Lines, Lures & Baits,
Fishing Accessories

Heb Manufacturing Company
Box 115, Chelsea, Vt. 05038
Fishing Accessories

Helin Tackle Company
4099 Beaufait, Detroit, Mich. 48207
Lures & Baits

John J. Hildebrandt Corporation
P.O. Box 50, Logansport, Ind. 46947
Lures & Baits, Fishing Accessories

The Hofschneider Corporation
848 Jay St., Rochester, N.Y. 14611
Lures & Baits

Hopkins Fishing Company
504 Washington Parkway, Norfolk, Va. 23517
Lures & Baits

Ideal Fishing Float Company, Inc.
2001 E. Franklin St., Richmond, Va. 23203
Fishing Accessories

Indian Head Sporting Goods, Inc.
Ripley, Miss. 38663
Rods & Reels, Fishing Accessories

J & M Manufacturing Company
P.O. Box 27272, Southport, Ind. 46227
Fishing Accessories

Jamison Tackle Corporation
3654 W. Montrose Ave., Chicago, Ill. 60618
Lures & Baits

Luhr Jensen & Sons, Inc.
P.O. Box 297, Hood River, Ore. 97031
Lures & Baits

Jeros Tackle Company, Inc.
111 - 16th St., Brooklyn, N.Y. 11215
Fishing Lines, Lures & Baits, Fishing Acces.

Louis Johnson Company
154 Deerfield Rd., Highland Park, Ill. 60035
Rods & Reels, Lures & Baits, Fishing Acces.

Johnson Reels, Inc.
1231 Rhine St., Mankato, Minn. 56001
Rods & Reels

Keating Floating Sinker Company
3901 High St., Denver, Colo. 80216
Fishing Accessories

Kebek Industries, Inc.
509 Victory St., Knoxville, Tenn. 37919
Fishing Accessories

Kent Sales & Manufacturing Co.
501 Dodge St., Kent, Ohio 44240
Fishing Accessories

Kodiak Corporation
Van Buskin Rd. & Erwin — Box 467,
Ironwood, Mich. 49938
Rods & Reels

L & S Bait Company
148 S. Vasseur Ave., Bradley, Ill. 60915
Lures & Baits

La Push Lures, Inc.
P.O. Box 429, Ellensburg, Wash. 98926
Lures & Baits

Lakeland Industries
Isle, Minn. 56342
Fishing Accessories

Land-O-Tackle, Inc.
4650 N. Ronald St., Chicago, Ill. 60631
Fishing Accessories

Lazy Ike Corporation
512 Central Ave., Fort Dodge, Iowa 50501
Lures & Baits, Fishing Accessories

Homer LeBlanc, Inc.
Northport, Mich. 49670
Rods & Reels, Lures & Baits

H. L. Leonard Rod Company
P.O. Box 393, Central Valley, N.Y. 10917
Rods & Reels, Fishing Accessories

Lindy Manufacturing Corporation
Route 7, Brainerd, Minn. 56401
Lures & Baits, Fishing Accessories

Lisk Fly Manufacturing Company
P.O. Box 5126, Greensboro, N.C. 27403
Lures & Baits, Fishing Accessories

Long Lure Company
P.O. Box 6, Savannah, Tenn. 38372
Lures & Baits, Fishing Accessories

Lure Corporation
20800 Chesley Dr., Farmington, Mich. 48024
Lures & Baits

Marathon Bait Company
Route 2, Mosinee, Wis. 54455
Lures & Baits, Fishing Accessories

Marylynn Lure Company
1303 Main St., Blue Springs, Mo. 64015
Lures & Baits, Fishing Accessories

Martin Reel Company, Inc.
P.O. Drawer 8, Mohawk, N.Y. 13407
Rods & Reels

Mason Tackle Company
Otisville, Mich. 48463
Fishing Lines, Fishing Accessories

Maxwell Manufacturing Company
P.O. Box 649, Vancouver, Wash. 98660
Rods & Reels, Fishing Lines, Lures & Baits,
Fishing Accessories

Maybrun Manufacturing Company
2250 Clybourn Ave., Chicago, Ill. 60614
Fishing Accessories

Men-Go Dot Line Manufacturing Company
402 Cogswell Rd., Silver Lake, Wis. 53170
Fishing Accessories

Mid-Lakes Manufacturing Company
3300 Rifle Range Rd., Knoxville, Tenn. 37918
Lures & Baits, Fishing Accessories

Mildrum Manufacturing Company
230 Berlin St., East Berlin, Conn. 06023
Fishing Accessories

Mill Run Products Company
1360 West 9th St., Cleveland, Ohio 44113
Lures & Baits, Fishing Accessories

Mille Lacs Manufacturing Company
P.O. Box 27, Isle, Minn. 56342
Lures & Baits, Fishing Accessories

Mit-Shel Company
640 South Fifth, Quincy, Ill. 62301
Fishing Accessories

National Expert, Inc.
2928 Stevens Ave., S.,
Minneapolis, Minn. 55408
Lures & Baits

Nature-Faker Lures, Inc.
108 W. Benton St., Windsor, Mo. 65360
Lures & Baits, Fishing Accessories

Nickelure Line, Inc.
1526 S. Dixie Ave., Vero Beach, Fla. 32960
Lures & Baits

Norman Manufacturing Company
2910 Jenny Lind Rd., Fort Smith, Ark. 72901
Lures & Baits

North American Sports Products, Inc.
18320 John R., Detroit, Mich. 48203
Fishing Accessories

Nu-Pak, Inc.
920 W. Cullerton St., Chicago, Ill. 60608
Fishing Accessories

Nutron Plastic Company
7975 W. 20th Ave., Hialeah, Fla. 33014
Fishing Accessories

Nylon Net Company
P.O. Box 592, Memphis, Tenn. 38101
Fishing Accessories

The Oberlin Canteen Company
P.O. Box 208, Oberlin, Ohio 44074
Fishing Accessories

The Orvis Company
Union St., Manchester, Vt. 05254
Rods & Reels, Lures & Baits, Fishing Acces.

Osalco., Inc.
7300 N.W. 23rd., Bethany, Okla. 73008
Fishing Accessories

Padre Island Company, Inc.
2617 N. Zarzamora, San Antonio, Tex. 78201
Lures & Baits

Palmer's Manufacturing Company
R.D. #1 - P.O. Box 222, W. Newton, Pa. 15089
Fishing Accessories

Parrish Industries, Inc.
1312 W. Lee St., Greensboro, N.C. 27403
Lures & Baits, Fishing Accessories

E. H. Peckinpaugh Company
P.O. Box 15044, Baton Rouge, La. 70815
Lures & Baits

Pedigo Pork Rind Co., Inc.
500 W. 10th St., Bowling Green, Ky. 42101
Lures & Baits

Penn Fishing Tackle Manufacturing Co.
3028 W. Hunting Pk. Ave., Phila., Pa. 19132
Rods & Reels

J. F. Pepper Company
604-606 Kent St., Rome, N.Y. 13440
Fishing Accessories

Perfection Tip Company
3020 E. 43rd Ave., Denver, Colo. 80216
Fishing Accessories

Peterson Manufacturing Company
P.O. Box 3709, Sarasota, Fla. 33578
Fishing Accessories

Phillips Fly & Tackle Company
P.O. Box 188, Alexandria, Pa. 16611
Lures & Baits, Fishing Accessories

Phillipson Rod Company
2705 High St., Denver, Colo. 80205
Rods & Reels

Plano Molding Company
P.O. Box 189, Plano, Ill. 60545
Fishing Accessories

Plas-Steel Products, Inc.
P.O. Box 176, Walkerton, Ind. 46574
Rods & Reels

Plastics Research & Development Corp.
3601 Jenny Lind Rd., Ft. Smith, Ark. 72901
Lures & Baits, Fishing Accessories

Plastilite Corporation
9409 N. 45th St., P.O. Box 235,
Florence Sta., Omaha, Neb. 68112
Fishing Accessories

Play-mor Products, Inc.
P.O. Drawer 740, 1507 Independence Ave.
Cape Girardeau, Mo. 63701
Rods & Reels, Lures & Baits, Fishing Acces.

Point Jude Lures, Inc.
P.O. Box 149, East Greenwich, R.I. 02818
Lures & Baits

Eddie Pope & Company, Inc.
25572 Avenue Stanford, Valencia, Calif. 91355
Lures & Baits, Fishing Accessories

Prescott Spinner Co.: See Arbogast

REB Manufacturing Company
P.O. Box 179, Pontiac, Mich. 48056
Lures & Baits

Ribbon Lure Company
53 Leitch Ave., Skaneateles, N.Y. 13152
Lures & Baits

The Richod Company
2314 High St., Natrona Heights, Pa. 15065
Fishing Accessories

St. Croix Corporation
North Highway 13, Park Falls, Wis. 54552
Rods & Reels

Sampo, Inc.
Noth St., Barneveld, N.Y. 13304
Lures & Baits, Fishing Accessories

Scientific Anglers, Inc.
4100 James Savage Rd., Midland, Mich. 48640
Rods & Reels, Fishing Lines

Seneca Tackle Company
P.O. Box 2841 — Elmwood Station,
Providence, R.I. 02907
Lures & Baits

Sevenstrand Tackle Manufacturing Co.
14789 Chestnut St., Westminster, Calif. 92683
Rods & Reels, Fishing Lines, Lures & Baits,
Fishing Accessories

Shakespeare Company
241 E. Kalamazoo Ave.,
Kalamazoo, Mich. 49001
Rods & Reels, Fishing Lines, Lures & Baits,
Fishing Accessories

Shellee Industries, Inc.
2516 Atlantic Ave., Brooklyn, N.Y. 11207
Fishing Accessories

Shoshoni, Inc.
East Highway 30, Meridian, Idaho 83642
Lures & Baits, Fishing Accessories

The Silicote Corporation
520 W. 14th Ave., Oskosh, Wis. 54902
Fishing Accessories

South Bend Tackle Co., Inc.: See Gladding Corp.

Sportcase, Inc.
204 Central Ave., Osseo, Minn. 55369
Fishing Accessories

Sportsman's Products, Inc.
841 E. 38th St., Marion, Indiana 46952
Lures & Baits

Steffey Manufacturing Company
404 Martin Dr., Irwin, Pa. 15642
Lures & Baits

Stembridge Products, Inc.
2941 Central Ave. — P.O. Box 90756
East Point, Ga. 30044
Lures & Baits, Fishing Accessories

Storm Manufacturing Company
P.O. Box 265, Norman, Okla. 73069
Lures & Baits

Stratton & Terstegge Co.
1520 Rowan St., Louisville, Ky. 40201
Fishing Accessories

Strike Master, Inc.
411 N. Washington Ave.,
Minneapolis, Minn. 55401
Lures & Baits, Fishing Accessories

Subria Corporation
P.O. Box 113, Montclair, N.J. 07042
Lures & Baits, Fishing Accessories

Sunset Line & Twine Company
Jefferson & Edwin Sts,
Box 691, Petaluma, Calif. 94952
Fishing Lines, Fishing Accessories

Symonds & Company
1414 S. Michigan Ave., Chicago, Ill. 60605
Fishing Accessories

Tack-L-Tyers
939 Chicago Ave., Evanston, Ill. 60202
Lures & Baits, Fishing Accessories

Tackle International, Inc.
P.O. Box 278, Sandpoint, Idaho 83864
Lures & Baits, Fishing Accessories

Tensor Corporation
333 Stanley Ave., Brooklyn, N.Y. 11207
Rods & Reels, Fishing Lines, Fishing Acces.

Tiki Lures, Inc.
1805 E. Eleven Mile Rd.,
Madison Heights, Mich. 48071
Lures & Baits

True Temper Corporation
American Tackle Division
1623 Euclid Ave., Cleveland, Ohio 44115
Rods & Reels, Fishing Accessories

Tycoon Fin-Nor Corporation
29 Essex St., Maywood, N.J. 07607
Rods & Reels, Lures & Baits, Fishing Acces.

U. S. Line Company
22 Main St., Westfield, Mass. 01085
Fishing Lines

Uncle Josh Bait Company
P.O. Box 130, Ft. Atkinson, Wis. 53538
Lures & Baits

Union Steel Chest Corporation
54 Church St., LeRoy, N.Y. 14482
Fishing Accessories

Varmac Manufacturing, Inc.
4201 Redwood Ave., Los Angeles, Calif. 90066
Fishing Accessories

Vexilar, Inc.
1531 E. Franklin Ave.,
Minneapolis, Minn. 55404
Fishing Accessories

Vichek Plastics Company
P.O. Box 97, Middlefield, Ohio 44062
Fishing Accessories

Walton Products, Inc.
P.O. Box 456, Atlantic, Iowa 50022
Fishing Accessories

Water Gremlin Company
4370 Otter Lake Rd.,
White Bear Lake, Minn. 55110
Fishing Accessories

Waterford Tackle Company
55 E. Pike St., Pontiac, Mich. 48058
Rods & Reels

Weber Tackle Company
133 W. Ellis St., Stevens Point, Wis. 54481
Rods & Reels, Fishing Lines, Lures & Baits,
Fishing Accessories

Erwin Weller Company
2105 Clark St., Sioux City, Iowa 51104
Lures & Baits, Fishing Accessories

Western Cutlery Company
5311 Western Ave., Boulder, Colo. 80302
Fishing Accessories

Woodstock Line Company
83 Canal St., Putnam, Conn. 06260
Fishing Lines

Woodstream Corporation
P.O. Box 327, Lititz, Pa. 17543
Rods & Reels, Fishing Lines, Lures & Baits,
Fishing Accessories

The Worth Company
P.O. Box 88, Stevens Point, Wis. 54481
Lures & Baits, Fishing Accessories

Wright & McGill Company
1400 Yosemite St., Denver, Colo. 80220
Rods & Reels, Fishing Lines, Lures & Baits,
Fishing Accessories

Yakima Bait Company
Box 310, Granger, Wash. 98932
Lures & Baits, Fishing Accessories

Zebco Division — Brunswick Corp.
6101 E. Apache St. — P.O. Box 270
Tulsa, Okla. 74115
Rods & Reels, Lures & Baits, Fishing Acces.